American-Jewish Filmmakers

American-Jewish Filmmakers

Traditions and Trends

David Desser and
Lester D. Friedman

University of Illinois Press
Urbana and Chicago

This book is printed on acid-free paper.

Library of Congress Cataloging-in-Publication Data

Desser, David.
    American-Jewish filmmakers : traditions and trends / David Desser
and Lester D. Friedman.
        p.   cm.
    Includes bibliographical references (p. 297) and index.
    ISBN 0-252-01564-9 (cl). — ISBN 0-252-06301-5 (pb)
    1. Jewish motion picture producers and directors—United States.
2. Jews in the motion picture industry—United States. 3. Jews in
motion pictures. I. Friedman, Lester D. II. Title.
PN1998.2.D47   1993
791.43′0233′092273—dc20   92-39669
                                                                      CIP

To my parents, Roslyn and Lee Desser,
and the traditions they instilled in
me by their example.

For two women who have helped direct my life:
my stepdaughter, Amy Pitt,
and my daughter, Rachel Friedman.

A member of a minority group is—if we are to speak existentially—not a man who is a member of a category, a Negro or a Jew, but rather a man who feels his existence in a particular way. It is in the very form or context of his existence to live with two opposed notions of himself. What characterizes a member of a minority group is that he is forced to see himself as both exceptional and insignificant, marvelous and awful, good and evil. So far as he listens to the world outside he is in danger of going insane. . . . What characterizes the sensation of being a member of a minority group is that one's emotions are forever locked in the chains of ambivalence—the ego in perpetual transit from the tower to the dungeon and back again.

—Norman Mailer
Cannibals and Christians

We Jews are not painters. We cannot depict things statically. We see them always in transition, as change. We are storytellers.

—Franz Kafka

Contents

Acknowledgments

At the University of Illinois at Urbana-Champaign, David Desser would like to thank his friends and colleagues in the Unit for Cinema Studies for their extraordinary kindness and patience: Edwin Jahiel, director; Richard Leskosky, assistant director; and Lyn Petrie, research assistant. A special thanks and deepest gratitude are due Debbie Drake who, with usually unfailing humor and grace, aided this project in numerous ways. The Department of Speech Communication, Jesse Delia, head, and David Swanson, assistant head, also provided valuable and welcome support, and the Committee on Jewish Culture and Society, which Michael Shapiro and Gary Porton co-chair, supplied a grant to utilize resources in New York City. Michael Shapiro also provided a sensitive and critical reading of chapter 1. A sabbatical leave enabled the beginning of this project; the humanities released time program of the UIUC Research Board enabled it to continue by relieving some teaching duties; and the Center for Advanced Study enabled completion of the manuscript.

In New York City, the staffs at the Museum of Broadcasting and the Jewish Museum, Broadcasting Division, were helpful and kind. Darilyn and Norman Desser, Miriam and George Kaeman, and Rita and Al Kalish provided hospitality over the years and demonstrated some of what is at stake in American-Jewish movie culture.

A debt to Cathleen Desser goes beyond words, and someday Madeline Desser will see her patience rewarded, too.

Lester Friedman gratefully acknowledges the assistance of the following people, without whose guidance the completion of this book would have been impossible. Eva and Eugene Friedman gave support and encouragement, and Delia Temes proved a compassionate source of wisdom and friendship. At the SUNY Health

Science Center, Sharon Osika-Michales provided expert secretarial assistance far beyond typing and proofreading, while medical librarian Peter Uva rendered valuable bibliographic aid. Many thanks as well to President John Bernard Henry and Dean Provost Donald Goodman for creating an atmosphere in which diverse ideas can flourish. At Syracuse University, two sympathetic colleagues, Owen Shapiro and Robert Arnold, provided intellectual stimulation. Steve Bucci, Rosemary Klein, and Mike Nelson gave their time generously to obtain many of the films analyzed herein, and, at the E. S. Bird Library, the expert research skills of Denise Stevens saved many hours. Lawrence J. Malley initiated this project while at the University of Illinois Press, and Ann Lowry provided sensitive editorial advice. Deak Rossell of the Directors' Guild of America helped with the survey discussed in chapter 1. Carolyn Friedman's patient cajoling forced the completion of this book; her high standards are a constant source of inspiration.

We appreciate the fine editorial guidance of Carol Weiland, executive director of the Jewish Heritage Video Collection at the Charles H. Revson Foundation. We are also grateful to the following sources for supplying stills: Jerry Ohlinger's Movie Material Store, the Anti-Defamation League of the B'nai B'rith, Orion Pictures, United Artists Corporation, Lorimar Motion Pictures, the Landau Company, Tri Star Pictures, Amblin Entertainment, Touchstone Films, Warner Brothers, Universal Studios, Columbia Pictures, 20th Century-Fox Films, Embassy Corporation, the Museum of Modern Art/Film Stills Archive, Kevin Brownlow, and the National Center for Jewish Film (Brandeis University).

CHAPTER ONE

Traditions of
American-Jewish Art

Although Jewish executives, producers, writers, performers, and directors dominate the American film industry, American movies before the 1960s rarely ventured very far beyond stereotypical Jewish characters trapped within conventional situations. From 1908, when Walter Selig moved his company to California, with the exception of Darryl F. Zanuck's 20th Century-Fox ("the Goy Studio"), Jewish creative artists and businessmen guided the destiny of America's largest propaganda machine. Their pictures influenced not only the millions at home, but also countless more abroad whose only view of America was cranked out by the studios of such ill-educated but streetwise immigrants as Louis Mayer, Carl Laemmle, Marcus Loew, Adolph Zukor, Harry Cohn, Jesse Lasky, the Warner brothers, and Samuel Goldwyn. How paradoxical that those films, which so accurately captured the country's spirit, almost totally ignored one of America's most prominent minorities. How ironic that those pictures, which forever froze our national experiences into unforgettable images, limited almost all references to the cultural and religious heritage of the industry's leaders.

A story about Harry Cohn of Columbia illustrates the prevalent attitude among Jewish moguls throughout the studio years. The director Richard Quine wanted to use a specific actor in a film. "He looks too Jewish," barked the irritated Cohn, adding, "around this studio the only Jews we put into pictures play Indians!" Louis Mayer (M-G-M) obviously shared Cohn's cruder sentiments when he told the dejected Danny Kaye, "I would put you under contract right now but you look too Jewish. Have some surgery to straighten out your nose and then we'll talk." Once, when an ailing studio chieftain checked into a hospital, he was questioned about his heritage for the institution's records. "American" he quickly responded, an answer that prompted a startled volunteer to ask, "but aren't you Jewish?" "Oh, yes" he added, "That too." "That too" aptly sums up the attitude of Jews in Hollywood, both on and off the screen, from the inception of movies until the end of the studio system in the late fifties. The attempt at almost total assimilation by the powerful men who ran the studios reflected itself in a de-Semiticizing of the action that took place in front of the lenses.

The death of Harry Cohn on March 2, 1958 signaled the end of one-man studio rule in Hollywood. Although Adolph Zukor lived until 1967 and Samuel Goldwyn until 1974, they retained little actual power. Many who replaced the old moguls in the industry's hierarchy were also Jewish, but they were American-born and had radically different worldviews than their immigrant predecessors. Some had degrees in management and accounting; most were college-educated. All were far removed, both physically and psychologically, from the old-country shtetls and immigrant experiences that helped shape the dictatorial Jewish studio bosses. Although some looked back nostalgically to the paternalistic studios and their erratic, colorful chieftains, most of this new breed realized that those bygone days were ancient history. Freed from a monolithic studio system that cranked out predictable assembly-line films supporting white, male, middle-class, Christian values, the movies from the 1960s onward provocatively mirrored the growing ethnic consciousness that marked the evolution of American history.

Thus, an emerging ethnic concern, coupled with the destruction of the old studio system, inspired film producers in the 1960s to transcend moribund racial stereotypes and create a cinema that confronted ethnic issues and characters with greater understanding, sensitivity, and sophistication. Ethnic consciousness in the American cinema is a fairly recent trend, however, one that sprung to life during the turbulent era of campus protests, Flower Power, and cultural upheaval. The United States of the 1960s prized individuality over sameness. The notion of a "great melting pot" that reduced everyone to blandly similar types, therefore, held little interest for people needing to proclaim their uniqueness. To discover who they were, many reached back to their ethnic origins, back to the customs and traditions that made their heritage—and, by extension, themselves—distinctive. And they liked what they found. Many saw ethnic identification as an alternative to a modern, computerized world of the fifties that rewarded uniformity and praised conformity. Ethnic affiliation, pride in belonging to a minority culture group, thus became important, one critical element in what has continued to be a nationwide obsession with ethnicity. Since the 1960s, minority-group members have found themselves scrutinized under the penetrating lenses of America's movie cameras, their traditions explored and their psyches dissected.

By the middle of the 1960s, therefore, American film directors found it possible to speak overtly about ethnic issues, to have ethnic characters clearly identified as such within their films, and to confront controversial issues with few fears of industry (or even audience) backlash. Jewish directors new to the cinema—for example, Woody Allen and Mel Brooks—found a freedom of expression absolutely unknown to earlier generations, while veterans such as Sidney Lumet found themselves suddenly free from many of the constraints that had shackled them throughout their television and early film careers. Faced with this new freedom of expression, Jewish filmmakers had no direct tradition, no previous examples or models, to draw upon in creating a visual art filtered through their Jewish consciousness. Of course, one might question the extent to which they contemplated or even desired to fashion a film art that was somehow specifically Jewish, but nevertheless the directors turned to Jewish themes and characters to take advantage of the ethnic sensibility characteristic of contemporary American culture. In so doing, however, they faced an empty past, a cinematic lacuna they attempted to fill with models drawn from other, earlier Jewish forays into art and popular culture.

The title of this book refers, in a sense, to a quest. Woody Allen, Mel Brooks, Sidney Lumet, and Paul Mazursky all work in a commercial context and thus are already a part of a system, a tradition of American cinema that stretches back to the late 1800s. But against this tradition of commercial filmmaking that tends to ignore issues of ethnic identity and culture, these directors established another tradition, one not necessarily in opposition to the dominant mode but existing alongside it. This tradition of a personal, often ethnically populated cinema is, of course, not solely the province of these four artists—or, for that matter, of American-Jewish directors. But it clearly unites a seemingly diverse group of artists into a reasonably coherent system. As such, it provides insight often lacking in the work of those scholars who totally ignore ethnic issues in their historical, esthetic, and theoretical examinations of American cinema.

To write as we do about directors will strike some as naive because commercial filmmaking is obviously a collaborative effort that depends on many people, technologies, situations, and conditions beyond the control, conscious or unconscious, of any so-called auteur. Yet, those involved in filmmaking know that almost all production crews function via a hierarchy. Anyone may contribute ideas, but one person (usually the director) must ultimately decide what is and what is not included in the final work. Beyond this, Allen, Brooks, and Mazursky all function as true auteurs, genuine authors overseeing every aspect of their films, from working on the script to casting decisions to musical selections to advertising campaigns. All three (and Lumet to an extent as well) also work repeatedly with the same people, both performers and crew members, creating an ongoing surrogate family and a recognizably visible universe from one project to the next.

It is true that American-Jewish writers remain the artistic group that critics and commentators most often scrutinize. Many scholars take a central theme and show how Jewish literary artists handle it. Both the scholarly community and the general public accept such explorations as academically, intellectually, and even emotionally valid. The imaginative products of such authors as Mary Antin, Saul Bellow, Abraham Cahan, Arthur Cohen, E. L. Doctorow, Bruce J. Friedman, Allen Ginsburg, Herbert Gold, Joseph Heller, Stanley Kunitz, Meyer Levin, Bernard Malamud, Hugh Nissenson, Cynthia Ozick, Chaim Potok, Norma Rosen, Henry Roth, Philip Roth, Gerald Stern, Edward Lewis Wallant, Jerome Weidman, Leon Uris, and Anzia Yezierska strike us as quite different and can be analyzed from various perspectives. Yet most, if not all, literary scholars who adhere to the concept of personal authorship would affirm that each writer's Jewish identity plays a significant role in his or her creative artistry. Even Norman Mailer, who includes few Jewish characters in his books and actively fights against his Jewish identity, is usually included in anthologies and critical works about Jewish authors.

Few studies of Jewish authors cite authorial verification or biographical facts to support their claims for the importance of Jewish identity in the works analyzed. In fact, critics usually interpret a Jewish author's direct denial of ethnic influence as a conscious evasion, a personal blind spot, or a psychological problem; more frequently, they ignore denials in favor of analyzing the work, not listening to the author. Scholars even scrutinize those novels, poems, and short stories lacking Jewish characters and having little apparent relationship to Jewish culture for Jewish points of view, attitudes toward characters, and thematic selections. Regardless of a Jewish author's past or present involvement with organized religion, current religious or cultural practices, and personal sense of group attachment or isolation, the underlying critical assumption is that the work of a Jewish writer must either overtly or covertly reflect a Jewish sensibility.

Like a generation of literary critics, we also seek to situate a group of texts within a stream of social, cultural, historical and ethnic factors. Our subject, however, is film instead of literature, and our focus is filmmakers instead of writers. Although the focus on these directors as the auteurs of their work does not blind us to the collaborative nature of the cinema, neither does it compel us to claim the uniqueness of these directors as individuals and as artists. In fact, this project is quite the opposite. We do not contend that "being Jewish" represents the sole determining factor in the movies made by these directors; rather, we assert that the importance of Jewish elements and motifs in their films has been insufficiently acknowledged and understood. We reject, therefore, the totally assimilationist perspective represented by writers such as Eric Lax, who claims, for example, that Woody Allen's Jewish background was merely "incidental" to his art (166). Primarily, we focus on what it means to be Jewish in the United States and how that fact colors the creation of a number of films by a handful of prominent American-Jewish filmmakers. Our methodology encourages viewers to recognize these films as part of a Jewish cultural tradition as well as an American cinema tradition, to draw conclusions about their relationship to a Jewish heritage in addition to an American experience.

We would also extend the concept of a tradition to situating these filmmakers within other artistic and intellectual contexts, particularly literature and drama. Clearly, they draw upon Jewish writers and playwrights for inspiration, sometimes in a direct way such as Mazursky's adaptation of I. B. Singer's *Enemies, A Love Story* and Lumet's of Edward Wallant's *The Pawnbroker* and E. L. Doctorow's *The Book of Daniel*. Allen himself is a Jewish writer and playwright. These filmmakers are, therefore, heirs to a tradition of Jewish artistic continuity, a long and varied history of Jewish intellectual and creative interaction within a mainstream culture that is not Jewish. Thus, the concept of "tradition" enables us to examine the range of issues raised by the varied films produced by this otherwise eclectic group of auteur filmmakers.

Three major traditions of Jewish art and expression exist for American-Jewish film directors to draw upon and incorporate in their work: humor, social justice, and "life-style trends." Each has an identifiable history in other art forms, particularly literature. In fact, one can see the literary roots of all three as they evolve from linguistic to visual icons, shifting from a read to a watched medium. Such a transformation involves far more than simple transcription; it involves a basic shift in both creative thinking and critical context. Yet before exploring this process, we must note one major structure, or formal pattern, that encompasses all these traditions: the bildungsroman.

The bildungsroman, or the education novel, certainly is not unique to American Jewry; it is, nevertheless, something more than merely one of many traditions into which writers may fit their work. For the Jewish hero, the education novel in which a sheltered, youthful protagonist enters the wider world of experience inevitably incorporates a bitter confrontation with anti-Semitism and the shock of social injustice. Thus, the bildungsroman provides both a subject (the education and growth from adolescence to adulthood) and a framework for a range of themes, including social conditions. In a 1952 essay Harold Ribalow drew up a list of fifty basic works of Jewish fiction written between 1917 and 1951. Twenty of the fifty novels on the list depict "the initiation into experience of a boy or youth, tracing his passage from innocence to awareness, his realization of the particular meaning of the life of a Jew in the American city" (Sherman 19). Similarly, Murray Baumgarten argues that Jewish writing clusters around an "informing myth," that is, "the marginal person emerges from the ghetto *shtetl* and seeks a place in the freer, more complex and cosmopolitan life of the city" (1).

Such observations contain two major elements of what might be labelled the American-Jewish bildungsroman, a variation or subgeneric type characterized by two important aspects: an urban setting and a marginal identity. Jews write "urbanals," not pastorals. An educative tale in the hands of Jewish authors was inevitably rooted in their decidedly urban experience: "City life offers a setting for the exploration of the historical ambiguities of the Jewish experience. In the process of emancipation, the city is also the bridge from tradition to modernity. It makes the move from communal status to ethnic and personal identity possible" (Baumgarten 1).

Jewish chroniclers of metropolitan life saw an urban existence as one in which Jews, as outsiders among other outsiders, could somehow fit, one that presents not only dangers but also possibilities.

"The city is transition," observes Baumgarten, "an emblem of the possibility of change, be it geographic, personal, social, cultural, or psychic" (8). Sam Girgus, too, points to the importance of the urban landscape in American-Jewish writing, noting that novelists often depict the city in ambivalent terms: violence versus excitement, rejection versus acceptance, and danger versus opportunity. More important, the "radical change" in the landscape of the modern American myth, from the frontier to the city, from a lateral to an upward mobility, represents a "major theme" in contemporary American-Jewish narratives (18). Finally, Leslie Fiedler observes that as society shifts its geographical and emotional focus, so the urban American Jew is "in the process of being mythicized into the representative American" (Schultz 5). This preoccupation with city life also characterizes the work of important American-Jewish directors, particularly the films of Woody Allen, Paul Mazursky, and Sidney Lumet.

Along with exploring the urban American experience, most American-Jewish novelists perceive of themselves as marginal to mainstream culture. This traditional concept of Jews as cultural hybrids—psyches trapped between the old and the new, between partial acceptance and partial rejection—forms the underpinnings of much critical work on Jewish creative artists and thinkers and much sociological writing about Jewish identity. Thus, for example, the sociologist Robert Park comments that once the Jew was no longer bound by the walls of medieval ghettos, "there appeared a person living and sharing intimately in the cultural life and traditions of two distinct peoples. . . . He was a man on the margin of two cultures and two societies" (Baumgarten 20). Thorstein Veblen saw such a marginal existence as necessary for Jewish creativity, arguing that "only when the gifted Jew escapes from the cultural environment created and fed by the particular genius of his own people, only when he falls into the alien lines of gentile inquiry and becomes a naturalized, though hyphenate, citizen in the gentile republic of learning, that he comes into his own as a creative leader in the world's intellectual enterprise" (473–74).

Some scholars, following on Veblen's idea, view marginality as a great advantage for Jewish creative artists, although they acknowledge that such a position necessarily incorporates a certain amount of psychological and emotional pain. For example, Max Schultz observes that "the tension between the old and the new generation, between ghetto and suburb, bar mitzvah and little league baseball, between synagogue and college, gabardine and Ivy-League suit, has spurred the Jewish writer to an evaluation of his heritage as a Jew, American, and modern man" (5–6). Similarly, Baumgarten claims that the modern American-Jewish writer "recounts the tale of the marginal person in quest of the promised city. . . . As he portrays the ambivalent situation of the modern Jew, he is led to question, challenge, and revise the premises of his work: exploring the proffered conditions of citizenship, he reflects upon its purposes" (136). Thus, Jewish artists' marginality allows them a vantage point denied other, more culturally absorbed, creative thinkers.

Yet marginality cuts another way as well. Ted Solotoroff concludes that the American interests of prominent authors of the 1950s and 1960s outweighed their Jewish concerns. It was not until the mid-1960s, he argues, that such Jewish (rather than American) issues as Israel and the Holocaust entered their work in any substantive manner. In addition, these writers looked to the Anglo-Christian tradition of English and American letters for their ancestors and themes, not to their heritage of Judaism, of Hebrew literature, or even of Yiddish culture. They were, as Solotoroff characterizes it, American writers who simply happened to be Jewish—the literary equivalent of the "that too" syndrome.

What such widely diverse writers as Alfred Kazin and Delmore Schwartz, Paul Goodman and Norman Mailer, Phillip Roth and Grace Paley, Lionel Trilling and Saul Bellow, Arthur Miller and Bernard Malamud never realized was that they stood at the end of what Solotoroff labels "the Diaspora mentality" (31). Suddenly, they seem "less marginally American than marginally Jewish" (31). Unable to give up the comfortable concept of marginality, however, Solotoroff establishes two new marginalizing issues. The first, an outgrowth of the former marginalization, is "the tensions between spiritual and secular being" (33). The second, and for Solotoroff more important, marginalizing experience is the relationship of American Jews to Israel. Thus, he concludes, "to the extent that American Jews are marginal Israelis, we find ourselves connected once again to the Diaspora and to the condition of radical doubt that has produced much of its salient modern fiction" (33).

Jewish youths making their way in the complex society of urban America, typically in relation to and in opposition with their family, undoubtedly form the major definitional characteristic of American-Jewish fiction described by Solotoroff and other critics. That this form should find its way into cinema seems quite problematic, because mainstream Hollywood cinema discourages notions of an overt, individualized author, a detectable narrating presence dictating events from behind the camera. In novels, issues of first-person narration and clearly autobiographical referencing are conventionally foregrounded in ways that film makes problematic, both as a commercial and discursive strategy. Thus, the repeated use of the bildungsroman formula in the works of Woody Allen and Paul Mazursky, for instance, indicates how structures, themes, and traditions from outside of the cinema would be more crucial than the cinematic past that preceded them.

Before turning to these specific traditions, one point must be firmly established, one aspect fundamentally understood: the absent tradition of Jewish art and expression. This missing tradition in Jewish art is Judaism. Characterizing this attitude is the thinking evident in Mordecai Kaplan's influential book *Judaism as Civilization* (1934), which argues that Jews are part of a "religious civilization" rather than a "religious denomination." American Judaism, for Kaplan, transcends mere religious rituals, allowing those who do not practice the traditional Jewish religion to still consider themselves as Jews. Karl Shapiro, one of the most important Jewish poets of the 1950s, observes that "the religious question is not my concern. I am one of those who views with disgust and disappointment the evangelism of the twentieth century and the backsliding of artists and intellectuals toward religion. The artist's contribution to religion must in the nature of things be heretical" (1).

Traditions such as humor, social justice, and life-style trends share a common secularity in that formal religious elements—or even overt belief in a transcendent being—play a small role within them. Further, the lack of Judaism itself is a structuring absence helpful in explaining the traditions that are present; it marks a key component to understanding why these particular traditions had such great appeal. How, and why, Jewish filmmakers adapted these traditions without returning the absence to Jewish art and expression remains one of our central concerns.

Humor

Hannah Arendt, in *The Jew as Pariah,* observes that "in Chaplin the most unpopular people in the world inspired what was long the most popular of contemporary figures. . . . Chaplin's own background and experiences taught him two things. On the one hand, it taught him the traditional Jewish fear of the 'cop'—that seeming incarnation of a hostile world; but on the other, it taught him the time-honored Jewish truth that, other things being equal, the human ingenuity of a David can sometimes outmatch the animal strength of a Goliath" (79–80).

A similar analysis of the Jewish elements in Chaplin's comedy comes from Albert Memmi in *The Liberation of the Jew:* "his eminently social humor, even the frail little character he invented, constantly battling brutes and the establishment, finding his only salvation in stratagems and the versatility of his intelligence" (204). Another critic, working with the same ideas and extending them, writes of Chaplin:

> Chaplin was an English Jew who was at pains always to deny or minimize his Jewish origins. At the same time his comedy was an abstract of Jewish humor, with the essential Jewish properties operating in the traditional Jewish manner, the only difference being that the Yiddish tags were removed so as to achieve a "universal" effect. The Little Fellow was the apotheosis of the *schlemiel*. His vulnerability and helplessness, his quick wit and ingenuity in self-preservation, his absurd affectation of dandyism, his infatuation with blond-haired, fair-skinned, voluptuously innocent maidens, whom he courted with eyes brimming with Jewish soul and sentiment, were the classic notes and signs of the Jewish comic hero. (Cohen 81–82)

This was not written by Joseph Goebbels, but rather by Albert Goldman. Nevertheless, we again see how Chaplin's Jewish humor is alleged to revolve around intelligence and ingenuity, the things available to the physically frail, intellectual Jew in a confrontation with the brutality and hostilities of the Christian world.

Such statements nicely encapsulate what might be taken as part of the essence of Jewish humor with perhaps one minor caveat: Charlie Chaplin was not Jewish. His father was not Jewish, his mother was not Jewish, and none of his grandparents were Jewish. He was not raised a Jew, did not attend Hebrew school, did not speak Hebrew or Yiddish, and did not particularly associate with Anglo-Jewish culture. How can we then account for this astonishing misstatement of basic facts? On the one hand, we might pay tribute to Chaplin's universality in that Jews can take him as their own. We might make the case that Chaplin, influenced by Jewish humor, deliberately adopted certain principles of humor primarily codified by Jews. Yet the kind and quality of humor to which the critics refer, the humor associated with Sholem Aleichem and the Eastern European Yiddish tradition, was contemporary with Chaplin, who did not speak Yiddish. In any case, these borrowed traits were, in Chaplin's case, visual rather than literary.

On the other hand, we might make the more likely case that immediate and future generations of comics borrowed from Chaplin the way that other silent, non-Jewish clowns (Harold Lloyd and Harry Langdon among others) borrowed from him. Certainly, a great deal of truth resides here. Future generations of Jewish comics did borrow from Chaplin (e.g., the Marx Brothers and Woody Allen), and he hit upon some timeless comic truths: that our sympathies lean toward the little guy, that the cynical outsider occupies a better position to offer commentary and satire on the mainstream than the smug insider, that looks can be deceiving, that inner spirituality is more important than outer materiality, and that physical grace is an objective correlative for a state of grace. Yet contrary to the positions of Arendt, Memmi, and Goldman, who are all Jewish commentators and writers, Chaplin is an essentially Christian filmmaker. The overarching themes of his finest films invoke a redemptive Christian vision revolving around self-sacrifice and charity as the highest forms of love.

In fact, the astonishing wrongness of these critics can be attributed less to Chaplin's universal appeal, his unintentional coincidence with Yiddish writers, or his instinctual command of comic theory than to a clichéd notion of Jewish humor. Of course, clichéd does not necessarily mean wrong; rather, it encapsulates a received wisdom that too often goes unquestioned. We can distinguish between the clichés of Jewish humor—and, more generally, the stereotypical analysis of the Jewish existential state that gives rise to the clichés about Jewish humor—and the actual experiences of real Jews. We may also distinguish between the clichéd and the actual by understanding that these analyses derive from a specific body of literary texts that grew out of a particular, and tragic, set of historical circumstances. Thus, the "literary Jew" springs from the lived experiences of Jews in specific circumstances—the lived experiences of American Jewry.

The clichéd Jew—the literary Jew—has entered the critical lexicon; he or she has been sufficiently introduced into popular discourse through mainstream newspapers and journals to become a clearly identified character type. The image, therefore, presents possibilities for use by American-Jewish artists, both in talking among themselves and in speaking to a gentile world. The literary Jew—the Jew-as-outsider, the little man, the schlemiel, the unintentional modernist, the arguer-with-God, the ambivalent thinker—is an available image to characterize (and often parody) the American Jew. These images, in effect, evolve into a tradition within which comic artists often fit characters and themes. But a lived experience of American Jewry remains equally available, a quite large but unique group of linked motifs and concerns which, taken together, define the specifics of Jewish ethnicity and the Jewish struggle with American culture and mores. These specifics of actual Jewish life in America have potentially as much artistic validity as the Jewish life in the Pale immortalized by Sholem Aleichem; they certainly have more direct connections to what constitutes Jewish humor.

There does seem to be an attitude toward life that can be called Jewish humor, a comic perspective derived from historical circumstances and made ever-fresh by both the continuation of these circumstances and the transmission of this humor. In his influential essay "Jewish Humor and the Domestication of Myth," Robert Alter cogently analyzes humor that is specifically Jewish. He points to "A . . . process of ironic or playful domestication of myth [that] is often observable when Jewish writers deal with heaven, hell and the realm of fantastic creatures in between" (*Imagination* 160). He further elaborates upon a European, Christian tradition that "characteristically conceives of suffering as a mystery, beginning with and drawing on the cultic or literary formulation of the mystery of suffering in Greek tragedy and in Christ's passion. Affliction is the medium through which man must realize his humanity; accordingly, he must view both himself and his suffering with the utmost seriousness" (156).

Juxtaposed with this tradition, Alter finds a Jewish point of view that "typically drains the charge of cosmic significance from suffering by grounding it in a world of homey practical realities" (156). Suffering is indeed embedded in Jewish humor. Derived as it is from the lived experience of Eastern European Jewry, how could it not be? But, "if in the tradition of Jewish humor suffering is understandably imagined as inevitable, it is also conceived as incongruous with dignity" (157). Thus, for Alter, Jewish humor remains firmly grounded in the common occurrences of daily life, events through which tragedy and suffering are drained of their pretentious grandeur.

Mark Shechner also expresses this idea of the cosmic combined with practical realities in "Dear Mr. Einstein: Jewish Comedy and the Contradictions of Culture." He views Jewish humor as characterized by "a sudden thrusting downward from the exalted to the workaday, from the tragic to the trivial, from the Hebrew to the Yiddish, from the biblical cadence to the commercial slogan" (148). As an example, he chooses Woody Allen's line, "my parents were very old-world people. Their values were God and carpeting." This paradox, this contradiction, expresses the essential opposition in Jewish wit: the sacred versus the profane. But we characterize this slightly differently, as the sacred versus the mundane. Again, Allen provides an example: "Is there a heaven, and if so, do they validate parking?" Allen's case reveals his subscription to these principles of Jewish humor, these supposed definitional characteristics, as quite deliberate—a tradition of Jewish humor that Jewish comics may choose to adopt.

The same idea may be seen in the figure of the schlemiel, that classic figure Albert Goldman compared to Chaplin. Ruth R. Wisse traces the origins of the schlemiel figure, again, to Yiddish authors. It was their response to a precarious existence in Eastern Europe and in opposition to the very real behavioral and cultural normative differences between Yid and goy. In *The Schlemiel as Modern Hero,* Wisse claims that "the *schlemiel* is used as a cultural reaction to the prevailing Anglo-Saxon model of restraint in action, thought and speech. . . . The American *schlemiel* declares his humanity by loving and suffering in defiance of the forces of depersonalization and the ethic of enlightened stoicism" (82). Such a figure demonstrates an essentially Jewish perspective by acknowledging that the distance between the silly and the sublime, the sacred and the mundane, is far less than we like to imagine. In fact, the sublime and the sacred both carry elements of the silly and the mundane.

The critic and writer Isaac Rosenfeld observes that Sholem Aleichem's comedy was built upon "the incongruity between man's ambitions and his impotence to achieve them" (Friedman, *Hollywood* 273). Such a statement defines tragedy as well as comedy, and therein lies the essence of much of Jewish humor's delicate mixture of the serious and the comic: the ability to laugh at humanity's ineffectual attempts to obtain what it desires, while at the same time to admire its attempt to strive beyond its means. Similarly, Saul Bellow observes in the introduction to *Great Jewish Short Stories* that in much Jewish literature "laughter and trembling are so curiously mingled that it is not easy to determine the relations between the two. At times the laughter seems simply to restore the equilibrium of sanity; at times the figures of the story, or parable, appear to invite or encourage the trembling with the secret aim of overcoming it by means of laughter" (12). The humor of America's great

Jewish comedians blends laughter and trembling, pain and pleasure, into a unified, organic whole. Perhaps the most succinct statement of this characteristic comes from Israel Knox, who, in his
essay "The Traditional Roots of Jewish Humor," characterizes it as
"the intermingling of the 'Is' with the 'Ought'" (327).

Several psychologists have explored Jewish humor, using the insights of their discipline to reveal much about both the personal
and the public functions of such jokes and stories. For example,
Howard Ehrlich sees all humor as an "act of self-disclosure . . . a
means by which a person tells those present something about himself" (383). Sigmund Freud concludes that Jewish jokes are distinguished by six particular characteristics: a sharp self-criticism of
the Jew; a democratic mode of thought; an emphasis on social
principles of Judaism; a revolt against Judaism; a concern with the
socioeconomic status of the Jew; and a generally skeptical outlook.
It is this first feature, "sharp self-criticism of the Jew," which has
drawn the most attention. Many thinkers quickly understand that
humor functions as a form of self-defense for the Jew: "It illustrates the cruelty of the Jewish fate, the futility and the unending
effort to come to grips with the cruelty. When the oppressed cannot
revolt, he laughs" (Memmi, *Liberation* 33–34). Yet this ancient art of
deriving what Josh Greenberg calls "the grin from the grim" often
turns inward, manifesting itself in a kind of auto-aggression in
which the butt of Jewish humor is often the individual Jew. Some
scholars suggest that this development results from the internaliza-
tion of negative Jewish stereotypes, whereas others believe that it
springs from the identification of Jews with their oppressors. As
Albert Memmi sees it, "the Jew's self-rejection and his rejection by
the non-Jews are so intertwined that it is sometimes difficult distin-
guishing between them. In making fun of himself, by this very
mockery, the Jew reveals his absurd preoccupations, the acrobatics
to which he resorts to face them, his complicated and ludicrous
adaptations to life in a too-harsh world, one which he can't face
unprotected. Jewish humor tells of the fundamental lack of adaptation of the Jew to non-Jewish society" (*Liberation* 45–46).

Thus, Jewish humor becomes an index by which personal preoccupations evolve into communal issues. It therefore grows out of
the themes that obsess the individual—fears of anti-Semitism, issues of assimilation, problems of intermarriage, and threats of
extinction—and documents the changing concern of Jews from
one generation to the next.

Sig Altman's book *The Comic Image of the Jew* represents a notable attempt to trace the role of comedy throughout Jewish art and place contemporary Jewish humor (and humorists) in a historical perspective. Three of his points contribute to an understanding of the films that we will discuss. First, the role of the jester has, for centuries, been important in Jewish culture. The *badken* or *marshallik* was a sort of Lear's fool, a figure allowed the privilege of caustic humor and social criticism without fear of reprisal. Such a persona has its most tragic incarnation in the form of Rubinstein, the half-madman, half-clown who spoke "dangerous truths" in the Warsaw Ghetto (Fein 235). Second, self-depreciating and self-ironic Jewish humor has been the constant companion of a people forced to live under someone else's rules, often-unwelcome inhabitants of someone else's religious state. This adaptation of the "Stepin Fetchit" demeanor to ward off possible aggression and make Jews seem as inoffensive as possible was a necessary tactic in a hostile world. An "I'll-Say-It-About-Myself-Before-You-Say-It-About-Me" attitude represents a defensive strategy strengthened by centuries of persecution, powerlessness, and paranoia. Third, Jewish humor has been an important component of Jewish literature from Sholem Aleichem, to I. B. Singer, to Philip Roth. An expression both of self-love and self-hatred, such humor became a part of the cultural heritage that Jews brought with them from country to country— modified for and by specific circumstances but drawing upon a history of discrimination, exclusion, and murder. Altman concludes that "the Jew is the comic figure par excellence in films," that the "very word 'Jewish' has become laden with humorous overtones," and that "Jewish identity is itself a kind of automatic comic device projected at an audience 'programmed' to receive it" (11, 49, 50).

Social Justice

Humor represents only one tradition into which American-Jewish filmmakers could place themselves, although it would be the dominant one. We have termed another "social justice," a tradition within which many Jewish film and television directors (as well as writers) had already placed themselves even before the openness of the 1960s. Some critics in America immediately before and after the war tended to characterize American-Jewish literature (novels, short stories, plays, and poetry) as being linked by "the cry for social justice." Thus, for instance, commentators often characterized the plays of Elmer Rice, Clifford Odets, and Arthur Miller as specifically Jewish, even when Judaism (the religion of the Jews) is virtually ignored and the protagonists are not typically identified as Jewish. For example, Enoch Brater writes of Miller, "social responsibility, man's behavior to man, becomes the universal theme Miller inherits from the Old Testament" (125). Baird Shuman argues that Odets' "concern with the themes of homelessness and alienation are outgrowths of the Jewish motif of exile" (103). Elmer Rice observes that "the dominant concern . . . should be with the attainment of freedom of the body and of the mind through liberation from political autocracy, economic slavery, religious superstition, hereditary prejudice and herd psychology" (Chametzky 76). Thus, much American-Jewish literature of the depression not only takes note of the economic circumstances of its protagonists, but also claims "that the class struggle dominates every human relationship and that Judaism is an opiate of the masses" (Sherman 74).

The first generation of American-Jewish novelists in America, of which Abraham Cahan is the greatest exemplar, could similarly fit Marxist or socialist models of thought within the context of the bildungsroman. The second generation, children of the depression, would often be even more overt in its leftist-influenced view of humanity and society, although the best of its novelists, Henry Roth and Daniel Fuchs, were more personally than artistically involved in the left. The aforementioned playwrights also fit comfortably into this category. At the same time as these first- and second-generation writers were linking their Jewish backgrounds and boyhoods to an emerging socialist consciousness, far more American Jews were actively participating in political movements of the left. Thus, while American-Jewish novelists would, for complex reasons, no longer find political reality a significant correlative for autobiographically derived characterizations after the war, American Jews would continue the tradition of political activism.

Attempts have been made to link the Jewish propensity to identify with political activism and social justice to Judaism, with specific exhortations in the Old Testament. Such attempts try to isolate precepts and commandments favoring social egalitarianism and universalism. This thesis, attractive although it may be in some circles, has at best a tenuous explanatory capability. In fact, Christianity would more likely have greater religious ties to secular liberalism which, given the history of Christianity itself and the nations that have embraced it, indicates that extra-religious factors must be brought to bear on the subject. By way of further closing the argument that Judaism is somehow responsible for social justice, we may also note that Jewish cries for social justice did not arise until the nineteenth century, and there were precious few major Jewish political thinkers until this period. Both the Industrial Revolution and the Jewish Emancipation, therefore, are necessary prerequisites to Jewish ties to leftist politics and, in many instances, the demands for social justice and Jewish involvement in radical revolutionary movements involve a requisite rejection of Judaism. The demand for social justice is primarily secular. It is not necessary here to account for the extraordinary ties that Jews have forged with leftist political movements. Rather, we need only note that this is so; it forms a viable, visible tradition within which Jewish artists may situate themselves.

Life-style Trends

Most American Jews did not turn to overt political activism, certainly not to socialism or communism. The most one can say is that throughout the twentieth century and into the 1990s, American Jewry stuck to the Democratic party in far greater numbers than did other white ethnic groups. Neither, however, did the majority return to the Orthodox Judaism of the pre-Emancipation days, certainly not to one or another of the Hasidic sects. American Jewry remains secular, a segment of society characterized by ethnic or cultural rather than religious ties.

Instead of turning to secular political movements, the majority of American Jews pursued the other available option away from Judaism: materialism and economic gain. In seeking this goal, and largely attaining it, they came to identify with the values of the mainstream middle class and helped shape those values by entering specific areas of American life. It is not an accident, therefore, that the films of Woody Allen, Mel Brooks, and Paul Mazursky most often explore issues from a middle-class perspective. By assuming these values, and in pursuing material gain as an end itself, American Jewry was also susceptible to the weaknesses of middle-class life, to the pressures that such a life inevitably exerts.

Such pressures of middle-class life manifest themselves in a variety of ways. For instance, just as studies by Braungart and Liebman point to an overrepresentation of American Jews within Old and New Left movements, one can similarly find them overrepresented in the cult phenomena that began in the 1960s—Eastern religions, transcendental meditation, and the "Moonies." This fact could be related to the numbers of Jews within psychoanalysis, on and off the couch. Shifts in family demographics and gender roles, also apparent in the 1960s, had equally significant effects; divorces are as common among Jews as among any ethnic group. A direct correlation also exists between educational achievement and career aspirations and, according to the 1991 National Jewish Population Survey, two and a half times more Jewish women graduate from college than do women who are not Jews. Jews are prominent within the world of diets, exercise, physical, and psychic health movements (pop psychology and philosophy). Jewish women are highly visible within social, community, or cultural organizations; they have been in the vanguard of the American feminist movement. None of this claims a commonality between the Jewish presence in pseudo-religious, pop psychology cults and the Jewish presence within the career women, feminist roles. Rather, it insists that both these phenomena are primarily middle-class in origin, and that Jews are predominantly middle-class.

Nor can we claim entirely that a susceptibility to shifts within life-style trends, or a tendency toward faddishness and cultism, is precisely a tradition. It is, after all, arguably a post-1960s phenomenon—a postmodern phenomenon. As such, it is too soon to call such a recent trend a tradition. Perhaps a tendency, then. Yet what we have termed "life-style trends" is a new tradition, a new option that reflects contemporary realities and is particularly, if not exclusively, Jewish.

Motifs of American-Jewish Life

The American-Jewish film directors who occupy the bulk of our study were born between 1922 and 1935 and were raised in urban environments, primarily New York and Philadelphia. During their youth, the image of Jews on local movie screens and in popular magazines and serious literary works, the status their parents occupied at home and on the job, and the goals to which they themselves felt they could aspire cut across specific familial terrain. These Jews were not mainstream Americans. The pressures these filmmakers-to-be experienced to conform and succeed were of a different order than those contemporary young people feel; the obstacles they faced were not the same as those of today. Without question, the lives of American Jews in the 1920s and 1930s differed greatly from the lives of most contemporary American-Jewish children. Jews in their thirties and forties might live in the same neighborhoods as their grandparents or great-grandparents did, but they likely inhabit high-rise condominiums, not over-crowded tenements. When Allen, Brooks, Lumet, and Mazursky matured, however, an individual's religious heritage played a domi-nant role in how he or she was perceived by the majority society; the very fact that these filmmakers were Jewish indelibly colored their particular worldview and, by extension, their artistic cre-ations.

By asserting this not particularly controversial view about Jewish generational differences, we can go on to isolate an interconnected series of motifs that define a good deal of the inner and outer life experiences of Jews born in the 1920s and 1930s.

The motifs of American-Jewish life subsequently enumerated do not merely define the Jewish experience in America. They in-fuse seemingly divergent Jews with the sense, if not necessarily the reality, of a shared background and a common fate. Even if all members of the community do not literally experience most of these motifs, the fact that they appear in books and plays, in movies and magazines, on television and in newspapers, and in comedy routines and poetry becomes—in and of themselves—part of the shared experience of that community. For example, most Jews never duplicate the experiences of Alexander Portnoy that Philip Roth details in *Portnoy's Complaint*, yet the book, in one form or another, is forever a part of their lives—as well as a part of Ameri-can culture. But the ways an artistic text such as Roth's novel rever-berates in the life of an American Jew cannot be wholly replicated in the life of an American who is not Jewish. By characterizing a diverse group of people, such texts inform a community; in effect, such motifs create shared experiences, which in turn mold a group into an identifiable subculture within a majority society. These mo-tifs thus build a public and a personal identity for those who func-tion within the specified group.

The linked, lived experiences of American-Jewish life have a function beyond defining the Jewish experience in America. They act as a kind of code and provide a sense of commonality, of shared background, of identity. A community forms around these shared experiences, not so much an actual community of Jews who live and work together, but a subculture manifested in popular culture, in Jewish novelists, comedians, and filmmakers referencing these motifs. These in-jokes spontaneously reference shared experi-ences; they enable hiding from "them" while at the same time ac-knowledging oneself to one's own. Jews now participate in virtually all walks of life, and if differences in religion and some daily activities do define the specifics of Jewish life in America, in general and in essence, Jews here are as American as anyone else. Yet to the resentment of some, the puzzlement of many, and the satisfaction of a few, Jews have somehow remained "Jewish" in this golden land of opportunity.

A Mosaic of American-Jewish Life

Jews have participated actively in American life since Colonial times. A handful, mostly Sephardic Jews from Iberia, settled in the soon-to-be United States during the eighteenth century, and throughout the first half of the nineteenth century a small number of prominent German Jews contributed greatly to life on the burgeoning American continent. Later in that century, Jewish soldiers fought on both sides of the bloody Civil War, part of the Blue and Gray armies that decided America's fate. Yet only in the twentieth century did Jews influence American life broadly and decisively. Their impact springs from the great wave of emigration (beginning in 1880) when one-third of Eastern European Jewry—tired of prejudice, pogroms, and poverty—sought a better life in America. Fully 90 percent of today's American Jews trace their ancestry to this mass migration.

The achievements of these immigrants, their children, and their grandchildren were miraculous by any standards. In a few short decades, Jews rose from the poverty of ghetto life to share in virtually all aspects of society. But with economic and professional success came a dizzying proliferation of problems and promises—a startling realization that many of the advances in the secular world endangered the traditional values in the religious realm. Indeed, the lives of these sons and daughters of immigrants vary so widely that no one characteristic adequately defines American-Jewish life—certainly not Judaism, practiced (or not) in an almost baffling variety of ways in the contemporary United States.

Four directors—Woody Allen, Mel Brooks, Sidney Lumet, and Paul Mazursky—clearly and dynamically highlight the unique tensions and cultural diversity inherent in contemporary American-Jewish life. Descended from immigrant Eastern European Jews, raised in New York City during the heady and difficult days before World War II, these directors were molded by forces that cast the modern generation that profoundly influenced American society, and that created a distinctive Jewish community. Their films reveal the tensions that being Jewish in America creates, as well as how the fusion of Jews and America fashioned a uniquely American-Jewish sensibility.

American Jewry of the 1920s and 1930s found itself in a reasonably secure, if often confusing, position. On the one hand, traditional American freedoms permitted entry into professions denied ancestors in Europe, and Jews rather swiftly climbed the ladder of socioeconomic success. Moreover, the fundamental American axiom separating church from state permitted—some argue even encouraged—American Jewry to abandon its religious roots and embrace these secular opportunities. Although leaders struggled to maintain a distinctive identity within a melting-pot society that welcomed and promoted the elimination of individual ethnic identity, many assimilated Jews quickly replaced religious observances with American customs. On the other hand, persistent pockets of anti-Semitism reminded even comfortable Jews that their position in American society was always open to attack. More critically, events in the outside world, especially the rise of Nazism during the 1930s, awakened American Jews to their potentially vulnerable status in any "host" country.

Even a superficial glance at the American-Jewish art before the war reveals a cauldron of creative activity that persistently scrutinized assimilation, examined alienation, and defined Jewish identity within a fluid national society. Living in the midst of such dichotomous times indelibly marked a generation of Jewish children torn between the traditions of the Old World and the novelty of the New. Moreover, being born and raised in a particular environment, New York City, amid particular neighborhoods and exposed to a similar range of social, intellectual, philosophical and religious forces, inevitably molded these artists; such a context made them acutely aware of certain critical issues. Thus, American-Jewish filmmakers born in the 1920s and 1930s seem particularly obsessed with intense examinations of self-definition. They relentlessly explore their relationship to the Jewish elements of their background and how that background both ties them to and divides them from the rest of American society. Their personal probes, therefore, often revolve around examinations of the greater society, their insights piercing deeply into American majority and minority culture.

Such a combination of the personal and the cultural creates some ironic situations. Thus, for example, American-Jewish filmmakers, along with a good portion of American Jewry, remain intimately concerned with such secular issues as social justice, racial equality, and diminished values in the materialistic American society. At first glance these preoccupations do not seem specifically Jewish issues, yet in the American cinema they become the special province of Jewish filmmakers. Take, for instance, the movies of Allen, Brooks, Lumet, and Mazursky. Almost all their films focus on assimilation into American society in one setting or another. These directors, in particular, explore the intricacies of Jewish life in America, presenting such complexities in a series of poignant, often humorous, always moving portraits.

We can conceptualize, indeed define, the cultural life shared by these directors by recourse to a linked set of issues. No single issue sufficiently defines American Jews, but taken together they constitute a magnificent mosaic of American-Jewish life over the last four decades. Enough commonalities, clear experiences, and tendencies exist to characterize this variegated life. Highlighting the parameters of this shared experience thus provides a perspective from which to view the films of these directors and appreciate how they integrate their Jewishness, their experiences as Jews in America, into their films. Indeed, it demonstrates how these experiences mold their films. Such a view should not diminish individual artistry. It should never blot out the unique personalities expressed in these pictures. Yet these important films clearly and significantly speak to the situation of contemporary Jews. As such, they provide an index to how being Jewish in America provides an intellectual, emotional, and philosophical foundation to express one's art and live one's life. Indeed, as the philosopher Martin Buber observes, Jewish history "does not consist of a sequence of objective events, but of a sequence of essential attitudes toward such events, and these attitudes are the product of collective memory" (147).

The Jewish Encounter with America

As the myth foretold, America did eventually prove a golden land for European Jews. Indeed, the United States played its role of host country differently from other host countries because American institutions rarely sanctioned official anti-Semitism. To be sure, earlier in the twentieth century "gentlemen's agreements" denied Jews entrance to certain country clubs, fancy neighborhoods, and prestigious universities. But for the most part, anti-Semitism festered in the psyches of individuals, not the precepts of American ideology. Although the nativist movement of the 1920s drastically limited immigration from Eastern Europe through World War II, and anticommunism slipped over into anti-Semitism during the early years of the cold war, these instances marked a tragic failure to live up to America's ideals, not a sustained, systematic reneging on them. Yet, despite a relatively hospitable environment, the threat of anti-Semitism still burns deeply in the consciousness of most American Jews, leaving a fear that the good times cannot last and that the pogroms will start any minute. As Abba Eban once wryly put it, "Jews are a people who won't take 'yes' for an answer."

One manifestation of this lingering sense of vulnerability remains an accompanying feeling of differentness that sometimes evolves into self-hatred. Norman Mailer provocatively asserts that "no anti-Semite can begin to comprehend the malicious analysis of his soul which every Jew indulges in every day" (Cuddihy ix). Albert Memmi claims this Judeophobia by Jews is a universal dynamic: "Every oppressed person . . . adopts as his own a part of the charge instituted against him: it is one of the internal dramas of oppression" (44). Jews identify so strongly with the majority culture that they internalize its beliefs, a system of values that may well stigmatize and reject them.

Even if one downplays the intimate connection between majority values and Jewish self-hatred, we still note the readily familiar number of "nose jobs" by Jewish women striving to emulate WASP ideals of beauty and the equally clear examples of Jewish men pursuing Gentile love goddesses (shiksas). At the very least, a significant number of Jewish artists and thinkers have recalled their own ambivalences, evidence of a basic uncomfortableness with their Jewishness. Philip Roth, for example, remembers that "reading *The Wings of the Dove* all afternoon long in the graduate-school library at the University of Chicago, I would find myself as transfixed by James's linguistic tact and moral scrupulosity as I had ever been by the coarseness, recklessness, and vulgar, aggressive clowning with which I was so taken during those afternoons and evenings in 'my' booth at the corner candy store." For Roth, these "seemingly inimical realms" of his experience mark twin poles between which he struggles to define himself: "the aggressive, the crude, and the obscene, at one extreme, and something a good deal more subtle and, in every sense, refined, at the other" (Girgus 120).

The critic John Murray Cuddihy calls this tendency "the Ordeal of Civility" in action—the Jew's attempt to mold his or her behavior, speech, and even thoughts into more "civil" (Christian, WASP) behavior. But the ordeal itself only creates a corollary feeling, the guilt of shame. As Anne Roiphe recalls, "when I went to a predominantly Gentile high school I became ashamed of my mother, whose clothes and manner were different from most of the other mothers, who wore oxford shoes with their blue stockings and understated tweeds over bodies that had played golf and done volunteer social work for generations. It was a matter of class mixed with ethnicity. I understood none of it. I experienced shame and shame for my shame" (171). There is, as exemplified in Roth and Roiphe, something to the notion of a Jewish sense of inherent inferiority, a feeling inevitably followed by a guilt for feeling ashamed of one's Jewishness.

The notion of assimilation refers, in the American context, to the myth of the melting pot, the ideal that all who come to the United States are welcome, their foreign identities melted away and replaced by Americanism. Conforming to this American ideal was both permissible and possible for immigrant Jews, especially because the American character was always "in process." Alternately, one could remain rather outside the mainstream of society, an option chosen by a number of religious sects such as the Amish or Orthodox Jews. Yet most Jews desired to modulate between assimilation and alienation, between Americanism and Jewishness. "It is clear . . . that the history of Judaism is also the history of the assimilation by the Jews of the cultural, social, and religious traits characteristic of their neighbors" (Neusner, *Stranger* 50). Jewish life in America flourished by not ghettoizing itself, by not cutting itself off from the cultural mainstream but by participating in all phases of life. Yet Jews in the United States never assimilated to the point of disappearing. American Jewry became American and remained Jewish, even if being Jewish meant something different than it did in the Old Country.

To immigrant Jews and their children, the Old Country was usually the Pale of Settlement in Poland and Russia, home to a third of the world's Jewry before the Holocaust. For these new Americans, the Old Country held little nostalgia. Unlike some other groups, Jews emigrated not simply to improve their lot financially; they came to save their lives, and they came to stay permanently. After all, they had no safe place to which they could return, so they brought their families and forsook their homelands. As bad as it got on the mean streets of the Lower East Side, these new Americans found it infinitely preferable to the poverty and pogroms of the Old World. Besides, life was clearly going to get better—if not for the hardworking greenhorns, then surely for their quickly acculturating children. And it certainly did.

In the years since the end of World War II, the Old Country, especially Jewish villages (*shtetlach*), has been painted with a fresh coat of romanticized nostalgia. Although much of American Jewry traces its roots to this bittersweet image, it provides little for a positive self-image, particularly for upwardly mobile Jews. Images of the Old Country remain suffused with pathos and tragedy; Jews too often play the role of victims and martyrs. Beginning after the war, however, novelists, playwrights and moviemakers forged a new vision of an old environment, a New Old Country: New York's Lower East Side and neighborhood New York (Brooklyn, Queens, and the Bronx). This is American Jewry's triumphant background, its roots. Jewish artists bathed this New Old Country in the soft focus of sentimentality. Jewish greenhorns suffered poverty and violence, but not the horrific death and destruction inherent within the European experience. The culture that American Jewry made in the Lower East Side and neighborhood New York—of attending Hebrew school and public school, of bar mitzvah lessons and baseball, of Sabbath services and Saturday night dances—represents a foundation for an American-Jewish identity, a new beginning that speaks directly to this new country.

Yet the creation of this new identity meant losing, at least partially, aspects of the older European identity. Among these losses was the almost total disappearance of Yiddish. Many European Jews before World War II were bilingual, speaking both Yiddish and the language of the host country (for example, Russian, Polish, and German); many also had a good command of Hebrew. Yiddish, however, was the language of Jewish daily life. In fact, it represented far more than a language; it created an international culture. Yiddish, the mother tongue (*mama loshen*) of the immigrant Jewish community in America before World War I, helped maintain links among Jews living in the various pockets of settlement throughout Europe, the United States, and South America. For more than forty years on the Lower East Side, Yiddish was as common as English, encompassing a thriving world of clubs, newspapers, theaters, films, and radio programs. Yet the uniqueness of the American experience, otherwise a triumph for Jewry, proved disastrous for the survival of *Yiddishkeit*, the world of Yiddish culture.

After only one generation in America, the number of Jews who spoke Yiddish as their primary language fell by one-third. Economic and educational success contributed to the elimination of Yiddish language and culture because they were tied so intimately

to Old World customs and ideals. As Jews moved away from tenements and ghettos, they shed their Yiddish culture as they often
changed their names or fixed their noses. Some expressions, of
course, still survive (as Yiddish is deliberately preserved by some),
perhaps primarily as a reminder of a family's roots, the remnants
of their life in the old neighborhood.

As Yiddish was lost in the accommodation to mainstream society,
Jewish expressions of identity could be found in the realm of economic and professional achievement: medicine, law, education, the
sciences, finance, and business. These areas of interest might be
termed "social professions," pursuits that rely strongly upon inter-
personal skills and communal activities in addition to requiring
high levels of intelligence, academic success, and a will to succeed—
values instilled into Jewish children by the dynamics of their family
life. American Jews, then, did not pursue simply secular activities,
but rather specific activities that demanded a social conscience and
a communal spirit.

Moreover, these activities grow out of the environment in which
Jews primarily lived, for Jewish life in America was (and remains)
primarily an urban one, as indeed Jewish life had been in Europe
before the Holocaust. In 1920 the Bureau of Jewish Social Research estimated the American-Jewish population as 3,600,800.
About half that number lived in New York City. Some estimates
placed the New York figure as high as two million. Substantial Jewish populations were also found in Chicago and Philadelphia, and
Cleveland, Boston, St. Louis, and even Los Angeles had large enclaves. Almost two-thirds of American Jews lived in major cities.
The pattern of urban living, far from decreasing with assimilation
and acculturation, actually increased. The 1957 Bureau of the
Census survey revealed that 96 percent of the Jewish population
over fourteen lived in urban places, 87 percent in cities with a
population of more than 250,000. Thus, Jews, who constitute a
little under 3 percent of the total population, account for 8 percent
of the total urban population.

Jewish involvement in the social professions and in city life provided a certain eye and ear for the constantly shifting trends of
popular culture. Urban life is remarkably sensitive to trends and
fads, especially among the middle class, that part of society most
broadly educated and attuned to societal shifts. Because American
Jewry is both a secular community and a profoundly middle-class
one, Jews assumed the values of middle-class morality and behavior
even before attaining the status. Thus, such a process enabled

America's Jews to escape the tenements of the Lower East Side, yet often left them profoundly ambivalent, even conflicted, about their status.

The clearest expression of these conflicts in contemporary American-Jewish life, as well as about the shifting trends within American society as a whole, may be found in an area of spectacular Jewish success: show business. The Jewish contribution to American show business, indeed to the idea and reality of a "show business" at all, is absolutely fundamental. While vaudeville, Broadway, radio, nightclub, and resort entertainment have been heavily Jewish since the turn of the century—from theater owners, to writers, to directors, to composers, to entertainers, and to audiences themselves—nowhere is the Jewish contribution to show business more total than in the movie industry. It may have been coincidental that the invention of the motion picture apparatus corresponds precisely to the great wave of Jewish immigration, but it is far from accidental that the spectacular growth of the American movie industry owes much to those same immigrants and their children.

The names of Louis B. Mayer, Irving Thalberg, Marcus Loew, Carl Laemmle, Adolph Zukor, Jesse Lasky, Joseph and Nicholas Schenck, Dore Schary, Harry, Jack, Albert, and Sam Warner, Samuel Goldfish, Harry Cohn, and William Fox may be known to only a relative few, but the companies they formed and ran—M-G-M, Universal, Paramount, Columbia, 20th Century-Fox, Warner Brothers—invigorated the hopes and dreams of an entire nation. These Jewish film producers, known not entirely affectionately as movie moguls, employed a veritable army of talent both in front of and behind the camera, many of whom were Jewish. The number of Jewish writers and actors, in particular, is amazing, as are the number of émigré directors who started in the 1920s, followed after the war by an entire generation of directors such as Allen, Brooks, Lumet, and Mazursky.

Jewish success in America, whether in the professions or in show business, results from American largesse and the dynamics of Jewish family life. Whether large or small, Jewish families possess unique characteristics. One of the hallmarks of traditional Jewish culture remains the emphasis on family. Although some traditional family dynamics might have changed in America (for example, less status accorded to fathers as religious leaders), Jewish homes remained predominantly child-centered. Children play central, tradition-sanctioned roles in almost all Jewish secular and sacred celebrations, those joyous, noisy rites of passage such as bar mitz-vahs, weddings, and religious holidays. Scholars often cite the concept of *naches,* the Hebrew word for pleasure or gratification that Yiddish adopted, as central to Jewish families. Marshall Sklare notes that "while it is possible to receive *naches* in many ways, there is only one true and abiding source of *naches:* that which is received from children" (1971, 87). Related to this concept is that of *kvelling,* "to beam with immense pride and pleasure." As Leo Rosten tells it, "only from your children can any parent derive such *naches* as makes you *kvell*" (201). Through the achievements of their children, American Jews of the immigrant, first, and even second generation define how triumphantly they have coped with American society and the success of their assimilation into mainstream life. Yet the pressures on children to succeed can cause ambivalence; sometimes hostility toward parents may result.

At the center of the Jewish family, the typical target for this ambivalence (at least in the popular literature and cinema) is the Jewish mother. The father, of course, plays an important part in the Jewish family, but the traditional role as material provider and religious scholar meant that a strong bond between mother and children usually existed in the Jewish household. This bond was intensified in America by the emergence of small families, an American-Jewish demographic characteristic correlating with increased economic success, social mobility, and educational achievement. Philip Roth memorably (and controversially) enshrined a certain image of the Jewish mother into American culture—an image Woody Allen and Paul Mazursky often reproduce.

For some, like Roth, Allen, and Mazursky, the pressures thrust upon young men lead them to look outside their backgrounds to gain validation or to rebel against tradition. One result of this is the cult of the shiksa. The Jewish presence in show business and the success of the extraordinary generation of American-Jewish novelists of the postwar era almost guaranteed that this particular term for a non-Jewish woman remains well known. Yet for all the seeming visibility of the shiksa in Jewish-produced art and entertainment, the reality of the situation is a bit more complex. Before the 1980s, more Jewish men than Jewish women married non-Jews. This is because Jewish men were more likely to come into contact with the non-Jewish world (for example, in college and on the job) than were Jewish women. Even so, until the 1980s intermarriage was rare; between 1900 and 1940, no more than 3 percent of American Jews married people who had been gentile at birth. Even in the decade following World War II, intermarriage rates were no higher than 6 percent. By 1990, however, the intermarriage rate rose to approximately 50 percent—one of every two Jews married a non-Jew. The shiksa image, then, has more to do with the creativity and conflicts of Jewish male artists and entertainers than with an overwhelming reality in American-Jewish life.

Thus, the particular talent of these East European heirs to centuries of wandering and accommodation blended with the unique characteristic of a rapidly urbanizing, essentially democratic society to allow Jewish immigrants relatively easy access to the American dream. The elements of specific cultural traits cultivated over years of a common religious heritage, an open country ready to welcome industrious settlers, a psychology already adjusted to minority status, a need to make America home rather than return to a homeland, and an intense desire to succeed here facilitated the rapid rise of East European newcomers from ghetto to country club. That which was lost—and gained—in this journey from alienation to affluence forms the central themes in the movies of Woody Allen, Mel Brooks, Sidney Lumet, and Paul Mazursky.

The American-Jewish Response to Judaism

The emergence of a large Jewish community in America in the late nineteenth century might, at the time, have looked like yet another example of the Diaspora—the exile from the Jewish homeland in Israel and the dispersion of the Jewish people across the globe that began with the destruction of the Second Temple in 70 A.D. But with a population larger than any in the world, and its own rich cultural legacy, American Jewry faced a new and distinct relationship to some fundamental aspects of traditional Judaism. In both biblical and literary analyses, scholars make much of the concept of exile (*Galuth*), of the Jew as eternally homeless, the so-called wandering Jew.

To Jews, or to Judaism more particularly, the concept of exile functioned as part of the Diaspora. For nearly two millennia, Jewish history concerned itself with the Diaspora and the hoped-for return to Zion. Exile and Diaspora, certainly until the founding of the state of Israel, remained unique to Judaism and to Jewish culture. A nation or a people may be exiled from their homeland without being dispersed, or may be exiled and dispersed without thereafter maintaining the image of a specific homeland as part of their national mythology. Yet although the Diaspora may be a fact of Jewish life, neither every Jew nor every Jewish community conceives of itself in exile. Assimilated Jews in Western and Central Europe before World War II—and in some thriving Jewish communities today, for example, England and France—and the American Jewish community have little emotional or intellectual connection with exile.

Yet even if the question of exile holds little theological force for many Jews, it still retains a strong mythological power, one often expressed in literature and art. The myth of the wandering, eternally homeless Jew, functions as a significant symbol for Jewish artists themselves. Thus, although the state of Israel renders the exile from the homeland obsolete and the Diaspora a matter of choice and not divine will, the myth of the wandering Jew retains its powerful hold. In particular, the choice to remain an American Jew, that is, to be Jewish and to stay in America, meant the reformulation of what it means to be Jewish, a redefinition of Jewishness in religious, ethical, and cultural terms.

For many American Jews, the Holocaust (along with Israel) provides the major link between the Jewish past and today's American present, as well as the major defining notion of American Jewry. The Holocaust was a European event, but American Jewry made it a major public issue and perhaps was able to do so because it feels so safe and secure in America. Yet American Jews who deal with the Holocaust in public discourse do so from two entirely different perspectives: 1) insisting upon its uniqueness as a Jewish catastrophe; and 2) seeing it as a warning to all groups that such an event must not be allowed to happen again to any people. In any case, the Holocaust, as a Jewish event, links American Jewry to the Jewish past and to each other as a community in peril and, of course, as a community, a culture, worth preserving.

By the same token, American-Jewish support for Israel, at least its basic existence and continuation as Jewish homeland, similarly links American Jewry to a Jewish past and an American present. American Jews vary sharply in their conceptions of Judaism, in their political leanings, and even in how much they identify themselves as Jews; yet, relative unanimity prevails when it comes to Israel. American Jews displayed a vested interest in modern Israel ever since its founding in 1948. Indeed, some scholars believe that the issue of Israel and the concept of the Holocaust remain as virtually the only concerns that unite American Jewry.

Yet is this true? Apart from identification with the Holocaust and Israel, what does it mean to be an American Jew? Jacob Neusner, a rueful yet perceptive critic of American Judaism, once remarked that "American Judaism has persisted although the Jews have largely ignored it" (*Stranger* 34). This is because the definition of "Jew" remains vague. Is it a religion, a people, an ethnic group, or a civilization? For the latter, see Mordecai Kaplan's influential work, *Judaism as Civilization*. Charles Silberman puts it best, perhaps, when he observes, "the fact that there is no way to stop being Jewish is the largest, and certainly the most puzzling, difference between Judaism and Christianity. In the Jewish self-definition, belief and practice determine whether one is a *good* Jew or a *bad* Jew but not whether one *is* a Jew; to be a Jew is an indelible status, from which there is no exit" (70). Even Judaism, the religion of the Jews, has many forms (e.g., orthodox, conservative, and reform) and is, in many of these, an ongoing, ever-developing set of religious beliefs and practices. Many observers note the relatively high percentage of Jews who belong to synagogues and yet observe minimal religious practices. These people define themselves as Jews not for their religious beliefs, but for their cultural identification. Minimal—at least, symbolic—connections to Judaism may remain but quite strong connections to Jewry, to Jewishness, abound.

Many American Jews found secular Judaism a substitute for religion. In some instances, secular fervor for social justice replaced the messianic fervor of Judaism. Thus, Jewish political involvement, especially in the liberal or leftist camps, has remained one of the most notable aspects of Jewish political behavior. Many immigrant and first-generation Jews were prominent in what has come to be known as the Old Left. Typically, this refers to the American Communist party and also encapsulates various socialist and leftist political ideologies (including Zionism in one of its most potent forms) in the prewar and war eras. The American Communist party was extremely active in union organizing in the teens and twenties, something near and dear to the hearts of the thousands of Jews in the needle and tobacco trades in New York. Similarly, in the 1930s, the party was the only organized political party to take a line against anti-Semitism, and even to call for laws making its propagation a crime (Liebman 506).

Jewish involvement with the Old Left died out because of the revelations of Stalinism—which harmed Jewish and Yiddish culture almost as gravely as did Hitler—after the war combined with the shift in the socioeconomic status of American Jewry. In transforming itself from a working-class to a middle-class group, such things as union organizing, working-class culture, and millenarian dreams of a classless society were swept away by economic success and social acculturation. Moreover, the cold war and its attendant anti-Semitism took some of the bloom off the Communist rose already wilted by Stalinism. This did not mean, however, that millenarian or messianic politics would find no home in the American-Jewish community when the Old Left faded. Far from it, for a younger generation of American Jews (part of the baby boom) would come to dominate in a political, even life-style, movement known as the New Left. American Jews were in the vanguard of the New Left, which came to life in the 1960s around the issues of civil rights, free speech, and protests against the war in Vietnam.

The preceding sketch of American-Jewish life emphasizes the extent to which being Jewish means more than a certain religious tradition subscribed to or rejected; more than a deep sympathy for Israel; more, even, than a particularly visceral response to the Holocaust. It means that the combination of these factors provides a range of shared experiences. Yet just as we acknowledged that being Jewish was not the sole factor that determined a director's artistic vision, so, too, the vision of a Jewish director need hardly confine itself to overtly Jewish issues. Indeed, the most uniquely Jewish issue, Judaism, appears infrequently in American-Jewish filmmaking. Therefore, we should not demand that a director such as Woody Allen deal with Jewish issues in each film, something he avoids doing. The same is true of Paul Mazursky or Mel Brooks, while Sidney Lumet, the most prolific of these directors, sticks to the old-fashioned vision of the director as craftsman, thus tackling an enormous and diverse range of projects. Yet because the Jewish experience in America encompasses unique qualities, we should expect these directors to manifest something that can be accurately described as a Jewish sensibility, a particular bent of mind that attracts them to certain issues and themes and a perspective that invigorates their films with a sensitivity that grows out of their Jewishness. We believe, therefore, that many of the films of Allen, Brooks, Lumet, and Mazursky that do not focus on overtly Jewish characters still reveal the influence of the American-Jewish experience.

Issues of social justice, personal freedom, and the right to express oneself predominate in the films of Woody Allen, Mel Brooks, Sidney Lumet, and Paul Mazursky. These filmmakers share profound similarities of background and experience, a background they have in common with much of American Jewry. What follows, then, will sketch the biographies of these filmmakers, paying particular attention to shared characteristics of time and place.

A basic outline of their film careers and dominant expressions of their interests will precede discussions of two of each director's major films: *Annie Hall* and *Crimes and Misdemeanors* for Allen; *The Producers* and *History of the World, Part One* for Brooks; *The Pawnbroker* and *Daniel* for Lumet; and *Next Stop, Greenwich Village* and *Enemies, A Love Story* for Mazursky. These pictures rank among the directors' major expressions of Jewishness. As such, they respond to the successes and tensions of American-Jewish life, to their own attempts to forge Jewish identity or to rebel against it, to their accommodation within a mainstream culture that has rewarded them with financial success and a good deal of fame. An analysis of their films, therefore, not only provides a journey into the world of four prominent American-Jewish filmmakers, but also illuminates the critical issues that preoccupy much of the American-Jewish community.

Results of Survey of American-Jewish Directors

During March and April of 1988, we sent a four-question survey to a hundred and seventy directors listed in the Directors' Guild of America directory:

1. What kind of Jewish background did you have, and what role, if any, does Judaism play in your life now?
2. Do you feel that being Jewish has influenced your work in terms of themes and characters that attract you?
3. Do you see yourself as working within a tradition of American-Jewish directors? If so, what elements characterize this tradition?
4. If you have included Jewish characters in your work, did you approach them differently than non-Jewish ones?

Sixty-one directors responded, fairly average for a mail survey. Because we selected the directors on the basis of their last names, we expected to reach some who were not Jewish and, indeed, several whom we contacted were not. The replies from the other participants constitute a broad spectrum of possible responses.

Perhaps the most predictable responses came from the few directors who either found little merit or argued totally against the idea of discussing the films of American-Jewish directors from an ethnic perspective. The first response we received, for example, accused us of providing "great ammunition for anti-Semites." Another respondent said that he did not think of himself as a Jewish director and felt that there was no way he could "separate my religious upbringing from the rest of the ethics I've learned over the years." Several characterized our survey as divisive because it separated Jews from the rest of the American society. One, who seemed particularly annoyed by our request for information, expressed the hope that he would not have to look forward to studies of American-Jewish "physicists, harpists, pizza-makers, bookies, and pederasts." A few directors found no real difference between "American-Jewish directors and any other ones," while one specifically wondered what "useful continuum goes from Mel Brooks to Woody Allen to Stanley Kubrick?" A lone voice argued that our research would be more valuable if we dealt with American-Jewish screen and television writers rather than directors because they were the actual creators of characters.

Many directors found their Jewish identity simply irrelevant to their daily existence and, we assume, to their artistry. For example, Alan Arkin observed, "my Jewish background was scant; my parents were more interested in politics than religion . . . and there was no religious training at all in my generation nor my parents' generation. As a result, Judaism plays little part in my conscious life. Being Jewish has played more of a part in the roles and plays offered to me than what I have accepted, and I don't see myself working within a tradition of Jewish directors or actors."

For another respondent, Elia Kazan is "the most American-Jewish director I can name, and he's not Jewish." Quite a few directors saw themselves as influenced by Jewish liberal idealism, not Jewish religion or culture. One noted that we are dealing with a "null hypothesis" and that he considers himself "a humanistic film-maker and my heroes are John Huston and Francois Truffaut." Another characterized himself as "ridiculously benighted" and saw Judaism as playing "no role" in his life. Responding to the question of the role of Judaism in his life, Russ Meyer emphatically answered, "ZERO!!!"

Several directors, however, delved into historical events that determined their personal sense of Jewish identity, citing the Holocaust in particular. Andrew Bergman, for example, defined his Jewish background primarily in terms of being the grandson of Holocaust victims: "My maternal grandparents were killed by the Nazis in France and that event is for me the central and indelible proof of my Jewishness . . . I work primarily in comedy. Comedy is the perspective from which I deal with the world. It is most probably a defense mechanism against the horrors of my background." Stanley Kramer asserted that "any Jew who lived during the time of Adolph Hitler is aware of his lineage." Another director observed that he felt "the historical importance of one's Jewishness is becoming more acute to me. I have developed an awareness of the greater bond between Jews and the importance of this bond in an increasingly intolerant world."

Many other directors, most of whom were nonobservant Jews or those who celebrated a few specific holidays like Passover or Hanukkah, discussed their Jewish identity somewhat vaguely. One expressed this rather cryptically: "Once Jewish-Always influenced." A few directors mentioned "humor, humanism, and civil rights" as personal characteristics springing from their ethnic background. Others included "social concerns, humanistic orientation, and political issues" as the main ways that their Jewishness influences their work. In a similar vein, several respondents cited "heart, humanity and an understanding of the nature of suffering" as the results of their Jewish upbringing. Some characterized the tradition of American-Jewish directors as encompassing "social conscience, sense of being an outsider, neurotic humor, and humanism," as well as "a permanent sense of social and human responsibility."

Jeremy Paul Kagan, whose father was a rabbi as well as a practicing psychologist, reported that making *The Chosen* had reawakened his interest in Judaism: "My philosophical perspective has been mostly inspired by my Jewish thought and ethics and therefore influences my attitudes on all subject matter and human personality." One respondent noted, "Judaism is so deeply instilled in me, it must surely play a dominant role in my thoughts and actions." Another identified a sense of community: "the fierce creative energy of the Jewish intellectual community (including its artists) has always provided both a foundation and a frame for me."

The sample of these answers accurately reflects the spectrum of responses we received. In many ways, our relatively small survey mirrors the general conclusions about ethnic consciousness and religious affiliation that others conducting similar research have noted: most American Jews identify with cultural traditions rather than with religious adherence. As Calvin Goldscheider points out, "religiosity is the only one of the ways in which Jews express their Jewishness. In the past, Judaism and Jewishness were intertwined, so that any change in religious expression represented a threat to Jewish continuity. This is no longer the case among contemporary Jewish communities" (165).

CHAPTER TWO

Woody Allen: The Schlemiel as Modern Philosopher

If the amount of scholarship and criticism devoted to an artist's works forms an accurate index of professional status, Woody Allen ranks in the forefront of contemporary American directors. He is written about more frequently than any other American director working today. Among contemporary directors, in fact, the amount of written text devoted to Allen rivals that of such world-renowned directors as Akira Kurosawa, Jean-Luc Godard, Federico Fellini, and Ingmar Bergman. Books and articles devoted to Allen match the stack of works devoted to such acknowledged directors in the pantheon of American cinema as John Ford, Alfred Hitchcock, and Orson Welles. Allen has even achieved cult status through the publication of some strange books devoted to him and his work.[1]

But Woody Allen remains neither the exclusive province of the academy nor the obscure object of the cultish. He has achieved a rare celebrity; he is as recognizable as any tabloid movie star, yet as respected for his work as any serious writer or political pundit. Even if his box-office success fails to measure up to some of his younger colleagues in Hollywood or New York, his status in American cinema is unique. He is a filmmaker who has almost total control over his projects, as well as almost totally insular working methods. Since 1969 he has been one of the most prolific of filmmakers, as well as one of the most respected and admired, in the United States.

Woody Allen has evolved into one of the few "public intellectuals" (the term is from Russell Jacoby) in America, a person working in the popular arenas of film, television, journalism, and literature who transcends the merely popular and transitory, but who never loses touch with this mass audience. The French critic Robert Benayoun, agreeing that Allen is "the only comic of international renown who can be described as an intellectual," feels that he "is the first to found a reputation on an instantaneous reaction to the great problems of our times" (71). This status as a public intellectual is aided by Allen's position as the director, writer, and star of most of his films; as such he creates a recognizable persona. Moreover, his films appear autobiographical, so, given his status as a celebrity, Allen can count on his audience knowing at least the basic outlines of his life. In addition, the use of recurring motifs across the length and breadth of his career, and the repetition of certain jokes and situations, enables Allen to affirm his status as a genuine auteur and gain acceptance as a personal filmmaker, or author, with a private vision expressed in a public medium.

At the same time, Allen often goes to great pains to deny the similarities between his art and his life. For example, he rarely engages in the kind of discourse typical of celebrities; he no longer appears on television talk shows (as he did in the late 1960s and into the early 1970s, although infrequently) and only occasionally does celebrity interviews. Although he jealously guards his privacy, Allen's habits, such as eating at Elaine's or playing jazz clarinet, are well known. Such dualities bespeak a profound ambivalence about the whole concept of celebrity, as well as Allen's precise function within an industry devoted to public exposure. Such confusion continues as one of the ambiguities recognizable within Allen's life and work. Indeed, the huge amount of publicity generated by the bitter separation and custody battle surrounding the breakup of Allen's long-term relationship with Mia Farrow in August of 1992 may have resulted as much from Allen's renowned reclusiveness as from the events themselves. Here, after all, was new fodder for the voracious tabloids and the equally curious public. A comment Allen made on television summed up this aspect of the whole sordid affair: "This is the first public appearance I've made in years, and all my dialogue is straight lines." No doubt Allen's ambivalence about celebrity slipped over into abhorrence while his private life was subjected to an unpleasant public scrutiny he long tried to avoid.

A great deal of this public, intellectual popularity, and the sometimes-controversial elements that accompany it, springs from Allen's engagement with his own Jewishness and the Jewish experience in America. One particular engagement with Jewry might be taken as emblematic of Allen's status as a public intellectual and some of the dangers associated with such a position. In "Am I Reading the Papers Correctly?" in the January 28, 1988 op-ed section of the *New York Times* (around the beginning of the *intifada*), Allen

Woody Allen on the set of *Crimes and Misdemeanors* with director of photography Sven Nykvist.

notes that he is apolitical and that his few political stances in recent years accomplished nothing. He then decries what he characterizes as violent and cruel acts by Israeli soldiers against "the rioting Palestinians." In a somewhat strained attempt to inject a little humor into the piece, he wonders if these soldiers are "the people whose money I used to steal from those little blue-and-white cans after collecting funds for a Jewish homeland." More seriously, he feels "appalled beyond measure" at these actions and calls on Israel's supporters to do whatever they can to "bring this wrongheaded approach to a halt."

The letter unleashed a handful of duly printed responses a few days later, some accusing Allen of being a self-hating Jew. "But then one shouldn't be surprised," said one letter-writer. "In all Woody Allen movies there has always been a subtle, yet cutting edge of Jewish self-hatred." Another letter-writer similarly castigated his stance, claiming that "it sounds a tad specious coming from an artist who, in his films and writings, exploits a now-extinct Jewish culture while scrupulously avoiding any references to Israel, the Holocaust or any other relevant Jewish issue." The most interesting responses, however, wondered why that particular event inspired Allen's first serious foray into print on the political scene, for example, "I don't recall seeing an Op-Ed article by Mr. Allen at the time of the *Achille Lauro* or after the slaughter of young children at Maalot or following the massacre of Israeli athletes at Munich." Sidney Zion, himself a Jewish public intellectual, similarly mused, "Funny that the first time Woody Allen lets us in on his devotion to Israel and his eternal outrage against her enemies appears in a diatribe against Israeli tactics in the rioting territories."

The letter-writers could and did link Allen's films to his editorial stance, and the motif of self-hatred appeared in the two separate forums. The charge of self-hatred sounds perhaps extreme, but the point about Allen's motivations for this first foray into political polemics is worth pursuing. Significantly, he took a very public stand on a major issue in which Jews could be seen in a negative light. Although Allen attempts to keep his rhetoric light, to defuse negative responses by his ingenuous introduction, he never states why Israel's actions are, to his mind, wrong. Apparently, the wrongness appears self-evident. Indeed, by pointing out that Israeli soldiers were "dragging civilians out of their houses at random to smash them with sticks" or were firing real bullets into crowds of demonstrators, Allen leads most readers to agree with him on the basis of Western values and simple human decency. Yet why was he not equally compelled to state these self-evident values when Arab violence was directed against Israel?

Allen chose not to answer his critics in the same journalistic forum of the *New York Times*. Rather, he selected another site to speak out again about Israel and the Palestinians, as well as to defend himself from some of the charges that had been leveled against him. This time, however, the forum was even more overtly Jewish than the *Times: Tikkun,* a leftist, liberal, intellectual journal overtly associated with Jewry. In an article entitled "Random Reflections of a Second-Rate Mind," Allen begins his ruminations with a recollection about seeing a Holocaust survivor eating at a trendy New York City restaurant and wondering about the vast difference between the man's life now and his death-camp experience. This inspires him to remember Elie Wiesel's statement that, upon liberation, the camp survivors thought about many things, but revenge against the Nazis was not among them. Allen remarks that he, who lived a comfortable, safe life in America, "think[s] of nothing but revenge" (13).

Yet from this historically and culturally specific tale of the Jewish experience, Allen goes on to wonder about the need, the humanity, of specifying a journal for Jews. "Aren't there enough real demarcations without creating artificial ones? . . . do I really want to contribute to a magazine that subtly helps promulgate phony and harmful differences?" (13, 14). Yet contribute he certainly did.

From such an ambivalent stance, we might conclude that Allen remains uneasy about his status as a Jewish filmmaker, a Jewish figure of importance. He clearly strives to deny his association with Jewry, yet he chose to write an op-ed piece about Israel and an article in a magazine exclusively identified as a "Bimonthly Jewish Critique of Politics, Culture and Society." Even earlier, many of the stories he published in the *New Yorker* convey a Jewish perspective and emerge from a distinctly Jewish consciousness. Predictably, in the pages of *Tikkun* he took as much punishment and received as much derision as he did in the *Times.*

Allen's career represents a virtual case history in coming to terms with tradition, with the search for an appropriate personal model of artistic creation sifted through a set of circumstances characteristic of a large portion of American Jewry. His films participate in the stream of American-Jewish art and literature that uses the structure of the bildungsroman to examine the emerging, maturing self and its relation to the world. His films, further, rely heavily upon the classic characteristics of Jewish humor and target aspects of popular culture. Allen's cinema, however, participates little in the search for social justice, a point for which he has been criticized, most often by Jewish critics. Instead, he reaches beyond the moment for larger social and religious truths. In this respect, Allen's cinema draws as much on other traditions as the Jewish ones identified in chapter 1, particularly relying upon the tradition of European art cinema exemplified for Allen, as for most audiences, by Bergman and Fellini.

Allen archetypically represents the American-Jewish artist in his reproduction of the absent tradition of American-Jewish art: Judaism. In fact, Judaism is the structuring absence of his mature films; his cinema is a constant working out of this missing link, a continual search for a substitute for Judaism. Jewish artists often manifest this absence through the search for social justice or the participation in popular life-style trends. For Allen, however, the cinema itself substitutes for Judaism. Although he began his film career by humorously parodying earlier films and film forms, his career has gradually explored the place of movies within a complete, meaningful life. This life will be lived in the predominant settings associated with American Jewry—urban America, often within the world of show business—but meaning will be derived from a search for the transcendent found in the movies.

Allen's search for traditions is also a matter of coming to terms with influences, many of which derive from Jewishness although he borrows from other significant traditions as well. In addition to the tradition of European art cinema, he draws upon the tradition of American silent comedy, especially the works of Charlie Chaplin, Buster Keaton, and Harold Lloyd. In fact, Allen's cinema progresses precisely by the degree to which he gradually abandons the established physical traditions of comedy in favor of a metaphysical approach exemplified by Bergman and Fellini.

Allen's reproduction of the image of the little man owes a specific debt to Chaplin, Keaton, and Lloyd, as well as to the schlemiel figure. The little man at odds with his environment remains an apt metaphor for the Jewish experience in history, but it persists as an equally potent contemporary symbol and is an often-used comic device. Allen's combination of the Jewish aspects of the schlemiel with the physical characteristics of the silent clowns presents an image of a man eternally bewildered by a hostile universe. In this respect, Allen typically reproduces the basic humor in the situations of classic comedies: of Charlie Chaplin's Tramp in the Alaskan Gold Rush, of Buster Keaton becoming a boxer or a general, or of Harold Lloyd's Freshman trying out for the football team.

Allen's filmic influences, then, are many. Confining ourselves to a discussion of the influences of Jewish tradition and experience in America on his films is not done with the intention of impoverishing them or denying the range of Allen's borrowings, transformations, or unique contributions. Rather, it is important to understand the particular nature of his films and the concerns they manifest by recourse to what is surely a fundamental influence on Allen's life: growing up Jewish in America. It is not our intention to reduce Allen in any way to the sum of his influences or his background, but rather to tease out the profound and personal aspects of his films by recourse to the definitional motifs of Jewish life in America.

Woody Allen—Allen Stewart Konigsberg—was born December 1, 1935 in Brooklyn. After graduating from Midwood High School, he attended New York University and City College of New York, without attaining a degree from either school. Allen began his career in show business as a gag writer, submitting jokes to newspaper and television personalities such as Walter Winchell, Earl Wilson, and Ed Sullivan. He then wrote for television shows, including "The Tonight Show" (1960–62) and, earlier, "Your Show of Shows" starring Sid Caesar, where he worked with other Jewish comic writers such as Mel Brooks, Larry Gelbart, Carl Reiner, and Neil Simon. At the urging of his agents Charles Joffe and Jack Rollins, he became a stand-up comic in the early 1960s, adopting the persona of the little loser, the schlemiel, in awe of women and unable to succeed with them. Accentuating his slight stature, glasses, and already thinning red hair, Allen's extremely self-deprecating humor focused upon his own shortcomings and failures. Little in his stand-up routines explored the politics of the day; he was no Mort Sahl and certainly no Lenny Bruce, except in his clever language and precise insights.

The kind of parody predominant in "Your Show of Shows" was equally evident in Allen's written humor, beginning in 1966 with his sketches for the *New Yorker*. Here he brilliantly replicated serious literary forms, such as the scholarly biography or the philosophical treatise, but filled them with inappropriate content, the humor resulting from an obvious clash between form and content. In "Yes, but Can the Steam Engine Do This?" he recreated the career of the Earl of Sandwich, whose accomplishment he likens to those of Da

Vinci, Aristotle, and Shakespeare. In a parody of the dramatic style of literary biography, Allen offered such gems as, "living in the country on a small inheritance, he works day and night, often skimping on meals to save money for food" (*Getting Even* 34). Other parodies included "Mr. Big" (a hard-boiled detective story in which the private eye searches the mean streets for God) and the writing styles of Dostoyevsky ("Notes from the Overfed") and Hemingway ("A Twenties Memory").

In addition to simple literary parody, the humorous style of the stories is extremely Jewish. Allen, for example, reproduces the essential strategy of linking disparate realms, especially the sacred and the profane. Often, he applies this tactic overtly to Jewish motifs, as in "Hassidic [*sic*] Tales, with a Guide to Their Interpretation by the Noted Scholar." Generally, however, the metaphysically serious rubs up against the hopelessly mundane, as when the philosopher Metterling proves "not only that Kant was wrong about the universe but that he never picked up a check" (10). Other one-liners demonstrate this subject as well, such as "eternal nothingness is O.K. if you're dressed for it," and "the universe is merely a fleeting idea in God's mind—a pretty uncomfortable thought, particularly if you've just made a down payment on a house" (31). Allen also combined parody and the yoking of disparate realms in the playlet *Death Knocks*. Here, a personified Death, inspired by Ingmar Bergman's *Seventh Seal*, plays gin rummy—not chess—with his unwilling victim. The victim wins more time, and Death owes him $28!

The *New Yorker* sketches clearly reveal a tension that structures Allen's entire career: his ability to link disparate realms for his own interests. As he began writing popular film comedies, he also created humor out of parodies of serious, intellectual subjects. In his film works, Allen would also move between the high-brow and the popular, although eventually his parodies of the serious would turn toward genuinely serious attempts at similar subjects. He then found himself in a struggle between intellectuality and popularity, as well as the serious and the humorous.

Finally, his early *New Yorker* writings confronted Jewishness and Judaism in a way that his films would only later. They reveal, through humor, an attitude toward Judaism that veers toward irreverence if not yet hostility. In the "Hassidic Tales," for instance, a woman asks a famous rabbi why Jews are not allowed to eat pork. "We're not? Uh-oh," he responds. In "The Scrolls," Allen rewrites the story of Abraham's command to sacrifice Isaac, with God telling

Abraham that He was only kidding, and chiding the patriarch for his gullibility: "some men will follow any order no matter how asinine as long as it comes from a resonant, well-modulated voice" (*Without Feathers* 27).

Between the writing of *What's New, Pussycat?* (1965) and *Casino Royale* (1967), Allen redubbed a Japanese spy thriller to create the comic *What's Up, Tiger Lily?* (1966). *What's Up, Tiger Lily?* also clearly demonstrates Allen's debt to Sid Caesar, particularly to a "Your Show of Shows" sketch parodying samurai movies, a cultural coup for a writing staff creating skits in the late 1950s. One of the least of the concerns in *Tiger Lily* was Jewishness. Yet, even here, Allen's ethnic sensibilities appear. The (Japanese) hero is called Phil Moscowitz, and a character calls for his rabbi after being shot. Brode concludes that this film enabled Allen "to introduce what will become a key theme: assimilation of Jews into non-Jewish lifestyles" (65). But such a comment, although astute, fails to see the larger issue. Rather than simply thematizing the issue of assimilation, Allen introduces Jewishness as a source of humor, the wellspring from which his unique comic perspective will derive its particular vision.

The specifically Jewish dimensions to Allen's work in the period leading up to *Annie Hall* were few and usually covert. He made his official directorial debut with *Take the Money and Run* (1969), which featured him as an incompetent criminal. Filmic parody and the schlemiel persona again dominated the film, which also incorporated a handful of ethnic gags. In this, his first film as writer-director-star, Allen began to focus upon his Jewish background and, as would often be the case in his later films, the images presented are disturbing. In particular, he gratuitously uses the image of a rabbi for broad humor. For example, as a prisoner, he ingests an experimental drug that has side effects that turn him into a rabbi—visually, a Hasidic rabbi. Much of the rest of the ethnic humor is subtle. The image of Allen's character being beaten by neighborhood bullies looks forward to the more explicitly anti-Semitic nature of such beatings claimed for the character of Zelig in the film of that name. Similarly, the hero's parents, absurdly disguised in Groucho glasses, squabble and snap at each other and condemn their wayward son at every turn.

More important than specifically overt ethnic humor, the basic situation of *Take the Money and Run,* as well as Allen's succeeding films for the next six years, represents a decidedly Jewish perspective in terms of his constant use of the "fish out of water" structure:

the difficulty of the little Jew trying to assimilate into a predominantly non-Jewish society. Allen's Virgil Starkwell desperately wants to succeed and fit in, even within the world of crime. Voice-over narration tells the audience that, indeed, "he wanted only to belong," and "he was unable to fit in with any aspect of his environment." (The parallels with *Zelig* continue to resonate.) But such a claim may provide a too simplistic, or at least too reductive, an explanation, for Allen is working in classic comic territory. The very sight of him portraying a would-be gangster and laboring on a chain gang makes the audience laugh, as the discrepancy between Allen's physical appearance clashes with the image we hold—even if derived from movies—of real gangsters. Similarly, Allen the neurotic urbanite as a Latin American revolutionary (*Bananas*), or Allen the disheveled bumbler as a feared revolutionary in a dystopic future (*Sleeper*), or Allen the frail coward as a Tolstoyan hero during the Napoleonic Wars (*Love and Death*) creates comic dissonance between competing images, a discontinuity that is inherently funny.

Allen again mimed the little man at odds with his environment, along with the disparity between image and reality, in *Bananas* (1971), his follow-up to *Take the Money and Run*. Working the same vein as "Viva Vargas," his short story of the same period, *Bananas* displays little feel for genuine political humor. Allen's essentially apolitical nature, his distrust of politicians and their solutions, generates little sympathy for either side of any political question. His heart, not his ideals, motivates him to make a powerful political statement. Two essential features of his awkward (and awkwardly named) protagonist, Fielding Mellish, are apparent. First, Fielding, a neurotic urbanite, is not only out of place amid Che Guevara-like Latino revolutionaries, but he is also out of tune with his Manhattan surroundings. He fears the urban jungle on the subway ride home from work as much as he later fears the steamy jungle of the mythic Latin American revolutionary sojourn. Here the classic schlemiel, the total nebbish, fails once again to master machines in his job as a product tester, a failing that mirrors his inability to succeed with women. Second, he undertakes a dangerous and foolish task precisely to impress a woman.

With *Take the Money and Run* and *Bananas*, Allen set his films on a stable and consistent course. The endearing schlemiel persona, combined with a caustic eye for popular culture and a penchant for the parodic, still characterize most of them. Lacking in these first two films, however, was a fourth component: a command of, and an appreciation for, the cinema. In both *Play It Again, Sam* (1972) and

Everything You Always Wanted to Know About Sex* (*but Were Afraid to Ask) (1972) Allen developed a more cinematic sensibility than had been apparent previously. Although Allen did not direct *Sam*, he adapted his own Broadway play with an eye toward opening it up for the screen and assumed the lead role under Herbert Ross's direction. More important, the near-religious awe with which he regards the cinema and the possibility that movies hold for transcending ordinary existence are evident.

Play It Again, Sam marked the first major statement of Allen's developing view of the cinema. In this parody of *Casablanca*, he reveals how the cinema dominates the hero's life (seemingly to his detriment), yet how it also provides a positive model of behavior—indeed, a positive worldview. Allan Felix (Allen's alter ego), a film buff, writes for a small, San Francisco-based movie magazine. Beyond simply making his living from watching films or even merely enjoying the movies, Felix defines his life by the images he sees on the screen. His dreams become flesh as he conjures up an image of Humphrey Bogart (Jerry Lacy), to seek advice about love and life. Bogey, a creature from the id for Allan Felix, presents a purified extract of the tough-guy, cynical Bogart persona. Thus, for example, Allan's failures with women since his divorce from Nancy (Susan Anspach) contrast starkly to Bogart's casually disdainful success with "dames." Nervously awaiting a blind date, Allan imagines himself as Bogey, having to slap the woman around when she begs him for more. Bogey's basic advice to Allan: "dames are simple— they understand a slap in the face or a slug from a .45."

The interpellation of imagined films within the film forms part of the larger pattern of *Play It Again, Sam*, which completely interpellates *Casablanca*. The film does not simply "borrow" the famous airport scene from Curtiz's classic, but rather transposes Casablanca to San Francisco, simultaneously transposing the minidrama of World War II to a mini-comedy of the war between the sexes. Allen's *Sam* is essentially a remake of *Casablanca* and possesses almost all of the film's key ingredients. In transposing the film to a contemporary locale and eliminating the larger surrounding issue of World War II, Allen's film domesticates the exoticism of *Casablanca* and lowers the stakes, precisely the definition of comedy (Jewish comedy, in particular): the domestication of myth. Allen, in occupying the place of Bogart in this remake, uses the implicit disjuncture between his screen persona and that of Bogart's to comic effect.

On closer examination, however, mere comedy, or even mere

parody, are not what is at stake here. Rather, *Sam* is about the relationship between film and life. The film poses two questions in its use of *Casablanca*. Can real life provide the opportunities for heroism that *Casablanca* gave Bogart, who had to sacrifice the woman he loved for a larger cause? Can movies provide a glimpse of transcendent moments that we can use in our own lives? *Sam* implicitly answers the first question affirmatively. Allan Felix does not give Linda up for the sake of the Allied cause (and does not really have to give up Linda, for she has already decided to go back to Dick), but for the sake of his friend. As Bogey tells him, helping a pal is a good thing to do. The second question is more problematic but precisely the one Woody Allen ponders in virtually all of his subsequent important films.

Everything You Always Wanted to Know About Sex* (*but Were Afraid to Ask), which followed *Sam* almost immediately, was inspired by a bestseller by Dr. David Reuben, a pop-culture phenomenon of the era. Allen's film, really a series of sketches, uses Reuben's actual headings for discussions of sexual topics. The sketches satirize rather than illustrate Reuben's points, however. Allen's particular genius moved him beyond satire to clothe the sketches in images drawn from another realm of popular culture: the movies. As Allen recognized in *Play It Again, Sam*, people take lessons from the movies. What happens on the screen greatly influences ideas, particularly images of romance and sex. Allen films each sketch in a different cinematic style, with the topic of each scene determining the particular style or form and greatly adding to the comedy. For example, "Do Aphrodisiacs Work?" is illustrated by a costume sketch in which the medieval world of alchemy and wizardry provides a fitting setting to ponder the pseudo-science of love potions. Similarly, "Why Do Some Women Have Trouble Reaching an Orgasm?" becomes a perfect parody of the world of Michelangelo Antonioni, whose films, for example, *L'Avventura, La Notte,* and *L'Eclisse* (1960–62), deal with existential angst, with the sterility of contemporary middle-class life accompanied by a propensity for sterile, near-empty mise-en-scène. Angst and ennui characterize the couple in Allen's exact reproduction (in color, not black and white, however) of Antonioni's sterile, passionless world. While choosing the proper parodic style, Allen learned to perfect his own cinematic technique.

Although David Reuben himself was Jewish, little beyond the sociological emphasis was "Jewish" in his book. Yet a number of the sketches (four out of seven) in *Everything You Always Wanted to Know*

About Sex cast characters as clearly Jewish. In "What Is Sodomy?" Gene Wilder stars as a "superstraight Jewish doctor" (Brode 129); in "Are Transvestites Homosexuals?" Lou Jacobi's character reads as clearly Jewish; in the concluding sequence, "What Happens during Ejaculation?" Allen himself (as a spermatozoon) exclaims "At least he's Jewish!" in reference to the person whose spermatozoon he is. The "What Are Sex Perverts?" sequence parodies the television game show "What's My Line?" and features a rabbi (Baruch Lumet, Sidney Lumet's father) whose secret fantasy is to be whipped by a statuesque shiksa while his wife eats pork. As Vincent Canby drily noted in the *New York Times* on August 7, 1972, the sketch "will not endear Mr. Allen to the Anti-Defamation League." (He was right; B'nai B'rith did protest the scene.) Beyond the possible cry of self-hatred, why introduce Jewishness at this point?

Let us return, for a moment, to Sig Altman's insightful recognition of the comic image of the Jew. The association of Jews with comedy, of Jews as being humorous, can help explain why Gene Wilder, Lou Jacobi, Baruch Lumet, and Allen himself play the roles that they do. Another reason concerns social class and comic discrepancy. Again and again it is apparent that Allen uses the disjunction between image and reality as a source of humor. For example, in *Bananas*, Allen, the neurotic Jew as Latino revolutionary, provides one instance of the strategy. The same dislocation operates in this case. Gene Wilder is not simply a doctor, but a psychiatrist.

Allen's own ventures into psychoanalysis, by now well known and a frequent source of one-liners in his cinema, immediately bring *Sleeper, Stardust Memories,* and *Zelig* to mind as containing jokes at psychiatry's expense. Allen pokes fun at both himself for being an analysand and at the analyst fallen victim to a mental aberration of his own. More important, Allen plays upon the image of the Jewish doctor-psychiatrist as an educated man of science, as assimilated into intellectual discourse, falling in love so inappropriately (not with a shiksa, but with a sheep). Alternately, Lou Jacobi's Sam is an average family man, a typical, middle-class husband and father. The sight of him prancing around in a dress is funny precisely because it deviates from middle-class norms. As Nancy Pogel has it, "for a moment he . . . achieves a moment of playful freedom" (61). This freedom from restrictions—from the middle-class morality that characterizes American culture and Jewish culture in America—is perhaps Allen rebelling less against Jewry than against the middle class. He remains equally as ambivalent about his social class as about his ethnicity.

In *Sleeper* (1973), his most assured and cinematically successful film yet, Allen directed himself opposite Diane Keaton for the first time; he was also the first filmmaker to give her an essentially comic leading role. Even more than in *Sam,* their chemistry was based upon one of the essential conflicts in Allen's films: Jew-WASP. The meeting and romancing of the WASP woman and the Jewish man primarily involves the man educating the woman and making her aware of the complexities of life. She, in turn, provides him with the confidence to be himself. *Sleeper* mines the genre of dystopic fiction, the creation of a future world gone awry. But rather than parody science fiction, as does Mel Brooks's *Spaceballs* (1987), *Sleeper* stands as a comic science-fiction film in its own right. Like most good science fiction (and most good comedy, for that matter), its alternate world comments primarily on the present rather than the future, on our world rather than our great-grandchildren's.

A strong use of regional humor and intellectual satire by no means exhausts the comic and serious aspects of *Sleeper:* its ethnic aspect is equally important. A memorably funny sequence involves the Jewish robot-tailors, whose humor stems from their anachronistic dialect and Bergsonian actions. Although funny, the fact that they are stereotypically Jewish also says something about the durability of ethnic stereotypes (which have negative connotations) and about the positive maintenance of ethnic difference. Like an earlier ethnic joke in the film—all of the men in this future society are impotent except those whose ancestors were Italian—this joke speaks of ethnicity as contributing toward a unique identity in a conformative world.

Jewishness is again invoked in an extended sequence revolving precisely around the question of identity. Having been reprogrammed into a new identity by the State, Miles Monroe (Allen) needs to be deprogrammed by the Rebellion. To accomplish this, the muscleman Erno (John Beck) and Luna, a shiksa (Keaton), undertake to initiate a scene from Miles's youth. They act out a seder (the Passover ritual meal) and mangle the Yiddish-inflected dialect of Miles's parents. Erno badly mispronounces "oy vey iz meir," and Luna tells Miles to "be quiet and eat your shiksa!" The double entendre, of course, completely bypasses those who do not have at least this one word of Yiddish at their command.

Significantly, this re-brainwashing does not quite work just yet, for Miles becomes, not his old self, but Blanche DuBois of Tennessee Williams's *A Streetcar Named Desire.* Nancy Pogel sees this moment as revelatory of how Miles's role as Blanche is as equally inappropriate for a Jewish boy as Luna and Erno's parent roles were for two WASPs (69). But this seems to be kvetching a bit, for Miles has assumed a role quite like his own: a frail, bewildered outsider unable to live in a cruel, cold, dehumanized world. That Miles becomes Blanche while Luna acts out Stanley partakes of the humorous tradition of cross-dressing, which made fortunes for the likes of Milton Berle and Monty Python's Flying Circus, among others. Equally important, Miles's transformation marks the second time in the film that Allen crosses gender. In the earlier brainwashing undertaken by the State to make Miles a citizen, he participated in a Miss America contest (as Miss Montana), thereby transforming the neurotic, urban Jewish man into an all-American, clean-living, rural WASP woman. Although we should not make too much of this "transvestite" comedy, or the earlier cross-dressing sequence in *Everything You Always Wanted to Know About Sex,* we can note that cross-dressing is *not* usually a part of Allen's repertoire; gender-crossing marks the most significant absence in the transformative powers of Leonard Zelig, for example.

The most likely reason for the unqualified comic and cinematic success of *Sleeper* springs from the basic image of the film: the alien. Good comedy involves a disjuncture between image and reality, between self-image and self-deception, between aspirations and actualities. Good comedy can also be built around the image of the little guy struggling to come to terms with a hostile universe, as well as by using the figure of the outsider who cannot—and does not want—to come to terms with his environment. Chaplin's Tramp demonstrates and apotheosises these assertions, however this image in *Sleeper* stems from the historic situation of Jews in a gentile world. Not only is the little Jew from 1973 an outsider in this dystopic future of 2173, but the State also perceives him as a hostile, intrusive, dangerous force who cannot be allowed to contaminate citizens. Because *Sleeper* is a comedy and not an allegory of the Holocaust, this futuristic society "reprograms" Miles Monroe instead of putting him to death. However, the sense of alienation he feels, the persecution he experiences, and the uncomfortable accommodation he makes to this repressive society are telling derivations of the historical situation of the Jews. The millenarian, utopian yearnings of American Jewry encounter the dystopic future (that is, present) that Jews have more often than not faced. That Miles finds solace only "in the two things that come once in life—sex and death" typifies Allen's solution to his historical and metaphysical situation.

"Sex and death" as the ultimate meanings of life become transformed slightly into *Love and Death* (1975), Allen's next film. *Sleeper* and *Love and Death*, again with Diane Keaton, remain his most completely "funny" films, precisely the kind of "earlier, funny ones" that the aliens of *Stardust Memories* wish Allen would continue to make. *Sleeper* demonstrated Allen's growing mastery of visual comedy; *Love and Death* demonstrated that a return to the verbal humor of his stand-up comedy days did not mean abandoning his evolving cinematic consciousness.

Love and Death takes its comic force from, again, the disjunction between image and reality, between form and content, between WASP and Jew. The film emphasizes the enormity of the disjunctures Allen uses. While he had perfectly inhabited the schlemiel persona and completely metamorphized into the schlemiel as "modern hero," his authorial genius now placed this schlemiel onto the epic stage. An obvious derivation from *War and Peace*—the film is set during the Napoleonic Wars, with Allen's alter ego, Boris, on a mission to assassinate the French general—*Love and Death* recognizes the contemporary impossibility of the epic. Indeed, following Tolstoy, the literary epic turns inward to Proust, James Joyce, "The Waste Land," and the comedy of Woody Allen. The film similarly derives much force from anachronism, from a modern sensibility at odds with a different epoch. As Foster Hirsch notes, *Sleeper* puts the very modern Woody Allen into a future in which his character has no place; *Love and Death* has the same strategy, except that it places the modern, urban neurotic into the pastoral past (70).

Although little of the film is explicitly Jewish, a few Jewish, or anti-Jewish, jokes do occur. For example, Boris says about Jewish women: "I hear [they] don't believe in sex after marriage." Yet, much of the comedy revolves around the sudden thrusting downward from the sacred to the mundane, a particular characteristic of Jewish humor. Nancy Pogel neatly describes Allen's humor in *Love and Death* as being "based on the incongruity between the weighty concerns and abstract rhetoric of philosophy and literature, and ordinary people's down-to-earth needs" (70).

For a film that seems to be only marginally Jewish, much of the humor in *Love and Death* derives from Jewish tradition, and the metaphysical musings keenly indicate its absence. Allen structures the film much as Bergman did for *The Seventh Seal*. However, Allen's film results in a series of cosmic jokes equal to his best *New Yorker* jottings. For example, Sonia (Keaton) is equally as philosophical as Boris (a reversal from Keaton's role in *Sleeper*). She commands Boris: "Look at this leaf. Isn't it perfect? And this one, too. Yes. I definitely think this is the best of all possible worlds." To which Boris replies: "It's certainly the most expensive." When, as a young boy, he meets Death, Boris asks, "What happens after we die? Heaven, Hell? God? [Pause.] Are there girls?" He needs a sign of God's existence, one small miracle, like his Uncle Sasha picking up a check. Allen also delivers one of his most famous religious pronouncements when he says of God, "the worst thing you can say about Him is that He's basically an underachiever."

Unsurprisingly, the only meaning that Boris can find in life is in love. His relationship to Sonia, and a sexual dalliance with a gorgeous countess, provide the sole semblances of value in a doomed existence. Yet love is fraught with peril. In a motif that will be repeated in *Manhattan, Stardust Memories,* and *Crimes and Misdemeanors,* we learn that people fall in love with the wrong person. Boris loves Sonia, but Sonia is in love with his brother, "a Neanderthal who can barely spell his name in the dirt with a stick" (Pogel 73). If love is irrational and usually unsatisfying, however, it is also interrupted by death. Love and death are the two things that come once in a lifetime.

Between 1965, with the writing of *What's New, Pussycat?* and 1975, with writing, directing, and starring in *Love and Death,* Allen was intimately involved in the production of ten feature films. He also continued to write short stories (publishing primarily in the *New Yorker*), made an occasional television appearance, and even produced three television specials. It is understandable, then, that in 1976 he took a break from filmmaking to star in a film that he neither wrote nor directed. The film, however, was not a mere diversion or a complete abandonment of the issues, motifs, and concerns that obsess him. If more overtly political than a typical Allen feature, *The Front* allowed him to express his usually private politics in a public forum.

The Front, the story of a small-time hustler (Allen) involved with blacklisted writers during the McCarthy era of the 1950s, carried forward three central motifs of Jewish life in America: show business (here television, in which Allen was employed during the 1950s); the importance of love relationships; and Jewishness itself. Although the script is never specific on the issue, one cannot miss the Jewishness of the blacklisted writers and stars with whom Allen's character Howard Prince (himself Jewish) comes into contact. With good intentions as well as personal anguish behind the film (end credits identify many of the cast and crew as victims of the blacklist), *The Front* had the potential to be a powerful indictment of the blacklist and the anti-Semitism that fueled much of it. Yet the typical Hollywood ending—Howard tells off the House Un-American Activities Committee—is a cathartic moment, mutes the political outrage, and avoids any notion of the origins and intentions behind the blacklist. Yet Allen's choice was well-intentioned. Perhaps the story, which could have been his own had he been older and more involved politically, inspired him to make films that did tell his own story in truthful, overt, and honest ways.

Following the huge commercial and critical success of *Annie Hall* (1977), Allen wrote and directed *Interiors* (1978), the first of three films of a trilogy that we term "Attack of the WASP Women." By his on-screen absence Allen declared these films to be "serious," as if a focus on Jews could only be funny and his mere presence denotes comedy and Jewishness. To a large extent, that is indeed the case, because Allen had long identified *Jewish* with *humor* and himself as an on-screen Jewish persona. As he told Douglas Brode, "my presence is so completely associated with comedy that when the audience sees me, they might think it's a sign for them to begin laughing" (179). Thus, he had to eliminate his on-screen presence in his three films about upper-middle-class angst and dysfunctional families. Allen, in an interview with Robert Benayoun, has expressed the notion that his earlier films were trivial, a syndrome of screen comedy going all the way back to Charlie Chaplin, whose first non-comic film, *A Woman of Paris* (1923), was the first of his own films in which he did not star. Chaplin could not resist injecting sentimental or supposedly serious motifs in even such comic films as *City Lights* (1931), *The Great Dictator* (1942), and *Monsieur Verdoux* (1947). He observed to Benayoun that his earlier films were "curtain raisers, entertainments, and desserts: they lacked substance. I felt trapped in a dead end." Through the use of such models as O'Neill, Chekhov, and, of course, Ingmar Bergman, whose *Cries and Whispers* lurks behind the scenes of *Interiors*, Allen tried to escape the trap of comedy (Benayoun 157). In a line worthy of Allen himself, Maurice Yacowar maintains the resultant film "can be described as a Chekhovian vision of an O'Neill family, expressed with Bergmanesque rigor" (*Loser* 186).

Interiors and the later films of the trilogy are important not because of their quality as cinema (by any standards, they are minor works), but because of what they reveal of the underlying tensions that structure Allen's best work. These tensions may be charted by a series of oppositions: Jew-Gentile, Man-Woman, Neurotic-

Psychotic, Mother-Father, Son-Daughter, and Urban-Rural. Although Allen has been accused of self-hatred, the peculiarly Jewish form of anti-Semitism, the WASP Women films reveal that he does not offer upper-class Anglo-Saxon values and behavior as alternatives to being Jewish. The WASP family of *Interiors* is comprised of three sisters, Diane Keaton, Marybeth Hurt, and Kristen Griffith (the Chekhov allusion must be clear), with a powerful, attractive father, Arthur (E. G. Marshall), and a cold, severe mother, Eve (Geraldine Page). The film focuses on how Arthur's desire to leave his wife for another woman affects Eve and the daughters.

We see the family as distant, uncommunicative, and unsupportive. The interiors of the title refer not only to the family's home, but also to the interior lives of the characters. The film evolves into a psychoanalytic case study of a dysfunctional family, exploring how family dynamics conspire to cause two of the daughters to have unhappy marriages and all to be inchoately yet clearly dissatisfied with their lives. Ultimately, their mother commits suicide, although the girls respond less to her death and more to their father's choice of a second wife, Pearl (Maureen Stapleton), a "vulgarian" constructed (but not mentioned) as Jewish.

The Jewishness of Pearl has been thoroughly explicated by Maurice Yacowar, who notes that "Pearl functions like Allen's Jewish hero in his comedies with Diane Keaton, in which the life-affirming Jew plays against and enlivens the controlled WASP" (*Loser* 191). He notes, too, that Pearl's "Jewishness is more a matter of class than religion, and her religious sense is primitive." This is consistent with how Allen views Jewishness elsewhere: the religious dimension, Judaism, is almost always absent from Jews in his films. As Pogel notes, "Pearl is associated with primitive mysteries . . . she is interested in voodoo and collects African fertility statues" (104). She does card tricks, which Woody Allen boasted proudly of being · able to do when he was interviewed by Benayoun (159). Pearl's place of residence, Florida (and, obviously, not northern Florida), and the fact that her former husbands were a jeweler and an orthodontist similarly help construct her as Jewish. Yacowar notes that Eve is Pearl's opposite. She spends a good deal of time in churches or cathedrals. Yacowar believes that a fundamentalist radio program to which she listens symbolizes her replacement by Pearl (191). In an interview on this program, a converted Jew tells of how wonderful it is to be a Christian, an idea later reversed by the Jewish woman replacing the Christian one in the family drama.

September (1988), the second film in the WASP Women trilogy, was a major departure. Yet it contains the ensemble acting that Allen had begun to use in *Interiors*. The frequently recurring show business milieu in this story concerns a famous, spoiled, monstrously egocentric actress (Elaine Stritch) and her mousy, timid, talentless daughter (Mia Farrow). The mother is not simply cold to her child, but cruel, her ultimate cruelty not revealed until the end of the film. The film, loosely based upon a famous incident in the life of Lana Turner, whose daughter (Cheryl Crane) shot Turner's gangster-lover (Johnny Stompanato), is the real-life stuff of melodrama, but Allen's film functions less like a Lana Turner soap opera than an Ibsen melodrama.[2] Unfortunately, Ibsen no longer works as an appropriate model even for theater, and his style is deadly dull on film.

In *Another Woman* (1988), the trilogy's most successful film, Allen moves away from a dysfunctional family and focuses on a more adult woman (Gena Rowlands), ignoring the neoadolescent whinings of adult-aged characters. The implicit psychoanalytic view of the characters of the earlier films here becomes explicit, with its focus on a philosophy professor who is exposed to the psychoanalytic process. Although the film appears indebted to Bergman's *Wild Strawberries* (1957) and *Face to Face* (1976), it lacks their obsessive use of close-ups to convey ultimate angst and the use of dreams and fantasies on the protagonist's part to convey symbolically what the drama cannot.

Almost every commentator has subscribed to the viewpoint that *Manhattan* (1979), produced on the heels of *Interiors*, remains one of Allen's finest filmic achievements. Far from following a trend, as in Allen's parodies of James Bond-style films early in his career, or from producing hollow imitations of master filmmakers, *Manhattan* marks a bold and original stylistic leap forward. The use of lush, black-and-white cinematography recalls the glorious black-and-white images of the 1930s, aided here by the equally lush strains of Gershwin melodies. Combined with the widescreen process of CinemaScope, *Manhattan* stakes out new esthetic territory.[3] The film's cinematography and mise-en-scène are every bit as studied and composed as are *Interiors*, but without the lifelessness of the more overt drama. Allen reappears on screen in the role of Isaac Davis, a clear and undeniable stand-in for Allen himself and a clear return to comedy. With its plot of Isaac's breakup with Mary (Diane Keaton), *Manhattan* obviously recounts Allen's breakup with Keaton during the film's production.

Significantly, the film's title foregrounds its setting, rather than the romantic components of the plot. Allen glorifies New York not only through the gorgeous cinematography that romanticizes the urban landscape, but also through voice-over. The film opens with a series of skyline shots, Allen's voice-over paying tribute to the city in a style that suggests film-noir. Using elegant shots of the Hayden Planetarium, he celebrates the city by showing how much there is to do in New York. He acknowledges the joys of city life by showing the variety of New York's inhabitants. For Allen, whose urban, Jewish neuroses often prevent coming to terms with his environment, New York represents home, as it does still for a large portion of American Jews. The city is the place of possibility, culture, and true inner life within urban (limited, but beautiful) exteriors.

Allen continually contrasts such an ideal with the compromises of personal integrity and the pitfall of succumbing to the quick, easy, and glib that also characterize contemporary urban life, with its overnight fads and forgettable fashions. New Yorkers in particular must appreciate the portrait of Yale (Michael Murphy, with whom Allen worked in *The Front*), who, instead of starting a small literary magazine, uses his money to buy a Porsche. Mary writes a novelization of a film; even Isaac has worked in television but retires to try and write a novel.

The Jewishness of Allen and of the milieu functions as a natural part of the environment, and, after ten years of filmmaking, Allen easily uses a shorthand to fill it in. We note the name *Isaac* as not only archetypally Jewish, but also referencing the Old Testament story of Abraham and Isaac. Can this biblical story of a son almost sacrificed in the name of religion possess some particular meaning for Allen? After all, we recall his humorous short story "The Scrolls" and note how the tale of Abraham and Isaac recurs again in *Stardust Memories*. This element of Jewishness, and of sacrifice, is humorously invoked when Isaac mentions one of his short stories, "The Castrating Zionist," which is about his mother not his father (psychoanalysis will not leave the scene). A section from his former wife's devastating critique of their marriage describes Isaac's "Jewish-Liberal paranoia." In a passing remark that subtly refers to the Holocaust, Isaac observes that the best way to deal with a group of neo-Nazis staging a march is not with satire but with bricks and bats. This is irony, or perhaps guilt, from a man whose greatest weapon has been comedy and satire, not physical violence. It also expresses the ambivalence of a man who would later be horrified at the use of bats on the part of Israeli soldiers dealing with the *intifada*.

The continuing absence of Judaism in *Manhattan* is also significant, as is the manner in which the existential Jew searches for a
substitute. As Allen told an interviewer, "there's no center to the
culture. We have this opulent relatively well-educated culture, and
yet we see a great city like New York deteriorate. We see people lose
themselves in drugs because they don't deal with their sense of
spiritual emptiness" (quoted in Pogel 119). The substitute for absent Judaism and the resultant sense of spiritual emptiness are
things Allen desperately tried to remedy in earlier films, which
espouse only two cures: sex and death. To these two things, which
come once in a lifetime, *Manhattan* proposes an addendum. This
addendum at film's end is foreshadowed by Isaac's angry reaction
to Yale and Mary, who denigrate many of his (and Allen's) cultural
heroes: Lenny Bruce, Gustav Mahler, Vincent Van Gogh, and Ingmar Bergman. Later, after breaking up with Tracy (Mariel Hemingway), Isaac speaks into his tape recorder, enumerating the
things that make life worth living: Groucho Marx, Willie Mays,
Mozart's Jupiter Symphony, Flaubert's *A Sentimental Education*, and
Tracy's face (see also Yacowar 201). Although in this list Tracy has
become an esthetic object, a work of art or a commodified cultural
icon, Isaac rushes across town to confront her. Thus, art and relationships make life worth living, as Isaac tries to salvage his relationship with Tracy. Tracy has the memorable, epigrammatic final
line of the film, encapsulating Isaac's existential, spiritual quest and
the moral lesson to be learned from it: "Look, you have to have a
little faith in people."

Manhattan marked the clearest, fullest expression to date of how
Allen wants to live his life. His continued willingness to confront his
inner feelings and personal situations led to *Stardust Memories*
(1980), a thinly disguised self-analysis in which Allen agonizes over
his public role as a comic filmmaker and the place of his art in his
life. Unfortunately, this deep introspection antagonized many fans
and almost all of the film's critics. Yet a careful viewing that goes
beyond Allen's apparent insults to loyal fans and the very act of film
criticism shows Allen's clearest target to be himself. His most vicious barbs are directed inward. Once again, the Jew, who might be
angry at the greater culture, misdirects his humor, victimizing himself. If *Zelig* is, in some sense, Allen's response to the attacks he
received following the release of *Stardust Memories*, *Stardust Memories* can also be seen as a precursor to *Zelig*, a film that similarly
focuses on a man with no personality, no meaning, of his own.

Set resolutely in the world of filmmaking, *Stardust Memories* struck many critics simply as Allen's fruitless attempt to imitate Federico Fellini's *8½* (1963). Both films focus upon filmmakers during a professional crisis; both use a combination of memory and fantasy from their protagonist's point of view to take the audience through a retrospective of their creators' lives. Allen even uses the idea of a weekend retrospective screening of his alter ego's movies to structure his film, much as Fellini's alter ego rehearses and recollects his earlier movies. Of course, the professional crisis of the protagonists, their inability to know what their next film will be, becomes their next film, the film we are watching, a pattern of Fellini's that Paul Mazursky also borrowed for *Alex in Wonderland*.

Stardust Memories catalogs several of Allen's other recurring concerns, those fundamentally linked to his Jewishness. The connections between love and death, for example, are once again apparent. Sandy Bates (Allen) tells Dorrie (Charlotte Rampling): "I'm *fatally* attracted to you" (201; emphasis in Brode). Similarly, the death of love strikes Allen's protagonist: he is unable to sustain his relationship with Dorrie; his relationship with Daisy (Jessica Harper) seems to come to a quick halt; and his difficulty in committing to a relationship with a relatively sane and healthy woman hopelessly compromises his relationship with Isobel (Marie-Christine Barrault). Sandy, much like Isaac Davis in this respect, also resembles Isaac by having a successful show business career and by starting, if not sustaining, sexual relationships.

Allen overtly invokes Jewishness by naming a character in a film-within-the-film Sidney Finkelstein, as well as by making the character an archetypal *echt*-Jew whose fondest desire is to rid himself of his domineering mother. Jewishness also permeates the troubled relationship between Dorrie and Sandy. Viewers can quickly pigeonhole the anorectic Dorrie as another of Allen's dysfunctional WASP women whose family dynamics lead her to the same profound psychosis that permeates the daughters in *Interiors*, the daughter in *September*, and the professor and psychiatric patient in *Another Woman*. In addition to a disturbed, troubled mother, Allen also includes strong hints of father-daughter incest. Pogel notes that during one of the quarrels between Sandy and Dorrie, the walls of his apartment display blow-ups of a newspaper headline about incest (138).

Dorrie represents more than dysfunctional WASP psychology, however. She also symbolizes superior social class, a world of wealth and travel, of servants and spas, denied Sandy Bates until his own success enables him to experience life's material gratifications. Allen neatly encapsulates these profound differences in psychology and social class in one moment of conversation. Sandy romanticizes the relationship with Dorrie's powerful, charismatic father and her institutionalized mother by juxtaposing it to his own upbringing: "Suicide was just not a middle-class alternative. My mother was too busy running the boiled chicken through the deflavorizing machine." He thus conflates social class and ethnicity. Only the rich kill themselves, he thinks, and only Jews serve flavorless boiled chicken. The brilliant comic conflation relies on the yoking of disparate realms that typifies Jewish humor and characterizes the best of Woody Allen's written and cinematic updating of the East European worldview.

The millenarian impulse, hinted at in *Sleeper,* parodied in *Love and Death,* and glimpsed in *Manhattan,* comes to the fore in *Stardust Memories.* But the cultural Jewishness of class and ethnicity represents just one aspect of Jewry that Allen brings up as he approaches Judaism (at least in passing) in a couple of key moments. Sandy's sister (Anne DeSalvo) reminisces to Isobel about the time Sandy protested against a school play based upon the biblical episode of Abraham's sacrifice of Isaac. Later, when aliens he imagines landing at a gathering of UFO believers berate Sandy for denying his comic gift and for his choice of women, he exclaims, "what are you, my rabbi?" By invoking Judaism within the context of UFOs and extraterrestrials, Allen admits people's metaphysical, millenarian impulses and rejects them explicitly. This scene in *Stardust Memories* draws much of its visual style from *Close Encounters of the Third Kind,* directed by Steven Spielberg, another Jew whose inability to believe in Judaism perhaps leads him to contemplate UFOs and extraterrestrials. Allen postulates that, at least for Sandy, his relationships with women (especially Dorrie) are substitutes for religion.

Juxtaposed against the millenarian impulse, and equally profound in Jewish culture, is the apocalyptic memory of Jewish history and religion. When a former friend from the old neighborhood bitterly compares his fate to Sandy's, the successful film director responds, "I was a lucky bum. If I was not born in Brooklyn, if I had been born in Poland, or Berlin, I'd be a lampshade today, right?" This overt invocation of the Holocaust, one of the few in Allen's cinema, in this context humanizes Sandy. We know that even if his worries about the universe are absurd, even if a viewing of *The Bicycle Thief* (1949) makes him feel guilty for making comic films and for feeling sorry for comparing his situation to the economic struggles of De Sica's victimized Romans, he still expresses some legitimate, sensitive concerns.

The Holocaust is discussed more overtly in *Hannah and Her Sisters*. Frederick (Max von Sydow) tells Lee (Barbara Hershey) that he has just been watching a television program about the Holocaust. Incredulous at the continuing puzzlement expressed by intellectuals trying to understand how it could have happened, he contends that "these are the wrong questions. Given how people are what's surprising is not how it happened, but why it doesn't happen more often." Allen immediately undercuts this brilliantly pessimistic insight by having Frederick continue, superciliously claiming that it does happen but in smaller ways, thus removing Jewish specificity from the Holocaust. Worse, Frederick remains the film's most unsympathetic character, which lessens the effect of what he says and allows it to be attributed simply to his egocentric misanthropy. Yet in this one moment of conversation in *Stardust Memories*, Allen allows the issue of the Holocaust to come forward as part of a pattern, a mosaic, of a complex life that—whatever the situation—remains informed by being a Jew.[4]

One could easily dismiss *A Midsummer Night's Sex Comedy* (1982) as a pleasant diversion following the complexities of *Stardust Memories*. Its retreat into an idealized rural setting, an idealized past, encourages one to see the film as Allen's attempt to leave aside his earlier, more depressing concerns. Having paid tribute to the urban exteriors of Manhattan, Allen now acknowledges something he only mocked or avoided previously: rural exteriors. Further, the change of setting and pace indicates Allen's desire to escape the soul-wrenching autobiography and equally intense criticism of *Stardust Memories*. In fact, between the release of *Stardust Memories* in 1980 and *A Midsummer Night's Sex Comedy* in 1982, no Allen production whatsoever occurred; 1981 marked the only year since 1970 without a Woody Allen film. With *A Midsummer Night's Sex Comedy*, Allen, obviously drawing upon Shakespeare (*A Midsummer Night's Dream*) and Ingmar Bergman (*Smiles of a Summer Night*, 1955), produces a comic pastoral with an unexpectedly bucolic vision of the countryside from urban America's essential citizen.

The very setting of *A Midsummer Night's Sex Comedy* reveals Allen's attempt to expunge Jewishness and thus comic anguish and self-criticism, at least for a while. So, too, the time period of 1906, when the majority of America's Jews were newly arrived and ghettoized, displaces Jewry almost entirely. Similarly, by eliminating the

WASP-Jew dichotomy, as seen in the very names chosen for the characters, Allen attempts to ignore Jewishness. Indeed, he solidifies the absence of Jewishness and Judaism by the rural setting, using shots of animals, and the spirit ball, which all create a pantheism to replace the absent Judaism. The only worthwhile pursuits are relationships and art, both the popular variety (the cinema) and high art as implied by the studied neo-Impressionistic compositions of the mise-en-scène and the muted colors (the film is in color unlike *Manhattan* and *Stardust Memories* and the predominate use of black and white in *Zelig* and *Broadway Danny Rose* that will follow it).

If in *A Midsummer Night's Sex Comedy* Allen abandons the Jewish persona, along with the painful interiorization and self-accusation that being Jewish entails, if he tries to retreat from autobiography and evade critical scrutiny, *Zelig* (1983), a technically stunning story of a fictionalized celebrity of the 1920s who was a "chameleon man," returns Allen to the critical concern with self. *Zelig*, the clearest expression of Jewish fear and paranoia ever produced in the cinema, reveals a desperate desire to fit in and achieve total assimilation within mainstream society. Like many of his short stories, *Zelig* displays not only a particularly Jewish theme but also a particularly Jewish appeal. In an in-joke of American-Jewish intellectual life, Allen uses real-life "witnesses"—Irving Howe, Susan Sontag, Bruno Bettelheim, and Saul Bellow, all of whom sit firmly in the pantheon of the American-Jewish intelligentsia—to comment upon and participate in this fictional story of an archetypally Jewish character.

Zelig's theme relies upon a powerful paradox and also employs one of the more intriguing cinematic experiments of any mainstream American film. Allen constitutes much of the film in the black-and-white newsreel style of the 1930s, complete with sententious narration. He actually integrates the fictional characters into extant newsreel or other types of footage. Thus, scenes of Leonard Zelig and Dr. Eudora Fletcher (Mia Farrow) standing at Times Square in the 1920s, or of Zelig waiting in the batter's box behind Babe Ruth or frolicking with celebrities at Hearst's San Simeon, seem to be actual nonfictional footage. Mia Farrow is cast in the role of Dr. Fletcher in the black-and-white sections of the movie, while Ellen Garrison portrays the older Dr. Fletcher in the modern, color sections of the film. Allen uses both fictionalized characters to comment upon the fictional Zelig and well-known contemporary figures, identified as themselves, who also analyze Zelig. This daring erasure of the lines between fact and fiction, appropriately through the medium of the cinema, which caused much confusion and dislocation among many of Allen's previous protagonists, is here used to comment upon the ambiguity of cinematic images in relating reality and constructing an image. It may thus be a comment upon the allegedly autobiographical nature of Allen's own films, an aspect that he takes pains to deny, even as he uses the stuff of his own life.

More daring is the film's meditation on celebrity, which is similarly reflective of Allen's own ambivalence about being a public figure. The picture is set during the jazz age and the depression, precisely when the motion picture industry solidified into a predominantly Jewish-owned studio system and became the first true mass medium. At the same time, the rise of radio, a second mass medium, contributed to the formation and development of the system of celebrity.

Although the setting for *Zelig* is critical for the technical gimmicks that Allen foregrounds (the integration of contemporary people into photographed scenes from the past), it remains equally important for a displaced meditation upon contemporary notions of celebrityhood. Allen uses the first generation of mass-mediated celebrity to comment upon the current obsession with celebrities. Celebrities are prized for their uniqueness and emulated by others, who wish they could be like these objects of worship and wonder. Movie critics, for example, write constantly about the unique persona, the special abilities, the one-of-a-kind attitude projected by movie stars or other celebrities. They cite charisma as the single most important attribute necessary for a movie star or celebrity. Yet Leonard Zelig possesses no charisma; he has no unique abilities, no persona. He evolves into a celebrity solely due to his ability to emulate other people. In a doubly ironic moment in the film, people on the street comment upon their wish to be more like Zelig, who merely takes on the characteristics of others.

The people whom Zelig becomes constitute one of Woody Allen's clearest ideological statements. Zelig typically transforms into a member of another ethnic or racial group, for example, Jews, similarly discriminated against. We learn, for example, that a Christian anti-Semitic radio program, "The Holy Family Christian Association," despises Zelig because he is a Jew who can disguise himself. Similarly, the Ku Klux Klan fears him as a triple threat: a Jew who can look like an Indian or a black. Early in the film Zelig metamorphosizes into an Italian and a black (a jazz trumpeter, perhaps recalling Allen's interest in the clarinet).

The first glimpse of the incredible changing man finds him as a Chinese in an opium den. Allen then extends Zelig's solidarity to include yet another group that is discriminated against: overweight people. Although the political aspect of change is tempting and something must be said for it, Zelig's transformations must be pre-eminently visible. His changes, his differences must be apparent. Thus, when he becomes less overtly ethnic, as when he turns into a Frenchman, Allen relies upon humorous stereotyping: beret and pencil-thin mustache. Later, when Zelig becomes a rabbi, he transforms into a Hasidic one because of the obvious visual components that such a persona entails. Thus, the idea of the visible underlies the most subtle joke in the film: a store advertises that it has pictures of Zelig as a Chinese, an overweight person, and an intellectual.

The most damning criticism of *Zelig* came, unsurprisingly, from a Jewish critic in a Jewish journal, *Commentary*. Richard Grenier noted that the origins of *Zelig* were not entirely fictional, that a real Zelig existed in the form of one Stephen Jacob Weinberg, who, however, took on roles of conspicuously high status. Critiquing Allen's film, Grenier wondered, "who, in the 20's, would have thrilled at the idea of a clever Brooklyn Jew managing to pass himself off as a Negro or a Chinese?" (62). Allen's shift of emphasis, then, adds to the idea of his political solidarity with repressed ethnic others. *Commentary*'s critic completely and (given the journal's conservatism of recent years) perhaps deliberately ignores this element of the film in a wrongheaded and obtuse criticism of it.

Yet if political solidarity with ethnic others is only subtlety situated in *Zelig*, Allen's incorporation of Jewishness is not. The Jewishness of Leonard Zelig, stated outright, links him directly to his creator, Woody Allen, further intensifying the authorial or autobiographical links between character and creator as well as the influence of Jewishness on both. Leonard Zelig is the son of a failed Yiddish actor named Morris Zelig, "whose performance as Puck in the Orthodox version of *A Midsummer Night's Dream* was coolly received." The humor of this wonderfully complex allusion resides in the audience's ability to reference a number of allusive levels. First, Allen based his immediate filmic predecessor to *Zelig* largely on *A Midsummer Night's Dream;* it, too, was "coolly received" (Pogel 175). More significantly, the once-popular Yiddish theater in New York notoriously "borrowed" other texts for its own purposes, Shakespeare included. *The Yiddish King Lear,* for example, was one of the most popular of these intertextual reworkings.[5] Finally, the notion of an "Orthodox" version of a Yiddish drama plays on the strands within Judaism—Orthodox, Conservative, Reform—and not within the secular Yiddish theater.

From the Yiddish theater background of the Zeligs, Allen moves to the urban environment. We learn that, although the Zeligs lived above a bowling alley, it was the bowling alley that complained of noise. This recalls the apartment house of Alvy Singer's youth in *Annie Hall*, situated below the giant roller coaster at Coney Island, although visually the Zeligs' neighborhood appears nearly identical to that of the Starkwells in *Take the Money and Run*. The anti-Semitic bullying meted out to Leonard similarly resembles Virgil's childhood. Whereas anti-Semitism could only be inferred from the earlier picture, however, Allen makes it explicit in *Zelig*. In fact, even Leonard's parents are complicit in the anti-Semitic bullying, a self-conscious recognition of the mechanism of Jewish self-hatred. Later in life, his sister, Ruth, and her domineering husband exploit Leonard horribly by exhibiting him at a sideshow.[6]

If his parents and family fail Zelig, then religion—Judaism— fares no better. As he recalls, "I'm 12 years old. I run into a synagogue and ask the rabbi the meaning of life. But he tells it to me in Hebrew. I don't understand Hebrew; he wants to charge me $600 for Hebrew lessons." Such a seemingly absurd situation speaks to numerous aspects of the American-Jewish experience, including the money-grubbing stereotype, the mystical confusions of Judaism, and the bemusement of young people attending Hebrew school amid their otherwise secular education and lives. The comedy that Allen finds in Judaism recurs in Zelig's transformation into a Hasidic rabbi (as he earlier "transformed" in *Take the Money and Run* and *Annie Hall*). In this instance, however, Allen again references anti-Semitism; the narrator says that "his transformation into a rabbi suggests to certain Frenchmen that he be sent to Devil's Island," quickly recalling the notorious Dreyfus affair.

If Judaism failed him, however, a particularly virulent form of anti-Semitism—self-hatred—almost destroys him. The link between self-hatred and anti-Semitism is most shocking when Zelig transforms into a major member of the Nazi party. Although awesome technical brilliance reveals the tiny figure of Leonard Zelig on the dais behind and screen right of the ranting and raving Adolph Hitler, the image of the little Jew, now an active member of the group that sought to annihilate his people, is mesmerizing. By this cinematic, even cultural, yoking of opposites Allen illuminates the tragedy of German Jews trying to assimilate into a mainstream

society that viewed them as enemies and outsiders to be slaugh-
tered. No visual, behavioral, or attitudinal amount of conformity,
real or imagined, saved the Jews nor, Allen likely notes, would it
save them in the future.

Zelig is thus an important demonstration of the mechanism of
self-hatred revealed by Allen himself, particularly as an artist who
simultaneously makes fun of Jewish culture and religion while he
reveals the tragic consequences of its underlying anti-Semitism.
That Zelig relates, therefore, an essentially Jewish story is stated
overtly in the film by Irving Howe: "When I think about it, it seems
to me that his story reflected a lot of the Jewish experience in
America; the great urge to push in, and to find one's place and then
to assimilate into the culture." Before saying this, Howe, previously
identified only by his name, is further identified as the author of
World of Our Fathers, the classic text about the Jewish experience on
the Lower East Side. Zelig's background, of course, is precisely this
Lower East Side, and he is a product of this "world of our fathers."

Zelig's desire to conform, to "assimilate like mad" as Howe says,
stems from Jewish fears of prejudice and feelings of inferiority.
Under hypnosis, Zelig reveals to Dr. Fletcher that he metamorpho-
ses because "it's safe" and "I want to be liked." The first sentiment
reveals fear, the second inferiority. Why is it dangerous to be different, and why would one not be liked if one is different? The answers to these questions, unfortunately, remain obvious, especially
to Jews, in particular those who lived during the 1920s and 1930s
when the film is set. Zelig first experienced feelings of inferiority at
school, when some very bright people had read *Moby-Dick* but he
had not. The choice of *Moby-Dick* is complex. Robert Stam notes
the four separate occasions in Zelig when Allen references *Moby-
Dick*. He concludes that perhaps the use of Melville's novel points
"reflexively to certain features of the Allen film, since Zelig's own
generic tapestry recalls the dense textual interweave of *Moby-Dick*
(*Subversive Pleasures* 208).

The allusion can also be seen as reflecting Jews' sense of alienation from mainstream culture. To push this a bit further, *Moby-Dick*
represents the ultimate American text, reflecting not just the high
cultural standards that alienate Jews, but the all-Americanness of
the novel's concerns: male-bonding, adventure, and the conquer-
ing of a wilderness. For that matter, it might be that *Moby-Dick*
represents an essentially Christian allegory from which Jews remain similarly alienated. Yet Allen attempts to establish a rapport
between Zelig and the audience, perhaps similarly conflicted over

their own intellectual and cultural identities. *Moby-Dick,* after all, symbolizes other books that are well known yet little read.

If Zelig experiences the fear of inferiority when he is ashamed of not having read *Moby-Dick,* he experiences the fear of difference when he enters a bar on St. Patrick's Day. This, we learn, is the first occasion of his metamorphosis: "My hair turned red, my nose turned up . . . began talking about the great potato famine." Zelig's transformation from one ethnic type to another is apparent immediately, and we see how the Irish, established in New York before the Jews and traditionally both proud and militant about their heritage, provide an implicit model of ethnicity that self-hating, assimilating Jews might better emulate.[7]

It is not ethnicity, Jewish or otherwise, that provides Zelig's ultimate redemption, however. Once again, in typical Allen fashion, salvation comes through love and the attempt to sustain a relationship. Yet redemption, at least at first, seems to come from another type of Judaic substitute, psychoanalysis. Zelig's condition, which Dr. Fletcher determines to be psychological, allows a glimpse into the psychoanalytic process, the talking cure. At their first meeting, Fletcher watches Zelig become a psychiatrist but not a woman. This provides the occasion for the first of many jokes at psychiatry's expense, familiar territory to Allen's aficionados. "Dr." Zelig proclaims that he studied on the Continent with Freud, but broke with him over the concept of penis envy—"Freud thought it should be limited to women." Later he claims to be treating four sets of schizophrenic Siamese twins, thus collecting fees from sixteen patients. The self-deprecation and feelings of inferiority that Allen expressed so memorably in his early films here return as Zelig whines about his need to get uptown, where he teaches a course in advanced masturbation. If he is late, the class starts without him. Yet for all the apparently psychoanalytic situations, nothing other than the love of a good woman and a few weeks in the country cures Zelig.

Although Allen provides a happy ending, he immediately undercuts it with a bittersweet coda.[8] Although Leonard and Eudora lived happily together, Leonard then died. Dr. Fletcher is still quite alive and not especially old in the present-day, color, sections of the film. More than that, we learn that Zelig's only regret about dying was not getting a chance to finish reading *Moby-Dick,* which he has just started. This coda, this anhedonic inability to enjoy life, separates Allen's vision of relationships from the simplistic redemption of best-selling novels and popular films. Even cured, even with the love of a woman and a life of contentment, the little Jew still possesses that lingering doubt that he is not quite good enough.

"Not quite good enough" similarly describes both the character of a theatrical agent portrayed by Allen in his next film and the clients his character represents. *Broadway Danny Rose* (1984), one of Allen's least autobiographical films, is one of his most affectionate.[9] Perhaps its marginally autobiographical element allows Allen to permit his affection for life's little losers to shine through. Certainly, the film relates to *Manhattan* because it shares the earlier picture's fondness for New York cityscapes, again photographed in black and white although deglamorized. Whereas *Manhattan* foregrounded New York by its very title, the city in this film recedes into the background; in fact, only Broadway is seen. *Broadway Danny Rose* belies the mythic and romantic implications of Broadway and becomes Allen's tribute to a slightly darker, much less glamorous side of show business. In a sense, *Broadway Danny Rose* is an alternative autobiography of Woody Allen, the story of what Allen's own show business career might have been but for the grace of God and a few lucky breaks. It is thus one of Allen's most overtly Jewish films.

Allen implicates the world of Broadway, his alternate autobiography, and of the Jewish milieu that dominates these worlds in the very first sequence of the film. A long-shot outside the Carnegie Delicatessen firmly establishes physical place and cultural milieu. Once inside the restaurant, the camera casually "overhears" two comics discussing their craft, one complaining that his old-standby Miami joke did not work the other night. Shortly thereafter, a group of seven comics again complains about the continuing decline of New York clubs. One (Will Jordan) speaks of how he came to be an impressionist and launches into a fine imitation of James Mason. The comics also begin to reminisce about the "Ed Sullivan Show" and mention Danny Rose.

In this world, nightclub comics hustle to make a living playing clubs; it is a world of old jokes borrowed, stolen, told, and retold. We later see many of Danny Rose's own clients, who occupy a lower rung on the show business ladder of success than the comics (Corbett Monica, Morty Gunty, and Sandy Barron) who sit swapping stories. Danny's pitiful clients include a blind xylophone player, a one-armed juggler, a singing bird act, and a husband-and-wife balloon-folding team. We even glimpse Danny Rose as a comic, precisely the kind of performer who horrified Allen's alter ego Alvy Singer in *Annie Hall* when he was asked to sell jokes to him.

Woody Allen's small-time theatrical agent Danny Rose proudly wears his Jewishness for all to see: here, a *chai* around his neck.

Woody Allen himself, of course, played nightclubs, college campuses (as he humorously tells his balloon-folding act they someday will), and appeared on the "Ed Sullivan Show." Had he less talent as a writer or less interest in filmmaking, Allen would perhaps still be struggling to make a living telling jokes to old Jewish people in the Catskill Mountains or Miami Beach. He would certainly be among the faded comics at the deli. For this reason, Allen uses Milton Berle, the apotheosis of success in old Jewish show business, as the ultimate triumph of Danny's only successful client, Lou Canova.

On a number of occasions Allen clearly implicates the Jewishness of the audience as well as the Jewishness of the comics. Early in the film, Danny desperately tries to book an act, any act, at Weinstein's Majestic Bungalow Colony (the New York Jews in the audience can be separated from the rest of the audience by the laughs this name evokes). Weinstein complains that old Jews do not want to see a blind xylophone player or a one-armed juggler. Danny then suggests Eddie Clark's penguin, who skates onto the stage dressed like a rabbi (more evidence that Allen views the appearance of rabbis as humorous). Later we learn that a hypnotist whom Danny handles has put a woman into a trance and cannot get her out. As the husband desperately berates the hypnotist in Yiddish, Danny tries to calm him by saying that if the wife does not awaken, he will take the man to a Chinese restaurant. For Jewish New Yorkers, especially displaced ones, the throw-away line is a vivid reminder of home.

The most Jewish aspect to the film, however, is Danny Rose himself. Allen's own Jewishness has always been overt, an inherent part of the persona he has created and shaped throughout his career. Here, however, he makes ethnicity even more obvious. Danny Rose, for example, wears a *chai* necklace, a well-chosen Jewish symbol for the character. A Star of David would have made his religious affiliation as clear, but the symbolism of the *chai* would be lacking. Against all odds and circumstances, Danny believes in life, the meaning of the Hebrew letter *chai*. He has learned a lesson from *Manhattan*'s Tracy; as the narrator Sandy Barron says, although Lou Canova was an overweight, washed-up alcoholic, "Danny has faith." On a number of occasions Danny exclaims, "*Emmis* [truth], my hand to God."

Danny's own Jewishness is further instilled by the deceased family he forever invokes to make a point. We hear of Aunt Rose,[10] Uncle Menachem, Uncle Morris, Uncle Sidney, Cousin Ceil (Ceil will also be the name of one of the young hero's Jewish aunts in

Radio Days), and Uncle Meyer. He describes his female relatives in the most unflattering terms: Aunt Rose looks like something you could buy in a live bait store, and Cousin Ceil like something in the reptile house at the zoo. These remnants of anti-Semitism and self-hatred spring from the self-deprecation of Allen's schlemiel persona, resurrected for this film.

Danny Rose bases his philosophy of life upon guilt and love. Although Woody Allen occasionally makes fun of the Jewish holy day of Yom Kippur (for example, in *Annie Hall* and *Radio Days*), Danny Rose understands the source of guilt. "Guilt is important," he tells Tina (Mia Farrow), whose own philosophy of life Danny compares to the screenplay for *Murder, Incorporated*. Guilt prevents us from committing otherwise horrible acts, and so a lack of guilt, a lack of some religious faith, leads to a horrible act—murder—in *Crimes and Misdemeanors*. "I'm guilty all the time," he continues, "and I never did anything." When Tina asks if he believes in God, Danny replies, "No, but I feel guilty about it!" To balance one's own sense of guilt requires a generosity of spirit toward others. Danny subscribes to his Uncle Sidney's philosophy in this matter: "Acceptance, forgiveness, and love." The concept of guilt comes alive for Danny when, horrified, he learns that the Rispoli brothers have badly beaten Barney Dunn after being told by Danny that Barney is Tina's lover, thinking the stuttering ventriloquist to be out of town entertaining on a cruise ship. Danny must make amends to Barney, and he does so by representing him as his agent.

Danny's admirable philosophy of life, however, never leads him to financial success. No more skilled as a theatrical manager than as a comedian, Danny's clients leave him behind as soon as they achieve even a modicum of success. Instead of interpreting this as his problem, or even as a failure in other people, Danny theorizes that people want to reject their earlier years, rewrite them, and deny their origins. Allen himself often speaks harshly about his own background, his family, his childhood, and his early days in show business, yet he never denies them. Danny's outlook on life leaves him a financial loser, but he emerges a winner in matters of the heart. By film's end, he has Tina, who originally tells Danny that his apartment looks like a loser lives there. Danny and Tina represent different philosophies of life, however Tina eventually moves over to Danny's position, even quoting back to him Uncle Sidney's watchwords, "acceptance, forgiveness, and love."

Douglas Brode maintains that *Broadway Danny Rose* "could be subtitled 'The Education of Tina,' since it is about her growing consciousness; the way she becomes worthy of Danny" (240). In this respect the film reproduces Allen's recurring motif of the shiksa's education by the Jewish man, as seen particularly in *Sleeper, Annie Hall,* and *Manhattan.* The Jewish man teaches his shiksa about the darker side of life, about guilt, death, and the need for love in a harsh world.

A harsh world is exactly the description of the environment of *The Purple Rose of Cairo* (1985), the follow-up to *Broadway Danny Rose.* This film presents a far darker and demythologizing view of show business than the previous work yet paradoxically makes even stronger the power and importance of the cinema, which becomes a crucial component in a dark and cruel world to compensate for the absence of Judaism. *The Purple Rose of Cairo* marks Allen's strongest statement on how the cinema replaces religion as a moral and ethical teacher. Both implicitly in cinematic parodies and explicitly in such films as *Play It Again, Sam, Manhattan,* and *Stardust Memories,* Allen uses the cinema to posit a model of how to act and how to provide a meaning to relationships. *The Purple Rose of Cairo* makes the religious dimension of the cinema overt. In addition, the relationship component becomes a function of the cinema in this story of a woman who worships the cinema and falls in love with a character who literally comes out of a movie.

Allen clearly links *The Purple Rose of Cairo* to *Play It Again, Sam,* with some important distinctions. In the earlier film, the protagonist conjured up a figure out of film (Bogart) to teach him about relationships, whereas in this film a figure steps out of a film to relate to the protagonist. Allen's 1985 film is linked to his own, earlier short story "The Kugelmass Episode," in which a character first steps into the world of *Madame Bovary* to relate to, and have relations with, the novel's protagonist. The couple then enters the real world. Similarly, Allen's film owes a debt to Buster Keaton's 1924 silent classic *Sherlock Junior,* except in Keaton's film a character walks into a movie and in Allen's a character walks out of a movie. In both films, however, the implications of these impossible acts are not ignored. Even in "The Kugelmass Episode," the consequences of the hero's actions are apparent; students in classrooms all over the country wonder, "Who is this character on page 100? A bald Jew is kissing Madame Bovary?" (*Side Effects* 67). When Keaton's protagonist enters a film, he becomes subjected to the laws of cinema in one of filmdom's most inspiring and brilliant montages. When Allen's filmic protagonist emerges into the real world, its alien laws provide a good deal of humor about the differences between reel and real life, a motif Allen often uses in his earlier films. The most amusing of these dislocations is the shocked look on film character Tom Baxter's (Jeff Daniels) face when Cecilia (Mia Farrow) tells him about babies and childbirth.

Yet Allen cannot resist a few jibes at the world of movies, especially the people who work in it. Cecilia ingenuously chides actor Gil Shepherd for claiming he created the character of Tom Baxter. "Didn't the writer do that?" she innocently wonders. Gil is easily diverted from getting Tom Baxter back into the movie whenever Cecilia begins to talk about Gil's acting talent. Although it is a cliché to say that actors are egotists, in this film at least the actor is compared to the character he creates. Equally clichéd, perhaps, is Gil's betrayal of Cecilia. He promises to take her back to Hollywood with him if she rejects Tom Baxter, thereby forcing him back onto the screen. After doing so, Cecilia learns that Gil returned to Hollywood immediately. Yet if actors' egos are large, so, too, are many of the characters'. After Tom leaves the film for the real world, the other characters begin to talk about how the film revolves around them individually. Here Allen demonstrates that there truly are no small roles, only small actors.

Allen also remembers that the classic Hollywood of 1935, of the major studios like RKO, the distributor of the (fictional) film-within-the-film *The Purple Rose of Cairo*, was Jewish. The name *Raoul Hirsch* is an amusing tribute to the Jewishness of the old Hollywood, but the fictional screenwriters Irving Sachs and R. H. Levine also make the same point.[11] Allen compares the Jewishness of the Old Hollywood to the Jewishness of the Old Testament, as *The Purple Rose of Cairo* makes most explicit his earlier links between the cinema and religion.[12] As word gets out, for example, that Tom Baxter has left the movie and entered life, a reporter shouts, "it's a miracle!" Near the end of the film, Tom asks the on-screen priest to marry real-life Cecilia to fictional Tom. When Gil complains about the legality of this, the priest angrily responds, "the Bible never says a priest can't be on film." In the most complex establishing link between cinema and religion, Cecilia takes Tom to a church and begins to speak of God, "the reason for everything . . . the universe." For Tom, God is understandable: "The two men who wrote *The Purple Rose of Cairo*, Irving Sachs and R. H. Levine." This is not only a complex joke about Tom's limited perceptions, but also a metaphysical allusion to the artist, significantly, the screenwriter, as prime creator. In addition, it is the second insistence in the film on the primacy of the writer. Because Woody Allen wrote the film (that is, *The Purple Rose of Cairo,* which features Tom Baxter, and *The Purple Rose of Cairo,* which contains Baxter's film within it), it contains another allusion to Allen's own identification with God, stated previously in *Manhattan* and *Stardust Memories.* He even manages to allude quite clearly to the importance of movie-going as ritual; like religion, the movies engender a familiar, repetitive pattern that bespeaks a timeless transcendence. As a woman patron who objects to the idea of a character leaving the film states, "I want what happened in the movie last week to happen this week. Otherwise what's life all about anyway?"

If *The Purple Rose of Cairo* demonstrates the developing faith in the cinema as a means of transcendence, then *Hannah and Her Sisters* (1986) marks a significant step in the evolution of Allen's attempt to mediate the binary conflicts between Jew and WASP, neurosis and psychosis, and self-hate and self-respect. Here, Allen appears in a predominantly serious film that uses the same basic structure as *Interiors:* three sisters in a dysfunctional family with a powerful, attractive father and mother, both of whom have emotional problems. As in *Interiors,* the sisters are at loose ends and jealous of each other. The middle sister, Holly (Diane Wiest), desperately seeks romance and a career and initially fails at both. Lee (Barbara Hershey), the youngest and a recovering alcoholic, involves herself in a dissatisfying relationship with a much older man (Max von Sydow) and then in an affair with Hannah's husband, Elliot (Michael Caine).

Unlike *Interiors,* however, *Hannah and Her Sisters* features Allen as a major character. To an extent, the film mediates its dramatic and comic elements, with Allen taking most of the comic sequences and the WASP family bearing the dramatic intensity. Structurally, therefore, Allen splits the film along the lines of WASP drama–Jew comedy. Allen portrays Mickey, another of his lovable losers and a schlemiel despite his success as a television producer, the former husband of the major character, Hannah (Mia Farrow). If a bit grotesque and a painfully comic caricature of a Jewish hypochondriac, Mickey still remains the focus of the film's major thematic moment, the recipient of a transcendent experience. Although he relegates the bulk of the film's comedy to this Jewish outsider, Allen also saves its most heartwarming, life-affirming moments for his Jewish persona.

The film also segments its WASP drama–Jew comedy along philosophical lines, perhaps expressed as an opposition between metaphysics and physics, between mental musings and physical couplings. Ultimately, Allen solves the metaphysical via the physical (and the esthetic), but until doing so he splits the film by the religio-philosophical musings of Mickey versus the physical, romantic intertwinings of Elliot, Lee, Hannah, and Holly. Two juxtaposed sequences make this clear. The first begins with an aphorism from Tolstoy: "The only absolute knowledge attainable by man is that life is meaningless." Mickey, via a voice-over, despairs of ever finding the meaning of life, especially if the great minds of the past have been unsuccessful. The humor of this sequence provides yet another example of the yoking of disparate realms, the sudden thrusting downward from sacred to mundane. Mickey quotes Nietzsche about the eternal recurrence of life, which depresses him because "I'll have to sit through the Ice Capades again." Juxtaposed to Mickey's musings, Allen places a sequence entitled "Afternoons" that contains only two scenes. The first features Elliot and Lee enjoying (except insofar as they are racked by guilt) an afternoon tryst at a hotel; the second accentuates Elliot with Hannah, as he agonizes over his treatment of her and she desperately tries to communicate with him. Thus the characters are segregated in their disparate realms.

However, this seemingly precise separation of comedy and drama, the metaphysical from the physical, Jew from WASP, seems more apparent than real. Although Mickey stands apart from the drama surrounding Hannah and her sisters, he had a relationship with Hannah and eventually establishes one with Holly. Further, in sequences that focus upon Mickey, Allen often integrates other characters in significant and interesting ways. "The Abyss," a sequence in the middle of the film (before the Tolstoyan despair), introduces the audience to Mickey's existential crisis. Upon learning that he does not have a brain tumor, he is plunged into doubt, desperate to find meaning in a life that eventually and inevitably will end. As Mickey ruminates about doing something drastic, Allen cuts to Elliot and Lee in a hotel room, making love for the first time. They are plunged into their own abyss, although one involving sex and guilt. A sequence late in the film, "Summer in New York," finds Elliot still agonizing over his inability to break away from Hannah or end his relationship to Lee, and Mickey discussing the meaning of life with a Hare Krishna acolyte. Both Jew and WASP, in their own private abysses, await a spark of meaning or insight.

The real links in the film between Jew and WASP, between metaphysical and physical, are forged by Mickey and Holly. At the end of the sequence introduced by the caption "the anxiety of the man in the booth"—a deliberate reference to Robert Shaw's play *The Man in the Glass Booth*, which has the Holocaust as a theme—Mickey remarks that "love is really unpredictable." Then the scene cuts to a scene onstage at the opera. Instinctively, the audience takes the opera to be an ironic commentary on the hyperactive, melodramatic musings of the hypochondriacal Mickey, perhaps as Allen uses Hollywood films to comment on his characters in *Crimes and Misdemeanors*. However, the architect, David (Sam Waterston), and Holly watch the opera from David's box at the Met. It is then clear that love—in the triangle of David-Holly-April—is unpredictable, because Holly agonizes over whether David prefers April to her. Retrospectively, however, we remember Allen foreshadowing love's unpredictability by linking Mickey with Holly in this subtle way. Later, he reestablishes the link between Mickey and Holly at the end of the sequence that began with the grim epigram from Tolstoy.

As Mickey muses that "maybe love is the only answer," he remembers a date he had with Holly. Although the date was horrible, they establish a relationship in the film's present. The relationship comes to fruition in the sequence "Lucky I ran into you," in which Holly bravely asks Mickey to read a script she has written. Mickey's admiration for the script brings them together again. With the song "You Made Me Love You" in the background, their eventual union seems inevitable. Yet this, too, has been preceded by another juxtaposition within an earlier sequence, "The big leap," which is memorable and hilarious.

The big leap primarily refers to Mickey who, searching for meaning and significance, explores the possibility of converting to Catholicism. Allen foreshadows the Catholicism in this sequence by earlier using comedy that is rare for him: antireligious humor that is not directed at Judaism. Although he is quite willing to poke fun at Judaism, he does not make jokes at the expense of other religions until early in *Hannah and Her Sisters*. Mickey, introduced in the sequence entitled "The Hypochondriac," is seen backstage as the producer of a television show similar to "Saturday Night Live." A network censor, come to complain about a sketch dealing with child abuse, claims that such a skit is unusable because it names names. This is not so, Mickey retorts, the sketch just refers to the pope! A short while later, Mickey's assistant (Julie Kavner) suggests substituting a sketch used earlier: "the Cardinal Spellman–Ronald Reagan Homosexual Dance Number."

It is hard to know if Allen sees this as funny for its own sake, or if he satirizes what passes for satire on contemporary American television. It is equally possible that he recalls an earlier, frustrating experience of his own: a show entitled "The Politics of Woody Allen" (1971), which PBS produced but never aired. One of its bits involved a nun commenting on the Allen character's sexual prowess by noting, "he's an unbelievable swinger, a freak" (quoted in Yacowar 104). Allen mitigates such jokes at the expense of Catholicism by a reverential treatment of Mickey's thoughts of conversion. Mickey goes to St. Patrick's Cathedral and watches respectfully as liturgical music pulsates in the background. Yet he also passes a store window that displays a picture of Jesus, whose eyes seem to open and shut as one shifts perspective. This example of Catholic kitsch at least indicates that Mickey (and Allen himself) seems unlikely to find purpose or affirmation in such a well-merchandised realm.

That Mickey thinks of converting to Catholicism becomes important and a fact that some audiences, perhaps, will not appreciate. After all, Allen never mentions the word *Jew* until the "big leap" sequence. That we recognize Mickey's Jewishness all along (and, in fact, take it for granted) is a function of codes: he is Woody Allen, a hypochondriac, and in some ways still the lovable schlemiel. To make this clear to all audiences, Allen has Mickey visit his parents, who question why someone raised as a Jew would want to become a Catholic. His mother slams her bedroom door in despair, and his father, Max, tries to reason with him. Mickey's father represents Jews who are not neurotic, questing, and intellectual like Mickey, but hard-headed, practical, and entirely down-to-earth. He wonders "who thinks about such nonsense" that concerns his son. When Mickey says that he needs to know how evil can exist, how, for example, could God have allowed the Nazis, his father, exasperated, responds, "how the hell do I know why there were Nazis. I don't know how the can opener works!"

This exchange represents yet another example of yoking disparate realms, thrusting the audience suddenly downward from the metaphysical to the mundane. From here, Allen cuts to Mickey entering his apartment and unpacking some Catholic "supplies" he has just bought: a crucifix, a picture of Jesus, Wonder Bread, and mayonnaise. Astute audiences appreciate how Wonder Bread and mayonnaise can be "Catholic," as the mangled Yiddish in *Sleeper*, or Annie Hall ordering a pastrami on white with mayonnaise and lettuce are matters of recognizing the cultural and ethnic codes at work in the humor. Of course, such things are not Catholic so much as they are goyish, and by their very goyishness it becomes clear that the answers to Mickey's question reside neither in Catholicism nor in any other religious system of belief. Although he gives up the idea of converting, Mickey still searches for real answers, and soon questions a Hare Krishna.

Although we appreciate the humor of Mickey's big leap, the sequence does not end with him, but rather moves to Hannah and her sisters at lunch. Holly, too, undertakes a big leap: she decides to abandon acting for writing. Both she and Mickey contemplate changes in their lives, another of the links that foreshadow their eventual union. Holly's big leap into writing is successful; Mickey's into Catholicism fails to solve his metaphysical problem. His dilemma is finally solved in the "Lucky I ran into you" sequence, in which he comes to an accommodation with life, accepting and living with its built-in limitations. As he tells Holly, he overcomes his crisis at the movies.

At his lowest ebb, Mickey seeks refuge in the comforting darkness of a movie theater. While the Marx Brothers cavort on screen in *Duck Soup* (1932), Mickey experiences an epiphany that allows him to accommodate the complexities, ambiguities, and evils of life. Here Allen again asserts the power of the cinema to endow life with meaning, this time in homage to one of his screen idols, Groucho Marx, to whom he also pays tribute at the start of *Annie Hall*. At the movies, Mickey finds the power of art and the sense of fun that enable him to continue to live in spite of his knowledge of the inevitable.

Mickey's revelation comes perilously close to a similar sequence in another Hollywood comedy, Preston Sturges's *Sullivan's Travels* (1941). Sturges's autobiographical stand-in, the film director John Sullivan (Joel McCrea), finds no satisfaction from making comedies. Like Allen's Sandy Bates of *Stardust Memories*, he agonizes about continuing to produce comedies in an increasingly dark world. Sullivan learns the lesson that comedy is good, when, as part of a prison chain gang, he watches a cartoon in a church. Hearing the raucous laughter of the impoverished church-goers and hardened, abused criminals, Sullivan is struck by the importance of laughter and the escape that it brings from everyday life. He can return to Hollywood and make comedies rather than pompous dramas about social situations and poverty.

Allen's point avoids the simplistic and self-serving message of Sturges because he makes no claims for the cinema's role in society. Further, Mickey's revelation represents merely the initial phase required for his redemption, for his transcendence of life's emptiness. He still requires Holly, demonstrating that romance, love, and relationships remain equally as important as the movies. Only after coming to terms with life and establishing a new relationship can Mickey be a real father (his children with Hannah are the result of artificial insemination). Holly announces her pregnancy at film's end, the third Thanksgiving of the picture, and Mickey can partake at last in this most important secular celebration.

The conflicts and contradictions that suffuse Allen's work reappear significantly and interestingly in *Radio Days* (1987). A follow-up to *Hannah,* the film is a seemingly affectionate tribute to his childhood and the meaning that radio had in Allen's life and that of his family's. On the one hand, *Radio Days* marks another of the films in which Allen is absent and is his first such film that does not focus primarily upon a woman. On the other hand, he is heard offscreen, in voice-over narration, throughout the film. This voice-over narrator, never named as Woody Allen, corresponds to a youngster, Joe (Seth Green), whom we do see and who is, obviously, not Woody Allen (nor named Woody Allen, although he looks like he will grow up to be Woody Allen). Yet the voice-over seems to be Allen's and is heard even before anything is seen. Thus, Allen modulates the film between a genuine autobiography, the tales of a real radio raconteur appropriately heard but not seen, and another of the thinly disguised fictions in his filmic canon.

The film's time frame is deliberately compressed and vague, as is memory. Although set in the early days of World War II, much of the film clearly takes place sometime before the war; for example, Joe, Aunt Bea (Diane Wiest), and her date see *The Philadelphia Story* (1940) at Radio City Music Hall, and one of Aunt Bea's dates abandons her on a highway when he becomes frightened by the infamous "War of the Worlds" broadcast of 1938. The film, again structured by alternating sequences (this time between the world of radio and the world of the family), represents another variation of WASP versus Jew. Although show business is a very Jewish business, here Allen codes it as WASP. For example, he segregates Mia Farrow—so to speak—from the Jews, as she occupies a place in the world of radio and never interacts with the family. Allen offers behind-the-scenes glimpses of radio programming under the guise of telling some of the radio stories collected over the years. He also provides scenes of family and neighborhood life to demonstrate clearly the meaning of radio to the family.

In *Radio Days*, the radio is the realm of fantasy, the world of hopes and dreams; it even assumes a religious aura. Allen explicitly contrasts the glamorous world of the radio stars to the drab life of the family. "Breakfast with Irene and Roger," for example, is contrasted to breakfast at the household (the family's last name is never given), much to the detriment of the latter. The world is structured of binary opposites: fantasy-reality, high (radio)-low (family), and sacred-mundane in yet another film that demonstrates the importance of popular art in ordinary life. Of course, part of Allen's strategy reveals the hollowness, shallowness, and phoniness of the radio (and, by implication, film) side of things. At the same time, he attempts to show the family as loving, sympathetic, nostalgic, and real. Regardless of the reality behind the radio, however, it allows the family members their moments of quiet transcendence.

Radio Days, in many ways, represents quite a daring, even risky, foray into Jewishness. Its portrait of class and ethnicity are far in excess of anything Allen has shown previously. Where Allen only covertly coded as Jewish the lower-middle-class background of Virgil Starkwell in *Take the Money and Run*, or merely glimpsed Alvy Singer's Jewish milieu in *Annie Hall*, or Sandy Bates's similar background in *Stardust Memories*, *Radio Days* immerses the audience in the dilapidated row houses of neighborhood New York. Constant worries and bickering about money might be played for laughs, but no one who lived through the depression or grew up only one generation removed from the ghetto can fault the accuracy of Allen's memories. Similarly, the fact that Uncle Abe (Josh Mostel) brings home fish night after night might have its humorous component, but the nutritional value of fish sustained many Jewish families during difficult times.

To this portrait of an extended family barely getting by, Allen adds one of the neighborhood, with the Commies on one side of the family and the Waldbaums, with whom they share a telephone line, on the other. Of course, the eternally snooping yenta lives across the street. And one day Mr. Zipsky from down the block runs amok, brandishing a meat cleaver while he runs down the street in his underwear.[13] Along with the component of economic class, impressively and accurately realized in *Radio Days*, Allen's foregrounding of the component of ethnicity, of Jewishness, becomes more problematic. In particular, two extended sequences make these portrayals of Judaism almost anathema to the Jewish community. The scenes should be seen as the images of the family members themselves—as ultimately either truthful or loving (if not both)—in order not to condemn the film as anti-Semitic.

The extended family of *Radio Days*.

The first scene involves Joe, who desires a Masked Avenger secret compartment ring. In order to pay for it, he steals the money he ostensibly collects "for a Jewish homeland in Palestine." The youngster tells his friends that Palestine means nothing to him, so he might as well use the money for the ring and some ice cream. The idea of stealing money intended to build a Jewish homeland, Israel, certainly verges on the sacrilegious; Israel is the secular religion of American Jewry (hence the furor over Allen's condemnation of Israel discussed earlier). To this already sacrilegious act Allen adds the rabbi's shocked reaction to little Joe's thievery. The rabbi, who teaches at the Hebrew school in the neighborhood, calls in Joe and his parents to inform them of their son's horrific theft. When Joe calls the rabbi his "faithful Indian companion," the incensed rabbi smacks the youth. His parents, insistent that they should be the ones to smack him, join the rabbi, and the three adults begin cuffing the boy about the head in a scene that rapidly leaves the realm of comedy. The rabbi is named Rabbi Baumel, the same name Allen gave to the rabbi contestant in the "What's My Perversion" sketch of *Everything You Always Wanted to Know About Sex,* perhaps an autobiographical act of revenge on some childhood disciplinarian and the continuing denigration of Judaism.

The second, extended, sequence is set on Yom Kippur, the Day of Atonement, the holiest day in Judaism, when Jews fast for their sins. The family's neighbors blast their radio and clearly eat, even feast, in defiance of the day's solemnity. Ultimately, Uncle Abe goes next door to confront these communists. While he is gone, the mother, Tess (Julie Kavner), relates to Aunt Ceil (Renee Lippin) a story of the yenta, Mrs. Silverman, who spotted the neighbors' daughter kissing a black man, an act visualized through Tess's voice-over. Upon seeing the kiss, Mrs. Silverman suffered a stroke, her teacup frozen on the way to her mouth. At this point in Tess's story, Uncle Abe returns home, spouting the hoariest party-line clichés about the only sin being the exploitation of the workers. Religion is the opium of the masses, Abe proclaims, immediately substituting the religion of communism for the religion of Judaism. Not only does Abe eat, but he also has pork chops, thus breaking the holy fast of Yom Kippur and eating *treyfe* (nonkosher food) in the same sacrilegious moment.

Uncle Abe's quick conversion indicates that his commitment to communism is as superficial as his understanding of and commitment to Judaism. He and the rest of the family follow religion only because the neighbors do and have no understanding of why they do so, nor any deeply felt emotional ties. When another neighbor does something else, they simply follow suit. Allen the filmmaker remains ambivalent about Yom Kippur, unsure of its significance and, for that matter, about God's role in modern Jewish life. When Aunt Ceil tells Abe that God will punish him, Abe's initial skepticism dwindles as he develops a severe case of heartburn. Thus, Allen clearly pokes fun at the superficial remnants of religious ritual, yet never brings himself to declare, with certainty, the death of God.

If God—or communism, for that matter—holds few answers, one sequence in the film offers a look at what does: the power of imagination and art to redeem ordinary lives and how the family can commune to make such a moment magical. Allen's voice-over relates which radio shows appeal to each family member. For Cousin Ruthie (Joy Newman), a little overweight and obviously Jewish like her equally overweight and Jewish parents, radio provides music, which provides an opportunity to escape her everyday life for a moment. The camera comes upon her as she lip-synchs and dances in turban and flowing skirt in front of a mirror to Carmen Miranda's "Down South American Way." Shortly thereafter her father and uncle see her and, instead of making fun of her or deriding her play, they join in the performance, becoming her backup group. This moment of quiet transcendence speaks of the liberatory possibilities of art and entertainment without the ponderousness of Allen's closing monologue in *Manhattan,* the sentimentality of the ending of *The Purple Rose of Cairo,* or the need for explanation, as in *Hannah and Her Sisters.* Although later in the film another radio program—a news report about a young child who is trapped in a well and then dies—provides another moment of warmth and peace for the family, the earlier moment provides visual insight into the transcendent moments that individuals and families occasionally achieve.

Allen next participated in an interesting, if not especially successful, experiment with an omnibus film, *New York Stories* (1989). Although intermittently attempted in Europe (Fellini was involved in three such films, Truffaut and Godard in another), such anthologies rarely appear in America. For *New York Stories,* three well-known directors, all intimately involved with New York City, each made a short film about some aspect of the city's life. Allen's contribution, "Oedipus Wrecks," with its classical and psychoanalytic implications, sounds like a hilarious glimpse into family dynamics.

Along with *Radio Days,* "Oedipus Wrecks" is Allen's most sustained look at parent-child relationships. The brilliant and funny conceit behind the film extends ideas first used in both "The Kugelmass Episode" and *The Purple Rose of Cairo*. A middle-aged son, Sheldon (Allen), plagued by the worst case of Jewish Mother in the annals of psychiatry, one day sees her disappear accidentally, courtesy of a magician's trick. He feels curiously liberated, now able to enjoy life with his shiksa girlfriend (Mia Farrow). One day, however, his mother manifests herself as a huge, cloudlike apparition in the skies above Manhattan, commenting for all to hear about her son's life. This drives Sheldon crazy. Talk about a super-ego! Talk about projection! Talk about guilt!

In desperation, he turns to a psychic, a cheap, pseudo-gypsy mystic (Julie Kavner) who, of course, is Jewish. The most interesting thing about the film, after the hallucinogenic apparition that is Mother, is that Sheldon abandons Mia Farrow's character and marries Julie Kavner's. This accommodation to his mother, marrying a Jewish girl although she has abandoned Judaism and substituted something else in its place, also represents Allen's accommodation to the Jewish community. Rather than give up the Jewish woman for the shiksa, he abandons the shiksa in favor of the Jew. This was not the pattern in the much earlier and more important *Annie Hall*.

Early in *Annie Hall* (1977), Allen delivers a long-take, static camera sequence that focuses upon a lengthy conversation between Alvy Singer (Allen) and his best friend Rob (Tony Roberts). The sequence begins in long-shot as Alvy and Rob converse on a Manhattan street, walking toward the camera. Primarily, the conversation revolves around Alvy's insistence that he is surrounded by anti-Semites. He claims that a television producer invited him to lunch by asking "Jew eat? Not, *did you* eat, but Jew eat?" Rob dismisses this perception as paranoiac raving. But Alvy has another example, that of a record clerk who insisted that the store was having a sale on "Wagner, Max, Wagner. Get it?" Rob responds by decrying the state of life in New York City and extolling the virtues of Los Angeles. Alvy sneeringly dismisses that idea with one of the two jokes in the film at Los Angeles's expense ("I won't move some place where the only cultural advantage is that you can make a right turn on a red light"; "L. A. is so clean because they take all their garbage and make it into television shows"). But the perception, real or imagined, of anti-Semitism and a love for New York City turn out to be two of the poles around which Allen structures this Oscar-winning film.

Annie Hall is a compendium of American-Jewish issues. Allen's autobiographical Alvy Singer and his relationship to the mid-western Annie Hall reproduce a central motif of American-Jewish literature and cinema: the Jewish male and the shiksa. Interactions between Alvy and Annie's family point out the ambivalent attitude toward WASP society and the phenomenon of Jewish self-hatred. Through a complex narrative structure, Allen cuts a swath through American-Jewish culture and history, pointing to Jewish involvement in political causes, show business, and the Jewish educational achievement in America. Alvy Singer, unable to feel happy about his life and searching for an ultimate meaning, evolves into a compelling Jewish archetype.

Of course, his archetypal status springs from the complex of problems he manifests as the urban, Jewish neurotic. His anhedonia (the inability to feel happiness, and the original title of the film) may be humorous, but it stems from a series of issues intimately associated with being Jewish. For example, his obsession with death manifests itself in everything from a concern with the dissolution of the universe (he stops doing his homework when, as a youth, he is confronted by this reality) to a constant replaying of the Holocaust in the form of re-viewings of the monumental French documentary *The Sorrow and the Pity*.[14] Alvy's inability to sustain a relationship (two former wives and the breakup of his current relationship demonstrate this) are also outgrowths of his anhedonia, itself a function of paranoia and self-hatred. He feels simultaneously inferior and superior. At the start of the film, Alvy quotes Groucho Marx's joke about not wanting to belong to a club that would have someone like him as a member. His two divorces from Jewish women apparently spring from this attitude of inferiority, self-hatred, and Jewish anti-Semitism. At the same time, upon establishing a relationship with Annie Hall, a WASP, he begins to remake her, forcing his obsession with death upon her and demanding that she obsessively view *The Sorrow and the Pity* and Ingmar Bergman films. He pays for her psychoanalysis and for her tuition for evening classes at college. Alvy's inferiority-superiority conflict eventually manifests itself in one of the film's most famous scenes: the split-screen dinner that compares the Halls and the Singers.

Announcing its own departure from normative filmmaking is only one of the ways *Annie Hall* contains its own excesses. It is the clearest autobiographical expression yet in Allen's cinema. The film even begins with Allen directly addressing the camera in the first person. The character, not announced as Alvy Singer, is therefore presented as Woody Allen, already familiar on the basis of his appearance in ten previous films and a handful of television programs. Even after being marked as Alvy Singer not Woody Allen, the autobiographical references predominate. Alvy Singer is a comedian who lives in New York and dates a woman named Annie Hall, just as Woody Allen is a comedian who lives in New York and dates Diane Keaton, the actress who plays Annie Hall. The film also repeats numerous gags from earlier Allen efforts. Thus, it appears to be a personal project of both Alvy Singer's (whose own memories, fantasies, and desires structure it) and of Woody Allen's (who, as the author of the text, may be permitted any excesses he desires).

The major narrative strategy of the film is the flashback. The film progresses something like the monological reminiscences of Alvy, whose direct address opens it. The film closes with Alvy again speaking via voice-over in the same wistful tone with which he opened his talk to the audience. However, in discussing his breakup with Annie Hall, he moves from an attitude of uncertainty and self-doubt to a more positive, accepting stance. From the self-depreca-tion of the start, he concludes that he has made a difference in Annie's life (he takes it as a major coup that Annie takes her new boyfriend to see *The Sorrow and the Pity*), and he concludes, more importantly, that relationships are the fundamental aspect of life. The film that opens with a classic joke closes with another, the one about a man who complains to a psychiatrist that his brother-in-law thinks he's a chicken. When the doctor suggests putting him in an institution, the man claims that they would like to, "but we need the eggs."[15] Relationships, too often temporary, still give meaning to life, itself short, horrible, and filled with doubt and death, but we need the eggs. What brings Allen to this conclusion, to this new maturity, is precisely the bulk of the film, the scenes that Alvy re-calls for the audience.

While Alvy sketches in his relationship with Annie Hall—their initial meeting, growing relationship, and slow breakup—he also provides glimpses of his early life, as if in recognition that where he comes from has made him what he is. Scenes with no direct narra-tive causality with Alvy's relationship to Annie Hall reveal his inner life. Although Allen calls the film *Annie Hall*, he focuses upon Alvy's thoughts, feelings, and background, not Annie's. Annie tells Alvy something of her life in Chippewa Falls, and we eventually see her parents, grandmother (the completely anti-Semitic Grammy Hall), and suicidal brother Duane. But they are seen through

Alvy's eyes. Similarly, although we see some of Alvy's past, it, too, is mediated through his eyes in scenes not so much constructed as flashbacks but as comic exaggerations of memories.

The majority of these memories focus upon his family life and childhood, and he recalls living near the ocean at Coney Island. The ocean will recur in *Radio Days* and is derived as much, perhaps, from Bergman and Fellini as it is from Allen's real autobiography. He lived near the ocean in the Midwood neighborhood of Brooklyn, but not so near as these films indicate. He admits that he exaggerates when he recalls that his apartment house sat literally under the roller coaster at the once-famous amusement park. Similarly, we take as exaggeration the constant arguments between his parents (again, much like *Radio Days*). One argument in particular reveals something of relations between Jews and blacks. A black cleaning woman apparently steals from the Singers. The father wants to forgive her because she is poor and clearly needs the money; the mother, less forgiving, recognizes that they themselves are hardly rich. In the ethnic enclaves of Brooklyn, relations between Jews and blacks always were much closer than between blacks and other white ethnics. This would, eventually, lead to much disharmony because the kinship and responsibility that Jews, an early ethnic success in America, felt toward blacks eventually led blacks to resent Jews.[16] A ridiculous argument cannot entirely displace Allen's serious invocation of Jewish–black relations.

Considering that the stereotype of the Jewish mother who smothers her son with guilt-inducing love is a constant in Jewish humor, its absence stands out in Allen's cinema. Annoyance and dismay seem more characteristic of Alvy's mother, as well as the few other mothers in Allen's work. In *Radio Days*, the most sustained image of the Jewish family in Allen's canon, the mother is less a harpy than usual and yet not particularly supportive. Alvy's mother certainly does not smother her son. For example, she reaches her wit's end when seven-year-old Alvy, realizing that the universe is expanding and will eventually break apart, stops doing his homework.

The horrors of family also appear in a part-memory, part-fantasy scene. The adult Alvy, with Rob and Annie, visits the old neighborhood, where they attend a party at the Singer household of the past, a party also attended by young Alvy. Young Alvy is dismayed by a family friend who, in an obnoxious effort to amuse, constantly harps upon his name, Joey Nichols (Nickles): "Remember my name: Joey Five Cents!" This is perhaps a universal component of adult life as seen through a child's eyes. More problematic is Rob's attitude toward another party guest. He interviews an aunt, an aging, overweight woman with a Yiddish accent, who claims that she "was considered the beauty of the family," a sentiment Rob and the audience take humorously. Too much self-hatred is evident here, as it is when Allen repeats the gag later in *Radio Days*. When the line is spoken by Aunt Bea to the father, he remarks, "Some competition!"

The image of Alvy's family finally comes to the fore in the split-screen sequence. Alvy, both dismayed and impressed by Annie's family during an Easter dinner, tells the audience that her family looks healthy and American, "not like my family." Claiming that the family looks American is an interesting slip of the tongue, for Alvy's family is also American; the Singers were all born in the United States. Allen's reference is obviously to the image of an American as a stereotypically healthy midwesterner, strong and solid-looking if somewhat bland.

When the Singers and another couple (presumably an aunt and uncle) are seen at the dinner table—the mother standing and everyone talking at once—the behavioral differences between them and the sedate, polite Halls are obvious. While the Halls speak of swap-meets and boating, the Singers discuss failure and disease. The ordeal of civility indeed! Yet for all the Halls' politeness and apparent all-Americanness, beneath their smooth exterior lies repression and psychopathology. The grandmother is an anti-Semite, the father is alcoholic, and the brother is suicidal. Allen/Alvy cannot reconcile the competing image of the WASP family. Although he condemns his own, he never elevates the WASP family in their place as an ideal.

His memories and fantasies of his family betray a profound ambivalence. So, too, does Alvy's choice of career: show business. Although a successful comedian (we see two scenes of him performing in concert and one scene on a television talk show), self-hatred is also directed toward his chosen profession. The references to California, home to most of show business, reflect Allen's continued denigration of television. The ambivalence is made even clearer when the horrors of Borscht Belt-type comedy appear in one of Alvy's flashbacks. A comic asks Alvy to supply him with jokes while he gives Alvy some idea of his "style"—all too reminiscent of the schmaltz of mediocre nightclub entertainers, such as Danny Rose to come.

Alvy's greatest ambivalence, however, manifests itself in how he deals with relationships. Because he is divorced from two wives, it seems fair to conclude that—because they were Jewish, where Annie Hall is not—he succumbed to self-hatred in rejecting them. The basis for this conclusion is supplied by Alvy/Allen himself in his quote from Groucho Marx. Yet not only does Alvy try to remake Annie in his own image, but his relationship with Annie also founders.

Allison Porchnik (Carol Kane), Alvy's first wife, meets him at a rally for Adlai Stevenson, who is running for president. Alvy, nervous before addressing the crowd, strikes up a conversation with Allison. When he learns that she is writing a thesis on "Political Commitment in Twentieth Century Literature," he stammers out a litany of descriptions that, she humorously remarks, reduces her to a "cultural stereotype." His catalog description echoes an early, humorous foray into reverse stereotype, "The Whore of Mensa," which originally appeared in the *New Yorker* and is reprinted in *Without Feathers*. In the story, the beautiful Sherry, "packed into her slacks like two big scoops of vanilla ice cream," works as a call girl for men who want not physical contact but intellectual discussions with sexy women. When arrested by the hero, Kaiser Lupowitz, she pleads to be let go, and her whole story comes out: "Central Park West upbringing, Socialist summer camps, Brandeis. She was every dame you saw waiting on line at the Elgin or the Thalia, or penciling the words, 'Yes, very true' into the margin of some book on Kant" (*WF* 39).

Compare the description of Sherry with Alvy's list of Allison's background: "New York Jewish, Left-wing, liberal, intellectual, Central Park West, Brandeis University, Socialist Summer camps, father with the Ben Shahn drawings, right . . . really strike-oriented, kind of red." Alvy invokes this cultural stereotype, a Jewish one, to pigeonhole Allison. The stereotype (which, like all stereotypes, has at least an element of truth) itself indicates the tensions and ambivalence that have accompanied American Jewry's success.

Alvy's second wife, Robin (Janet Margolin), is equally Jewish but intellectual rather than political. The humor in this case is also specifically Jewish. At a party in their apartment, he complains to Robin that he is tired of having intellectual discussions with people who write for *Dysentery*. When Robin corrects him by saying *Commentary*, he quickly tells her that he has heard that *Commentary* and *Dissent* have merged to form *Dysentery*. The gag is more than simply a pun, of course, for both journals are Jewish and intellectual, and the idea of their merger is funny because they are diametrically opposite politically. Thus the audience appreciates the fact that these publications are real, as well as the fact that they have different stances. It is a throwaway line, funny, as Jonathan Rosenbaum notes, without being particularly meaningful (99). Yet the gag is within a Jewish realm and thus highlights Allen's continued ambivalence and, by invoking diametrically opposed Jewish journals, the contradictions and contrasts within the American-Jewish community.

Alvy's former wives also indicate his changes in status, his economic and professional success. He moves from a lower-middle-class apartment house underneath the roller coaster in Coney Island to a more bohemian life-style, probably in Greenwich Village, and then, finally, uptown. We see him with Allison in their semi-bohemian apartment, with books strewn about and a mattress on the floor. It is just after November 1963, and Alvy agonizes over the Warren Commission's findings in the John F. Kennedy assassination. For all of the overt importance of the scene (Alvy wonders if he is just using the Kennedy conspiracy theories as an excuse to stop sleeping with his wife), it also reveals Alvy at a time when he was not quite as well to do as he will later become in his apartment with Robin.

The change in physical geography is also reflected in the look and attitude of the two wives. The modest, politically committed Allison's long hair is worn free, and she uses a minimum of jewelry and makeup; the more confident, assertive, socially committed Robin wears a hairstyle, makeup, and jewelry that are in the latest fashion. The next step, of course, is to the non-Jew, the WASP, the shiksa.

Alvy's economic and professional success mirror that of American Jewry's. The apartment house of his youth in Brooklyn represents the New Old Country of memory in the period from 1910 through 1940; the first generation of Jews born in the United States typically moved away from the tenements of the Lower East Side to Brooklyn or Queens. The move away from Brooklyn after World War II, seen in Alvy's relationship with Allison in the 1950s and early 1960s, indicates the economic success of postwar Jewry as well as the intellectual sophistication of the second and third generation, which was aided by the public school system and the fine, free colleges of New York. Even Alvy's profession mirrors the explosion of Jewish nightclub comics and television writers in the 1950s. Finally, by the late 1960s, Jews had it made in America for all to see; economic, political, and social success was manifested by an increased visibility in entertainment, law, medicine, publishing, and politics.

Alvy's economic and professional success also translates into his success with women. *Annie Hall* essentially eliminates the schlemiel persona from Allen's repertoire, or at least the schlemiel who must pay to work behind the scenes in the burlesque house, as Victor Shakapopolis does in *What's New, Pussycat?* Just as Alvy's life-style in *Annie Hall* marks a major economic leap from his characters in *Take the Money and Run, Bananas,* and *Sleeper* (in which he was the proprietor of a health-food store before his untimely loss of time), so, too, his former alter egos would envy his success with women. Alvy married two beautiful women, has a current girlfriend of note, and even dates a number of attractive women following his breakup with Annie Hall.

Clearly, Alvy's/Allen's success with women is partly a function of his economic and professional success. But his confidence as a man stems in equal part from his greater sense of self-worth as a Jew. The image of Jews as weaklings, as nervous, neurotic urbanites, physically slight and athletically nil, was always belied after the war. For example, Jews were a major presence in boxing and basketball. Revelations of the Holocaust certainly contributed to an image of Jews as victims and aided the stereotype of the weakling. To be sure, Woody Allen's own persona enhanced this image in the early part of his career. But the image of Jews after the capture and trial of Adolf Eichmann in 1961 and the victory in the Six Day War of 1967 (and changed by such films as *Exodus* [1960] and *Cast a Giant Shadow* [1966]) applies equally to Allen, especially once he had established himself as a significant filmmaker. Of course, two attractive Jewish former wives and an attractive current, shiksa girlfriend represented Allen's reality in 1977.

The professional and sexual success manifested by Alvy Singer are traits that Allen continued in later films. He also continued the basic dissatisfaction, the pervasive sense of unease, that characterize Alvy Singer and are manifested in his anhedonia. This sense of unease often stems from anti-Semitism, real or perceived. We have already noted the "Jew eat" conversation, and Annie Hall's description of Grammy Hall as anti-Semitic (which Alvy will solidify when he calls the old woman a "classic Jew hater" in the Easter-dinner scene) should also be emphasized. Yet how much of Grammy's overt anti-Semitism results from Alvy's paranoia (as Rob claims in the "Jew eat" sequence)? When Alvy is seen in the beard and garb of the Hasidic Jew, it comes not from Grammy's point of view, as

Brode claims (178), but rather from Alvy's imagining of Grammy's point of view.

The sense of unease also stems from the recognition of death, whether in the form of the universe that is constantly expanding until it will break apart or in the form of the Holocaust. Although the recognition of death may, therefore, spring in part from the historical memory of anti-Semitism and possibly its continuing remnants, it also comes from the recognition of the absence of God. Despite all the talk of death in *Annie Hall,* it remains one of the least overtly philosophical of Allen's films. The major manifestations of ontological concerns are a joke about cheating on his metaphysics final ("I looked within the soul of the boy sitting next to me"); a rejection of Duane's suicidal vision ("I'm due back on planet Earth now" is his response to Duane's poetically chilling death wish); and a quick joke at the expense of Judaism (in the split-screen dinner scene the Singers have no idea why they fast on Yom Kippur). A joke also occurs at the expense of popular religion. On his disastrous date with Pam (Shelley Duvall), the *Rolling Stone* reporter, she claims that a youthful maharishi is god. Alvy replies, "I think I see god now, coming out of the men's room." Again, Jewish humor (which Allen has made his own) typically thrusts downward from the sacred to the mundane. The joke, more at the expense of fads than of religion, finds its target in the gullible culture of youth. In addition to the maharishi, Pam makes claims for a handful of rock performers as gods.

Because its philosophical and metaphysical musings are minor, religion remains less important in *Annie Hall* than in other Allen films. The same holds true for esthetics. Although Alvy is a dedicated movie-goer, films provide an opportunity to discuss other issues. Films are serious, whereas television is not, but not in themselves capable of imparting meaning to life. Films hardly provide the glimpses into the transcendent that Allen would come to recognize in *Manhattan, Stardust Memories,* and *Hannah and Her Sisters,* for example. Similarly, the redemptive power of art to remake reality, although alluded to by the fact that Alvy writes a play based on his relationship with Annie but gives it an ending in which Annie returns to New York with him, provides little greater meaning to Alvy's efforts.

At the ending of the film, Alvy and Annie are apart. While the soundtrack returns the audience to Alvy via a voice-over, the image track directly derives from Michelangelo Antonioni's *L'Eclisse.* The Italian film ends on a long-take of the cityscape where the protagonists were supposed to meet but do not. The space, empty of the main characters, becomes a final symbol of the emptiness of their lives. The cityscape, similarly significant in *Annie Hall,* is where Alvy and Annie were once at home together; it now stands sadly, metaphysically empty. Because Alvy's anhedonia is generalized—and Allen is not explicit about what bothers his protagonist—the audience is left simply with death. Nothing can be put in its place except relationships that inevitably fade.

That relationships do not simply fade but may also lead to death seems the unhappy conclusion of *Crimes and Misdemeanors* (1989). In earlier Allen films, romance or marriage leads to something like death (as, for example, in *Annie Hall, Manhattan, A Midsummer Night's Sex Comedy, The Purple Rose of Cairo,* and even *Hannah and Her Sisters* and *Radio Days*). But never before has Allen's vision of relationships been so grim. One relationship ends in murder; another deteriorates to the point of outright animosity between the couple; yet another promises love until one member opts out and chooses someone else. Although one-night stands have been unsuccessful in previous Allen films (as seen in the memorable sequence with Shelley Duvall as the *Rolling Stone* reporter in *Annie Hall*), the disastrous date alluded to but thankfully never shown in detail in *Crimes and Misdemeanors* casts an unpleasant pall over much of the film.

Crimes and Misdemeanors must be reckoned important for Allen because it recasts and reworks crucial dichotomies that structure his previous films; more importantly, one dichotomy is almost completely eliminated. Allen again uses a comparative structure built around two sets of characters, as implicated by the title *Crimes and Misdemeanors.* The crimes and misdemeanors correspond to the opposition of drama to comedy (even tragedy to comedy in the classical sense), while Allen, as in *Hannah and Her Sisters,* relegates his own role to comic misdemeanors. He has, however, eliminated the WASP versus Jew dichotomy, a central conflict in much of his earlier work. In a strange way, the central Jewish character acts much like Allen's gentile figures. Not only is he well-to-do and serious, well-behaved and thoughtful like the WASPs in *Interiors* and *Another Woman,* but he is also a criminal, like the mother in *September,* a murderer. Although the title *Crimes and Misdemeanors* recalls Dostoyevsky's *Crime and Punishment,* the film lacks the comic tone of Allen's earlier, Russian-inspired *Love and Death,* which overtly mocks Tolstoy's *War and Peace.* More significantly, *Love and Death* draws much of its comic force from the inappropriate sight of the little Jew on the vast epic canvas; *Crimes and Misdemeanors* provides a genuine Dostoyevskyan protagonist. Although a Jew, he is, like Dostoyevsky's heroes, obsessed by a powerful loss of faith, gripped by a compelling existential angst, and possessed by a profound sense of guilt. The fact that he neither seeks nor finds pseudo-Christian redemption but is "saved" in a far different manner than Dostoyevsky's hero marks a difference in Allen's worldview, but not a comic difference. That the protagonist, the criminal, lives happily ever after is central to Allen's vision of the silence of God, the question of faith, and the significance of art in a meaningless world.

To begin to explore this film, and its significance for Allen's developing vision, it is necessary to first focus upon the comic character played by Allen himself in a role that represents a partial return to the schlemiel persona. The lovable loser so prominent in Allen's previous work also characterizes Cliff, a documentary filmmaker of rather modest means and minor reputation. Trapped in a loveless, sexless, marriage—Cliff rather crudely claims that "the last time I was inside a woman was when I visited the Statue of Liberty last year"—his one genuine pleasure comes from periodically taking his niece to the movies. However, he soon meets a very pretty and intelligent television producer, Hallie (Mia Farrow), while working on a project he abhors. Not only does he develop a romantic interest in Hallie, but the couple also share other joys in life: movie-going and Cliff's work, especially an in-progress film on Louis Levy, a Holocaust survivor turned philosophy professor. That Levy echoes sentiments apparent throughout much of Allen's previous work is clear from the many inserts in which he appears. In fact, the first film-within-the-film sequence finds the professor discussing the biblical tale of Abraham sacrificing Isaac, recalling the other occasions upon which Allen has invoked this tale and raising implications for the ontological questions the film poses. Profound questions of faith and of justice, both implicated by this biblical story, resonate throughout *Crimes and Misdemeanors*.

Significantly Cliff, the schlemiel, does not win in this film. It was said of silent clown Harry Langdon that he embodied the little man watched over by God. The same could be said of other great silent clowns, like Chaplin and Keaton, who had profound impact upon Allen's work. Although it is more problematic and ambiguous, the same might be said of the schlemiels of Yiddish literature who have similarly influenced Allen. In *Crimes and Misdemeanors*, Allen demonstrates that the schlemiel exists forever at the mercy of a hostile universe; the loser, no matter how lovable, cannot and will not win.

Cliff's marriage continues to deteriorate, his hoped-for relationship with Hallie dies, and in perhaps the cruelest cut of all, Louis Levy commits suicide, thereby ruining Cliff's film and blighting the optimistic message he hoped to convey. The little man watched over by God becomes a cosmic joke because God does not exist, or if He does, He is blind to the plight of those who most need Him. Allen's God is no longer merely an underachiever; He is vast, indifferent, and sightless.

The blindness of God may be a Jewish-American variation on Bergman's *The Silence of God,* but Allen develops it through a conscious, recurring motif of eyes and vision. He confines the motif of blindness to the serious side of the film—the crimes—as if to explain the other, less serious side. The film's serious hero, Judah Rosenthal (Martin Landau), is an eminent ophthalmologist. One of his patients, a rabbi, is going blind. Late in the film, Judah recollects a conversation with his lover Dolores (Anjelica Huston) in which she recalls her mother telling her that the eyes are the windows of the soul. After Dolores is dead, Judah looks into her eyes and then tells his brother that nothing is behind her eyes any longer. Finally, and most significantly, Judah tells a crowd gathered to pay tribute to him that his father repeatedly told him that "the eyes of God are on us always." Perhaps, he only half-jokes, this is why he became an eye doctor. This belief that God sees everything first paralyzes him from contemplating Dolores's murder seriously and then plagues him after the deed is done.[17]

Another sort of blindness also extends to Cliff and to the misdemeanors side of the film. Cliff literally does not see what Hallie values in Lester (Alan Alda), for instance. To him, his brother-in-law is a pompous windbag and the worst kind of show business Jew: a Sammy Glick with intellectual pretensions. Indeed, it is hard not to agree with Cliff. So why does Hallie ultimately agree to marry Lester and willingly leave Cliff to go to London, as Tracy did to Allen's alter ego in *Manhattan?* Although we romantically, perhaps naively, assume that Tracy might eventually return to Ike, Hallie returns married to Lester, much to Cliff's dismay. She merely claims that Cliff does not know the real Lester. Another bad judge of a would-be romantic partner is Cliff's sister, a single mother who tells Cliff of her disastrous encounter with a man she met through the personal advertisements. Instead of making love to her while she was tied to the bed, he defecated on her. As Cliff relates the incident to his own wife (who receives the tale rather coolly), he only expresses bemusement at human sexuality.

But something more than bemusement clings to the images of relationships in this film, and something much more lethal than blindness. In both the crimes and the misdemeanors of the account, things go seriously wrong with romance. Cliff, who lives in a hopelessly unhappy marriage, remains unable to establish a solid relationship with Hallie. Judah Rosenthal, seemingly happily married, engages in an affair for more than two years. Because his mistress proves unwilling to break off the liaison when he has had enough, Judah instigates her death. Although we might interpret the failure of Cliff's relationship to Hallie and Judah's to Dolores as a rejection of the Jewish man–shiksa pairing, often a failure in Allen's earlier films, it has never ended in murder as it does in *Crimes and Misdemeanors.*

In fact, for all the separation between crimes and misdemeanors, two murders of a sort really occur in the failed Jew–shiksa relationships. In one, the Jewish man has the shiksa killed; in the other, the shiksa kills the Jewish man's beliefs. Obviously, Allen wants his audience to pay primary attention to the relationship between Judah and Dolores, just as Judah's own doubts and crises receive primary attention at the expense of Cliff's. But it is also necessary to pay attention to how Allen compares the differing Jew–shiksa relationships. On the one hand, for example, in each instance the relationship is broken off by a long-take scene. In the major relationship, Judah breaks off with Dolores in her apartment. Here Allen shoots a lengthy long-take sequence of almost four minutes' duration, deceptive because it involves seven major reframings of the conversation. On the other hand, Hallie is in the park when she breaks off with Cliff, and the long-take is slightly less than two minutes in duration and consists primarily of a tracking shot that becomes a static two-shot. It is clear that Judah wishes to end the relationship with Dolores and will, in essence, murder her; yet Hallie ends the relationship with Cliff and essentially "murders" his idealism.

The fact that Hallie kills something vital in Cliff becomes apparent in his rather strange response to her announcement of her marriage to Lester and her statement that she truly loves him. "This is my worst fear realized," he says. What precisely does Cliff-Allen mean? It is not the fear of anti-Semitism (à la Alvy Singer) because Hallie marries another Jewish man or the fear of peer ridicule that distresses Isaac Davis. Allen specifically tells us what this fear means a short while later, when Cliff offers almost the same exact response to Judah's pseudo-fictional account of murdering Dolores. Thus, the only way to appreciate what Hallie has

Hallie (Mia Farrow) breaks up with Cliff (Woody Allen)—another of the crimes and misdemeanors in the film of the same name.

murdered in Cliff is to understand the significance that murdering Dolores has for Judah.

In Judah Rosenthal, Allen creates the modern Jewish man as confident adult, possessing a loving family, status in his field, and recognition in his community. Judah is certainly no schlemiel, no erstwhile Isaac sacrificed to some arbitrary God. Instead, he is a patriarch, a father and father figure, a scientist, and a devout rationalist, a skeptic with doubts about God but with, significantly, a solid Jewish education and philosophical basis from which to question his own beliefs. Although Allen does not present Judaism in completely positive terms, he includes none of the negatives of earlier pictures: no arbitrary insertions of comic Hasids or satire on religious beliefs. Judah, at the start of the film, thinks of himself as a modern Job who wonders why God punishes him with Dolores, who threatens to expose him to his wife as an adulterer and, later, to the community as an embezzler—a Bathsheba to his David.

Thinking back to his childhood education in the synagogue and his own father's faith and belief, Judah's unpunished murder strengthens his doubts about the existence of God. At his lowest point he returns to the New Old Country of neighborhood Queens and remembers a typical seder, with his father, Sol, quietly proclaiming his religious faith. Judah also recalls the alternative voice, that of cynical reason, symbolized by his Aunt May, who invokes the powerful facts of the Holocaust as proof of God's absence. To Aunt May's question about God punishing him, Sol answers: "He won't punish me, May, he punishes the wicked." May's incredulous answer can only be: "Oh, who, like Hitler? Six million Jews burned to death and he got away with it!"

Sol will not hear of doubts. And Judah remains, until the end, torn about his own beliefs. For him, the murder of Dolores, the most heinous crime he can commit, must ultimately be taken as a test of God's presence, just as on a much larger scale the Holocaust created a monumental rift in Judaic theology. That Judah is a murderer, whereas the Holocaust Jews were murdered, is perhaps Allen's disguised response to the deterioration of Jewish ethical standards (as indicated earlier in his response to Israeli handling of the *intifada*). When he goes unpunished, Judah takes grim satisfaction in proving his father, as well as previous generations of Jewish thinkers, wrong.

Judah's stance, however, does not go entirely unchallenged. Juxtaposed to him is Ben (Sam Waterston), a modern rabbi. Ben is another father (his grown daughter's wedding party is the film's final scene) and father figure in this surprisingly traditionally Jewish film in which religion, philosophy, and education are the provinces of men. Judah's mother is not identified in his flashback to the seder, and Judah's wife (Claire Bloom) is a minor character. Ben and Judah engage in philosophical, theological discussions—twice in Judah's office and once in Judah's imagination—in which Ben and his father are conflated as the voices of optimistic faith and believers in a just God and world; Abraham is willing to accept God's decrees.

On the one hand, Ben and Sol both maintain that "God sees." In the face of Judah's doubts, Ben has faith. In the face of Judah's belief in the harshness of life and the pitiless nature of the universe, Ben maintains a firm belief in a moral structure that has real meaning and the possibility of forgiveness underpinned by a higher power. Ben firmly believes, has faith, because if God does not see, if He does not exist, "it's all darkness." Not only does Ben echo Judah's father, but he also makes explicit the search for values and eternal verities for which Allen has searched during the course of his cinema. He ultimately allows Ben to be something of a final image in the film.

On the other hand, Judah's conviction that God does not exist is confirmed precisely by Judah's opposite, Cliff the schlemiel. Against Ben's optimism versus Judah's pessimism, Allen juxtaposes Louis Levy's optimism against Cliff's schlemiellike pessimism. Unfortunately, Professor Levy disappoints Cliff and thus supports Judah. Upon learning of Levy's suicide, Cliff, shocked, says: "He'd seen the worst side of life, always was affirmative. . . . Always said 'yes' to life, 'yes, yes.' Today he said 'no'." Why he said no—why he "went out the window"—is seemingly left open. Levy is a Holocaust survivor yet contemporary life drives him to suicide (perhaps like another Levi, Primo Levi), another ironic reversal of the image of the Holocaust. The implications of Levy's action might be seen by juxtaposing him to Lester because Cliff makes a film about each man.

Levy leads what philosophers call the examined life and says things that are meaningful and challenging, whereas Lester, for all his pontifications, sounds like a typical Allen pseudo-intellectual, for example, the man at the movie theater in *Annie Hall* confronted by Marshall McLuhan. Yet the world basically ignores Levy while it rewards Lester, who brags that he never graduated from college and yet college professors teach courses devoted to his work. (The same is true, of course, of Woody Allen, who must wonder how much of Lester is in himself.) Similarly, Allen also compares Lester with Judah in one of the film's subtlest juxtapositions. As Judah remembers his father's certainty that "the righteous will be rewarded and the wicked will be punished for eternity," Allen cuts to Lester on a date with Hallie, whom Lester will later marry.

Because Cliff makes a television documentary about him, he is implicated in Lester's success. In a deontological rather than teleological argument, Allen wonders whether the good of making a film about Levy justifies the bad of glorifying a man like Lester. Thus Lester prospers while Levy dies just as the film about Lester will air on television; the one of Levy will never be completed. Because both Levy and Lester are Jewish and work in areas in which Jews excel (academia and show business), Levy's suicide can be viewed as an index of how contemporary Jewry, and the world at large, substitutes false values for worthwhile ideals in the pursuit of success. Levy's suicide, however, is merely a prelude to Cliff's greatest personal disappointment; Hallie leaves him for Lester. His worst fears are realized: God cannot orchestrate justice in the world because there is no God.

To substitute for God, especially for religion, we once again find movies. Movies function, initially, as counterpoint to the film's action, an implicit commentary upon the differences between real life and reel life, a motif prominently featured in *Play It Again, Sam.* Following a number of key dramatic scenes, the film cuts to movie scenes of a similar nature, except they function as comic irony. A discussion of marriage and divorce early in the film leads to a clip from Hitchcock's *Mr. and Mrs. Smith* (1941), itself a comedy about marriage and divorce. When Judah first contemplates murder, Allen cuts to a sequence from *This Gun for Hire* (1942), in which Laird Cregar similarly asks another man to commit a murder for him. It is a rather humorous scene, especially taken out of context. Later, when Judah learns that a police detective wants to speak to him, Allen cuts to a clip of Betty Hutton singing "Murder He Says" from *Happy Go Lucky* (1943). These inserts from Hollywood movies are motivated within the world of the film by the fact that Cliff watches them. Movies directly relate to Cliff himself; after Hallie tells him she is going to London for four months, we see a montage sequence from *The Last Gangster* (1937) in which time passes slowly for the imprisoned Edward G. Robinson. It is obviously meant to express Cliff's feelings of entrapment and the slow parade of weeks

before Hallie's return. Allen intends, and his audience understands, that these sequences are symbolic commentaries upon the
ways movies often treat serious themes.

Differences between Hollywood movies and real life come to the
fore when Judah tells Cliff about his idea for a movie. He describes
an act he did previously in this movie: commit a murder, feel some
guilt about it, and overcome it with hardly a memory or guilt feeling left. "One morning," says Judah, "he awakens [and] the crisis
has lifted." Cliff wonders if the man can ever really go back to the
way things were.

> *Judah:* With time it all fades.
> *Cliff:* Yes, but then his worst beliefs are realized.
> *Judah:* Well I said it was a chilling story, didn't I?

Judah goes on to claim that, in reality, we all rationalize and find
ways to live with our sins, mistakes, and dreadful deeds. Cliff wants
a different ending rather than Judah's happy one: "I would have
him turn himself in. . . . Because in the absence of God . . . he is
forced to assume that responsibility himself. Then you have tragedy." Judah replies, "But that's fiction. . . . If you want a happy
ending you should go see a Hollywood movie."

Allen wants us to be certain, then, not to mistake this movie for a
Hollywood movie; the happy ending that is Judah's (and Lester's)
but not Cliff's represents the way things are in the world. Thus,
he intersperses other Hollywood movies into the film and further dissociates himself from Hollywood movie-making by having
Cliff's job be that of a documentary filmmaker. Of course, he as-
signs himself the role of the uncompromised, who will not bend to
the will of the system, whether television or Hollywood. It is thus
important for the audience to learn that Cliff was formerly an editor for newsreel footage. He quit, presumably, because he no
longer wanted to be a party to the kinds of distortions that commercial news perpetrates upon the public. Cliff's earlier documentaries
include a film on leukemia and one on acid rain. Allen does not
make such films, although he is fond of injecting a fatal disease or
two into his movies, for example, ALS in *Stardust Memories* or the
dreaded brain tumor of *Hannah*.

Instead of interpreting Cliff's films as Allen's guilt feelings for
not making movies of a more politically or socially engaged nature,
however, we see them as symbolic of Allen's. They stand in for
Allen's movies and for him not giving in to the system that demands upbeat or positive movies like a profile of the phony Lester.

Therefore, Cliff's latest film becomes a philosophical meditation from Louis Levy, just as *Crimes and Misdemeanors* is a philosophical meditation from Woody Allen: although not quite the tragedy that Cliff wants Judah's movie to be, it is not quite the comedy that Allen has made previously. If not a tragedy, the film is an anticomedy wherein the murderer goes unpunished and the little schlemiel remains a loser, wherein the righteous are not rewarded and the wicked prosper.

It is no surprise, therefore, that the film should end with a conflation of Cliff's and Allen's film, in which Allen allows voice-overs of Louis Levy to accompany images from earlier in the film itself. It is also no surprise that what Professor Levy has to say is suspiciously similar to what Allen has said for years: We are the sum total of our choices; only through the capacity to love do we give meaning to an indifferent universe and, despite our misery, find joy in simple things like family, work, and the hope that future generations might understand more than ours. But we must take our joy only in moments and believe in love despite overwhelming evidence to the contrary. As proof of this, scenes from earlier in *Crimes and Misdemeanors* give way to images of Ben, sightless but enjoying the company of friends and relatives who have gathered together. For a filmmaker and a film viewer, going blind must be an event of monumental pathos, evidence of God's willingness to inflict suffering. Nevertheless, Allen feels that our faith in life must be blind, as is the rabbi who dances with his daughter at her wedding at the film's end.

Notes

1. See, for example, Dee Burton, *I Dream of Woody,* David Wild, *The Movies of Woody Allen: A Short, Neurotic Quiz Book,* and Graham Flashner, *Fun with Woody: The Complete Woody Allen Quiz Book.*

2. Along with Chekhov and Bergman, Ibsen has also been a model for Woody Allen. In addition to the Ibsen-derived structure of *September,* in *Annie Hall,* Alvy's second wife, Robin, complains at one point that she has a headache, "like Osvald's in *Ghosts.*" In *Hannah and Her Sisters,* Hannah starts the film fresh from a theatrical triumph in *A Doll's House.*

3. *Manhattan* is one of the few American films to be released to home video in the letter-boxed format, which, by blacking out portions of the top and bottom of the screen, preserves the aspect ratio of CinemaScope, a contractual demand on Allen's part.

4. The Holocaust also recurs more subtly in *Shadows and Fog* (1992), Allen's

film adaptation of his one-act play *Death* (*Without Feathers* 45–106) by way of Ingmar Bergman's *Sawdust and Tinsel* (1953). If the paranoia that pervades the entire film springs from a monstrously arbitrary murderer who stalks the vaguely middle-European village in which the film is set, one instance (not in the original play) clearly calls forth the scapegoating of European Jewry by the Nazis. Allen's little-man hero, Kleinman, comes upon a scene of black-clad police rounding up a Jewish family (indexed by their name). The police tell him that although he is "one of them," he is okay for now, but that he should mind his own business or he will be next.

5. A handful of academic film critics have applied the notion of "the dia-logic," from the theoretical writings of Mikhail Bahktin, to the cinema of Woody Allen. In this view, one text "argues with [another], agrees with it (although with conditions), interrogates it, eavesdrops on it, but also ridicules it, parodically exaggerates it" (Pogel 8). Linked to the dialogic is "'the carni-valesque,' the Rabelaisian, festive comedy that served as Mikhail Bahktin's model of subversion and revitalization in the dialogic imagination" (Pogel 190). The medieval carnival, "in which people took to the streets in costume, in which the vulgar parodied the polite and sacred to symbolically destroy all convention and restriction" (Pogel 222–23) found its greatest exemplar, ac-cording to Bahktin, in the works of Rabelais. Such critics as Pogel and Robert Stam see Allen, especially *Zelig*, as continuing this tradition. Of course, none claims that Allen was influenced by Bahktin, rather, that Bahktinian "dialog-ism" can be used to shed light upon Allen's cinema and its significance. We feel that Allen's dialogic and parodic penchants owe much to Yiddish theater as a direct influence, itself symptomatic of modern Jewish mediations with the dominant culture; Jewishness, as expressed in the Yiddish theater and the work of Woody Allen and Mel Brooks, for instance, is itself dialogic. As Stam notes, in Bahktinian terminology, "the theatre that 'fathered' Zelig was a the-atre full of transformations and boisterous polyglossia" (210).

6. The scenes of Leonard at the sideshow recall a film released shortly before *Zelig*, *The Elephant Man* (1980). Is it too much of a coincidence that *The Elephant Man*, the story of someone whose difference made him a horrifying celebrity, was brought to the screen as the first project of Mel Brooks's newly formed Brooksfilms? Allen, in these scenes at the sideshow and in Zelig's transformations, and Brooks by producing *The Elephant Man* and his own films, continue to identify with outsiders and "monsters."

7. Links between Irish and Jew are a dominant feature in silent and early sound cinema in the United States, exemplified by *Abie's Irish Rose*. (See Lester Friedman, *Hollywood's Image of the Jew*, chapters 1 and 2; and David Desser in *Unspeakable Images*.) John Murray Cuddihy (himself of Irish extraction writing sympathetically of the Jewish experience) attempts to draw links between the two groups based on structural similarities between Irish persecution at the hands of the English and Jewish persecution at the hands of the Russians. Cuddihy maintains that both groups were "latecomers to modernity." (See also Stam, *Subversive* 214–15.)

8. We earlier noted that one of the traditions Allen uses is silent comedy,

drawing on the work of Buster Keaton, among others. The tone of the ending of *Zelig* is reminiscent of Keaton's quite outrageous ending to his classic comedy, *College*. Keaton has pitifully pursued the heroine throughout the film until he finally wins her via his athletic skills. A coda following their happy union reveals them in a series of still images that quickly take them from marriage to family to old age, with the film closing on a shot of their tombstones side by side.

9. If *Broadway Danny Rose* is marginally autobiographical in terms of Allen's life, it also derives some of its parameters from the biography of co-star Mia Farrow, who was once married to Frank Sinatra. Nancy Pogel notes the resemblances of Allen's film to a minor Sinatra vehicle called *Meet Danny Wilson* (193). She also makes some labored comparisons between *Broadway Danny Rose* and *The Godfather*, without, however, recalling the fact that the character of Johnny Fontaine in Coppola's film (the character whose desire for a part in a movie leads to the infamous horse's-head-in-the-bed scene) is allegedly based on Frank Sinatra. More to the point, however, is a wicked in-joke that Allen delivers. Tina (Mia Farrow), in Danny's apartment, sees a picture on his wall. "Who's this?" she asks. Danny responds incredulously, "Who's this? That's Frank!"

10. One hopes that Aunt Rose was on his mother's side of the family, lest there was a time when her name was Rose Rose! It is more than likely, however, that Danny Rose is a stage name. Having probably changed his name from a more obviously Jewish one, for example, Rosen or Rosenberg, gives Danny one more thing to feel guilty about. The paradox of Jewish entertainers changing their name only to become intimately associated with Jewishness can be found all the way back to Asa Yoelson, who became Al Jolson, and forward through Allen Stewart Konigsberg, who became Woody Allen.

11. Nancy Pogel, otherwise an astute observer of Allen's films, has transposed Irving Sachs (Sax) and R. H. Levine to "R. J. (*sic*) Sax and Irving Levine" (205).

12. Although we speak of the "Jewishness" of Allen's religious implications, Pogel notes that purple roses are associated in Christian mythology (her term) with crucifixion and rebirth. "Roses are associated with the mother of Christ and with Cecilia, one of the most innocent martyred saints in Christian literature" (190).

13. Can Allen be referencing a scene in Akira Kurosawa's *Dodeskaden* (1970), another portrait of a poor neighborhood and the specific types who inhabit it, in which a man runs amok, brandishing a samurai sword? Allen is familiar with the Japanese cinema. In one scene in *Annie Hall*, Alvy and Annie stand in front of a movie marquee that prominently features *Chushingura*, a classic Japanese tale. Similarly, in the later *Husbands and Wives* (1992), at one point we see Jack (Sydney Pollack) and Sally (Judy Davis) standing outside a theater whose marquee displays *Ran*, a film Kurosawa directed in 1985.

14. *The Sorrow and the Pity* is not primarily "about" the Holocaust, although it is hard not to reference the Holocaust in any story of the Nazis and their collaborators. In fact, within the film, Alvy and Annie discuss the movie in

terms of how they would stand up under torture, how their own notions of heroism would quickly dissipate in the face of a truly powerful foe. Alvy jokes that Annie would crack the moment her Bloomingdale's charge card was taken away. The choice of *The Sorrow and the Pity*, directed by Marcel Ophuls, a French-Jewish filmmaker (his father was Max Ophuls, a German-Jewish film-maker who worked in Germany, Hollywood, and France) is a complex issue. At the time of the making of *Annie Hall*, perhaps Allen had no Holocaust film of similar complexity and magnitude to reference; or perhaps he wanted only to reference the Holocaust obliquely. (Ophuls's own *Memory of Justice*, while overtly about the Nazi horrors, was released at the same time as *Annie Hall* was in production and therefore not yet known to Allen.)

15. "But we need the eggs" gives title to Diane Jacobs's early, excellent work on Allen.

16. This is a subtle acknowledgment of Jewish-black relations in New York City. Allen intended a clear recognition of the deterioration of relations between Jews and blacks in a scene that was shot for the film but never used. Alvy's mother, in a flashback, complains that the neighborhood has changed "now that the element has moved in." Alvy complains about this attitude: "The element. Can you believe that? My mother was always worried that 'the element' would move in. It's like a science-fiction movie." Then, in a science fiction movie called *The Invasion of the Element*, a moving van arrives and a black family emerges. See Jonathan Rosenblum, "Notes Toward the Depreciation of Woody Allen."

17. Coincidentally, almost simultaneous with the release of *Crimes and Misdemeanors*, the author Lynn Sharon Schwartz published *Leaving Brooklyn*, another story set in the Jewish New Old Country, focusing on vision, and featuring an ophthalmologist with a sex drive beyond the bounds of marriage. Although Schwartz's story centers on the memories of its female protagonist, as in Allen's film, the eye troubles are clearly symbolic.

CHAPTER THREE

Mel Brooks: "Farts Will Be Heard"

Mel Brooks (Melvin Kaminsky) never camouflages the causal relationship between his Jewish perspective and his comic work. Indeed, he persistently demonstrates and explicitly acknowledges how the latter springs from the former. In both his interviews and his films, Brooks incorporates Jewish motifs and concerns, a repetitive pattern as easily recognizable in his earliest works as in his most recent picture. Often referring to himself as "your obedient Jew," a phrase squeaking with mock obsequiousness while affirming his outsider status, Brooks plainly situates himself, his work, and his humor within a recognizable Jewish tradition that integrates his personal history with his people's suffering:

> Look at Jewish history. Unrelieved, lamenting would be intolerable. So, for every ten Jews beating their breasts, God designated one to be crazy and amuse the breast-beaters. By the time I was five I knew I was that one. . . . You want to know where my comedy comes from? It comes from not being kissed by a girl until you're sixteen. It comes from the feeling that, as a Jew and as a person, you don't fit into the mainstream of American society. It comes from the realization that even though you're better and smarter, you'll never belong. (Zimmerman 57)

Such a comment assumes that suffering constitutes a large segment of Jewish history, while it recognizes comedy's role in the midst of such tragedy. In fact, Brooks's statement goes further, expressing an instinctive understanding that comedy relieves, if only temporarily, the pain and horror of historical intolerance. This cultural anguish finds a direct parallel in Brooks's personal experience, where his physical appearance and religious heritage limit his participation in everything from the traditional rites of puberty to acceptance into mainstream American life. Yet, once again, grief and bitterness become crucibles that forge comedy rather than existential despair or violent recriminations. For Brooks, being a Jew

Mel Brooks directs Cleavon Little on the set of *Blazing Saddles* (1974).

means being tied to a specific tradition from which he draws both his inspiration and his comic vision.

One finds this constant reaffirmation (some might call it an annoying redundancy or even obsessive paranoia) of Jewishness throughout Brooks's career. Take, for example, his 1966 *Playboy* interview, ironically placed between interviews with Fidel Castro and Malcolm X. Brooks begins by proclaiming that he is "spectacularly Jewish," and then goes on to assert that many top comedians are Jewish because "when the tall, blond Teutons have been nipping at your heels for thousands of years, you find it enervating to keep wailing. So you make jokes. If your enemy is laughing, how can he bludgeon you to death?" (Siegel 266).

Comic riffs about always being afraid, feeling pursued, defending yourself through humor, connecting suffering with comedy, and sensing personal difference characterize almost all of Brooks's interviews and movies. Flash forward to the April 1991 American Comedy Awards, a show honoring Carl Reiner with its Lifetime Achievement Award. Steve Martin introduces Brooks as Reiner's "illegitimate son" and asks for a few words about his longtime friend and collaborator. Addressing the star-studded audience as "Ladies and Jews," Brooks's voice grows steadily more strident as he indignantly castigates Reiner first for not being funny and second for forcing him to assume a false identity: for twenty-five years he pretended that he was a Jew when he was really a gentile from Waco, Texas. (The real Waco Kid?) Finally, Brooks rips off his "false" nose, begins yelling in a Texas drawl, and vows never to utter "any more of that Jew talk." A few moments later, a convulsed Reiner thanks Brooks for channeling into humor his deep-seated anger over having to pay homage to someone less talented. Brooks builds all his films on his indignation, attacking serious topics such as bigotry, intolerance, and greed through comedy.

For Brooks, the very fact of being Jewish provides a framework, a cultural context, for viewing the world, a perspective he never totally casts aside. Take, for example, his seemingly offhand response to Lisa Mitchell about the current (1978) trend toward sexual permissiveness and nudity in films: "Sex—like eating Jewish foods such as chopped liver and gefilte fish—should always be a totally private matter" (63). Not only does his remark make the obvious equation between sex and food, but it also relates to both from a particularly Jewish point of view. Even a gentle foray into the world of speculative thinking brings Brooks back to the past rather than forward into the future, when he told *Omni*'s Jeff Rovin that he could be persuaded to go to Mars if "I could get a light-as-a-feather matzo ball. You haven't been able to get one on Earth anymore, since the old Jews from Odessa and Kiev (his mother's birthplace) started to die" (Rovin, "Last Word" 130). In a more serious moment in 1982, Brooks related his difficulty finding funds for *Frances* (a Brooksfilms Production) in terms of his cultural history: "You hold your hat in your hand, and you plead and cajole and beg to get a few rubles—like a peasant, a *muzhik*.[1] It's like the way *goyim* relate to Jews anyway. They don't think we're serious because they don't give us land. If they thought we were serious, they'd give us land. That's the one thing they don't give us, so they think we're just transient and funny" (Sragow 59).

The comment clearly betrays Brooks's frustrations with a system that deals with him on predominately one level; it also displays his anger with the anti-Semitism faced by his forebears. Most important, however, the analogy Brooks draws—between himself as the modern moviemaker scouring Lotus Land for money and not being taken seriously, and his peasant ancestors denied the right to own land and thus being marginalized—explicitly connects him to this tradition of bigotry, exclusion, and hatred. In fact, as many interviews attest, Brooks filters most of his basic emotions through his Jewish sensibility, even his anger. For example, after "serious" critics panned *The Producers*, he exploded to Albert Goldman: "My comedy is based on rage. I'll show those cockamamie *cahiers* critics. I'll make a movie that'll bend their bagels. . . . We Jews have upward mobility, you know. We're short people but we know how to grow" (Holtzman 254). Such an outburst contains much to be analyzed, from Brooks's acknowledgement that rage fuels his comedy, to his inclusion of Yiddishisms, to his notion of Jews triumphing over physical limitations, to his ethnocentric assumption that *cahiers* critics even have bagels that he can bend.

Like the three other American-Jewish directors discussed in this book, Mel Brooks started his career in television. He was, in fact, the acknowledged master of skit creation for "Your Show of Shows," a program that established the comic gold standard for the medium. From February 25, 1950 until June 5, 1954 (160 performances), Brooks dominated a noisy swarm of writers that formed the most illustrious collection of gagmen ever assembled to work on one television series, including, at various times, Sid Caesar, Howie Morris, Carl Reiner, Larry Gelbart (creator of "M*A*S*H"), Imogene Coca, Joe Stein (writer of *Fiddler on the Roof*), Neil Simon, and Mike Stewart (writer of *Bye Bye Birdie* and *Hello, Dolly!*). In addition to employing these luminaries, Caesar's show also provided a start for an anemic-looking, red-haired young writer who, although initially hired as a typist, eventually challenged Brooks for the title of America's comic genius—Woody Allen. An enduring part of television history, "Your Show of Shows" provided comic inspiration well beyond its initial run, a legacy that encompasses such parody-loving, skit-oriented programs as "The Carol Burnett Show," "Saturday Night Live," and "In Living Color."

One need not look very far beyond "Your Show of Shows" to ascertain the roots of Brooks's comic method. Parodies piled upon parodies, more than a hundred during the "Show of Shows" run, provided audiences with enough laughs to make Caesar and his gaggle of writers the kings of the tube, their antics captivating an estimated weekly audience of more than twenty-five million viewers. Brooks consistently worked on parodies of musicals ("Star Struck" instead of *A Star Is Born*), dramas ("A Trolleycar Named Desire" for *A Streetcar Named Desire*), gangster pictures, westerns ("Dark Noon" instead of *High Noon* and "Strange" instead of *Shane*), foreign movies ("La Bicycletta" instead of *The Bicycle Thief*), and melodramas. His contributions often contained detectable Jewish overtones. When Imogene Coca asks "Strange" why he seems so thirsty, for example, he responds, "I had a herring for breakfast" (Yacowar, *Method* 36). Such early training eventually led him to fashion a more sustained parody of the popular James Bond movies, resulting in "Get Smart," the highly successful, still syndicated television series he created with Buck Henry in 1964. Here Brooks's bumbling superspy Maxwell Smart, CONTROL Agent 86, frustrates the evildoers of KAOS by incompetently fumbling along the path to success, along the way introducing the phrase "sorry about that, Chief" into the national lexicon. In 1975, Brooks attempted to repeat his television series success with "When Things Were Rotten," a parody of the Robin Hood legend that lasted only from September until December of that year.

Because Brooks bases his personal brand of humor so heavily on parody, we need to explore, at least briefly, what distinguishes this specific type of humor from other forms of comedy. "Transpose the solemn into the familiar," said Henri Bergson, "and the result is parody." Such a reversing of the serious and the usual, of the awe-inspiring and the customary, illuminates one crucial component of parody: Laughter results when redundance replaces reverence. Essentially, then, the transposition of the important and the usual forces reevaluation of our veneration of the solemn, allowing us to approach even the most serious of subjects with a broader range of attitudes—including, of course, the humorous.

Bergson's observation provides a solid starting point for understanding the lure of parody, but it does little to clarify why this particular comic configuration so pervades artistic creations in the latter part of the twentieth century. Indeed, not since the neoclassic age of English literature—a period of sustained parody practiced by such poets as Pope and Dryden, essayists like Swift and Johnson, and novelists like Fielding and Stern—has this particular mode of expression so permeated all levels, forms, and styles of modern culture, from fashion to architecture, from painting to music, from philosophy to film.

Like the creators of that earlier age, many of the best contemporary artists appear acutely aware of, and habitually intimidated by, their predecessors. Their work, therefore, demonstrates a profound and persistent tension with the products of the past; they engage in an unmistakable and highly emotional battle with their predecessors that the critic Harold Bloom accurately labels "the anxiety of influence." Parody represents one method of dealing with the burden of the past. By employing this methodology which, by its very nature, must recognize and ultimately incorporate the power of previous texts, contemporary artists who parody older works engrave continuity, a tradition, into modern culture. Simultaneously, however, their reshaping of these previous texts proclaims how much their own time differs from the past, a creative activity that simultaneously highlights likeness as it spotlights uniqueness. As Linda Hutcheon, who defines parody as both "repetition with critical differences" (20) and "authorized transgression" (76), theorizes, "it [parody] is not a matter of nostalgic imitation of past models; it is a stylistic confrontation, a modern recoding which establishes difference at the heart of similarity. . . . Its appropriating of the past, of history, its questioning of the contemporary by 'referencing' it to a different set of codes, is a way of establishing continuity that may, in itself, have ideological implications" (8, 110). Parodies, as Hutcheon points out, tacitly assume both the reader's and the creator's knowledge of the older text being mocked, an assumption based on their joint understanding of textual codes, cultural systems, generic conventions, and artistic models.

The act of parody, therefore, inherently yokes the past with the present, establishing an ongoing dialogue between the original work and its parodic offspring. Such an exchange affords artists the luxury of maintaining a tradition while still commenting critically upon it. Through this dynamic interchange of the new with the old, a process Hutcheon formally labels as "trans-contextualizing" (101), parodists compare and contrast today's world to yesterday's. For example, "the mock epic did not mock the epic; it satirized the pretensions of the contemporary as set against the ideal norms implied by the parodied text or set of conventions" (44). By this juxtaposition of the past and the present, the process of parody forces modern artists to compete directly with their predecessors. A parody of "Paradise Lost," for example, would inevitably bring up comparisons between the skill of Milton and the parodist, as well as between the themes of the two works. Such an intimate linkage inevitably spotlights the dirty little secret that lurks within all parodies, no matter how hip or how clever: It is easier, and consequently less creative, to poke fun at something that already exists than to produce something new. In other words, all parodies both great and small remain derivative rather than original creations because without a previous text to comment upon the parody would never exist. At the same time they irreverently deride canonized texts, parodists must, on some level, feel deeply insecure about being matched against the giants who preceded them.

All of Brooks's films are parodies, but his particular mediation of this process clearly springs from a distinctly Jewish perspective. Sanford Pinsker, expanding on the comments of Ronald Sanders about pastiche, sees parody as particularly attractive for people living in bifurcated cultural situations because it is built "from nearly equal shares of imitative reverence and ironic distancing" (249). In one sense, therefore, Brooks's parodies function as complex responses to life as a Jew in America. On the one hand, such a structure allows Brooks ample room to comment upon traditional American myths and iconography, to allow him to critique an essentially gentile culture from the perspective of the outsider.

As Ella Shohat argues, "parody, which tends to be a marginalized artistic practice, is especially important for the discussion of how marginalized ethnic and racial groups can critique not only explicit racist enunciations, but also what the political theorist Stuart Hall calls 'inferential racism,' that is, those apparently naturalized representations whose ethnocentric and racist propositions are inscribed in them as a set of unquestioned assumptions" (238). *Blazing Saddles*, for example, explodes the myth of the democratic West by foregrounding the blatant racism inherently a part of what textbooks paint as the triumph of civilization over savagery. *Spaceballs* takes this critique into outer space, and *Young Frankenstein* into the nineteenth century. On an even grander scale, *History of the World, Part One* deflates several golden eras of Western culture, demonstrating that such ages were far less than golden for those not in power—and Jews never were in power.

Brooks has stated that he parodies genre because he likes "a background to work against, a milieu" (Yacowar, *Method* 2). Indeed, that background usually represents a traditional melting-pot mentality, a cultural hegemony dominated by a white, middle-class, masculine, and decidedly gentile worldview. Brooks's films make explicit the implicit assumptions about race, religion, and gender that support the ideology inherent in typical westerns, musicals, mysteries, science-fiction films, and horror movies. He exposes the cultural doctrines hidden behind the curtain. Yet Brooks's movies all alternate between a yearning to partake uncritically of that cultural tradition and an understanding that such total assimilation is never possible. In order to mediate the tension produced by these mutually exclusive desires, Brooks adopts an attitude of comic superiority and pokes fun at the very traditions that exclude him. Again, Brooks speaks to this very issue when he claims, "you cannot have fun with anything that you don't love or admire or respect" (Young 33). Be that as it may, Brooks continually questions the conventions of our most revered genres, showing how typical conventions change when the perspective of the storyteller moves from the center to the margins. In essence, he turns the language of the dominant culture back onto itself, seeking both to accommodate and criticize American ideology.

Parody, as many commentators have noted, is also a vehicle for emotions far beyond the limits of simple humor. In *Against the Apocalypse: Responses to Catastrophe in Modern Jewish Culture*, David Roskies demonstrates how various forms of parody flourished even during the Holocaust in ghetto songs and writings. He further describes how Jewish writers from ancient times, up through the medieval ages, and into the relatively modern eras of S. Ansky and Sholem Aleichem used parody to channel their anger and respond to their status as minority members within a predominately gentile culture, often by irreverently "making the [sacred] text seem for a while crazy and corrupt" (19).

Brooks's sacred text, of course, is the screen not the Scriptures, but Roskies's description of how parody functioned in earlier epochs of Jewish culture aptly characterizes Brooks's method. Certainly, his barely disguised anger and disgust fuel Brooks's indignant attacks upon Nazis in *The Producers,* anti-Semitism in *To Be or Not to Be,* greed in *Silent Movie* and *The Twelve Chairs,* intolerance in *History of the World, Part One,* and racism in *Blazing Saddles.* Within this broader context, therefore, parody powerfully reaffirms Brooks's Jewishness and gives him a structure within which to question some of the sacred American and cinematic values inherent in our culture.

If Brooks's use of parody speaks to his perpetual sense of alienation from and affection for American culture as embodied within his movies, his continual use of a Yiddish-inflected accent and the incorporation of actual Yiddish words and phrases within his pictures draw him directly back to his immigrant roots. Such affectations spring directly from his upbringing within the insular Eastern European communities of Brownsville and Brighton Beach, where he spent the early part of his life, and of the Borscht Belt circuit of the Catskill Mountains where he honed his instinctive comic talent into razor-sharp parodies and sketches.

Brooks's parents, his father from Danzig and his mother from Kiev, and his extended family of grandparents, aunts, and uncles filled his youthful world with Yiddish stories, off-color jokes, puns, and homilies. So pervasive was this early immersion into Yiddish language and culture that young Melvin Kaminsky innocently assumed that English was the language of children and Yiddish that of adults: "When I was a little boy, I thought when I grew up I would talk Yiddish, too. I thought little kids talked English, but when they became adults, they would talk Yiddish like the adults did. There would be no reason to talk English anymore, because we would have it made" (Yacowar, *Method* 63).

Such an upbringing, as Brooks himself admits, could not but leave lasting imprints, even when Kaminsky evolved into Brooks: "The roots of my humor are in very old-fashioned Yiddish comedy . . . which is based on some failure—making fun of the inept, which is cruel. . . . So Jews taking off on unfortunates, it's always compelling. Because you're saying in a strange way, 'Oh thank God, it's not me.' You enjoy the humor because you are not the butt of the joke. It's cruel but effective" (Carter 271). With this basic Yiddish context in mind, it is easier to understand Brooks's often-repeated distinction between comedy and tragedy: "Tragedy is if I cut my finger. Comedy is if you walk into an open sewer and die" (Tynan 94). The central difference, of course, revolves around the dissimilar responses to an event that happens directly to the individual—when even a small misfortune becomes the stuff of tragedy—and an event that happens to someone else—when even a fatal accident can be humorous because another person is the victim. Such an observation certainly functions as "cruel but effective."

Although Brooks incorporates many Yiddish elements into his television parodies for Caesar, as well as into his Oscar-winning short *The Critic* (1962), his most famous expression of these formative years remains his classic recordings as the 2,000 Year Old Man: "2,000 Years with Carl Reiner and Mel Brooks" (1961), "2001 Years with Carl Reiner and Mel Brooks" (1962), "Carl Reiner and Mel Brooks at the Cannes Film Festival" (1963), and "2,000 and Thirteen" (1973). A clearly Jewish character from the Old Country, one who comments on the cycles of history in response to questions by straightman Reiner, Brooks's alter ego almost fulfilled his naive childhood expectation: He came as close as he could to speaking Yiddish as an adult. "I really wailed," says Brooks about these adroit mixtures of practiced routines and improvisations with Reiner. "I could hear my antecedents. I could hear five thousand years of Jews pouring through me. . . . Within a couple of decades, there won't be any more accents like that. They're being ironed out by history, because there are no more Jewish immigrants. It's a sound I was brought up on, and it's dying" (Yacowar, *Method* 52). As this quotation indicates, Brooks's incorporation of Yiddish accents and expressions represents a personal act of faith and memory. They draw him back to his roots, to his connection with an almost exclusively Jewish environment that retrospectively assumes utopian proportions. Such a dialect, beyond its obvious comic intentions, marks Brooks as a Jew, a descendent of someone not born in this country. As such, it puts definable limits on the possibilities of assimilation because a person speaking this type of broken English remains permanently alienated from the high culture of any given epoch of American life. In this sense, then, Brooks's Yiddish clearly establishes his separateness from gentile life while simultaneously creating a clear connection with the voices of Jewish immigrants and their children.

"Being an American-Jewish comic," observes Sanford Pinsker, "is often a delicate balancing act between keeping in touch with these voices and incorporating them into one's act" (249). In his articulate discussion of modern writers, Murray Baumgarten analyzes the role of Yiddish in a diverse series of such American-Jewish novelists as Bellow, Kaplan, and Roth. Basically, he says, modern Jewish writing is part of the "history of Jewish interlinguistics," and what he concludes about these authors seems equally true of Brooks: "It is important to note that the individual passes out of his or her original community and yet is measured by the ability to remember it. Leaving behind old habits, the critical thinker takes along old values. Self-definition depends on the honoring of two commitments: his independence can be maintained only insofar as he recognizes his traditional values. He must continue to search for a new order within himself that reconciles past and present and fits both to the modern framework" (31).

In this sense, then, Brooks becomes an interesting example of Bahktinian polyphony, one of the independent voices that never melts seamlessly into the dominant, flat discourse of modern-day America. Such a Bahktinian formulation represents more than simple sounds in different registers; instead, it conjures up the presence of dissimilar perspectives and ideologies of the "social and ethnic diversity . . . fundamental to every utterance" (Stam, "Bakhtin" 259, 260). The use of Yiddish, therefore, provides Brooks with an alternative voice that comments, often satirically, upon the uniformity of American culture and values and calls them into question.

Several elements appear consistently across Brooks's oeuvre. First, his persistent inclusion of what many critics and viewers characterize as vulgarity—his enthusiastic embrace of bad taste often incorporating scatological references and activities—stamps Brooks as directly descended from an American-Jewish comic team who also struck their contemporaries as low class and common: the Marx Brothers (who seem an equally appropriate model for Brooks's dialect comedy). "You've been accused of being vulgar," said one interviewer. "Bullshit!" said Brooks (Siegel 266). For Brooks, as for the Marx Brothers, genteel society's avoidance of bodily functions represents a suppression of natural responses. On a somewhat higher level, this suppression symbolizes a hypocrisy bred of class distinctions and cultural affectations. "Good taste is meaningless," Brooks told Arthur Cooper. "It's not a factor in art" (102).

For a sympathetic critic like Kenneth Tynan, who likened him to Ben Jonson, or like Frank Manchel, who called him the American Rabelais, Brooks's bad taste simply pricks "the public's absurd pretensions. . . . Using bad taste as a weapon to right the world's social wrongs is a long tradition that Mel inherited from great film clowns. . . . Brooks brings to it a sense of anger growing out of his Jewish heritage and battles with anti-Semitism. Gifted with a fertile imagination, he delights in attacking phonies and bigots" (Manchel 62). Using a more Freudian perspective, Maurice Yacowar claims that "for Brooks as for Freud, comedy is man's highest defense because it openly confronts ideas that are generally deemed shameful or painful. . . . So Brooks' robust vulgarity is central to his moral and psychological purposes. . . . He extols the more sublime rigor and honesty of the freed and open energy, that will confront man in all his weakness and embarrassment, that will follow through the consequences of man's consumption, whether culinary or cultural" (*Method* 169). This "robust vulgarity" certainly provides Brooks with a weapon with which to bludgeon pretension, a method by which he assaults precious American shibboleths ranging from the theater, to the myth of the West, to psychoanalysis, to history, and to romantic love.

Brooks's most famous cinematic instance of this impulse toward scatology is the farting-around-the-campfire scene in *Blazing Saddles*. Yet even this element of Brooks's work is filtered through a distinctly Jewish consciousness: "Farts are a repressed minority. The mouth gets to say all kinds of things, but the other place is supposed to keep quiet. But maybe your lower colons have something interesting to say. Maybe we should listen to them. Farts are human, more human than a lot of people I know. I think we should bring them out of the water closet and into the parlor" (Yacowar, *Method* 103).

Farts as a "repressed minority" that might have something "interesting" to say! Farts as detested outsiders ghettoized in the bathroom! Farts as more human than some people! Certainly a perspective that pleads for toleration for farts—which somehow manages the figurative leap necessary to equate them with history's misfortunate "others"—displays an understanding that comes directly from the personal experience of being suppressed and ignored, of being perceived as smelling up polite society. For Brooks, who won a bitter fight with Warner Brothers to keep the campfire scene in the picture, this particular moment restored life to an artificial genre; it blew the winds of realism into a desert of mannered affectation: "Shakespeare said hold the mirror up to life; I held it a little behind and below" (Yacowar, *Method* 102–3).

Western film directors had expertly staged bonecrushing barroom brawls and violent shootouts, had gleefully depicted savage Indian massacres and ferocious wagon-train attacks, had skillfully choreographed cruel bank robberies and desperate stage holdups, but from the early silent days on, observes Brooks, "wind was never

broken across the prairie . . . no one has had the courage to produce a fart" (Yacowar, *Method* 103). Far more to the point, Brooks
understands that as farts force people to acknowledge their bodies,
their connection with the animals, so his film tactics force society to
face its less desirable activities. "As long as I am on the soapbox,"
Brooks told Charles Young, "farts will be heard!" (35).

Although an obsession with scatology represents Brooks's
coarser side, his more refined sensibilities inform those films in
which he neither appears nor receives credit, the movies released
under the imprint of his production company, Brooksfilms: *Fatso*
(1980), *The Elephant Man* (1980), *My Favorite Year* (1982), *Frances*
(1982), *The Fly* (1987), and *84 Charing Cross Road* (1988). In one of
the few articles to deal with his contribution to these pictures,
which he begins by promising "to try to act like a serious Jewish
person," Brooks told Marc Kristal that Brooksfilms is "a wonderful
vehicle for me to convey my own more muted and complicated
passions" (25). Mel Brooks neither wrote nor directed any of these
films; yet, one of the intentional similarities between these diverse
works remains that, except for *The Fly* and *84 Charing Cross Road*,
each was made by a director working on his or her first major
motion picture (Anne Bancroft, David Lynch, Richard Benjamin,
and Graeme Clifford). Credits aside, however, Brooks took an active role in the editing and casting of the films. Most important, he
functioned as script supervisor (he had substantial input, for instance, into the writing of *The Elephant Man)* and salesman. "I'm a
better salesman than I am anything else," he bragged to Kristal,
comparing this talents to that of a Jewish merchant. "I should have
worked on Allen Street, on the Lower East Side, selling dark suits
to Jews who didn't need them" (27). Alan Schwartz, Brooks's attorney, speaks of Brooksfilms partly in terms of how the "street kid,
Brooklyn born and ghetto-bred" still seeks acknowledgment from
respectable segments of society, painting him as possessing "a little
Jew mentality about the way the big wasp world feels about him"
(Kristal 28).

However much Brooks hungers to express his serious side, to
gain approval for his ideas as well as his farts, he still understands
that Brooksfilms are better off without his name prominently ap-
pearing in the credits: "You put the name Mel Brooks on something and the public expects riotous comedy, and they end up with
something that has cellos and violins in it" (Kristal 27). Yet, as Kristal notes, all Brooksfilms products are similar in that they feature a
central figure, either ostracized or even brutalized by society, who

finally attains some sort of triumph and transcendence. Such a similarity is not coincidental, as Brooks himself notes in one of his few perfectly serious comments on the role of art and the artist: "One of the purposes of art is to make things right that are eternally wrong. And the job of the artist is to paint a picture of life as truly and honestly as he sees it, and add that extra dimension of hope, and of fantasy, and of dream" (Kristal 28). Yet even within this seemingly rarefied context, Brooks explicitly justifies his actions by harking back to his Jewish perspective: "Maybe it's part of the whole Jewish thing—'I pledge two dollars anonymously for the crippled children.' It makes you feel good to do something like that. . . . Somewhere in the Talmud it tells you that you must return a portion of your gain in this world. You must give it back" (Kristal 26, 28).

The "Jewish thing," as he puts it, endows Brooks with a point of view beyond the mere tallying of profits and the making of sequels; instead, it gives him a deeper historical perspective and wider sense of artistic philanthropy. As the farting speaks to our animalistic nature, so the Brooksfilms ultimately applaud our spark of divinity. They recognize the unfeeling, savage side of society, as well as the individual acts of kindness and decency that grace existence.

Although Brooks sometimes separates slapstick farce from serious concerns, no such bifurcation occurs in his persistent references to the Nazi era and the Holocaust. Although he did volunteer to fight during World War II, and at one point had the dangerous job of deactivating land mines ahead of the rapidly advancing Allied infantry (Adler and Feinman 20), Brooks's failure to engage the hated Huns directly apparently left him with a permanently thwarted sense of duty, an obsessive feeling of "unfinished business" that continues to haunt him. His most direct contact with Nazi troops, quite fittingly, was verbal rather than physical. Immediately following the Battle of the Bulge, the Germans erected a loudspeaker to spew propaganda at Brooks and his fellow American soldiers. To retaliate, Brooks set up his own loudspeaker and serenaded the Third Reich's finest with a raucous rendition of Al Jolson's "Toot-Toot-Tootsie." Perhaps Brooks felt this particular choice was apt punishment for the Germans' sins. More likely, he innately recognized the irony of forcing Hitler's elite troops to listen to an archetypal American pop tune, one, coincidentally, made popular by a Jewish performer. In any case, one can only imagine how the confused, defeated and dispirited Germans responded to this improvisational performance. Yet Brooks's feeling of not doing enough persists. As late as 1987, we see him almost salivating over the thought of producing the following movie: "I want to do a David Lynch unconscious treatment of the secret mind of Adolf Hitler, a Samuel Beckett-ish adventure dealing with unconscious truths. . . . Joseph Goebbels would be represented in some insane, symbolic way—Goebbels based on power and Goring on sexual perversity. Eva Braun would represent the people—the innocent people—swallowing everything, believing a lie, being seduced. It could be an incredible picture" (Long 104). Clearly, such sentiments come from a man still passionately entangled with this subject matter, still overwhelmed by brooding anguish whenever he contemplates the topic.

Brooks attacks Germans in almost all his films, from the recognizable German accents of Nurse Diesel (*High Anxiety*) and Frau Blucher (*Young Frankenstein*), not to mention his own German scientist role in *The Muppet Movie* (1979), to more frontal assaults in *The Producers* and *To Be or Not to Be*. Even his records with Reiner incorporate this preoccupation, particularly "Carl Reiner and Mel Brooks at the Cannes Film Festival." Here, he plays Adolph Hartler, head of the Narzi Film Company, who claims his SS tattoo really stands for "Simon Says," that Hitler's main error was losing the war, and that *Judgment at Nuremberg* was an unfair misunderstanding of the "camp" situation ("Don't you send your children to camp in the summer, also?"). On an earlier album, Brooks becomes Lopez de Vega Diaz, a Peruvian coffee plantation owner who constantly slips back into his native German accent and cannot help bragging about the Nazi's military prowess.

Hearing Brooks assume these roles reminds us of Jean Piaget's discussions about "ghost reaction" in *Play, Dreams and Imitation in Childhood*, in which the father of developmental psychology observes that the sources of imitation are the childhood fears and uncertainties that pervade daily existence. Imitation allows mastery of that which frightens us the most, because by using mimicry we can forge an accommodation with our terror by "assimilating it to ourselves . . . [by] becoming at one with it" (Corrigan 4). On a less personal level, Brooks's creation of characters like Hartler and de Vega Diaz, of Nurse Diesel and Frau Blucher, prompt us to consider how easily the post-World War II political order accommodates the remnants of Nazi Germany, how quickly the world forgets or chooses to overlook the atrocities committed in the name of racial purity and the Fatherland.

As in so much related to his films, one need not look very far from the Jewish perspective to discover his motivation: "Me? Not like the Germans. Why should I not like Germans? Just because they're arrogant and have fat necks and do anything they're told so long as it's cruel, and killed millions of Jews in concentration camps and made soap out of their bodies and lamp shades out of their skins. Is that any reason to hate their fucking guts?" (Yacowar, *Method* 17).

Although such intense, barely contained fury clearly motivates his persistent assaults on the Nazis, Brooks channels his indignation into comedy rather than tragedy. He understands that a simple laugh often stimulates the brain more than a long-winded, well-meaning speech. Thus, he places himself in a long and honored tradition of those artists who communicate serious values through laughter, a distinguished line of creators that stretches from the ancient Greek playwrights to the modern black comedians. All dictatorships, of course, view the humor directed at them as subversive blasphemy. For example, anyone in Germany or the countries it conquered who made anti-Hitler jokes could be put to death. The Allies, recognizing the power of humor, often dropped cartoons deriding Hitler behind enemy lines. Similarly, Brooks drops his humor directly on Hitler and his theories. He clearly understands that nothing is alien to comedy, even the worst catastrophes in history: "The more serious the situation, the funnier the comedy can be. . . . The greatest comedy plays against the greatest tragedy. . . . If you throw it [comedy] against the hard wall of ultimate reality, it will bounce back and be very lively" (Yacowar, *Method* viii). To appropriate David Roskies's description of Sholem Aleichem's work, Brooks struggles to laugh at the trauma of history.

Like Brooks, Woody Allen also communicates serious values through laughter and, because they represent different aspects of Jewish comedy, a brief comparison seems useful before examining Brooks's films in greater detail. Brooks, himself, has commented on their relationship, drawing particular attention to their shared immigrant Jewish roots: "No wonder Woody Allen and I are great. We are not Brooks and Allen; we are not some *department store*. We are Konigsberg and Kaminsky. Now *those* are names, like Tolstoy and Dostoyevsky" (Young 35). As if to validate this point of similarity, of bloodlines that go beyond the relatively short history of American existence, both directors eventually made a film inspired by Russian literature and set in the Old Country: Brooks's *The Twelve Chairs* and Allen's *Love and Death*. One need not search very far to find other biographical similarities, including their New York upbringing (both were born in a Brooklyn tenement), their long years in psychotherapy (which both, as with Mazursky, satirize consistently in their pictures), their non-WASP physical appearances, their romantic relationships with non-Jewish women, and their affection and respect for Fellini's films and those of the Italian neorealism movement (particularly *The Bicycle Thief*). Brooks and Allen both also share a love of music, although the chosen instruments of each indicate the men's individual temperaments and comic styles: Brooks plays the drums and Allen the clarinet.

Brooks and Allen also share a similar career history that has evolved into a working situation in which they star in, write, and direct their own pictures. Each started in television and even worked together for awhile on "Your Show of Shows," although Brooks wrote far longer for that enterprise and made a more central contribution to it. In addition, one of Brooks's earliest filmmaking experiences (with Reiner) was to juxtapose humorous dialogue to a poorly produced Italo-French production, *The Titans* (1966), much as Allen did to a Japanese film in his early effort *What's Up, Tiger Lily?* (1967). Because their pictures usually involve reasonable budgets and inevitably produce a profit, Brooks and Allen have both attained a certain degree of independence from the shifting financial sands of the turbulent film industry. Each director also surrounds himself with a repertory company of compatible performers with whom he works over a series of pictures: Brooks uses Madeline Kahn, Harvey Korman, Ron Carey, Dom DeLuise, Marty Feldman, Gene Wilder, and Cloris Leachman. Allen's films often involve Tony Roberts, Diane Keaton, and Mia Farrow. Occasionally, they even share a talented collaborator behind the camera, as is the case with film editor Ralph Rosenblum. On *Spaceballs*, for example, Brooks's coproducer was Ezra Swerdlow, who was associate producer on *Radio Days*, production manager on *Hannah and Her Sisters* and *Broadway Danny Rose*, and unit manager on *Zelig* and *Stardust Memories*. Finally, both directors use genre parodies to critique American myths, although Allen gave up this strategy reasonably early in his film career.

Because our basic premise revolves around the belief that Allen, Brooks, Lumet, and Mazursky express certain thematic similarities, it seems understandable that Allen and Brooks share a similar worldview growing out of their perspective as Jews struggling to succeed in a gentile world. For example, both display a constant uncomfortableness, a sense of displacement bordering on paranoia, with the Christian world surrounding them. Brooks's vision of a non-Jewish midwesterner as someone who "drives a white Ford station wagon, eats white bread, vanilla milkshakes, and mayonnaise" (Adler and Feinman 105) differs little from Allen's attempt to become a Christian in *Hannah and Her Sisters*. Similarly, Brooks's conception of everything between New York and Los Angeles as "John Wayne country" (Young 35) springs from the same sensibility Alvy Singer displays in his famous Easter dinner scene with Annie Hall's family.

Almost all of both Brooks's and Allen's important personal themes evolve from their deep-seated sense of being out of place in a culture that values tall, blonde beachboys and traditional, Christian upbringing. Both men so internalize the notion of "otherness" that it becomes the lens through which they view the world, although Allen combats this acceptance of negative self-images with intellectual pirouettes and Brooks with primal screams. No matter the tactics, the result remains the same. Each still suffers from what Yacowar aptly characterizes as "an unattractive man's dream of beauty . . . [and] the immigrant's clumsy embarrassment amid suave sophistication" (*Method* 169). For Kaminsky and Konigsberg, American life represents a series of compromises and accommodations, of disappointments and narrow escapes. Each confronts the ever-present fear that only one distinction makes America truly different: Its anti-Semites are more polite.

Even with these similarities, Brooks's style of filmmaking remains quite different from Allen's. As Gene Wilder, who acted in the films of both men, described their comic sensibilities to Kenneth Tynan, "the way Woody makes a movie, it's as if he were lighting ten thousand safety matches to illuminate a city. Each one of them is a little epiphany—topical, ethnic, or political. What Mel wants to do is set off atomic bombs of laughter" (65). Andrew Sarris, embroidering upon Wilder, concludes that Allen is "more cerebral" and Brooks "more intuitive," but that Allen lacks Brooks's "reckless abandon and careless rapture" (Sarris, "Funny Bone" 71). Pushing these distinctions even further, Maurice Yacowar argues that Brooks's films embody a Dionysian spirit against Allen's Apollonian tendencies and casts the Brooks versus Allen competition as "part of the civil war between Jewish intellectuals and Jewish philistines. . . . the beginning of an era of cultural affluence and alienation and of increasing fragmentation of audience sensibilities" (*Method* 36). On some essential, deeply felt level, then, Allen and Brooks share a feeling of wary accommodation, of temporary permanence. For all their apparent emotional overtness, psychological angst, and popular success, each still watches the world through hooded eyes, waiting nervously for the knock on the door that will reaffirm his difference from the center of American society.

The Twelve Chairs (1970), Brooks's second feature, hearkens directly back to the Old Country, to a world young Melvin Kaminsky heard about in stories and songs throughout his childhood. Such tales left a lasting impression and, during his tenure on "Your Show of Shows," Brooks devoted himself to reading Russian literature, particularly the novels of Tolstoy, Gogol, and Dostoyevsky. Later he enthusiastically gushed to *Time*, "My God, I'd love to smash into the casket of Dostoyevsky, grab that bony hand and scream into the remains, 'Well done you goddam genius!'" (Holtzman 255). Lucille Kallen, another Caesar veteran, saw Brooks's compulsive novel consumption as part of "an ancient Jewish respect for literature," one encouraged by coworker Mel Tolkin (Holtzman 255). Thus, after being deeply wounded by the critical attacks on *The Producers*, Brooks rather naturally turned for renewal and inspiration to the Russian culture he knew so intimately, specifically the comic novel *Diamonds to Sit On (Drenadstat Stuler)* by Ilya Ilf (Fainzilberg) and Yevgenyi Petrov (Katayev): "*The Twelve Chairs* for me was Russia. I'm a Russian Jew, and finally, I could bathe in everything Russian that's in me. . . . Chairs are Jewish to begin with. You come in, 'Take a seat'" (Yacowar, *Method* 96). (The same book was the source for a 1936 comedy, *Keep Your Seats*, and a 1945 film, *It's in the Bag*, also a Soviet film.) Brooks spent about a year writing the script and another six months revising it, describing the latter process with typical metaphors: "We attacked that script like we were Nazis in September 1939, entering Poland, that's how fiercely we attacked that script. And it acted like Israel in 1948, brave and courageous, fighting for its life" (Adler and Feinman 89). For all his love of Russian literature, for all the warm feelings evoked by his childhood memories of his ancestral homeland, Brooks's film displays little hazy nostalgia for a country steeped in anti-Semitism.

The film follows the misadventures of three incompetent treasure hunters searching for a fortune in rubles hidden inside one of a set of twelve dining-room chairs confiscated by the triumphant communists. Ron Moody stars as Ippolit Vorobyaninov, an impoverished aristocrat whose mother-in-law stashed the jewels away during the darkest days of the Revolution. On her deathbed, she reveals her ruse to her son-in-law and also confides in the corrupt Father Fyodor (Dom DeLuise), an unscrupulous priest who immediately sets forth to recover the riches for himself. To help best the rapacious prelate, Vorobyaninov reluctantly joins forces with an engaging con man, Ostap Bender (Frank Langella), a facile conniver willing to do almost anything to beat the new, bureaucratic system (the Housing Ministry contains different bureaus for various household items, including a Bureau for Furniture Not Used in Other Bureaus) and obtain his fortune. Together, these two very dissimilar men form an uneasy alliance of shared need and mutual mistrust, another example of the male bonding so prevalent in Brooks's films. As many critics quickly noted, the film breaks down into a series of comic chases and confrontations spread across the Soviet Union, an episodic structure that allows Brooks ample opportunities to indulge in dialect humor, slapstick, burlesque, and satire—not to mention parody. Brooks also continues his songwriting efforts; here, he adds lyrics to a Johannes—"a short man in a wig, but nice"—Brahms melody and comes up with a tune that aptly summarizes both his attitude and an archetypically Jewish perspective toward life: "Hope for the Best, Expect the Worst." Shot in Yugoslavia on a relatively small budget of $1.4 million, only half of *The Producers'* cost, *The Twelve Chairs* paints a grim portrait of life under the communists.

The Twelve Chairs represents Brooks's least overtly Jewish picture and remains his most cynical film. The negative portrait of Father Fyodor, a hypocrite who preaches ethical values he continually transgresses, springs from a Russian-Jewish hatred of such figures from organized Christianity, those religious zealots who instigated pogroms, fed anti-Semitic feelings, and used Jews as political pawns. "The Church must keep up with the times" Fyodor sarcastically argues, deceitfully justifying his secular search as a holy pilgrimage. He remains unredeemed throughout the film, a man willing to shave his beard, remove his cassock, and abandon his religious vows for the sake of personal wealth.

By emphasizing the greed of the former nobleman and the priest, two representatives from the upper ranks of Russian life under the czar, and then augmenting it with the figure of Bender, a man of the new order obsessed with the same overwhelming avarice, Brooks demonstrates that social systems may shift, but essential human selfishness remains constant. This maniacal lust for riches also thematically ties *The Twelve Chairs* to *The Producers*, even though the latter film presents a darker, decidedly more pessimistic, vision of humanity's essentially rapacious nature. The picture's most cynical moment occurs when Bender convinces Vorobyaninov to overcome his repugnance and masquerade as an epileptic begging for charity, an action that humiliates the proud aristocrat and demonstrates how easily the masses can be duped. In a final slap at culture in the service of greed, Bender summons up sympathy and rubles from the curious onlookers by pleading, "give from the bottom of your hearts for a victim of the same disease that struck down our beloved Dostoyevsky." In this new order, the revered names from the past are invoked simply to elaborate upon the con of the present.

"Everybody's the same," Brooks said about the film's theme, "eternal need and eternal greed" (Adler and Feinman 91). Perhaps the only mitigating action in this saga of cupidity lies in Brooks's major deviation (other than eliminating most of the female characters) from his source material. In the novel, Vorobyaninov ultimately cuts Bender's throat to make sure he alone gains complete possession of the last chair and its hidden riches. The film, however, has the jewels found by a man named Kaminsky and used to build the Moscow Railway Workers' Communal House of Recreation, a rather appropriate representation of human social activity so highly placed within this director's American-Jewish value system. Brooks's own role as Tikon, who sounds suspiciously like the 2,000 Year Old Man, hearkens back the old days, the prerevolutionary days of Brooks's ancestors, yet even here the film never sinks into mawkish sentimentality. Vorobyaninov severely mistreated Tikon, although the former servant favors his master's strict discipline over the bland conformity of his new comrades.

Although some critics argue that the maturing relationship between Vorobyaninov and Bender functions as another positive value within the film—indeed, many of Brooks's movies highlight this creative sense of male camaraderie—here such an interpretation strains the edges of credulity. Vorobyaninov's willingness to employ Bender's epilepsy hoax seems more pathetic than progressive, as more the acceptance of corruption than a corrective to it. *The Twelve Chairs* clearly demonstrates how Brooks draws upon his cultural past and love of Russian literature, but he never forgets that such times, for Jews in particular, were both harsh and cruel. As one of the lyrics in "Hope for the Best, Expect the Worst" expresses this notion of our emotional and psychological immaturity, "the world's a stage, we're unrehearsed."

Brooks went from the steppes of Russia to the plains of America's mythical West for his next picture, *Blazing Saddles* (1974), which he wrote with Norman Steinberg, Andrew Bergman (who wrote the original story "Tex-X"), Alan Uger, and Richard Pryor.

For seven months he established and sustained a writing environment resembling the old Caesar days (when the staff often parodied western films), isolating himself and the other writers "in a single room, turning on the tape recorder, and throwing lines at each other" (Adler and Feinman 100). The resulting plot revolves around the quick-witted Bart (Cleavon Little), a black railroad worker turned sheriff sent by Governor William J. LePetomane (Mel Brooks) to rescue Rock Ridge from greedy land-grabbers led by Hedley Lamarr (Harvey Korman) and his right-hand man Taggart (Slim Pickens). The townspeople, however, initially respond to Bart's color not his cleverness and castigate him with racist epithets. Only Jim (Gene Wilder), a drunken bum once known as the fast-drawing Waco Kid, helps Bart, much to the annoyance of the town's assorted Johnsons: Olsen (David Huddeston), Reverend (Liam Dunn), Howard (John Hillerman), Van (George Furth), Gabby (Claude Ennis Starret, Jr.), Harriett (Carol Arthur), and Dr. Sam (Richard Collier).[2] Eventually, Bart wins their respect, along with the loyalty of Lamarr's two deadliest allies, the sexy Lilly—"The Teutonic Titwillow"—Von Shtupp (Madeline Kahn) and the hideous strongman Mongo (Alex Karras).[3] *Blazing Saddles* was a spectacular hit, earning more than $45 million and contending for the crown of "funniest movie ever made."

Because Brooks calls *Blazing Saddles* "a Jewish Western with a black hero," we understand this film as an extended performance in blackface, his pointed attack on racism also functioning as a strike against anti-Semitism. By foregrounding ethnic confrontation, this stinging parody assails the implicit racist ideology of the genre and, by extension, of the mythic tradition of the Old West that informs it. Certainly, Brooks's frontal assault on bigotry provides a refreshing corrective to those patriotic celluloid hymns that either elided ethnic issues altogether, totally demonized Native Americans, or painted frontier life as the cradle of idealized democracy.

The film's first scene announces its alternative, typically Jewish, perspective. A group of white racists demands that black railroad workers perform for them: "When you were slaves, you sang like birds. How about a good old Nigger work song?" An incredulous Bart leads the suave response, as the group's silky harmony gracefully slides through Cole Porter's cosmopolitan lyrics in "I Get a Kick Out of You." Objecting to this sophisticated melody, the cowboys insist on something more stereotypical, "Swing Low, Sweet Chariot" or "De Camptown Races." In fact, they gleefully break into the latter tune, slapping their knees and dancing with clumsy gyrations that amuse the smirking blacks. Sanford Pinsker labels such moments "Jewish Camp . . . which wrenches the expected out of context and makes it fend for itself somewhere else. The zigzagging alterations are symptomatic of deeply divided impulses in American-Jewish life—to swallow the popular culture which surrounds it, to, in a word, assimilate *everything;* at the same time, to remain separate, slightly superior, culturally intact" (249). More important, Brooks immediately places the audience alongside the blacks. They own the gaze, and we quickly assume their perspective even though they clearly represent the outsiders within the traditional conventions of this genre. Such a move establishes the ethnic perspective that allows for a continuous exploration of the racist ideology that accompanied the westward expansion of America.

Sometimes we laugh at such stupidity, but at other times the film strikes a far harsher note, as when Taggart forces Bart and his friend to test for quicksand, reasoning that "horses, not Niggers, are too valuable to waste." But Brooks pushes the condemnation even further by having Taggart save a handcart from sinking while leaving the desperate men to fend for themselves. Then, when the men finally drag themselves to safety, Taggart tells them "the break is over" and laughingly includes the racist admonition, "don't just lay there getting a suntan." Not only are blacks lower on the economic and social scale than animals, but apparently they also rank below the equipment. Equally telling about blacks' status in the West is Taggart's comment when he hears Bart has been named sheriff of Rock Ridge: "Here we take the good time and trouble to slaughter every Indian in the West, for what? Just so they can go and appoint a sheriff that's darker than the Indians." In fact, Lamarr counts on the essential prejudice of Rock Ridge's citizens to further his plans to destroy their town, an ironic twist on how demagogues (even humorous ones) ferment intolerance to accomplish their own ends. Thus Brooks squarely faces the racial implications of the western, the notions that Indians were robbed of their lands, minorities were impressed to build the great transcontinental railroads, and blacks were discriminated against throughout the entire westward migration. Such ideas undercut the official history of the West, that grand and glorious tale of triumph and of manifest destiny. The ideas of thinkers, like Frederick Jackson Turner, that the frontier was the crucible of liberty, the well-spring of democracy, and creator of a composite nationality strike Brooks as laughably naive or even downright dangerous.

Bart eventually triumphs over the forces of social injustice by using his superior wit (he defeats Mongo with a candygram), or by slyly conforming to racist stereotypes to further his own ends (he escapes the welcoming committee's violence by appealing to their bigoted notions about black people). Bart uses the latter approach again to infiltrate Lamarr's gang of history's bigots (Lamarr is an Equal Opportunity Employer) when he lures some unwary Ku Klux Klansmen by purposely distorting his voice and syntax, then exclaims in a high-pitched tone, "where all de white wimmen at?" Apparently, the white community feels far less threatened by a black man who fits neatly within these stereotypes than by one who seeks to move beyond constricting images and clichés. But such tactics, even done smugly and in the cause of survival, take minority group members only so far because they simply reinforce racist imagery and acquiesce to the dominant ideology's hegemony. Brooks's grander solution to racism is for oppressed minorities to band together, to force whites to recognize their power and abilities. Thus, to save their town, the white residents of Rock Ridge must join forces with blacks and Chinese railroad workers, although they initially refuse to unite with the Irish. Such a union mutually striving for a single goal is the best Brooks has to offer in the way of racial harmony, even though the seemingly simplistic solution may appear outmoded in the cynical 1990s.

Earlier, Brooks takes a swipe at one of the western's most pervasive images, the lumbering line of Conestoga wagons slowly winding their way west to settle the land and tame the savage frontier. Here, however, we see Bart's family cut off from the main party, their wagon forced to occupy the same symbolic position as those southern blacks required to ride in the back of the bus. When the inevitable Indian attack on the train does occur, the lone wagon must circle around by itself, a dog chasing its tail. As the frightened family awaits certain death at the hands of the savage heathens, Brooks intrudes on the western's mythology by presenting a Yiddish-speaking chief (Brooks himself). Amazed at finding blacks ("shvartzers"), the chief commands his warriors to let the family go in health: "Loz em gaien. . . . Abee gezint." Other phrases appear elsewhere in the film, including a nervous town resident intoning "Gottenyu" (Oh, God!); Lamarr calling Taggart a "provincial putz" (a fool); Lili (whose last name is Yiddish slang for "to fuck") claiming she is "fablunged" (lost); as well as various assorted "oyes!" and "schmucks." But the use of Yiddish in the wagon train scene takes

on deeper significance. Brooks instinctively understands how tragically appropriate it is that the West's most conspicuous outsider,
the Native American, should speak in the tongue of history's traditional outsider, the Jew, as he lets live America's most abused outsider, the black.

Such a reading treats Brooks's intention sympathetically, yet several elements of the scene shed a somewhat harsher light on the
events that unfold. First, the Yiddish word *shvartzer* has the denota-
tive meaning of *black* (as an adjective) or of *Negro* (as a noun), but its
connotative meaning remains far closer to a derogatory racist epi-
thet, mainly *nigger*. Second, Brooks's frightened black family contains fairly stereotypical figures: the heavy black mammy, the ineffectual father, and the round-eyed young boy. In addition, the
chief's final words, with a Yiddish accent, as the wagon pulls away
to safety—"They're darker than we are [he shivers]"—is reminiscent of Taggart's comments when he learns about Bart's appoint-
ment as sheriff of Rock Ridge. One also wonders about the ap-
propriateness of one minority group member speaking in the
language of another. Does this, in essence, rob Native Americans of
a voice? By simply lumping oppressed people into one group, by
actually denying them their separate voices, their distinct sounds,
Brooks perpetuates the vision of white racism, a worldview that
sees all nonwhite groups as the same. One could make a case, therefore, that Brooks's use of Yiddish here undercuts the plight of the
Native Americans in the West as well as in the cinema, because they
become simply another alien culture overrun by the dominant ideology that spawned westward expansionism. Of course, such a
reading represents the harsher side of this archetypal Brooksian
moment, one that sees the injustice done to the Jews but ignores
those that minority groups do to each other.

While we offer two competing, but not necessarily mutually exclusive, readings of the Yiddish Indian sequence, no such problems
cloud Brooks's vision of organized Christianity. As usual in his
movies, formalized church activities offer only hypocrisy when
dealing with racism. The devout people who piously fill the
wooden pews of the picturesque church on the prairie pray faith-
fully every Sunday but show little tolerance or charity for the West's
outsiders, particularly those so markedly different. Even Rock
Ridge's spiritual leader, Reverend Johnson, enthusiastically participates in the general bigotry and racist name-calling, and also utters
more foul language than any other character in the movie. For

example, during the prayer he offers for the salvation of Rock Ridge, he ponders, "Oh, Lord, do we have the strength to do this mighty task in just one night, or are we just jerking off?"

Reverend Johnson's portrayal resembles Brooks's other images of the church, ranging from the greedy prelate in *The Twelve Chairs* to the sadistic inquisitors in *The History of the World, Part One,* to the silly minister in *Spaceballs.* Brooks finds little comfort in the kind words and gentle messages of official Christianity. As a student of the Holocaust, he fully knows that few Christian leaders did anything to aid those suffering in the concentration camps; as a student of Russian literature, he understands that anti-Semitism remains deeply embedded within Christian dogma. Married to Anne Bancroft, who is not religious yet from a strict Italian-Catholic upbringing, Brooks considers Jews and Italians to be cut from similar emotional and cultural cloth. Yet his love for Bancroft aside, Brooks's comments to *Newsweek* reveal the deep-seated distrust of Christians that formed part of his early years: "When I was brought up, the thought of marrying someone who wore a crucifix would cause people to spit three times to avoid the evil eye" (Cooper 103). Such emotions never fully disappear from Brooks's works, and he never misses an opportunity to spit in the face of organized Christian religion.

It is also necessary to consider the relationship between Bart and the Waco Kid. As played by Gene Wilder, the Kid can be read as Jewish, although this probably has more to do with looks, manner, and associations with Wilder's other films than with any internal evidence Brooks provides. It is clear, however, that the man called "deputy spade" by the good people of Rock Ridge is the only white man in the film without racist tendencies. As a drunk and a nonracist, he stands as much apart from Brooks's vision of western society as does Bart. Their relationship, in fact, is one of the many homoerotic love stories that characterize Brooks's films: Bialystock and Bloom (*The Producers*), Vorobyaninov and Bender (*The Twelve Chairs*), Frankenstein and the Monster (*Young Frankenstein*), Funn and Eggs and Bell (*Silent Movie*), and Lone Starr and Barf (*Spaceballs*). Although all of these films contain female love encounters, they center on the search for masculine companionship, a trait Brooks well recognizes: "The love story between two men . . . seems to be one of my motifs. Maybe my heaviest. I mean I do love the fellowship of men. It's in all my pictures" (Yacowar, *Method* 89). For Bart and Waco, these connections are made linguistically as well as visually. Both characters appear as self-referential creations totally cognizant of their stock roles within the typical western. Each, however, manages to transcend such conventions because his modern sensibility endows him with an aura of smug superiority that sees him as participant but somehow still outside the action. For example, Jim consoles Bart by reminding him that "these are simple folk, the common clay of the New West. You know—morons." Such an understanding remains evident from their first meeting in the jailhouse ("are we black?") until they ride off together, in a chauffeured limousine that reeks of star status, into the sunset so prominent in westerns. On an extra-diegetic note, Wilder's interplay with Cleavon Little foreshadows his more enduring cinematic interaction with another black performer, Richard Pryor, one of the movie's co-writers and Brooks's first choice to play Bart.

The self-referential nature of *Blazing Saddles* finally takes over the film's narrative in the final section, as the inhabitants of the western crash, quite literally, into a musical being shot on the adjoining set. Brooks forces confrontation of the facade that passes for fact in cinema, as he calls attention to the audience's gullible willingness to accept what it sees on the screen or the television set as truth rather than fabrication. In the final shoot-out, punch-out, and breath-out between Lamarr's gang and the good guys, the citizens of Rock Ridge and their minority allies build perfect plywood duplicates of their town and themselves—flat images that substitute for reality. During the fight, Brooks's camera pans upward to encompass the landscape of Warner Brothers studio in Burbank hidden behind the movie set, now clearly delineated. But the demystification goes further. With a crash, the furious battle on the dusty streets of Rock Ridge smashes into the adjoining set, a sophisticated musical directed by Buddy Bizarre (Dom DeLuise). In a truly Godardian manner, this scrambling of iconography destroys any remaining vestige of willing disbelief, forcing us to acknowledge how easily we can be, and usually are, manipulated by those seeking to present a particular vision of American history and culture in the cinema. As Maurice Yacowar observes, "Brooks's point is the essentially arbitrary choice of language for a world view. The musical, the western, any Hollywood type, provides only one of several alternative visions and values systems; none monopolizes truth or history" (*Method* 114). In this case, the vision Brooks attacks is the racist ideology propagated by white, Christian men who ignored the accomplishments of the minorities who helped settle the West.

Not content with this melange of competing conventions,

Brooks now plays with cinematic persona, as Korman/Lamarr escapes, at least momentarily, to the darkened safety of Mann's Chinese Theater, where he watches the activity in *Blazing Saddles*. Yet this is a western and the villain must die, so Bart pursues him off the screen, through the musical set, to the audience, and out into the mean streets of Hollywood. There, he shoots him (in the groin, of course) and watches as the evil state procurer dies, his face falling on the immortalized-in-concrete feet of Douglas Fairbanks. Jealous to the end, Lamarr's last words combine both his jealousy and knowledge of film history: "How could he do such fantastic stunts with such little feet?"

This colliding of conventions is more than simply mindless mayhem. As Brooks described his "surrealistic epic" to Kenneth Tynan: "The official movie portrait of the West was simply a lie. What I did when the gunfight spilled over onto the Busby Berkeley set with the fifty dancers was what Picasso did when he painted two eyes on the same side of the head" (120). Such an essentially Cubist perspective makes perfect sense for an American Jew struggling to understand the conflicting value systems that surround him and fighting to comprehend what ties him to (and separates him from) the rest of American society. From Brooks's perspective, the "rugged individualists" who settled America brought with them the bitter seeds of prejudice so prevalent in European cultures.

Although some might gag at the audacious Brooks brashly equating himself to the most famous painter of the twentieth century, or even to linking him with Godard, the point remains that such a consciousness about his work does help to take him beyond the realm of instinctual buffoon. Brooks's bold, scatological, slapstick humor masks serious observations about our national heritage forged on the frontier between savagery and civilization, much as his comedy in *The Producers* hides some trenchant comments about America's preoccupation with the Third Reich. His portrait of the bigoted western townspeople of Rock Ridge attacks the "frontier ethics" that fashioned the traditional American value system, showing them tainted with prejudice, hypocrisy, and intolerance. In fact, the entire film reverberates with a Jewish sense of outrage and alienation that forces Brooks to focus on the problems faced by outsiders in the Old West, those cut off from the center of society by their race, color, or religion. Brooks's frontier of bigots and racists, his vision of America the prejudiced, comically inverts the paean to liberty propagated by several generations of Hollywood directors, most notably John Ford. Yet his condemnation contains a sense of sadness, of longing, of wishing that the myth was indeed true. In *Blazing Saddles,* Brooks's emotions yearn to embrace the traditional elements of the western myth, but his outsider's intellect recognizes the hollowness at its center.

From the plains of America's mythic west, Brooks next journeyed to a fog-enshrouded castle for *Young Frankenstein* (1974), his parody of horror films. The movie is based on Mary Shelley's famous tale of scientific hubris and parental responsibility, which the director James Whale turned into a classic 1932 movie that Brooks remembers as one of his childhood favorites. Brooks even told Kenneth Tynan how he cracked up his eight-year-old friends by singing "Puttin' on the Ritz" in Boris Karloff's voice (68). Shooting the movie in black and white, as well as resurrecting the original laboratory set from Whales's groundbreaking feature, Brooks incorporates many of the by-now classic characters from horror fiction and B-movies: the brilliant young scientist (Dr. Frankenstein's grandson Frederick, Gene Wilder), the huge monster (Peter Boyle), the lovely fiancee (Elizabeth, Madeline Kahn), the wooden-armed police inspector (Inspector Kemp, Kenneth Mars), the hunchbacked laboratory assistant (Igor, Marty Feldman), the pretty ingenue (Inga, Terri Garr), and the faithful housekeeper (Frau Blucher, Cloris Leachman).[4] Brooks also incorporates early film transitional devices, such as vertical and horizontal wipes and iris in and out.

Yet for all its old-fashioned mise-en-scène, *Young Frankenstein*'s characters have a modern consciousness of their roles within the Frankenstein legend, even mugging to the camera with sly smiles of understanding. By working in a genre that continually recycles its stock characters and clichés, Brooks has ample room for parody and caricature. Yet what becomes critical is how his Jewish sensibilities twist the usual conventions of the horror film, often inverting its basic ideological concerns from a preoccupation with the cruelness of the monster to an exploration of the callousness of society.

The dynamic elements inherent within the horror film, best explained in Robin Wood's essays on the subject, strike a particularly resonant note in Brooks's psyche. Wood expands on the common analogy between dreams and films by arguing that movies are both "the personal dreams of their makers and the collective dreams of their audiences—a fusion made possible by the shared structures of a common ideology" ("Return" 25). Given this supposition, he offers a basic formula for the horror film: "normality is threatened by

the monster." Such a simple and general formula yields three vari-
ables: normality, the monster, and the relationship between the
two. The third variable, says Wood, constitutes the essential subject
of the horror film. Wood's ideas shed some interesting light on
Young Frankenstein. What happens, for example, if the filmmaker
finds himself or herself in conflict with the dominant ideology and,
like Brooks, identifies with the outsiders in history rather than the
ruling classes? For a director who brings a marginalized mentality
to all his films, the question of why society ostracizes the monster
becomes much more important than what the monster does to
alienate society. Why the monster attacks normality receives more
attention than how normality repels the monster. Brooks's comments regarding *Young Frankenstein,* therefore, are particularly revealing: "It deals with the ignorant vs. the intelligent. The mob vs.
the intelligent people. . . . The story of Dr. Frankenstein addresses
itself to the fear quotient. The monster is just symbolic of his mind,
and the mob hates his mind, they hate his imagination" (Atlas 57).
On the one hand, these sentiments sound suspiciously like a director whose own creations have not been properly appreciated; more
important, they remind us of Brooks's earlier comments about
never being good enough or being allowed to join mainstream culture because of being Jewish.

These feelings provide Brooks with a particularly sensitive perspective from which to view horror films: an outsider who identifies
more with the creator and his monster than with symbolic representatives of traditional social order. Brooks clearly identifies with
this homely monster, a creature so driven to fit in, to belong, that he
dons white tie and tails to join his maker in a duet of "Puttin' on the
Ritz" before the Bucharest Academy of Science. Avidly reading the
Wall Street Journal at the movie's conclusion, the monster eventually
gains the acceptance he so ardently craves, but middle-class society
almost destroys his fragile spirit.

While the monster seeks a connection with his creator, his sole
"relative," the young doctor struggles to escape from his heritage.
Calling himself "Fron-ken-shteen," rather than by the more infamous Frankenstein, Frederick heatedly denies any affinity, either
emotionally ("he was a kook") or intellectually ("his work was doo
doo"), with his notorious grandfather. He even dreams about not
being a Frankenstein. Such name-changing, of course, bears directly upon the substitution of *Brooks* for *Kaminsky,* an erasure of
cultural identification Brooks always regretted: "I thought if I ever
did anything important I'd change it back to Kaminsky" (Young

35). Yet Brooks never denies his Jewish heritage; in fact, he obsessively and explicitly refers to it in all his films and interviews. By the film's ending, however, Frederick, like Brooks, reconciles himself to his lineage and proudly proclaims the bond between himself and his progenitor.

The scene that most clearly displays Brooks's Jewish perspective on the Frankenstein legend occurs when the doctor soothes his distraught creation. In the original novel, a virtual meditation on parental (and, by extension, scientific) responsibility, Mary Shelley condemns Dr. Frankenstein for so callously abandoning his creation. As soon as Shelley's Dr. Frankenstein beholds his creature's "dull, yellow eye" open, he is "unable to endure the aspect of his being," and "breathless horror and disgust" fill his heart (57). At this early stage, the creature is a rather friendly, love-starved being called to life by a creator who abandons him in abject horror, a rejection based solely on an outward appearance fashioned by the very man who spurns him.

The failure to love, therefore, is not the creature's; it is the creator's. Indeed, the monster later rises to a level of moral understanding unsurpassed by any other figure in the novel, lecturing his maker on the responsibilities of creation: "How dare you sport thus with life? Do your duty towards me, and I will do mine toward you and the rest of mankind" (Shelley 99). In his quest to duplicate "the first principle of life . . . the cause of generation," Victor Frankenstein mistakenly substitutes cold, abstract logic for the warmth of human friendship and parental love. He deserves punishment for ignoring the duties owed to family members and loved ones, not for mocking God or going beyond the bounds of nature in his scientific mission to create life.

Unlike his fictional counterpart and cinematic precursors, Brooks's Dr. Frankenstein realizes that "love is the only thing that can save this poor creature" and resolves to risk his life to "convince him that he is loved." Abandoning the detached scientific mode, Frederick becomes, in effect, a Jewish mother, providing the almost suffocating acceptance so necessary to soothe the creature's battered psyche: "Look at that boyish face. Look at that sweet smile. Do you want to talk about physical strength? Do you want to talk about sheer muscle? Do you want to talk about the Olympian ideal? You are a God! You are not evil. You are good."

When these sentiments motivate the powerful creature to moan aloud and shed tears, Dr. Frankenstein literally evokes maternal pride and affection: "This is a nice boy. This is a good boy. [Frankenstein caresses the monster and rocks him tenderly back and forth.] This is a mother's angel. And I want the world to know, once and for all and without any shame, that we love this boy. [The monster sobs as Dr. Frankenstein cradles him in his arms and kisses him gently on the head.]"

It seems clearly appropriate that by accepting his fearful progeny, Dr. Frankenstein also acknowledges his past; immediately following the scene of maternal pride and ambition, he pronounces his name in the proper manner, accepting his past as part of his present. Finally, he willingly sacrifices a segment of himself for the son, as Brooks specifically comments: "the creator loves his creature so much that he risks his sanity and his life to help his brain child survive. In our picture, Dr. Frankenstein starts out like Yahweh and winds up like Christ" (Yacowar, *Method* 127). In essence, Brooks recreates his own fondest images of childhood, transforming Dr. Frankenstein from a heartless scientist who brings life into the world only to abandon it into a preening Jewish parent who delights in demonstrating his "offspring's" talent and intelligence.

In addition to this image of Jewish family life, Brooks includes other familiar motifs from American-Jewish culture. For example, Kahn is incarnated as a finicky, self-obsessed Jewish-American Princess whose hints of sex represent nothing but perpetual foreplay, much to Dr. Frankenstein's anguish. Early in the film, for example, she refuses to kiss Frederick good-bye because she fears he will smear her lipstick, mess up her hair and nails, or wrinkle her new taffeta dress. Later, in the castle, she sends him frustrated from her room, leaving him to contemplate her frigidity. Similarly, Garr's blonde Scandinavian appears as another incarnation of Brooks's obsession with buxom bimbos, a variation of the sexually alluring shiksa so much a part of American-Jewish films and books.

Young Frankenstein incorporates several of the other motifs present in the works of Allen, Mazursky, and Lumet. For example, show business appears, rather incongruously, in several moments, including when the doctor performs in front of his class (he uses the stock phrases of a second-rate magician) and the actual performance of "Puttin' on the Ritz." Similarly, the monster's desire to belong is another example of assimilation-alienation, and society's rejection of him results in his loneliness and exile. In addition, one might call it something of a Jewish fantasy, even wish fulfillment, to exchange some mental power for some sexual enhancement, precisely what happens to Dr. Frankenstein during his mutually beneficial trade with the monster: brains for length. As Brooks added farts to the western, so he enlarges the horror film by including penises.

If *Young Frankenstein* looks nostalgically backward to the black-and-white days of Hollywood in the 1930s, Brooks's next film, *Silent Movie* (1976), reverses the clock even more by recreating the free-wheeling days before the coming of sound. Yet its economic perspective remains firmly set in the Hollywood of the 1970s, a community where hostile takeovers by large conglomerates threatened the traditional studio hierarchy. The plot revolves around the efforts of a gigantic corporation, Engulf and Devour (read Gulf and Western), to swallow the bankrupt Big Pictures Studio and replace its "Current Studio Chief" (Sid Caesar) with grubby New York businessmen who demonstrate no real feelings for making movies. Director Mel Funn (Mel Brooks) and his partners Marty Eggs (Marty Feldman) and Dom Bell (Dom DeLuise) round up Hollywood's biggest stars, including Burt Reynolds, Liza Minnelli, Marcel Marceau (who utters the film's only dialogue), Paul Newman, Anne Bancroft, and James Caan, to make a silent movie comedy and save the studio. Brooks even spells out their progress in a series of *Daily Variety* headlines reminiscent of an earlier time. Along the way, Funn falls for Vilma Kaplan (Bernadette Peters), a femme fatale hired by the rapacious CEO of the company (Harold Gould) to drive Funn, a reformed alcoholic, back to the bottle. At first it works, but as in all good slapstick comedies, she realizes she loves Funn and joins his campaign to rescue Big Pictures Studio. Clearly a reflexive film that delights in its overtly self-referential nature, *Silent Movie* offers the perverse irony of seeing Hollywood's most relentless talker purposely gagging himself.

Silent Movie provides a series of interesting examples of Brooks's most important dictums regarding comedy: "Never, never try to be funny! The actors must be serious. Only the situation must be absurd. Funny is in the writing, not in the performing" (Yacowar, *Method* vii). Apparently, Brooks understood this lesson early in his life, even before his career as a professional comic. When asked in a 1966 *Playboy* interview what was the first funny thing he ever said, Brooks instantly replied, "Lieutenant Faversham's attentions to my wife were of such a nature I was forced to deal him a lesson in manners." Not too funny, certainly, until he went on to explain that he uttered this line to "an elderly Jewish woman carrying an oil-cloth shopping bag on the Brighton Beach Express" (Siegel 266). Taking this early example at face value, one immediately grasps how such an unfunny line, probably taken from some overblown melodrama or historical epic, becomes funny only in conjunction, or perhaps even more accurately in juxtaposition, with the particular situation in which Brooks said it.

Such an understanding of the relationships of action, dialogue, and setting strikes at the heart of this comic method. Brooks instinctively grasps how two serious elements intermingle to form comedy, an epiphany that underpins all his movies, even this one bereft of spoken dialogue. It also accounts for the moments that move beyond the comedy, the junctures when tender emotions sliver through the comic facade and surprise us with their power. Think of Vorobyaninov writhing in mock spasms at the conclusion of *The Twelve Chairs,* or when Bart and the Waco Kid ride off at the end of *Blazing Saddles,* or the scene between Frederick and the monster in *Young Frankenstein.* Such moments transcend slapstick and scatology, broad farce and clever parody. Indeed, they rival the serious scenes in the movies that Brooks parodies, providing ample evidence of his ability to wring emotions that are not humorous from a scene.

Silent Movie foregrounds show business, a constant Brooks motif, as the director pays tribute to the tradition of silent slapstick comedy. Yet, as almost always happens in his pictures, the Brooks persona finds it impossible to fulfill the roles handled with such seeming ease by gentile leading men during Hollywood's earlier eras. The strategy of never measuring up, of being present at the right time with the right people but inevitably doing the wrong thing, permeates Brooks's films. Take, for example, his pseudo-idyllic affair with Vilma Kaplan, whose first and last names seem at odds with each other. Their romantic scenes always turn out poorly, as idealization gives way to prosaic reality. Even his fantasies betray him. A romp through lush natural surroundings that begins with the couple holding hands and dancing in circles inexplicably turns into a hurdle race, complete with Mel and Vilma stripping down to their underwear. When they ride on a fanciful merry-go-round, her wooden horse doesn't merely slide gracefully up and down; its tail lifts and out drops chunk after chunk of horse excrement. For the Brooks persona, the masculine images of the past only highlight his own limitations. No matter the context, he can never measure up to the cinematic idealizations that haunt his imagination, figures of light and shadow internalized by American society.

Like *Silent Movie,* Brooks's next film, *High Anxiety* (1977), places Brooks's character into a clearly recognizable situation. He becomes an innocent Alfred Hitchcock hero trapped in a hostile environment that threatens to overwhelm him. Brooks is Richard H.

(Harpo) Thorndyke from Harvard University, a psychiatrist who comes west to take over the directorship of the Institute for the Very, Very Nervous. But the Nobel-winning doctor, who wears his Phi Beta Kappa key prominently displayed on a gold chain, has an Achilles' heel. Like another famous Hollywood hero, he suffers from vertigo, or high anxiety. Although a plot revolving around a beautiful woman's (Madeline Kahn) kidnapped father, the dirty dealings of two institute employees (Harvey Korman and Cloris Leachman), the reunion with a beloved teacher (Howie Morris), and a plan to frame Thorndyke for murder provides sufficient opportunity for slapstick and scatology, Brooks concentrates more energy on direct parodies of famous Hitchcock moments. He includes the shower scene from *Psycho* (1960), the bird attack from *The Birds* (1963), the tower climbing from *Vertigo* (1958), the setting of *Spellbound* (1946), the picture taking from *Rear Window* (1954), and many other allusions. Such parodies also take the form of visual homages, although, as one might expect with Brooks, each contains a distinctively humorous moment of recognition. For example, a long tracking shot from the garden to the dining room ends abruptly when the camera crashes into the glass door and shatters a window pane. Later, the equally inept camera literally hits a brick wall as a technician mutters, "maybe no one will notice." Such reflexive moments draw attention to the artifice of filmmaking, as well as the often ignored artificiality of the entire production.

As *Silent Movie* focuses on show business, so *High Anxiety* emphasizes another American-Jewish concern, psychoanalysis. When he was between twenty-three and twenty-nine, Brooks participated in two to four sessions of psychoanalysis each week in a period characterized by persistent insomnia, severe dizzy spells, prolonged vomiting between parked cars, and a generally worsening psychological condition:

> It was a choice of that or suicide. I had low blood sugar, a chemical imbalance, plus the normal nervous breakdown everyone goes through from adolescence to adulthood. It comes with the suspicion that only an incredible amount of failure is there to greet us. . . . In addition to relieving the early duress, analysis helped me later in my life with my writing, because I'm less inhibited and more in touch with unconscious realities. . . . If it did nothing but crush my societally taught sense of shame that was enough, that was plenty to free me. (Fleischman 10)

Even admitting his debt to therapy, Brooks revels in making fun of the process. For example, he happily recounts how a psychologist once told him that he was one of the healthiest persons he had ever met. One night Brooks found himself standing next to the man in a public bathroom and urinated on his shoe. The psychologist, as Brooks tells it, immediately retracted his professional evaluation (Young 35). Before *High Anxiety,* Brooks assumed the role of learned but absurd psychiatrists—Dr. Hall-Danish and Dr. Akiba ben Hollywood—as early as the recordings with Reiner. He was also a psychoanalyst from the Vienna School of Good Luck and, upon learning from Freud himself about the Oedipus complex, exclaimed "with a Greek, who knows? But with a Jew you don't do a thing like that even to your own wife, let alone your mother" (Yacowar, *Method* 46). In *High Anxiety,* Brooks comments several times on the expense of psychiatry; for example, the old professor reminds Thorndyke of the most important thing to remember: "never take a personal check." Thus Brooks's personal debt to psychotherapy does little to deflect his humor from this eternally ripe sacred cow.

In many ways, Hitchcock is the archetypal WASP director, whose central male characters (played by Robert Donat, Rod Taylor, James Stewart, Paul Newman, and Cary Grant) and female characters (Doris Day, Tippi Hedren, Janet Leigh, Grace Kelly, and Kim Novak) rarely betray a hint of ethnicity. It is therefore not surprising that Brooks, who clearly admires the "master of suspense," cannot help but inject his particular brand of Jewish humor into this ethnically sterile environment. Sometimes it is as simple as including realistic, often scatological, details into a scene devoid of such realism, as when the bird droppings pelt Thorndyke:

> The world—or at least the *birds* of the world—have a habit of doing exactly that. And if you are Mel Brooks, they will do it on your head. But the world is not an inherently evil place, nor should one reject it out of hand in favor of more spiritual, presumably less scatological realms. The vision that can see both the bird droppings and the world's beauty strikes me as very Jewish indeed. After all, birds have tormented Jewish heads since the days of Tobit. Mel Brooks has simply found a new wrinkle for a very old, very Jewish story from the *Apocrypha.* In both cases the human condition is not an Either/Or proposition; rather, it is likely to be both/and. Somehow Jews learn to make an uneasy accommodation to that reality. (Pinsker 254)

A similar accommodation occurs after Thorndyke's lecture on sexuality, when the following question-and-answer session disintegrates into infantile language after a father arrives with two young daughters. Thus, penis envy becomes pee-pee, excrement becomes cockie doody, vagina becomes woo woo, and breasts become balloons as an increasingly uncomfortable Thorndyke struggles to enlighten his colleagues without offending the children. Such a moment not only comments on linguistic pretentiousness, but also on the childlike immaturity that rests just beneath the surface of most intellectual jargon.

The most overtly Jewish scene in *High Anxiety* occurs at the San Francisco Airport, when Brooks and Kahn don ill-fitting clothes, adopt broad Yiddish accents, and masquerade as an old, obnoxious Jewish couple from New York City in order to sneak past a policeman who thinks that the psychiatrist is a calculating murderer. "Remember," Thorndyke tells the nervous Brisbane, "if you're loud and annoying, psychologically people don't notice you." Brooks is keenly aware that much of his humor, not to mention his entire career, hinges upon precisely these qualities because he rarely shies away from being, to some degree or another, both loud and annoying. Yet, the last thing Mel Brooks desires is to remain unnoticed.

Although the ruse stands on shaky psychological footing, Brooks and Kahn fight loudly over trivial questions, arguing why or why not they should take celery back home, debating the relative merits of airline bloody marys, disagreeing over whether Murray Weintraub is alive or dead, and demonstrating dissimilar versions of Morris Turtletaub's limp. The gambit is most successful when Thorndyke's gun sets off a beeping security machine, making him the focus of precisely those guards he sought most to avoid. Yet all is not lost. Spinning into a frenzy of words and actions, at one point even requesting passage back to Russia because he has become "the mad beeper," Thorndyke's K-Mart version of the 2,000 Year Old Man so befuddles the hapless guards that they help the raving psychiatrist onto the plane and do not search him.

Dramatic and psychological motivations aside, this scene smacks of self-hatred rather than loving recreation, as Brooks employs the broadest possible markers of cultural difference to delineate his Old World Jewish figures. Maurice Yacowar typifies the sympathetic commentators who rationalize the scene, claiming that it allows "Brooks to affirm his own ethnic roots, in counterpoise to his character's suave Sinatra and slick psychiatrist image" (163). Such a reading, although tempting in light of Brooks's other inclusions of Jewish culture within previous movies, still seems directly at odds with the scene's tone. To grant him the benefit of the doubt, Brooks probably sees these characters as comic rather than offensive, as garnering a quick laugh instead of creating audience embarrassment or even antagonism. But for a filmmaker with such a highly attuned Jewish sensibility, such scenes prove particularly disappointing because they do little but perpetuate negative stereotypes about Jews.

Unlike his journey into the modern Hitchcockian world of *High Anxiety,* Brooks returned to the historical past to confront his emotional obsession with the Nazis in *To Be or Not to Be* (1983). Although Brooks never ignores an opportunity to kick the Third Reich in its collective balls, this is the only film in which he specifically uses a historic timeframe: occupied Poland (the Old Country motif again) during World War II (1939). Of course, Brooks has the advantage of twenty-twenty hindsight; he knows that the Nazis were eventually defeated. Yet such knowledge never fully assuages his hunger to pound them one more time, express his pain over the loss of Jewish lives, declare his anger that few Christians aided the Jews, and voice his fear that the Nazi mentality is alive, well, and resting comfortably in America. The film is also the directorial debut of Brooks's choreographer Alan Johnson, who was responsible for the dance numbers in the *The Producers* and *History of the World, Part One.* It may seem strange, therefore, to call the movie a Mel Brooks film; he appears in the film but receives no script writing credit and lists himself as producer but not director. Yet we think it fair to include this film within Brooks's oeuvre because he produced it for his own company, Brooksfilms; it pairs (for the first time) him with his wife, Anne Bancroft; it contains many motifs and themes found in his other projects; and he had heavy input into the script and shooting. The film also functions as one of the direct links between contemporary Jewish directors and those of the past; it is a remake of Ernst Lubitsch's justly famous 1942 film.

Like its predecessor, the modern *To Be or Not to Be* follows the fortunes of a Polish acting troupe involved in an outrageous scheme to save the Polish underground during World War II. Frederick Bronski (Brooks), head of a popular theatrical company, is a hammy thespian who aspires to Shakespearean majesty, while his wife, Anna (Anne Bancroft), tires of his posturing and engages in secret rendezvous with a handsome young Polish pilot, Lieutenant Andrei Sobinski (Tim Matheson). Unfortunately, the Germans interrupt this bedroom farce by invading Poland. Escaping to England, Sobinski discovers that the kindly Professor Siletski (Jose Ferrer), an expatriate returning soon to Warsaw, is really a Nazi infiltrator intent on destroying the local underground. Meanwhile, the Bronskis struggle to salvage their careers and save their homosexual hairdresser Sasha (James Haake) and their Jewish actors and staff, Lupinski (Lewis J. Stadlen) and Mrs. Gruba (Estelle Reiner), from being deported and killed. The two plots finally merge as Sobinski rushes home to stop the duplicitous Siletski and continue his affair with Anna. Using a series of ruses based on theatrical disguises, including a segment where Bronski must impersonate Hitler, the actors outwit the strident Captain Schultz (Christopher Lloyd) and the lumpish Colonel "Concentration Camp" Erhardt (Charles Durning), eventually flying to freedom beyond the reach of the Germans.

As even this cursory plot summary demonstrates, *To Be or Not to Be* is as much about show business as *Blazing Saddles* is about moviemaking, again demonstrating that art is a necessary part of life and life often an intricate creation of art. Such an intimate intertwining blurs the distinctions between fact and fantasy, a motif that appears consistently in most Brooks movies. Sometimes, as in the case of the western myths exploded in *Blazing Saddles,* romanticized visions of how things "should have been" coat our consciences by ignoring harsh realities that demand more attention. Other times, as in *The Producers* or *Silent Movie,* show business fantasies inject a significance into life, providing the impetus to range beyond the mundane demands and petty limitations of daily existence. In *To Be or Not to Be,* show business has a far more practical purpose. It is the sensitive indicator of a society's tolerance for diverse, or even obnoxious, ideas. For example, when the fearful Polish censors close down Bronski's satiric review "Naughty Nazis," the persecution of people who disagree with prevailing opinions inevitably follows the censorship of different ideas. Brooks, like Lubitsch before him, understands that art is never neutral; even seemingly harmless comedies can strike fear into powerful dictators, for they show the emperor without his clothes. What one laughs at, one can fight against and easily imagine defeating. Brooks, therefore, applauds Lubitsch's belief that art can function as an effective weapon against tyranny, whether by employing direct dramatic assaults or covert comic strategies.

In Lubitsch's *To Be or Not to Be,* Greenberg's recitation of Shylock's famous speech from *The Merchant of Venice* constitutes a submerged threat on behalf of his people. In the later film, however, the Jewish elements become far more overt, an expected change because in 1942 Lubitsch did not know the magnitude of Hitler's slaughter of European Jewry. Lupinski never downplays his Jewishness. After another actor crosses himself, Lupinski makes the sign of a six-pointed star; later, he wears the all-too-familiar yellow Star of David on his arm. Even more important, when Lupinski acts out the same passage from Shakespeare's play, he reinserts the words "hath not a Jew," so obviously absent from Greenberg's more universalized plea for tolerance and understanding.

A second subplot that involves Jews concerns the costumer, Mrs. Gruba, and her ever-increasing band of fleeing relatives. Bronski eventually allows the fugitives to hide in the theater's basement and then masterminds their escape to England disguised as clowns. (Because Bronski never hides in the cellar, we assume his character is not Jewish, a rather strange irony for a performer-director who almost always plays his roles with a distinctly Jewish intonation.) The segment provides another complex visual representation of the lengths to which minorities go to camouflage themselves and adopt benign images that make them appear safe to the ruling classes. Much as Sheriff Bart uses stereotypical black dialect to defeat his enemies, these Jews paint their faces into frozen smiles to slip past those who would torment and ultimately murder them. The fact that they escape directly through the theater adds additional significance to Brooks's use of show business as a method to help defeat tyranny.

In addition to specifying the story's Jewish elements, the remake incorporates another group of victims totally ignored in the original: gays. In previous films, Brooks bashes gays with unashamed glee, from the swishy caricatures of Roger DeBris (Christopher Hewett) and Carmen Giya (Andreas Voutsinas) in *The Producers,* to the mocking of Mongo and the girlish dancers in *Blazing Saddles,* to the Hermit-Monster scene in *Young Frankenstein,* to such other asides as the James Caan segment in *Silent Movie,* Brooks inevitably goes for the easy joke on the subject.

In *To Be or Not to Be,* depending on one's perception, he either makes amends for earlier, nasty portraits or simply continues his litany of gratuitous assaults upon aging queens. It seems clear, however, that Sasha is intended to be sympathetic; the film admires his wit and invites us to share his discomfort when he moans about the "pink triangles clashing with everything," although coordinating colors will soon be the least of his worries. Because Brooks values show business so highly, it is soaring praise when Bronski exclaims: "Without Jews, fags and gypsies, there is no theater." Yet for all of this well-meaning sentiment, Sasha never moves far beyond stereotypical images. Perhaps his funniest moment is eavesdropping as Sobinski tells Anna about his love of flying, using images that get increasingly more sexual and excite Sasha as much as they do Anna. Such scenes provide few correctives to previous Brooks pictures that simply recycle clichés and do little to humanize these figures.

Several other elements operate on a psychological level in *To Be or Not to Be*. Brooks's fixation with the Third Reich and the Holocaust has been discussed previously. Yet it is puzzling why, in his most direct treatment of the issue, he takes the role of a Polish Catholic actor who pretends to be Hitler. (Jack Benny, in the original, never masquerades as the Fuehrer.) Ironically, Charles Durning plays Colonel Erhardt with the high-intensity lunacy audiences expect from Mel Brooks and—as Brooks often does in relatively small roles—steals the picture. Why this strange inversion? Perhaps Brooks found it too difficult, or even too painful, to play the part of the Jewish victims or an SS colonel. Perhaps the parts were merely too small, although he took lesser roles in earlier pictures. More likely, Brooks was stretching his range, seeing if he could discipline himself and actually play a semidramatic lead. To this end, other psychological questions arise. How much of Mel Brooks identifies with Bronski's desire to shed his comic persona and play Hamlet? What part of Mel Brooks quivers when he adopts the part of a second-rate performer who fears his beautiful wife (played by his real-life wife) will engage in affairs with younger, handsomer men? Has Melvin Kaminsky ever worried that the princess will wake up to find herself married to the toad? Whatever the answers to such speculations, *To Be or Not to Be* is Brooks's clearest expression of his continual battle with the forces unleashed by the Third Reich.

At the end of *History of the World, Part One* (1981), Brooks included "Jews in Space," a trailer for a segment of *History of the World, Part Two*, along with "Hitler on Ice." Perhaps he had *Spaceballs* (1987) in mind then, for the picture takes him light years away from the settings of his previous films. Yet one can easily see the recurrent Brooks motifs warp speeding their way to outer space. Here the evil leaders of planet Spaceball, having foolishly squandered their precious atmosphere, have devised a secret plan to take every breath of air away from their peaceful neighbor, the planet Druidia. President Skroob (Brooks), the unscrupulous planet Spaceball ruler, orders the flagship of his starfleet, under the command of Lord Dark Helmet (Rick Moranis) and his assistant, Colonel "Chicken" Sandurz (George Wyner), to abduct her royally spoiled highness Princess Vespa (Daphne Zuniga) from her loving father, King Roland (Dick Van Patten). He plans to blackmail Roland into trading Druidia's air supply for the life of his only daughter. But along comes space cowboy-for-hire Lone Starr (Bill Pullman) and his trusty copilot Barf the Mawg (John Candy), who rescue the ungrateful Vespa and her plucky robot maid Dot Matrix (whose voice is that of Joan Rivers and movements are Lorene Yarnell's) to pay back his debt to the galactic godfather, Pizza the Hut. Finally learning to control the power of the "Schwartz" from the wizened wise man Yogurt (Brooks), Lone Starr comes to understand himself and recognize his destiny with Vespa. Of course, all turns out for the best as evil planet Spaceball is defeated, and Lone Starr discovers he is really a prince and marries the now-repentant Vespa.

Again, Brooks peppers the script with overtly Jewish elements and familiar motifs. Because this is a Mel Brooks movie, for example, Nazis hide just around the next asteroid. The soldiers from planet Spaceball dress like Third Reich refugees, with Colonel Sandurz clearly resembling a storm trooper. The Spaceballers also employ German phrases, answering "Jawohl" and addressing their leader as "Herr Helmet." Brooks's fascination with reflexive sequences is also evident as Dark Helmet and Colonel Sandurz pick up a videocopy of *Spaceballs,* put it on the monitor, and use it to discover where Lone Starr and company are hiding. With a postmodern wink at intertextuality, their video library contains Brooks's previous features. In particular, however, Yogurt sounds strikingly like the 2,000 Year Old Man. Brooks calls his creation a "Yiddish Delphic Oracle" and, indeed, the outer-world Buddha employs a Yiddish phrase by calling Lone Starr's ring "bubkes" (something worthless, a trinket). The pint-sized wizard lives in a medieval chamber that resembles the Temple of Doom and, as Dot Matrix exclaims, "it sure ain't Temple Beth Israel." (During the film's production, Brooks developed a painful allergy to Yogurt's golden makeup, which he described as "a classic example of Jewish gilt.") Given this lineage, it comes as no surprise that Yogurt's power derives from "the Schwartz," a Jewish version of George Lucas's "the Force." He also plays on the stereotype of the Jewish businessman-cum-huckster; Yogurt owns the merchandising rights to all *Spaceballs'* product lines, from tee shirts to toilet paper.

Princess Vespa, like Yogurt, also displays attributes commonly associated with a Jewish stereotype, particularly the sexist incarnation known as the Jewish American Princess (JAP). The first clue appears when she is about to marry the perpetually sleepy Prince

Valium (Jm J. Bullock) in the First Intergalactic Temple (Reformed), an obvious reference to the liberal Jewish synagogues of modern America. Vespa, who drives a white Mercedes, has been so grossly pampered by her overly indulgent father that she demands he risk the entire planet and its inhabitants to save her. Later, she tempestuously refuses to abandon her doomed ship without salvaging her matched luggage and selfishly claims that she cannot live without her industrial-strength hair dryer. She even shoots a guard for mussing her perfect hairstyle. When the intrepid band of heroes wanders hopelessly across the barren desert, most hunger for a drop of water; Vespa, the "Druish Princess," calls for room service. The evil Dark Helmet traps the helpless Vespa, torturing her not with physical punishment or psychological terror. Instead, Helmet calls in Dr. Philip Schlotkin (Sandy Helberg), a prominent plastic surgeon who threatens to replace her beautiful, straight nose with her old, ugly, bumpy beak. When even this cruel tactic fails, Helmet tells the crestfallen physician to get back to the golf course and work on his "putz." Schlotkin agrees but vows, "I'll still have to charge you for this."

For all his subsequent success, Brooks's first feature, *The Producers* (1967), remains his most overtly Jewish picture, although critics attacked his outrageous stereotypes of Jewish characters. So, for example, Max Bialystock (Zero Mostel), a fat, vulgar, boisterous conniver, anxiously seduces rich old ladies to obtain funds for his rotten plays. His name reverberates with Jewish references: a "bialy" is a type of "Jewish" roll, and Bialystock (Poland, the Old Country) was the site of a major ghetto uprising against the Germans. His reluctant partner, the timorous accountant Leo Bloom (Gene Wilder), experiences overwhelming fits of nervous hysteria and calms himself by caressing a fragment of his tattered baby blanket. Bloom's name, too, resonates with Jewish allusions, for it alludes to James Joyce's famous Jew, Leopold Bloom in *Ulysses*.[5] Together, the two mismatched associates embark upon a money-making scheme to find the worst play ever written, finance it far beyond actual production costs, close the drama after one performance due to disastrous opening-night reviews, and keep the excess funds as under-the-table profit free from IRS suspicions. Unfortunately for the maladroit schemers, the play they select, *Springtime for Hitler*, turns into a runaway smash on Broadway.

Brooks's characters represent a compendium of Jewish clichés that could easily be lambasted as blatantly anti-Semitic: the cunning Jew who unscrupulously fleeces others, the money-hungry Jew

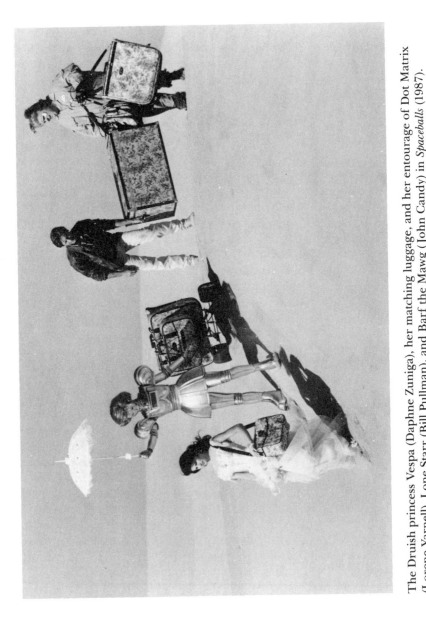

The Druish princess Vespa (Daphne Zuniga), her matching luggage, and her entourage of Dot Matrix (Lorene Yarnell), Lone Starr (Bill Pullman), and Barf the Mawg (John Candy) in *Spaceballs* (1987).

who sacrifices morality on the altar of immediate riches, the manipulating Jew who trades on the finer emotions of others for his own gain, the garish Jew who flaunts his wealth at the least opportunity, the parasitic Jew who lives off the talent of others, the wimpy Jew who is easily bullied by more powerful personalities, the unethical Jew who cheats in business ventures, the neurotic Jew who is unbalanced but brilliant, the sexually insecure Jew who exploits women, the ostentatious Jew who lavishly spends more than he earns, and the clever Jew who becomes the victim of his own cleverness. This catalog of "the Jew who" seems almost endless—and almost always in bad taste.

So why is all of this so funny? In *The Producers*, the Jewish characters, however unappealing, are far more attractive and lovable than the people they exploit. In particular, Brooks mercilessly parodies the talentless homosexual director Roger DeBris (Christopher Hewett); the spacy rock star Lorenzo "LSD" St. DuBois (Dick Shawn); and the sentimental Nazi Fritz Liebkind (Kenneth Mars). Compared to this trio of deranged maniacs, his two Jewish characters seem harmless and fun-loving. The Nazi, as might be expected, receives the brunt of Brooks's venom, a bitter but hilarious diatribe against those who insist on perpetuating the Fuehrer's memory while conveniently forgetting his terrible deeds against humanity. Liebkind describes his pathetically bad play as a "gay romp with Adolph and Eva in Berchtesgarden," never appreciating the irony implicit in his frivolous characterization. He frequently longs for Hitler's resurrection, forcing Bialystock and Bloom to sing "Deutschland über Alles" with him and wear swastika armbands. In fact, he only agrees to sell his play because he thinks it will be a "way to clear the Fuehrer's name" and show once and for all that Hitler "was a nice guy who could dance the pants off Churchill." Yet the very fact that Bialystock and Bloom will sacrifice their principles for a profit, as well as join forces with this Nazi at the end of the movie, indicates a great deal about the willingness of modern Jews to ignore the tragedies of the past and do business in the present.

Surely, then, something lurks not too far beneath the surface content of this absurd situation. Indeed, Brooks's comic intentions resemble Chaplin's in *The Great Dictator* and Lubitsch's in *To Be or Not to Be*. All three confront the Nazi menace and expose it the best way they can: They make people laugh at the obscene absurdity of the Master Race's pretentious superiority by turning its sanctimonious leaders into dumb stumblebums and its vicious ideology of racism into pathetic farce. *The Producers* obviously arises from feelings of pain and outrage. Some cry about the Holocaust, but others find themselves reduced to bitter laughter when faced with a tragedy so enormous that it defies rational understanding and human comprehension. As Brooks observes, "More than anything, the great Holocaust by the Nazis is probably the great outrage of the Twentieth Century. There is nothing to compare with it. So what can I do about it? If I get on the soapbox and wax eloquently, it'll be blown away in the wind, but if I do *Springtime for Hitler* it'll never be forgotten. I think you can bring down totalitarian governments faster by using ridicule than you can with invective" (Fleischman 8).

Truly, Brooks's tears mingle with his laughter. He remains fearfully cognizant that the Nazis' message of loathing and malice will live far longer than the brick and stone monuments designed by Albert Speer. He recognizes that hatred of others transcends any particular era or historical period, although certainly the German fascists raised it to new levels. Instead, it creeps into every culture, every society, waiting for the right moment, or the right people, to harness its power for their own ends. Anti-Semitism is thus a state of mind that needs only the proper atmosphere to assert its force.

Almost all the motifs discussed previously originate in *The Producers*, but the show business image dominates the film from a particularly fascinating American-Jewish perspective:

> It [*The Producers*] was an extended exercise in parody, albeit one that was American-Jewish to its very bones. Brooks' film not only saw the Broadway musical through Hollywood eyes, but, even more important, it saw the creators of that culture through eyes at least one generation removed. . . . The days of the old scenario in which Mickey Rooney gazes into Judy Garland's eyes and says: "Let's put on a show!" are over. To make a production happen you need money. And to make it happen on Broadway, you need a producer like Max Bialystock. (Pinsker 246)

Indeed, the scheme to get rich by producing a show (although a flop) on Broadway springs fullblown from minds overdosed on Hollywood movies, particularly those wonderfully naive musicals in which "putting on a show" solves life's thorniest problems. The most vivid single image of Hollywood's power to influence us occurs during Leo's frenzied dance around Lincoln Center's Revson Fountain, as he sheds his repressed mentality and joyously yells "I want everything I've ever seen in the movies!" Thus the dancer becomes the dance or, to put it another, less comfortable, way, the monster merges with its creator. In *The Producers*, the begetters of

America's most pervasive myths become seduced by their own opulent fantasies. They have come to believe their own advertising hype, their own saccharine version of the American Dream.

Yet the film cuts even deeper; it attacks the lengths producers go to make money, including collaborating with unrepentant Nazis, and the depths to which audiences will sink to be entertained. One need only conjure up Brooks's maniacal vision of a stage filled with "singing and dancing" Hitlers earnestly auditioning for Bialystock and Bloom's new production to understand the desperate idiocy and callous crassness that fuels show business. An instant replay is history, and not much is remembered beyond last week. The past events that do limp into the present are perceived without context or understanding, so Hitler simply becomes another piece of fodder gobbled up by the era's ravenous appetite for cultural kitsch.

On a deeper note this points to a total sense of irresponsibility that accepts all manner of ideology as worthy of iconographizing and all famous people as equally eligible for the cult of personality. Here Brooks mingles history and fantasy, personality and performance, introducing a bizarre yet hypnotic Busby Berkeley-esque musical extravaganza using images directly drawn from the Third Reich. For example, the leggy, overendowed showgirls wear Wagnerian costumes, beer-and-pretzel bras, and German eagles on their heads. Dancing stormtroopers link arms to form a human, revolving swastika. Cut loose from their historical moorings and placed within the comforting conventions of the Broadway musical, these totems of terror evoke laughter rather than fear, a strange acknowledgment of the power of art over the reality of life.

Brooks's anger reaches far beyond businessmen with the sheer audacity to present a musical called *Springtime for Hitler,* however. By having it become a resounding hit, Brooks assaults an American public willing to find humor, however grotesque, in the Third Reich. Bialystock and Bloom fail to produce their flop because they underestimate their audience's deadened sensibilities. They pick a subject they think is universally repulsive and assume that no feeling person could find it otherwise. Ironically, however, their awareness and compassion far outstrips that of their callous audience, which totally ignores the historical reality that lurks beneath the surface of the musical. Although most critics understand how Brooks assails the American public's easy assimilation of Nazi Germany's horrors, only Maurice Yacowar points to the wider, more disturbingly profound implications of the satire: "Bialystock's expensive lesson is that there is no moral absolute that he can confi-

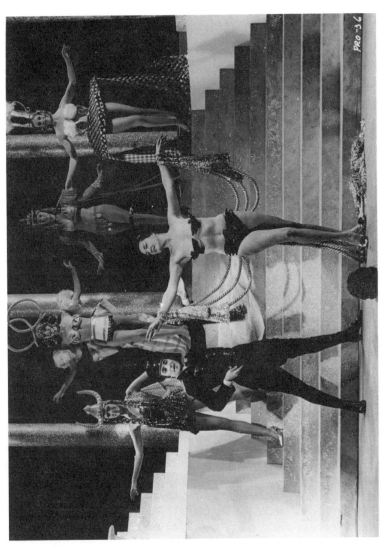

Nazi kitsch, as Busby Berkeley meets the Third Reich in *The Producers* (1967).

dently offend, either on Broadway or in Western Civilization (As We Know It). There is no sure distinction between Right and Wrong in his society's ethics, even for the hardy criminal spirit who wishes to pursue the Wrong. So what he thought would upset his audience pleases them immensely" (*Methods* 75).

Surely, this is the point: In a world drifting among subjective values, even Hitler can be reborn as a figure of fun rather than of fanaticism. Beneath the vulgar exterior of the crass comedian, the coarse bravado of the scatological filmmaker par excellence, beats the heart of a fire-and-brimstone moralist who castigates the trivialization of horror and the commodification of terror. This is a strange instance of the mouth biting the hand that feeds it. Brooks, who has made a career of shocking audiences with his grossness, condemns viewers for their jaded sensibilities which, at least in some measure, have accounted for his success. Like the court jester, he makes fun of his patrons yet expects that we will reward him for his honest cleverness.

Where then does Brooks find value? If *The Producers* is emblematic, he finds it in the male camaraderie epitomized by the relationship between Bialystock and Bloom, certainly an odd couple of staggering proportions. Many commentators trace how their relationship parodies conventional musical romances, from initial dislike to romantic courtship to committed partnership. In addition, the portrait clearly partakes of father-son feelings (the day in the park when Max buys Leo a balloon), as well as the union of Max's Dionysian spirit with Leo's Apollonian intellect. Or, in Sanford Pinsker's more prosaic terminology, "the partnership of Leo Bloom and Max Bialystock was arranged in that peculiarly Jewish heaven where there is a lid for every pot" (247). Whatever the yin and yang of these two men, their affection clearly transcends any con game or tasteless musical. Again, one may speculate about numerous personal (Brooks was just eight years old when his father died) and professional reasons why such male bonding permeates Brooks's movies. More to the point, it grows out of a Jewish sense of fatality, the idea that land and wealth, power and position, may vanish in the wink of an eye or a ruler's change of heart, but personal affection remains a powerful bond that lasts beyond the whims of fortune. For Brooks, such feelings define the best parts of life, the most enduringly human of emotions. At the end of *The Producers,* Bialystock and Bloom become "prisoners of love" (along with the repentant Fritz) in the best sense of that phrase; they are bound by chains of choice, not obligation.

Unlike *The Producers,* which contains the semblance of an ongoing narrative, *History of the World, Part One* takes us on a free-form, burlesque jaunt through time from the prehistoric ages, to ancient Rome, to the Spanish Inquisition, to the French Revolution, complete with sonorous narration by Orson Welles. This time, Brooks trains his parodic sights on the historical epic, those sprawling, lavish and ill-informed cinematic clinkers that reduce the sweep of history to clichéd love stories with casts of thousands played out against exotic backdrops. Yet the most fascinating aspect of the film is its subversive view of history lurking beneath the typical Brooksian urination jokes, the unfortunate homosexual jibes, and the persistent sexist leering. Brooks has the temerity to examine, albeit humorously, some of the most revered periods of history from the perspective of common people rather than the great, defining personages of the eras. As such, he implicitly disputes the evolution of the world as mediated through a predominately white, male, Christian, European perspective. Ella Shohat, one of the few critics to take the film seriously, correctly observes that it "is told from a marginalized perspective; the periphery moves to the center. . . . Brooks's presentation of history recalls that of the *Annales* school of historiography, which shifts the emphasis to peripheralised communities, in contrast to dominant historiographical accounts that focus only on the powerful" (241–42). By thus shifting the point of view, Brooks simultaneously alters the values and forces consideration of the groups that lost their gamble with historical inevitability.

In the segment concerning the Roman Age, for example, Brooks plays Comicus, a woefully inadequate stand-up comedian-philosopher forced to suffer the sarcastic barbs of bureaucratic hacks before he can get his unemployment allotment. Finally, his agent Swiftus (Ron Carey), a reference to superagent Swifty Lazar, gets Comicus his big break, and he performs at the pantheon of entertainment: Caesar's Palace (another allusion to Brooks's television days and the famous Las Vegas resort). Brooks envisions Caesar's imperial court as an elaborate game show, the emperor presiding as a crazed Monty Hall with the power of arbitrarily awarding life and death sentences to his hapless subjects. Initially, Comicus' act delights the besotted revelers. The drunken Caesar (Dom DeLuise), in particular, loves his invectives at the expense of the lowly Christians ("they're so poor they have only one God"). Lulled into a false sense of security by his riotous triumph, ignoring the whimsical cruelty of his host, Comicus momentarily forgets his benefactor's blubbery corpulence and launches into an abusive tirade of fat jokes that drives the rotund emperor to such murderous apoplexy that he orders Comicus killed immediately. So much for comedy's power to puncture tyranny. So much for the security afforded by art. The short segment clearly demonstrates the delicate balance, the artful little dance, that those without power or rights must learn in societies where a smile often hides a sneer and, with little warning, boisterous laughter can turn into a sentence of death.

Meanwhile, another outsider finds himself a victim of Roman justice. Josephus (Gregory Hines), a captured Ethiopian slave from 125th Street, claims to be Jewish so he will not be served to the lions, who only munch on tender Christians. Even his sprightly rendition of "Hava Nagilla," accompanied by accomplished tap dancing, fails to convince his dubious captors, particularly after they look inside his rags and discover his uncircumcised penis. Joining forces in the manner of Bart and the Waco Kid, Comicus and Josephus hide among the Vestal Virgins, a gaggle of blonde shiksas, and spy on the Roman senate, whose motto is "Fuck the Poor." They also manage to watch Moses (also played by Brooks) part the Red Sea and then get robbed and furiously curse his assailant in Yiddish.

The black slave and the Jewish comic, along with a renegade Vestal Virgin, finally escape to Judea aboard a ship that has "El Al" on its sail. Here, in an inspired bit of byplay, Comicus finds himself a waiter at the Last Supper. "All together or separate checks?" asks Comicus of Jesus and his solemn disciples. "Jesus!" curses the distraught Comicus; "Yes," Jesus responds. Finally, Leonardo da Vinci arrives to paint the group, and his famous picture of the Last Supper now contains a grinning Comicus. "Just another Jew," Brooks seems to imply. Such a view from the underbelly of the Empire, from the citizens carelessly ground beneath its heel, forces a rethinking of those grand and glorious toga epics that celebrate that power that was Rome.[6]

Like Moses parting the Red Sea (as well as his earlier dropping of one tablet, thus providing ten commandments instead of the original fifteen), Brooks includes many specifically Jewish elements in the film. The scene that instigated the most controversy is the segment dealing with the Spanish Inquisition. Here, as in *The Producers*, Brooks uses a lavish musical number to deal with horrible historical events. Once again, as in *To Be or Not to Be*, Brooks takes the role of a zealot bent on destroying the Jewish people, this time playing Torquemada, the vicious Grand Inquisitor who murdered thousands of Jews. Shohat sees this assumption of the murderer's role as a form of "metaphorical cannibalism," as "playfully masquerading as the enemy" and engendering a laugh that "exorcises the community's latent collective fears" (246). Like Piaget's comments, such a reading points to an obvious truth but fails to explore the profound emotional schizophrenia inherent in adopting the image of the torturer, even if that image vibrates with comic intentions. Albert Memmi argues persuasively that "every oppressed person adopts as his own a part of the charge instituted against him: it is one of the internal dramas of oppression" (*Liberation* 44). So, too, Sander Gilman discusses "the illusionary definition of the self, the identification with the reference group's mirage of the Other" (*Self-Hatred* 2). Instead of seeing himself as a victim, Brooks unconsciously identifies with these powerful figures of persecution, even as he does his comic best to destroy their image of strength and superiority. Such an "internal drama of oppression" indicates a deep division within his psyche that has profound ramifications within the American-Jewish community, a devastating split that intellectually undermines anti-Semitism while it emotionally rejects the weakness of its victims.

Throughout this sumptuous Busby Berkeley parody, complete with nuns swimming synchronized routines in a gigantic pool, Brooks intersperses shots of Jews undergoing various forms of painful torture at the hands of cruel priests. Christian charity is conspicuously absent. In fact, the lines of the song Brooks (and Ronny Graham) wrote to accompany the sequence clearly communicate the director's feelings about religious fanatics who persecute Jews under the guise of saving their souls. Torquemada, in particular, revels in such devotional torture and explains:

> We have a mission to convert the Jews.
> We're gonna teach them wrong from right.
> We're gonna help them see the light
> And make them an offer they can't refuse.

The Spanish Jews have done nothing to warrant this horrendous treatment. One is simply "flickin' chickens and suddenly dese goys break down my walls." Another is sitting in a temple, minding his own business, listening to some lovely Hebrew music when "the papist persons plunge in/and they threw me in a dungeon/and they shoved a red-hot poker up my ass." Within a broad, farcical context, Brooks depicts Jews as victims for simply being different than their Christian neighbors. More important, as was the case in the Roman segment, a person without power has little control over the whims of those who dictate the conditions of life.

As in *The Producers,* Brooks attacks anti-Semitism, as well as other forms of persecution, through his Swiftian blend of slapstick and scatological comedy. In *History of the World, Part One,* Jews suffer various forms of torture because they will not convert to Christianity, from being slapped into stocks to functioning as human slot machines to losing their skulls rather than their skullcaps. "Is it polite? Is it considerate? To make my privates a public game?" laments one poor victim. The comic-book approach in both films encourages laughter at suffering, but Brooks's intention always remains deadly serious. "Nothing can burst the balloon of pomposity and dictatorial splendor better than comedy. Comedy brings religious persecutors, dictators and tyrants to their knees faster than any other medium. In a sense, my comedy is serious, and I need a serious background to play against. That's why, for example, the Spanish Inquisition was so perfect for me. Poking fun at the Grand Inquisitor, Torquemada, is a wonderful counterpart to the horrors he committed" (Friedman, *Jewish Image* 236).

"So come on, you Moslems and you Jews," sings the jubilant Torquemada, "you'd better change your point of views." Point of view, of course, is precisely what Brooks's film is all about. By urging laughter at the prejudices of earlier generations, Brooks forces his audience to confront the destructive nature of religious excess as well as the brutal consequences of intolerance.

Ella Shohat theorizes that Brooks, "by associating traditional musical forms with recognizable marginalized communities, . . . calls attention to their traditional exclusion from the musical's communal harmony" and that the Inquisition episode "visualizes the Catholic mass as if drawn from a horror film" (243). In a wonderfully apt analysis, she draws a connection between the Purim carnivalesque tradition and this particular segment: "The *Purimspiel* tradition celebrates the prevention of genocide through Esther's outwitting of the oppressor. It is the biblical Esther's sexuality— here transformed into the erotic kitsch of Esther Williams—that redeems the Jews" (245). Such a sophisticated grasp of Brooks's methodology demonstrates how his Jewish consciousness informs his very images, perhaps in ways beyond his rational comprehension. Whether Mel Brooks did or did not make a conscious connection between Queen Esther and Esther Williams remains beside the point. The fact is that his movies scream out their intimate connection with the fundamentally same American-Jewish consciousness that informs the works of Mazursky, Allen, and Lumet. A non-Jewish Mel Brooks would not be Mel Brooks. His culture, his ethnic heritage, colors who he is and what he believes on such an intensely personal level that his films only reveal the tip of the psychological iceberg: "My comedy is big-city, Jewish, whatever I am. Energetic, nervous, crazy" (Pinsker 248).

Mel Brooks never stops engaging in what he calls "Jewish fencing" (Rovin, "Film" 28), and he never runs out of opponents: historical figures and critics, bigots and buffoons, monsters and morons. For Brooks, Jewishness encompasses far more than cultural signposts or arcane ceremonies. It lives and breathes. It offers a host of approaches to the world, a multilayered way of seeing which separates Brooks from most other directors. "Humor is just another defense against the universe" (Yacowar, *Method* 6), he is fond of saying. Such a claim, of course, comes only from a man who finds the universe a hostile environment, whose sense of history tells him that this may simply be one more pause in his people's seemingly endless migration.

For Brooks, the comic and the tragic cannot be pried apart. His comic style grows out of his anarchistic, postmodern vision, and that fractured perspective comes directly from his experience of the world that remains firmly wedded to his understanding of himself as an American Jew. "Comedy, not tragedy," claims Wylie Sypher, "admits the disorderly into the realm of art" (Corrigan 24), and few artists relish the disorderly so much as Mel Brooks. Disorder casually but definitively disputes the fragile hold that rationality exercises in our lives. In the opening section of *History of the World, Part One,* Brooks shows how comedy evolves out of tragedy—the cavemen laugh after a man is eaten by a dinosaur. Such an image springs from Brooks's consciousness, which can assimilate the horrors of history and still keep laughing, knowing that if he stops laughing he will go mad.

Notes

1. Like Morroe Rieff in *Bye Bye Braverman,* Brooks has it wrong. "A muzhik was not a peasant. A muzhik was a member of the middle agrarian class which Stalin wiped out by the millions. The millions!" (Markfield 13).

2. Knowing Brooks, one wonders if all the Johnsons are an allusion to the vernacular usage of *Johnson* as a substitute for penis, or simply to the most gentile name he could imagine.

3. Confusion over this last character's name caused Brooks some acute embarrassment when Terry Boyle, the father of a retarded child, wrote a letter

to the *New York Times* (March 31, 1974) accusing the director of poking fun at children with Down Syndrome by calling the creature "Mongol," as in Mongoloid children. Brooks hastily wrote a response, citing the correct spelling of the name and claiming he used it to pun on his favorite bongo player, Mongo Santa Maria. When a scared Rock Ridge resident in a serape sees the muscle-bound bully enter town, he yells out: "Mongo . . . Santa Maria!" (Adler and Feinman 108). *Shtupp* is a Yiddish word which, in common parlance, means *to fuck*. In fact, Brooks almost called the film *She Shtupps to Conquer*, playing off his love of Oliver Goldsmith's drama.

4. In a sly historical aside, Brooks names Leachman's character after Gebhard Lebercht von Blucher (1742–1819), a German military leader who commanded the Prussian army, which defeated Napoleon at Leon and fought alongside the British at the Battle of Waterloo.

5. Brooks told Kenneth Tynan, "I don't know what it meant to James Joyce, but to me Leo Bloom always meant a vulnerable Jew with curly hair" (108).

6. As Woody Allen starred in a Paul Mazursky film, *Scenes from a Mall*, so Paul Mazursky here plays a bit part as a Roman soldier for Mel Brooks in this segment.

CHAPTER FOUR

Sidney Lumet: The Memory of Guilt

Using the standard of critical attention that has been applied to Woody Allen, Sidney Lumet would not seem to be a major director. Scholars write little about him, certainly compared to Allen or even to Brooks and Mazursky. Such an absence, however, speaks less of Lumet's importance than about the prejudices and gaps in film scholarship. Lumet suffers from the fallout from the *politique des auteurs* as promulgated by Francois Truffaut in 1954, as he brusquely rejected the "tradition of quality," which meant the literary-derived cinema that had come to dominate French film after World War II. Most of Lumet's finest films are based firmly in preestablished texts, in particular in plays, novels, and nonfiction crime stories.[1] In addition to this auteurist bias, the wave of formalist criticism that catapulted the likes of Martin Scorsese, Francis Coppola, and Brian de Palma to the forefront of American cinema in the 1970s provided no place for Lumet's narrative-driven films.

Lumet, then, found himself in a time warp, neither part of the classical Hollywood generation of authentic auteur directors (Hitchcock, Ford, Hawks) nor the younger cineastes of the 1960s and 1970s (those mentioned previously, as well as Peter Bogdanovich, George Lucas, and Steven Spielberg). Thus, he fell into a void in scholarship, along with such other commercially successful but critically ignored directors as Elia Kazan, Fred Zinnemann, and, more recently, Sydney Pollack. Lumet's eclecticism, his undertaking of diverse genres and various approaches, makes him hard to pigeonhole, unlike his cohorts Sam Peckinpah and Arthur Penn. Whatever the reasons for this relative neglect, Lumet should be recognized as a major American filmmaker whose perspective is decidedly American Jewish.

Outside of official academic circles, Lumet does command respect. His vast output of more than three dozen films provides one index of his status. He has directed more pictures than any major filmmaker of our time. Similarly, the number of Academy Award nominations garnered by his films represents a tribute to the respect he commands in an industry notorious for its shifts and fleeting tastes. Although he may lack the immediate personal style or obsessive set of themes critics isolate with satisfied glee, Lumet is rarely a mere hired hand on an enormous series of projects. Although not every film is a major work, most demonstrate his intense commitment to certain social themes and issues. Many of Lumet's most artistically successful films foreground particularly Jewish issues, but even his others demonstrate the profound influences and crucial legacies that growing up Jewish in America provided him.

A deep and abiding commitment to social justice dominates Lumet's cinema. This commitment often takes the form of complex responses to complicated issues, sometimes alienating him from what should be his major supporters. Thus his important film of the Holocaust, *The Pawnbroker* (1965), remains mired in controversy from those who object to its "universalization" of a specifically Jewish theme. Similarly, Jews and Leftists vilified *Daniel* (1983), his film of the Jewish Old Left and the Rosenberg execution, arguing that his portraits betray the facts. We count these two films as Lumet's finest achievements and will strive to redeem them from such ideological pillorying. But Lumet never avoids controversy within the sphere of social justice.

Lumet represents Woody Allen's darker double, his doppelganger. As with Allen, critics and filmgoers associate Lumet with New York City. However, as Jonathan Rosenbaum notes, "part of what makes the Manhattan in *Manhattan* so 'attractive' . . . is the nearly total absence of blacks and Hispanics" along with the total lack of racism in any of Allen's films (99). Lumet documents these urban blights in great detail. The cityscape dominates his landscape, as it does Allen's, but the presence of a multiracial, multiethnic mise-en-scène is unmistakable and not merely tokenistic. Rather, Lumet builds a number of his finest films precisely on the conflicts that rage within a multicultural society. Allen's finest achievements spring from comedy, yet he often ranges into dramas; Lumet's major efforts arise in drama, but he often works within comedy as well. But although Allen's dramas prove at best uneven, Lumet's comedies remain intellectually interesting even when unfulfilling.

Lumet and Allen also share another profound similarity, the sentiment best expressed by Allen's Danny Rose: "Guilt is important . . . I'm guilty all the time and I never did anything." The question of guilt, of people who feel guilty and often are guilty (al-

Sidney Lumet directs *Q & A*.

though of precisely what) is exactly where Lumet finds his drama; it dominates his cinema. Guilt becomes a recurring motif that stretches across the boundaries of his cinema and most clearly defines it. From his very first feature film *Twelve Angry Men* (1957), in which a jury must decide the guilt or innocence of a young man on trial for murder, to *Q & A* (1990), in which a lawyer must determine the question of guilt and responsibility on the part of a maverick policeman, guilt links the diverse parts of Lumet's varied and complex canon. In *Murder on the Orient Express* (1974), a minor but quite popular effort, all of the suspects are guilty. In Allen's work, guilt often appears as comic and is expressed in the inability to feel happiness and enjoy life. Characters in Lumet's films often must pay an even dearer price for their guilt.

An injunction that is virtually biblical informs Lumet's conception of guilt, that of a father's guilt being passed on to his sons and implicating them profoundly. Fathers and sons, or structurally similar pairings (e.g., teacher–student or older man–younger man), are rampant in Lumet's cinema. Families are also, necessarily, dominant. Although family life is a central motif in American-Jewish life and art, it is hardly unique to Jews. A particular kind of family dynamic, an overwhelming focus on children, characterizes Jewish life in America. Yet most American films are characterized by the lone hero; the arresting image of the self-made man, who is literally without background or family, cuts across American genres. Lumet's insistence on the centrality of family life clearly distinguishes his films. From his early success with *Long Day's Journey into Night* (1962) to the underappreciated *Running on Empty* (1988), questions of family loyalty in confrontation with the guilt of a family member drive the best of Lumet's films. Along with actual families, he uses surrogate families, especially the police, as in the trilogy *Serpico* (1974), *Prince of the City* (1981), and *Q & A*. A different sort of family, albeit an untraditional one, structures another important film, *Dog Day Afternoon* (1975).

The guilt of an individual member, which in turn threatens the fabric of the family, allows Lumet to explore Old Testament questions of guilt and responsibility. The dynamics of family life also involve the individual and the family with the larger social sphere, especially the political realm. In his introduction to an interview with Lumet, Gavin Smith calls him "one of the only surviving political filmmakers in American cinema" (32). Sometimes the political content of his films may be disguised, although it usually rests clearly at his films' centers. An awareness of the historical period and a sensitive eye for nuance allows one to see how *Twelve Angry Men* was a definitive rebuttal to the lynch mob hysteria of the McCarthy era" (Smith 32). Less historical perspicacity reveals the political condemnations behind *Power* or the rejection of sixties' revisionism in *Running on Empty*.

As much as his movies demand social justice, and as much as family dynamics along with questions of guilt and responsibility dominate them, Lumet's most powerful central motif comes directly from Jewish tradition, specifically Judaism: the injunction to remember. Lumet structures his two most compelling, and most compellingly Jewish, films via flashbacks, situating his story around characters who always remember; in fact, they cannot forget. *The Pawnbroker* and *Daniel* become celluloid Haggadahs (the Passover text that recalls the Israelites' escape from bondage in Egypt). Like the Haggadah, these films commemorate, they do not celebrate. It is as if they are drawn from the canon of Judaism, itself dominated not by celebrations but by commemorations, by days of remembrance and atonement, of wandering and guilt. Even a seeming mere entertainment such as *The Morning After* (1986) revolves around an actress's inability to remember a murder she may have committed.

Lumet's background seems to have been tailored to induce him to produce the kind of films he would later make: close family ties, especially to his father; a boyhood spent in the depression; work in the realistic, activist political New York theater of the 1930s; and an immersion in Jewish culture, particularly the secular culture of *Yiddishkeit*, especially the Yiddish theater. His background in New York theater, radio, and his youthful acting forays into films were thus politically as well as ethnically tinged.[2]

Born in Philadelphia in 1924, Sidney Lumet is the son of Baruch Lumet, a Polish émigré actor who rose to modest success as a member of the Yiddish Art Theatre run by the famed Maurice Schwartz, Yiddish theater's most beloved figure. At the age of four, Sidney made his own stage debut in New York's Yiddish theater, the Lumets having moved to the Lower East Side when he was two. Constant activity in Yiddish theater and radio soon combined with a transition to more mainstream pursuits on Broadway, where Lumet appeared in the original production of *Dead End* in 1935. Yet Jewishness was not completely absent from these Broadway productions; Lumet appeared in such Jewish-themed plays as *The Eternal Road, Morning Star,* and *Journey to Jerusalem* between 1937 and 1939. Many plays in which Lumet appeared were, like *Dead*

End, primarily social problem dramas, for example, *Brooklyn U.S.A.* and *One Third of a Nation,* also in the period immediately before the war. The ability and the willingness to bring ethnic and social concerns to varied, mainstream audiences were hallmarks of the New York theater during the depression, and thus provided a significant background for Lumet's later filmic concerns, as well as a lesson in how to present them.

At the start of the war, Lumet enlisted in the Army Signal Corps, service that was followed by his immediate reimmersion into activist and ethnic theater. In 1946 he replaced Marlon Brando in the role of David in Ben Hecht's *A Flag Is Born.* As Stephen Bowles describes it, "the play was staged to aid the American League for a Free Palestine. The story followed the post-war plight of the Jewish people to establish a homeland and pleaded for a Jewish consolidation" (7). At this point, Lumet's interests turned toward directing, but one more acting role in 1948 indicates his continued commitment to Jewish issues. *Seeds in the Wind* is the story of a group of Jewish youths, victims of the Nazi terror, who attempt to start a utopian community.

Lumet began directing feature films fully ten years before Allen, Brooks, or Mazursky did. Whereas the life-style revolts and increased ethnic consciousness of the 1960s allowed them almost immediate freedom to focus on social issues, Lumet began his directing career during a time of more repression and conformity, the myopic vision of ethnic blandness that characterized the 1950s. Thus it is no surprise that Lumet's first film with a specifically Jewish focus, *The Pawnbroker,* did not appear until 1965. Yet Lumet's directing career was characterized by his early concern for social justice, a perspective sifted through a focus on urban, ethnic families that has captured his attention from the beginning of his long career. His start, however, was not in film but in television, the so-called golden age of the 1950s.

The golden age of television had much in common with the theatrical world in which Lumet spent his youth. It was characterized by enormous activity and, in business parlance, it had enormous need for product. Stephen Bowles estimates that Lumet directed as many as five hundred shows, beginning in 1951 and continuing throughout the decade (8). This enormous output enabled Lumet to receive the kind of training in directing and the staging of actors previously available only to the first generation of filmmakers (for example, D. W. Griffith directed as many as five hundred short films for the Biograph Company between 1908 and

1912). Equally as important, live television drama also provided its fair share of ethnic, activist, social drama. Paddy Chayefsky, for example, wrote two Holocaust-themed teleplays for the "Philco Television Playhouse" in 1952: "Holiday Song" and "The Reluctant Citizen." Similarly, *Judgment at Nuremberg,* one of the major films of 1961, was originally produced as a television drama in 1959. Herbert Brodkin was a seminal influence on Lumet in this period; the men worked together on the "Alcoa Playhouse," which Brodkin produced. Brodkin, an activist producer and a dramatic predecessor to the more comically inclined Norman Lear, would remain in television, creating and producing "The Defenders," an influential dramatic series focusing on lawyers. His greatest achievement, and a landmark on American television, was "Holocaust," the 1978 miniseries that went on to international success and controversy.[3]

Both television and the theater would remain significant influences on Lumet's career in motion pictures, inaugurated in 1957 with his theatrical film directing debut *Twelve Angry Men.* The film, produced by its star Henry Fonda, began life as a television drama in 1954 for the "Alcoa Playhouse." Although the writer, Reginald Rose, had worked previously with Lumet during their respective stints on the weekly dramatic series, Lumet did not direct the television version of the award-winning courtroom drama. It was directed by Franklin Schaffner, who would also go on to a career in feature films. *Twelve Angry Men* was one of many theatrical films that began life as an original television drama; *Marty* (1956, script for television and film by Paddy Chayefsky), *Requiem for a Heavyweight* (1962, television and film script by Rod Serling), and *Judgment at Nuremberg* are the most famous, along with *Twelve Angry Men.*

The continued decline of the film studios in Hollywood and the excitement of live television based in New York (where it drew upon a new generation of actors who found a great deal of work in the theater and on television) created a space for a younger, differently trained generation of film directors. In addition to Lumet and Schaffner, such notable directors as Arthur Penn, Martin Ritt, John Frankenheimer, and William Friedkin, among others, emerged from this creative milieu. *Twelve Angry Men* originated from this decline in Hollywood's dominance of film production and creativity. What is now an all-star cast, including Martin Balsam, Lee J. Cobb, Jack Klugman, E. G. Marshall, and Jack Warden, was then only the beginning of a new generation of actors trained at the Actors Studio and cutting their teeth on weekly television

dramas. But the particulars of this teleplay-turned-Oscar-nomi-
nated-screenplay rest in the sensitivity toward ethnic issues and the
search for social justice characteristic of American-Jewish writers
and directors.

Gavin Smith's characterization of *Twelve Angry Men* as a definitive
rebuttal to the lynch-mob hysteria of the McCarthy era is indeed
apt; the film is both an anticonformist tract and a plea for legitimate justice and civil rights. In this story of a lone juror who must
convince his eleven fellow jurors of a young man's innocence,
Lumet and Rose repudiate the "go-along" mentality of the 1950s,
but the lynch-mob hysteria recalls the real lynchings that recurred
with tragic frequency as blacks demanded civil rights. Lumet's directorial debut thus continues a tradition of American social problem films, specifically the antilynching films of the 1930s and 1940s
best exemplified by *Fury* (1936) and a key sequence in John Ford's
Young Mr. Lincoln (1939). The cycle reached its peak with *The Ox-
Bow Incident* (1943). Indeed, it is possible to view *Twelve Angry Men*
as Henry Fonda's rectification of the social injustice he could not
prevent in the earlier film.

In the 1930s and 1940s, however, the rejection of mob rule and
frontier justice by well-meaning Hollywood film producers repressed a central element in the lynchings that plagued the South,
for nowhere in these earlier films is the victim a black man, as the
tragic victim almost always was. (The most famous nonblack victim
of a lynch mob was a Jew, Leo Frank, in 1915.) Lynchings and other
violent forms of intimidation made a nasty reappearance in the
South after the war, especially given the increased activity in the
area of civil rights protests, which began in earnest in 1954, the
same year as Rose's original teleplay for *Twelve Angry Men,* after the
landmark school desegregation decision in *Brown v. Topeka Board of
Education.* The film version of *Twelve Angry Men* does not disguise
the all-too-frequent targets of the lynch mobs. The jury room, although not quite the frontier justice of *The Ox-Bow Incident,* represents only the veneer of decorum and fair play, for all of the jury,
save one, wish to convict and sentence the accused to death. But in
rejecting the conformity of McCarthyism, *Twelve Angry Men* equally
rejects racism, as Fonda's character (none of the characters have
names, they are referred to as Juror #1, #2, etc., Fonda is Juror
#8) shames the others into admitting that their basis for judgment
rests upon the fact that the defendant is Puerto Rican. Lumet not
only makes it abundantly clear that the jurors have stereotyped
images of blacks and Puerto Ricans, but also, and more important,

that such stereotypes can have tragic consequences. Conformity, especially when it disguises racism and prejudice, can kill.

Lumet's work between 1957 and 1965 is characterized by a love of New York City, where all the films were shot; an immersion in the particularly New York (and Jewish) world of the theater; and a sensitivity toward issues of self-fulfillment (life-style trends), family, and ethnicity. Thus *Stage Struck* (1958) is, as Lumet says, "a sort of Valentine to the theatre," and *That Kind of Woman* (1959) uses New York locales to tell the story of woman who must choose between love and money. Although neither film particularly pleases Lumet, he claims that part of his motivation in making them was that "I could do them both in New York" (Bowles 13–14). He turned down the opportunity to direct the film version of Lorraine Hansberry's acclaimed play *A Raisin in the Sun* because it meant filming in Hollywood (Bowles 14). Yet it is significant that he was offered the film at such an early point in his career. The offer indicates Lumet's demonstrable sensitivity toward issues of race, family life, and the urban environment.

The theater provided the setting and source for Lumet's next three films. He directed adaptations from three of America's most significant playwrights: Tennessee Williams, Arthur Miller, and Eugene O'Neill. *The Fugitive Kind* (1960), a reworking of *Orpheus Descending*, was the first of Lumet's two adaptations from Williams, both of which are set in the South. The second, *Last of the Mobile Hot-Shots* (1970), is based upon *The Seven Descents of Myrtle* and studied interracial tensions. It was part of an increased sensitivity in American movies toward major political and social issues, a movement in which Lumet was a leader. As Maurice Yacowar notes in a study of film adaptations of Williams's plays, Lumet's version of *The Seven Descents of Myrtle* increased public awareness of racism, and, by casting Robert Hooks, who is black, in the role of Chicken made the issue obvious (Bowles 25). *The Fugitive Kind*, however, favored psychology over sociology in a more typical Williams tale of repressed lust in the steamy South. That Lumet was interested in exploring Williams's specific concerns testifies to his desire to understand and explore the varieties of contemporary life and culture; that neither film was particularly successful speaks to some of the vast differences between urban New York and rural Dixie.

Yet Lumet's commitment to exploring southern life and its contemporary problems did not end with adaptations of Tennessee Williams, nor was it dampened by the cool reception that greeted these films. As Stephen Bowles relates, from 1958 to 1961, Lumet and Reginald Rose tried to make *Black Monday,* a film about reactions to enforced school integration in a southern town (16). He also attempted to adapt William Styron's *The Confessions of Nat Turner* (to be called *Nat Turner*), a project put on hold in 1969 following the commercial disappointments of Lumet's films in the preceding few years (Bowles 25). Lumet finally realized a major project concerning the civil rights struggle in the South with *King: A Filmed Record* (1970), a compilation documentary concerning Martin Luther King's efforts, with some new footage directed by Lumet and Joseph L. Mankiewicz, and produced by Ely Landau. The venture redeemed the earlier failure to make *Black Monday.*

In the meantime, *A View from the Bridge* (1961), adapted from Arthur Miller's play, found Lumet back on home territory with a story of ethnic Brooklyn family life. The working-class milieu of New York's docks was reproduced by location photography to lend authenticity to the poignancy of this portrait of new émigrés in conflict with an older, ethnic generation. This, his third theatrical adaptation, both solidified Lumet's reputation as a major American film director and showcased his sensitivity toward issues of family life and questions of guilt.

The Irish background of Eugene O'Neill appears in virtually every scene of his clearly autobiographical *Long Day's Journey into Night,* which Lumet filmed in 1962. Yet Lumet is clearly in synch with O'Neill; in fact, he directed *The Iceman Cometh* for television in 1960, working for the first of many times with Ely Landau, and won an Emmy for his efforts. As Bowles observes, "Carlotta Monterey O'Neill was so impressed by the production [of *The Iceman Cometh*] that she awarded Lumet the rights to all subsequent productions of O'Neill's plays over which she had control" (17). Critics generally regard *Long Day's Journey into Night* as one of the finest theater-into-film adaptations in Hollywood's history. The cast, which included Ralph Richardson, Katharine Hepburn, Jason Robards, Jr., and Dean Stockwell, accounts for the praise, but this intense vision of a tormented family in which each member feels guilty for the fate of the others strikes a particularly resonant chord with Lumet. Like O'Neill, he was the son of a famous theatrical father, and the uncertainties and excitements of the theater predominated both men's childhoods.

The pattern of adapting from other sources (most of them theatrical) and the prolific output established by his first half-dozen films in the same number of years would be characteristic of Lumet throughout his career. A focus on urban life and life-styles, family, and contemporary social issues also defines his versatile and nearly unceasing output. With *Fail Safe* (1964), he began to expand his social criticism, moving from the personal to the global. He was also more than the director of the film, assuming the role of coexecutive producer.

In retrospect, the film remains surprisingly optimistic despite the horrific nature of its conclusion, in which New York City is deliberately subjected to atomic bombing by decision of the president. (No doubt Lumet's special love for the city made this ending especially poignant for him.) A hopefulness pervades the film, with its vision of well-meaning and sensitive world leaders working together to avert total global destruction when an accident unleashes the Air Force's nuclear capabilities. With Henry Fonda cast as the president, the image of politicians and the military moves beyond benign and into the positive. Filmed as a response to the Cuban missile crisis and adapted from a popular novel by Eugene Burdick and Harvey Wheeler, *Fail Safe* could not take into account the assassination of President Kennedy. Instead, it seems to reflect the optimism of the Kennedy years. The vision of the corruption in such future productions as *Serpico, Prince of the City, Q & A, Network,* and *Daniel,* as well as that of the political process itself as seen in *Power,* constitute responses to the assassinations of the Kennedys and Martin Luther King, as well as to the Watergate affair.

Fail Safe turned Lumet's attention to novels, thus expanding his horizons, although the theater continued to remain a plentiful source of material. Although *Fail Safe*'s ending is somewhat optimistic, the gloom and doom that pervade much of the film harkened back to the atmosphere of *Long Day's Journey into Night* and anticipated *The Pawnbroker* and *The Hill* (1965).

The Pawnbroker, the first of Lumet's films adapted from an American-Jewish novel, will be discussed subsequently. Yet it is important to note here how Lumet's vision darkened, even compared to the tormented psychologies exposed in his adaptations of Miller, Williams, and O'Neill. He responded to contemporary American society of the 1960s by focusing more deeply on questions of social guilt and responsibility, on the relationship between the State and the individual, and the duty each owes the other.

With *The Pawnbroker,* Lumet immersed himself deeply in painful issues of American and American-Jewish life and offered commentary and critique on current social problems. With *The Hill* (his first of a handful of British-made movies), he removed himself from an American setting to comment upon universal truths in under-

standing guilt and responsibility. *The Hill* continues the vision of the
Nazi concentration camps seen in *The Pawnbroker,* with its setting in
a military prison camp. A harsh condemnation of bureaucratic
brutality, the film recognizes how systems, state institutions, demor-
alize and thus dehumanize people subjected to mindless rules and
authority.

With the exception of *Bye Bye Braverman,* Lumet's films following
The Hill and through 1974 are of little critical interest. In *The Group*
(1966), he again turned toward a novel for source material in an
attempt to provide a sympathetic portrait of a group of upper-class
women. Comparisons between this film and *Bye Bye Braverman* reveal where Lumet's true sympathies lie, however. Other British
films, for example, *The Deadly Affair* (1967, from a novel by John le
Carré) and *Murder on the Orient Express* (1974, from a novel by
Agatha Christie), represent the kind of mere entertainments that
Lumet has made throughout his career. Other films, for example,
Child's Play (1972), notable for using its setting in a Catholic boys'
school to examine the question of guilt and responsibility, and *The
Offence* (1973), with its focus on an exchange of guilt between a
criminal and a policeman, simply demonstrate Lumet's recurrent
concerns despite his varied projects.

Bye Bye Braverman (1968) is a major, fascinating exception to the
wide-ranging topics of films Lumet made between 1966 and 1974.
At the time of its production, he claimed that it was "the most
personal picture I've ever made" (Bowles 23). Considering that the
film is an almost completely faithful transposition of Wallace Markfield's *To an Early Grave* (1964), this is an interesting statement.
Lumet's claim that the characters are "everyone I grew up with.
Me, in fact" reveals the commonalities of American-Jewish life,
especially among American Jews born and raised in New York City
in the 1920s and 1930s. It is thus no surprise that Markfield was
born in New York City in 1927, nor that the Jewishness of the film's
four protagonists revolves as much around their urban background, interest in literature and popular culture, jobs in the academy or other intellectual fields, insecurities, neuroses, family, and
sexual conflicts as it does their being born into the religion of Judaism.

Lumet immediately sets his film in New York City, opening after
the credits on a long-shot of the Manhattan skyline, a subtitle informing the audience that "Leslie Braverman's friends live here."
Even before this establishing shot, however, Lumet specifically introduces Jewish New York under the credits (in a strategy that

anticipates the animated title sequence of *Garbo Talks*), with particularly piquant images of the old neighborhood shown through
what appear to be period photographs and home movies. Following shots communicate the shared bond between filmmaker and
audience, for example, the pushcart society of the Lower East Side;
the four friends going to see the Italian neorealist classic *Shoeshine*
(1946); three of the friends walking on a college campus, while the
fourth bellows forth from a podium about the political issues of the
day. Although there is no sound over these images, they provide an
archetypal picture of the Jew as political activist. Following the
credits and the establishing shot, individual vignettes introduce
each protagonist.

Morroe Rieff (George Segal), Felix Ottensteen (Joseph Wise-
man), Holly Levine (Sorrell Booke), and Barnet Weinstein (Jack
Warden) each live in a different part of Manhattan, neighborhoods
that become indexes of their characters. Thus Morroe Rieff, on the
Upper East Side, has more pretensions of fitting into mainstream
society than did the Village-dwelling Leslie Braverman, who has
recently died. Felix Ottensteen, on the Upper West Side, is a Yiddish writer from the Old Country who might be loosely based on
I. B. Singer, who lived on Manhattan's Upper West Side, home
to aging intellectuals who fled the Village's encroachment by the
youth culture of the 1950s and 1960s. Holly Levine's apartment, on
the Lower West Side, shows him trying to sustain an intellectual,
bohemian life-style; he is a contributor to the small literary journals. Barnet Weinstein's apartment on the Lower East Side indicates his attempt to be hip and up-to-date. In an attempt to hide his
age, he wears a toupee, which he removes when he learns of Braverman's death. Lumet is highly conscious of how a neighborhood
reveals character; in Markfield's novel, Morroe lives on the Upper
West Side. His move across town from West to East in a change
from novel to film not only has each of the four friends living in a
different part of the borough, but it also solidifies Morroe's change
from a youthful, Village-dwelling bohemian to staid, middle-class,
and middle-aged. Lumet and Markfield view the Lower East Side
as the New Old Country for America's Jews in general, and Greenwich Village as the New Old Country for Jewish intellectuals.

As the neighborhood symbolizes each character, so each character represents a part of American Jewry. Morroe Rieff makes his
living as a fund-raiser for Jewish causes. The film never reproduces
the centrality of Morroe's connection to Jewish causes, as well as the
irony with which it is expressed. When asked in the novel by Inez

Braverman, "You're still doing . . . the fund-raising work?" Morroe replies, "Still in the Jewish business." The film elides this comment, but Morroe is again a fund-raiser. The ability to contribute to such causes as Israel, Soviet Jewry, Jewish charities, or to local chapters of Jewish organizations, which in turn give to national and international causes, remains important in American-Jewish life. Morroe's specific contributions to fund-raising include writing speeches and brochures, thus reproducing the stereotypical Jewish propensity for verbal and intellectual dexterity. Morroe, however, secretly fantasizes about being a serious writer and feels guilty for not making a living as a genuine intellectual as Braverman does. Like the other characters, he has an impressive command of popular culture as well as a commitment to mainstream liberal causes. Morroe and his wife both possess the knowledge and political passion characteristic of American Jewry. She (Zohra Lampert) corrects her husband's pronunciation and definition of *muzhik:* "A muzhik was not a peasant. A muzhik was a member of the middle agrarian class which Stalin wiped out by the millions. The millions!"

Felix Ottensteen, the Yiddishist, is certainly not one of the happy-go-lucky, wise fools of Chelm popularized by Sholem Aleichem; he is cast out of a darker mold, out of Singer's Old Country passions. He complains of having to earn extra income by talking to Jewish women's organizations about Philip Roth. Over the bright side of the image of Jewish family life as supportive (perhaps oversupportive), Ottensteen casts a dark shadow in his relationship to his son, Max, who begs his father for yet more money. When the older man refuses, his son berates him for being cheap, a trait that allegedly shortened the life of Max's mother (a recollection of *Long Day's Journey into Night*). Later, Ottensteen berates God for taking Leslie Braverman's life and offers Max's in exchange, "no questions asked."

Ottensteen is as tragic and forlorn as the lost world of Yiddish in America. Political activism was important in Yiddish society, the world of the Old Left, and Ottensteen reprimands his son for complaining about being too tired to write. He tells Max that once upon a time there were poets who put in fourteen, sixteen hour days in sweatshops and still managed to write. They even tried to make revolutions. When Max says there are no more revolutions to make, Ottensteen quietly, bitterly, tells him, "I'll mail you a list." Such is Ottensteen's continuing ethnic commitment, expressed even more forcefully a short while later. Upon seeing Holly Levine's Volkswagen, Ottensteen refuses to ride in it: "Ottensteen is a simple person and an individual. He knows how to love, he knows how to hate. Thusly, when Sholem Asch [a major Yiddish writer] turns no good, he doesn't talk to Sholem Asch. And when the Germans kill six million of his people, he doesn't ride in [spits] German automobiles." It is one of the film's two references to the Holocaust, the other coming in a recitation Morroe delivers at the cemetery to the gathered gravestones. That the first mention of the Holocaust should come from Ottensteen is in keeping with his tragic mien.

Felix's dignity and mournfulness contrast with both Holly and Barnet, who represent Jewish participation in intellectual life and popular culture. Holly's introduction, unlike Morroe's and Felix's, is comic, the balding, overweight, would-be major figure on the New York intellectual circuit sits in front of his typewriter, in dread of the empty page. After much mindless fussing, he is determined to commit his latest review to posterity. Inspired, he writes, "Certainly, Prof. Gombitz' essays, gathered together for the first time, yield pleasure of a kind." He sits back and admiringly recites this bit of poetry to himself, until suddenly he is plunged into doubt and begins to agonize over the opening "certainly."

Barnet Weinstein is equally filled with doubts. In bed of a Sunday morning with his girlfriend, who is Jewish, Barnet tries to convince her to visit his mother. A brief argument ensues and then ends as Barnet snuggles up to her and murmurs lovingly, "Whose young liberal intellectual is it? . . . Who has the talent? Who has the promise? Who will write the definitive piece on Lawrence?" His girlfriend's "you, and you, and you" bring him back to manhood. Similarly unmanned when he learns that Holly might teach a course on popular culture, "From 'Little Nemo' to ''Lil Abner,'" Barnet challenges Holly to a game of comic-strip trivia. That Holly is equal to the challenge, and that Morroe seems quite as knowledgeable as his companions, shows the film's recognition of the peculiar Jewish fondness for the popular taken seriously, at least as a source of knowledge and pride. The men wield their knowledge as a weapon, just as Ottensteen's more serious memories of *Yiddishkeit* and the Holocaust momentarily shame his younger companions as they forget the occasion of their reunion: Braverman's funeral.

That the four friends miss Braverman's funeral service completely—and the audience learns little of Leslie himself except as conceived of by his friends—remains unimportant. Holly's comment that Leslie was "a secondary talent of the highest order" shows the ambivalence they continue to feel about themselves and others. Indeed, once Lumet establishes the four as character types, the film becomes literally a tour of the city, abandoning Manhattan for a ride through neighborhood Brooklyn: the immediate move out of the New Old Country of American Judaism and the continuing residence of ethnic New York. Through high-angles and long-shots, Holly's shiny red Volkswagen is shown navigating territory that is unfamiliar for the friends, who vainly search for the cemetery, as well as to movie-goers who live outside Manhattan. We clearly see a Spanish enclave, with its neighborhood bodega, and a Hasidic community, its distinctively dressed men going about their modern business.

An accident confronts them in the unlikely form of a black Jewish cab driver (Godfrey Cambridge), whose verbal facility, if not his intellectual pretensions, are a match for Braverman's wayward friends. Lumet characterizes the cabbie almost precisely as he appears in the novel, save for the extreme but not total deemphasis on the use of Yiddish (which itself characterizes the transformation from book to film) and the fact that he is black. A role written as "white," just like the character of Arnold Billings in *Power*, becomes more meaningful in the simple but significant casting of a black actor. Rarely referred to, but there to be seen, the ethnic transformation indicates Lumet's insistence on the recognition of ethnic pluralism at all levels, in all aspects of society, even in *Braverman*'s Jewish New York and *Power*'s WASP Washington.

Because the film is relatively plotless, its themes must be extracted from its characters—what they say, what they do, and who they are. In a sense, the major theme of the film becomes contemporary American-Jewish life itself. Some of the accommodations Jews make to get along in modern society are evident in the characters' problems, neuroses, ambivalences, fears, and hopes. Morroe, the main protagonist, stands most clearly for mainstream Jewish society, at least with his compromises; he abandons Greenwich Village, puts aside his own creative writing, and is insecure about what he does and, therefore, what he is. But Ottensteen's bitterness toward his son and Barnet and Holly's insecurities about their intellectual (and sexual) prowess have made the men lose some of their roots. Leslie Braverman thus functions as the man they each could (and should) have been, a braver man than they.

The most sustained glimpse of what Jewish culture has lost in accommodating contemporary mainstream society can be found in the nameless rabbi (Alan King) who delivers the eulogy at what the

The four friends meet a black Brooklyn Jewish cab driver in *Bye Bye Braverman.*

friends take to be Braverman's memorial service. The sermon, adapted closely from Markfield's novel (shortened, brought a little closer to colloquial speech, and updated slightly with current references), is a brilliant repudiation of the ordeal of civility, a complete rejection of WASPish behavioral models of stiff-upper-lip and emotional repression. "Bereaved family and friends," the rabbi intones at the start of his eulogy,

> we live in a time, a generation, a society when it's supposed to be not nice to bellyache over the pain and trouble of living. Feel, but don't cry, take punishment, but don't show. Keep everything nice, neat, under control. Keep everything inside. . . . Everybody is a James Bond. Life and death no one cares about like they used to. I remember once upon a time you celebrated a birth and mourned a death, and in between you recognized, clear and simple, you were growing older, you were aging and dying every minute. And when a man died no one was afraid to make a scene, no one was ashamed to grieve out loud. Nowadays they can't wait to bury and forget. Make it quick, Rabbi, simple and quick.

The rejection of the ordeal of civility recognizes the inevitable pain of life, not simply that one is dying every minute (Woody Allen, of course, is in total sympathy with this realization), but that life represents a series of compromises with the body and with God. The rabbi angrily denounces a universe in which every pleasure is greeted by an equal and opposite pain, a Jewish variation on Newton's Laws.

> The body is telling you every second how you have it too good. Did you look a little too long and with too much pleasure at the grandchildren? Take a few palpitations. Did the wife pick up a nice bedspread and covers for the couch? Let her have a low back pain. Did you get a particularly first-class haircut from the barber? Here, here's a cavity, or a little piece off the bridgework. Did you get a perfect fit in a cheap suit right off the rack? Pay for it with acid in the stomach and a trifle too much albumen and sugar in the blood. Did the father-in-law send a postcard from Miami and a box of mixed-fruits? Give him a stone in the kidney, a swelling in the prostate. Let us pray.

This part of the eulogy is taken almost word for word from the novel (147), with the exception of "let us pray." But this coda makes even more clear the theological complaint that the rabbi registers and brings his speech in line with Jewish humor, linking the mundane with the sacred. Further, the pleasures that the rabbi lists, along with the pains that inevitably accompany them, are specifically relevant to many Jews. Equally central to Lumet's understanding of the American-Jewish tradition is the rabbi's final complaint. He speaks of the deceased's inability simply to go along and not make waves, thus becoming something of a "special case. But if we have no room in this world for special cases, then whose fault is it?" Braverman's friends have lost a little of their specialness, and that is their tragedy, their fault. They should have been braver men. Lumet makes sure that his cinema, however, is filled with braver men, with special cases.

Bye Bye Braverman is remarkably faithful to Markfield's novel. Lumet's take on the life of Frank Serpico rings equally true. *Serpico* inaugurates Lumet's mature interest in exploring the contemporary scene, being the first film of a trilogy devoted to the New York City Police Department, with *Prince of the City* and *Q & A* comprising the second and third installments.[4] The films are related not simply by their focus on the NYPD, but because of their central concern with "dirty cops," who have broken the laws they are sworn to uphold. How do guilty cops and other officers respond to such guilt? The three films also recognize how the police department interacts with and affects other social institutions, especially the family. The films extend the notion of family as they overtly acknowledge how their policemen-protagonists conceive of their colleagues as members of a family. Indeed, *Prince of the City* is intimately concerned with exploring literal families that contrast to and are at odds with the police-as-family. Lumet also includes other law enforcement institutions, such as citizens' oversight groups and political committees. The police trilogy thus uses the department as a microcosm of all social institutions, demonstrating how one institution inevitably interacts with others, how institutions affect and constrain the actions of individual members, and how these members, in turn, affect the institution and the greater society.

Lumet goes beyond exposing mere police corruption; his concern has been with corruption in a variety of social institutions—television news, political elections, and governmental bureaucracy. He never highlights lone individuals who oppose corruption, never creates isolated heroes in the mainstream American literary and cinematic tradition. Rather, he examines the complex nature of such institutions, the moral ambiguities often attached to membership within an institution, and the failure of important institutions such as the media, police, and government to uphold their promise to society and the individual.

The police apparently fascinate Lumet beyond the failure of the justice system to serve the people, beyond the concept of guilt and the way it affects the family. As the premier instrument of physical authority, the police represent the State at its most potentially intrusive, corrupt, and violent. The State killed the family of Sol Nazerman in *The Pawnbroker*, of Daniel Isaacson in *Daniel*, and threatens the fabric of the family in *Running on Empty*—all among Lumet's most powerful films. That their protagonists are all Jewish surely seems no coincidence in terms of Lumet's deeply felt response to these dramas. As the Jewish director turns his concerns to the potential victimizers, it is also no coincidence that he produces equally powerful films.

Lumet intimately ties the corruption of the police department to racial prejudice, ethnic stereotyping, and favoritism (a connection made even stronger in *Q & A*). The department's corruption strikes at its very heart. Its material corruption and graft, all taken for granted, are outgrowths of its pervasive racism and prejudice. For example, Inspector Sidney Green (John Randolph), claims that the only way to succeed on the force is to possess "an uncircumscribed shamrock between your legs." Perhaps such discrimination eventually caused him to become part of Internal Affairs. Subtle pressure is also brought to bear on Serpico when his first precinct commander, Captain McClain (Biff McGuire), deals with his complaints by inviting him to Catholic officers' prayer meetings. Serpico must join the select religious enclave to be protected, yet at the same time his criticisms will be deflected. The corrupt Bronx police complain to Serpico about black and Hispanic criminals; unlike Italian gangsters, blacks and Hispanics must continually be intimidated to make payoffs.

The corruption of the police department, in terms of the prejudice and discrimination that infests it, appears most subtly in the attitudes that the police manifest toward civilians. The other officers, even Serpico's would-be mentor and coreligionist Captain McClain, finally ostracize him when they learn that he has taken his complaints outside the department. As they see it, he has betrayed them. It is evident that, in some profound sense, Serpico always remains an outsider. He has few friends on the force and, unlike the police in *Prince of the City*, spends virtually no time socializing with other officers. In this sense, Serpico rejects the image of the force-as-family, he also rejects aspects of his actual family. Although he socializes with them, he deflects their matchmaking attempts. His brother even chides him for moving out of the old neighborhood. Already apart from the police, Serpico's reaction to the force's corruption alienates him even more. The many-leveled corruption that infests the institution upon which he had pinned his dreams eventually destroys his career and family.

Frank Serpico cannot live with the guilt that surrounds him, that is with the sins of others. Danny Ciello (Treat Williams), the prince of the city in Lumet's 1981 fact-based film, finds that he cannot live with his own guilt and sins. In trying for expiation, Danny becomes a tragic figure in an epic drama of corruption and its devastating effects. Indeed, *Prince of the City* is a classical tragedy; an aristocratic hero (a prince, of sorts) is brought low by the sin of pride in thinking that he could do and have it all. The film even boasts something like a five-act structure. Five distinct sequences, each introduced by a subtitle, plunge the one-time prince of the city inexorably into a whirlwind of betrayal, self-doubt, and self-delusion. The tragedy that forms the basis of *Prince of the City* revolves around the pervasiveness of corruption and how difficult it is to be extricated from it. As in *Macbeth*, corruption taints all relationships, including friendship and marriage.

Typically for Lumet, there is an abundant Jewish presence in the urban-ethnic enclave of the New York City Police Department and legal world of New York and Washington. His filmic world remains constant, whether through a shot of a Hasidic Jew as part of a crowd of onlookers gawking at Bill Mayo's body, a handful of lawyers like Blomberg (a criminal), the prosecutors Kantor and Goldstein, or a cop whom an Italian mobster refers to as a "matzoh eater." Lumet's evident delight in the character of Gus Levy (Jerry Orbach) is unsurprising considering that the film was adapted from Robert Daley's book by Jay Presson Allen (writer of *Just Tell Me What You Want* two years before *Prince of the City*) and Lumet himself (his first credited screenplay). It is perhaps an in-joke that Gus does not simply go undercover in the garment industry (a very Jewish trade), but that the company for which he allegedly works profits for the first time through his efforts. But it is surely no joking matter when Gus refuses to come in and tell the federal agents anything. Being alienated from Gus hits Danny harder than any other occurrence in the film. It may be, as Special Investigative Unit partner Joe Marinaro (Richard Foranjy) claims, that "Gus is one tough Jew," but it may also be that doing the right thing in a corrupt world and sticking to moral principles in an amoral time is truly a tragedy as it threatens the bonds of family and friendship.

The multiethnic group that comprises Danny's unit in the SIU represents a tribute to the possibility of crossing ethnic boundaries in the contemporary urban world, a sign of New York's specialness.

The inability to cross such boundaries, however, underlines the tragedy of *Q & A*. The fictional story (adapted from a novel by an Hispanic judge) again boasts a script by Lumet himself.[5] This is the most personal of the three films because Lumet receives sole screenplay credit and also casts his daughter, Jenny Lumet, in the pivotal role of Nancy. The product of what is euphemistically called a "mixed marriage," Jenny Lumet's own multiracial background (she is the daughter of Lumet and Gail Buckley, an African American whose own family, the Hornes, is multiracial)[6] makes her an apt symbol for the promise of ethnic harmony. In the film, she is the daughter of an Hispanic mother and a black father, a patrimony that caused the breakup of her engagement to the Irish-American Aloysius (Al) Francis Reilly (Timothy Hutton). The relationship stands for the promise as well as the failure of ethnic harmony, of the continuation of racism, however subtly or overtly in contemporary life, and the possibility of its elimination.

The theme of police corruption again pervades the film, this time symbolized by police willingness to work outside the law and, more significantly, by the presence of racism at all levels of the department. Racism corrupts as much, if not more, than the temptation to profit from drugs, prostitution, bribery, and extortion that the police vainly attempt to resist. In the film, the highest levels of law enforcement are corrupt. At the start, Lieutenant Mike Brennan (Nick Nolte) cold-bloodedly murders a Puerto Rican and then plants a gun on him. Brennan's actions in this pre-credit sequence thus discredit him and what he has to say. When he is seen shortly thereafter regaling a group of officers with war stories from his early days, the audience knows that he is not a mythic, tough cop bravely fighting mobsters who have no respect for the law, but rather a foul-mouthed thug. The film continually villainizes Brennan, as he threatens Al and the two officers assigned to investigate the shooting. By the time Brennan's actions as a murderer are thoroughly explicated, the film long since condemns him as racist, misogynistic, and homophobic.

In *Q & A*, as in *Dog Day Afternoon* earlier, Lumet castigates society's marginalization of certain groups based upon their race, gender, or sexual preference. He explores the links between police activities against criminals and police harassment of subcultures and marginalized groups, for Brennan is not the only personified villain in *Q & A*. The film has even bigger fish to fry in the form of Kevin Quinn (Patrick O'Neal), chief of the Homicide Bureau of the Office of the District Attorney, County of New York, for whom Al works. It is clear from the first time that he is seen that Quinn is a villain. When Al introduces himself as Aloysius Francis Reilly, "but my friends call me Al," Quinn calls him Francis. Although viewers eventually learn that Quinn motivates Brennan's killings, undertaken to protect Quinn, a candidate for attorney general, from a murder he committed twenty-five years earlier, Quinn has been villainized by his own racism. In their first scene together, Al tells him that the people in Harlem have it tough, but Quinn castigates the younger lawyer, saying "if you want to be the house liberal, we'll transfer you back to Mr. Bloomenfeld's office" (which also implicates the Jew as a liberal). Quinn further insists that Al's father, a policeman, was "part of a tradition built by our people." Even when Al demonstrates his distaste for Quinn, the candidate-to-be asks Al to join his team. Quinn cannot conceive of anything having more value than ethnic ties, no matter how corrupted they have become or to what ends they have been put. When Bloomenfeld (Lee Richardson) later claims that Quinn is "a prick . . . a racist, and an anti-Semite and a prick" we believe him.

But if the villains are racists, even the good guys suffer from the taint of prejudice in *Q & A*. Chappy and Val (Charles S. Dutton and Luis Guzman), the black and Hispanic detectives investigating Brennan with Al, continually engage in racist banter. Although the remarks seem to be good-natured jibing, Lumet sees them as a continuation of harmful, dehumanizing stereotypes as the costs of racism, sexism, and homophobia become clear throughout the film. Even Bloomenfeld, the stalwart liberal, is infected, and exhibits self-hatred and anti-Semitism. Introducing Al to Preston Pearlstein (Fyvush Finkel), he says, "When Jesse Jackson used the word 'hymie' he meant him." When Bloomenfeld refuses to allow Al to expose Quinn because such a massive murder scheme reflects upon the department, we realize his level of corruption and see his anti-Semitic outburst as a clue to this sad state of affairs. When Al says he will take his story outside the department, Bloomenfeld threatens the removal of his father's pension, upon which Al's mother depends. Al's father, it seems, was also on the take, not in a big way but enough to have his detective rank revoked posthumously. Al's plaintive "you're breaking my heart, Bloomy" convinces viewers that institutional corruption, as was the case earlier in *Serpico* and *Prince of the City*, ruins friendships, families, and society. That it might even ruin the hero, that even the good-natured, solidly liberal, law-abiding Al might also be tainted is Lumet's most important hypothesis.

That Al may be racist, and thereby corrupt, causes the young man considerable agony, particularly at the film's end. He wonders why Brennan and Quinn thought that he would play along with their murderous coverup: "What made them think I was one of them?" It is not because Al is the son of a policeman and a former policeman himself, and not because Al shares their Irish-American background. Rather, Al wonders if it was because he, too, is a racist. Six years earlier Al had been shocked when he met Nancy's black father, causing her to break off their engagement. Was his reaction honest surprise or racist hatred? He told Nancy that he loved being in love with her, that their unlikely union—he the son of an Irish policeman from Queens, she the daughter of a Hispanic woman from the Bronx—held promise for the entire city, as well as for their own lives. Should one, unguarded moment ruin their lives? Did that moment reveal a racist tendency that infects him as well? Al solves this dilemma by choosing to fight the racism that surrounds him by fighting the racism within himself.

While Al agonizes over his own possible racism, Lumet challenges the audience with what is perhaps the most ethnically mixed cast of characters ever committed to celluloid. Italian mobsters interact with Puerto Rican drug dealers, who interact with black, Hispanic, Irish, and Jewish policemen, associations that eventually devolve into two characters of uniquely ethnic persuasions: Alfonso and Armand Segal, Cuban-Jewish killers. To an Italian mobster, this means "no hits on Saturdays"; to the Hispanic policeman, it means that they are "Cuban Hebes." The intriguing Segal brothers remain minor characters, however. Yet more challenging, Lumet focuses not only on ethnic others, but also sexual others through his glimpses of transvestism and homosexuality.

In Mike Brennan's murderous rampage he kills, among others, Jose Malpica and Roger Montalvo, notable less for their Hispanic background than for their homosexuality. In both instances, the powerful, overbearing Brennan uses the men's sexual preferences to tempt them. They go to him less out of attraction than of fear. Lumet further condemns Brennan for taunting them for their sexuality before brutally strangling them. The pathos that Lumet wrings from the murders, especially that of Malpica ("International Chrysis"), a transvestite, demonstrates his willingness to challenge audience attitudes about race, gender, and sexual preference. A short scene in a transvestite nightclub, another scene with a transvestite prostitute terrorized by Brennan, and Jose's character him/herself are all part of Lumet's intention of giving voice and vision to marginalized, repressed groups, a proclivity demonstrated earlier in *Dog Day Afternoon* and one of his primary sociopolitical concerns.

Although a middle-class audience's attitude toward these characters would perhaps not be as murderously homophobic as Brennan's, they would perhaps be uncomfortable enough to initiate the process of self-examination that Lumet wishes. Al, for example, faces the demons within himself at film's end. Before cleansing institutions that are corrupted by racism, sexism, and homophobia and beginning to restore the promise of society, Lumet feels that self-examination is necessary to erase personal racism, sexism, and homophobia. The personal is political; the political is personal.

The setting among gritty urban cops obviously appealed to Lumet, for in the summer of 1992 he released *A Stranger Among Us.* Perhaps only marginally related to the police trilogy, but obviously in keeping with Lumet's knowledge of New York and its Jewish communities, this film remains one of the very few American commercial works to focus on orthodox Jewry, specifically, Hasidism. (*The Chosen,* directed by Jeremy Paul Kagan in 1982, comes to mind as another exception.) In structure and tone, Lumet's film, from a screenplay by Robert Avrech (writer of the made-for-television "Scandal in a Small Town" [1988], which dealt with anti-Semitism in a public school) clearly recalls Peter Weir's *Witness* (1985). Indeed, industry wags quickly dubbed Lumet's film *Vitness*. Both focus on a policeperson, Harrison Ford in Weir's film, Melanie Griffith in Lumet's, who goes undercover in an isolated religious community. The cops become audience surrogates; their ignorance of the communities into which they (temporarily) try to fit allows the films to offer glimpses into the lives of these seemingly anachronistic, spiritually devout sects. In both, modern society, the outside world, is castigated for its hostility and emptiness; in both, the violence and greed of the greater society threaten the peace and stability of the bucolic, stable, and loving communal lives of these holy people.

The differences between the two films are instructive, however. The Australian Weir finds an objective correlative between the simple but holy state of his people and the pastoral beauty of the landscape they inhabit. But Jews, as indicated in our opening chapter, do not write pastorals; they create "urbanals." It is quite correct to say, as screenwriter Avrech did in the *Jerusalem Report* on August 13, 1992, that "the Amish have this bucolic, pastoral landscape . . . this sea of golden wheat, and they all look wonderful" (45). But we disagree with his contention that "the hasidim . . . in contrast, are seen within the framework of a horrible urban nightmare where nobody looks good." Instead, Lumet renders the brownstones of lower-middle-class Brooklyn and the neon canyons of midtown Manhattan's diamond district with a documentarylike accuracy. And if the blond, blue-eyed healthiness of the Amish in their wheat fields must be compared to the darker-haired, wan Jews in their book-lined homes and kosher kitchens, Lumet carefully imbues both characters and their interior settings with a healthy yellow glow bespeaking comfort and light.

Lumet uses one of his favorite technical devices to structure the film, cross-cutting for comparison and contrast. Used most extensively in *Daniel* to compare past and present, here it introduces and compares the life of Detective Emily Eden (Griffith) with that of the Hasidic Jews, represented by Ariel (Eric Thal), adopted son of the chief rabbi (Lumet regular Lee Richardson) of the (fictitious) Gencher sect. The film's opening scene, in fact, presents us first with the Hasidim: exterior shots of the Brooklyn landscape, followed by a shot of Ariel teaching in a *cheder* (religious school for boys). The initial words in the film are in Hebrew. Thus Lumet establishes the Jewish setting first, and only then gives us the central protagonist, Detective Eden, at work, as she and her partner (Jamey Sheridan) make an arrest at a nightclub. This pattern of cross-cutting between Emily and the Hasidic community continues until one of the Hasids is murdered while at work in the diamond district. Then Emily goes undercover among the Hasidim to investigate if one of the community members might be the murderer.

The image of the Jews that Lumet presents early in the film is a rather stereotypical one. The Jewish men are seen teaching at the *cheder,* praying in the synagogue, and studying Talmud in the evening—with Ariel also hard at work trying to solve the mysteries of the *kabbalah,* the book of Jewish mysticism. The women, alternately, inhabit mainly the kitchen, preparing sumptuous meals, or are seen in the dining room making the sabbath blessing. To be sure, Lumet depicts the specificity of Jewish orthodox life realistically, but his imagery feeds the stereotype of the Jewish man as intellectual and spiritual, not physical. As if to counteract this stereotyping, however, Lumet has Ariel save Emily at the end, somewhat improbably shooting a handgun (with which, needless to say, he has no prior experience) with great accuracy. Lumet, and the film, thus try to have it both ways. On the one hand, we see Emily's attraction to Ariel, how she prefers him to her partner. Ariel's spirituality and intellectuality attract her to him, in contrast to the cruder advances of her fellow detectives, including another, nonreligious Jewish detective, Levine (John Pankow). Lumet thus advances the values of religiosity, spirituality, intellectuality, and pacifism as more attractive than the rough-and-tumble world of police work. On the other hand, having advanced the ideal of intellectual and spiritual life as more appealing, more sexy, than the violence-prone physical world of the cops, the film insists that Ariel also be physically capable, that he participate in the violence that viewers of American cinema have come to define as true masculinity. Essentially an entertainment more in line with his lesser efforts, *A Stranger Among Us* still demonstrates Lumet's ongoing commitment to New York's ethnic enclaves and the value of the city's multicultural quality.

Lumet draws two of the three films of the NYPD trilogy from real-life characters and events, while *Stranger Among Us* is set in an ethnic Brooklyn neighborhood. The same is true of *Dog Day Afternoon*, which also stars Al Pacino. An almost-immediate follow-up to *Serpico* (it was preceded by an adaptation of Larry McMurtry's *Leaving Cheyenne*, entitled *Lovin' Molly* [1974], another of Lumet's attempts to deal with the South), *Dog Day Afternoon* represents not so much the flip side of Pacino's earlier role, but another story of alienation. Frank Serpico may be a policeman and Sonny Wortzik a crook, but they have much in common. Both are ethnic New Yorkers, part of a powerful subculture that makes great demands upon them and from which they deviate at some cost; they each try to break away from their ethnic backgrounds and from mainstream society. Both the police department in *Serpico* and the heterosexual norms of marriage and family in *Dog Day Afternoon* fail the quirky, nonconformist heroes.

Where Frank Serpico and Sonny Wortzik deviate, however, becomes the most challenging aspect of *Dog Day Afternoon*, for Sonny is not simply alienated—or even marginalized—from mainstream social institutions. He is positively on their outermost fringes. Sonny is not simply gay, and the film is not merely a positive portrait of an alternative life-style; rather, Sonny robs a bank to finance a sex-change operation for his male lover, Leon (Chris Sarandon). Lumet challenges his audience to continue to sympathize with this odd protagonist. The "special case" about which the rabbi spoke so eloquently in *Bye Bye Braverman* recurs here in a very dramatic way.

In a densely written essay that discusses the political readings possible in and around *Dog Day Afternoon*, Fredric Jameson makes a number of points which we may turn to our purpose to demonstrate links between Lumet's film and other works within the American-Jewish canon. He claims, for example, that the film "initially seems to inscribe itself . . . [within] the existential paradigm, in the non-technical sense of this term, using it in that middle-brow media acceptation in which in current American culture it has come to designate *Catch-22* or Mailer's novels. Existentialism here means neither Heidegger nor Sartre, but rather the anti-hero of the sad-sack, Saul Bellow type" (41). This antihero type, to which Jameson links Sonny, is apparent not only in Bellow's work, but also in Malamud's and Roth's (42–43). That each of these authors is Jewish, including Joseph Heller (the author of *Catch-22*) would be too mundane for Jameson to acknowledge.

What for Jameson becomes a critique of the film on this level—he calls this nontechnical existentialism part of a "regressive tradition" (41)—becomes the continuation of a tradition that allows the inarticulate and marginalized to be recognized. That *Dog Day Afternoon* represents Lumet's continuation of this tradition is accurately phrased by Jameson himself, who notes that "Sonny's story ceases to express the pathos of the isolated individual or the existential loner in much the same way that the raw material from which it is drawn—that of marginality or deviancy—has ceased to be thought of as anti-social and has rather become a new social category in its own right" (43). As John Murray Cuddihy speculated in *The Ordeal of Civility*, Marx, Freud, and Lévi-Strauss, as Jews alienated from the mainstream of society, turned their marginality into a new worldview. They eliminated the margins by redefining the center. So, too, Lumet, uses the materials of real life to challenge the concept of center versus margin by questioning both the concept of authority and who has the right to determine society's values.

Jameson also teases out some of the implications of the choice of locales in which the film's action is set, particularly "the ghettoized neighborhood with its decaying small businesses gradually being replaced by parking lots or chain stores." He then notes how the film establishes a relationship between Sonny and the people he holds hostage: "everyone in the [bank] is nothing but a salaried employee of an invisible multi-national empire, and then, as the film goes on, that the work in this already peripheral and decentered, fundamentally colonized, space is done by those doubly second-class and under-payable beings who are women, and whose structurally marginal situation is thus not without analogy to Sonny's own" (46).

The changing neighborhood recalls *Serpico*, Lumet's earlier sketch of the shifts in urban life, while the homology between criminal and victim extends to one between criminal and audience. The crowd that gathers around the robbery to watch the confrontation between Sonny in the bank and the police surrounding it roots for Sonny and chants "Attica! Attica!" It symbolizes the crowd watching the film (Jameson 43). The sympathies expressed for the real-life robbers, the subjects of the film, are matched by the sympathies of the filmmakers and of the audience.

This sympathy for Sonny extends beyond feeling sorry for an underdog and rooting for him, although surely no criminal in a serious crime film is more of an underdog than Sonny. Rather, Sonny's inevitable doom represents the nadir of individualism, the ultimate demythification of the power of the individual to defeat the forces of the State, and the recognition that the American mythos changed fundamentally after Vietnam and Watergate. The FBI agents who thwart Sonny and Sal's attempt to escape to the airport are as icily competent as Sonny and Sal (John Cazale) are nervously incompetent. From his politicized perspective, Jameson sees FBI agents as representing "the essential impersonality and post-individualistic structure of the power structure of our society." Jameson notes (48) that the film implicitly compares the FBI agent with the local police chief, Maretti (Charles Durning), whose powerlessness is symbolized by his "impotent rages and passionate incompetence" juxtaposed to "the cool and technocratic expertise of his rival," the FBI man.

> The FBI agent . . . comes to occupy the place of that immense and decentralized power network which marks the present multinational stage of monopoly capitalism. The very absence in his features becomes a sign and an expression of the presence/absence of corporate power in our daily lives, all-shaping and omnipotent and yet rarely accessible in figurable terms, that is to say, in the representable form of individual actors or agents. The FBI man is thus the structural opposite of the secretarial staff of the branch bank: the latter present in all their existential individuality, but inessential and utterly marginalized, the former so depersonalized as to be little more than a marker . . . of the place of ultimate power and control. (50)

What Jameson sees in Marxian terms, we see in American-Jewish terms. The origins of Lumet's political sentiments may be found in the historical situation of the Jewish people, subject in their past to exactly that immense and decentralized network of faceless, expressionless, depersonalized power that plagues the hapless Sonny. Many more such manifestations of State power appear in Lumet's cinema: the FBI again in both *Daniel* and *Running on Empty*, and the ultimate expression of depersonalized power and State terror, the Nazis in *The Pawnbroker*. Sonny is, essentially, a schlemiel—the schlemiel as tragic hero. Like the protagonists in many of Lumet's other films, his search for the American dream allows his victimization by a system that depersonalizes and marginalizes him. Sonny the schlemiel experiences his moment of glory, however, his fifteen minutes of Warholian fame come as he plays to the crowds that watch his hopeless standoff with the police.

Although the crowd in *Dog Day Afternoon* is omnipresent, Lumet carefully delineates another force that, seemingly on Sonny's side, is also part of his downfall: the news media, especially television. It is only fitting, therefore, that Lumet's next film would implicate this other system in the betrayal of the ideals of the American dream. It might seem that, in critiquing television, Lumet bites the hand that once fed him, but he holds nothing back in criticizing a system in which he was once a vital part. To aid him, he enlisted another television veteran, Paddy Chayefsky.

It was perhaps inevitable that Lumet and Chayefsky would eventually team, the only surprise was that it had not happened earlier than *Network* in 1976. After all, both New Yorkers are almost the same age (Chayefsky is a little less than eighteen months older than Lumet); both are Jewish; both served in the army during the war; both were connected to the theater in New York immediately after the war; and both were intimately involved in the golden age of television. Indeed, Chayefsky's name is almost synonymous with the period. He wrote episodes for the *Danger* series that inaugurated Lumet's directing television career. More significantly, both men are oriented to realistic dramas that situate characters in recognizable social settings. Even more important, neither man abandoned his Jewish background in his works. Chayefsky is notable for such modern classics of the Jewish theater as *The Tenth Man* and *Gideon*.

A major theme apparent in Chayefsky's impressive oeuvre could be characterized as how contemporary institutions, ranging from religion, to capitalism, to governmental bureaucracy, to the health-care system (seen in his Oscar-winning screenplay for *The Hospital*, 1971), have failed the individual.[7] Lumet, of course, shares the same concerns, as particularly evident in *Serpico* and *Dog Day After-*

noon. Network, a biting satire, provided familiar territory—television—to both men, both concerned about the country as it falls victim to the industry that nurtured them.

Network's verbal dexterity and much of its social satire emanate from Chayefsky; Lumet sympathetically transforms script to film. Yet what John Clum describes as Chayefsky's dominant motif remains as equally true of Lumet: "What Chayefsky clearly mourns in his work is the loss of spiritual values and, in its wake, the loss of love and compassion" (127). This sentiment aptly describes the underlying themes of Allen, Brooks, and Mazursky, as well as Lumet and also encapsulates a central problem in American-Jewish secular life. If Howard Beale (Peter Finch) can be seen as Chayefsky's spokesman, the mad prophet issuing jeremiads to a corrupt world, perhaps the protest is too extreme. When Beale exclaims to an enraptured audience, "First you've got to get mad. You've got to say 'I'm a human being, goddamnit, my life has value,'" he speaks not only for Chayefsky, but also for Lumet, who is often concerned with the dehumanization of people based on their race, ethnicity, or sexual preferences. But surely Beale's assertion that everything people know has been learned from television is an exaggeration, if not entirely too pessimistic a conclusion. Beale's extreme (and extremely depressing) remarks challenge the audience. It is Max Schumacher (William Holden), however, who is really the viewers' surrogate and the character through whom Chayefsky and Lumet speak.

Max is a veteran of that era of television news symbolized by the near-mythic image of Edward R. Murrow, who is invoked frequently in the film. Like Lumet and Chayefsky, Max Schumacher tries desperately to hold on to the values that inspired him early in his career. Faced with a younger generation, themselves raised on television, who see life in terms of ratings points and audience shares, Max becomes depressed. He also, however, seems bewitched by the programming dynamo Diana Christenson (Faye Dunaway). Eventually the couple will break up, not because Diana ruins Max's marriage (he alone did that), but because she remains incapable of giving and receiving true love. As Max observes, "she's television generation—she learned life from Bugs Bunny."[8] Diana's generation has been dehumanized by television and the way that everything in life is grist for the images and sound bites of television's mill.

As Howard Beale expresses it, "war, murder, death equals bottles of beer." The film's final sequence makes this brilliantly clear as

Lumet focuses on four television screens whose sound blends into one barely intelligible track, Howard Beale's death ironically juxtaposed to a commercial for Life cereal. Lumet is vague about what Max will do in such a world. Voice-over narration tells the audience that "this was the story of Howard Beale, the first known instance of a man who was killed because he had lousy ratings." But the real death, according to Chayefsky and Lumet, is an entire generation that has no idea how to live and, aided by the reductive nature of television, has lost the essential meaning of life in the pursuit of the almighty dollar. What to do about this is similarly left vague. What happens to Max is unknown; what will happen to society is more important.

Before directing *Just Tell Me What You Want*, a resolutely high-intensity film of a Jewish businessman's near-obsessive, albeit comic, love for a shiksa about half his age, Lumet returned to adapting theatrical originals as he had early in his career. Neither *Equus* (1977) nor *The Wiz* (1978) remain especially important films, but neither did Lumet entirely abandon his particular slant on the contemporary condition. *Equus,* for example, is concerned with memory. In this story of a middle-aged psychiatrist treating a disturbed adolescent boy who has horribly blinded some horses, Lumet recreates structurally a father-son relationship while exploring the nature of guilt.

Lumet lived in England for a time in the 1960s, and felt at home with the contemporary psychological English milieu that Peter Shaffer, a Jew who is British, wrote about. On the other hand, Lumet felt equally at home with the *The Wiz*, which features some of the most imaginative adaptations of New York locales since the glory days of the Astaire-Rogers films.[9] The stylized story of the black urban experience was familiar to Lumet not simply because of his own ethnic urban background, but because of his wife's and mother-in-law's. Lena Horne, mother of his then-wife Gail Buckley, has a prominent role in this black-cast version of *The Wizard of Oz*. Lumet was as comfortable in the pathos and poignancy of the film's ending, which glorifies family life, as he was in its earlier, expressionistically suggestive scenes of sweatshop labor, an environment all too well known to New York Jews in the world of our fathers on the Lower East Side.

Television, and show business in general, figures prominently in *Just Tell Me What You Want* (1979). The emptiness of a life devoted merely to material acquisitions, to ratings and profits, is also revealed in this comedy adapted by Jay Presson Allen from her own novel. The film's story line deals with show business, Jewish-shiksa relationships, and New York City. The urban perspective and attitudes of Max Herschel (Alan King) and Bones Burton (Ali MacGraw) are the characters' most immediately recognizable attributes. Indeed, even before the credits roll, the two are seen on a New York street, separately entering an expensive department store in midtown Manhattan. Each is clearly at home on these streets, which do not look particularly mean from the perspective of the jewelry counter at Bergdorf-Goodman. As the film develops, Max's attitude toward rural life becomes clear via numerous ironic comments. When he speaks of his wife (Dina Merrill), recovering in a sanitarium in Wisconsin, he sarcastically speaks of "all that dumb clean midwestern air" that will cure her alcoholism. At another point, trying to call Bones, he learns that she is spending the weekend in a rustic cabin in Vermont and cannot be reached by telephone. "In Vermont without a [telephone] number? That's ridiculous on the face of it!" He then insists that his secretary try every number in Vermont: "How many numbers could there be in Vermont!"

Max's perspective is more than simply urban; it is strictly New York. California, especially Southern California, comes in for substantial lambasting, as it does in Woody Allen's films. Mike Berger (Tony Roberts, who always betrays Allen when, in Allen's films, he moves to California), a character of somewhat ambiguous status, is given a line of great subtlety about the rivalry between the two coasts: "The hardest thing about California is getting over being ashamed of loving it." Here, the sentiment is taken with a grain of salt, but it is repeated frequently in other forms in the films of Allen and Mazursky; Woody Allen has a similar line in Mazursky's *Scenes from a Mall*. Even the suburbs of New York do not qualify as places for quality living. When Max thinks that he is being tricked by Mike Berger and his grandfather Seymour Berger (Keenan Wynn), who sell some holdings to an alleged corporation in New Jersey, Max promptly exclaims: "Who the hell lives in New Jersey? I'll tell you who lives in New Jersey! Cousins live in New Jersey!"

This dismissive urban perspective, which is typical of New York, becomes a Jewish perspective in Lumet's films. He humorously alludes to Max's and Seymour Berger's Jewishness in their first meeting, when they discuss health issues. In fact, Max is quite health-conscious, constantly riding an exercise bicycle and possessing more medical knowledge than the doctor he browbeats early in the film. Before getting down to business, Max and Seymour discuss the latest colon care theories and agree to disagree over the question of fiber. When Seymour asks for "a glass of tea," it is clear that he is from the Old Country (a fact made clear, in any case, by his heavy Eastern European accent). The world of business, in which both Max and Seymour are engaged, although not specifically Jewish, has, of course, become associated with Jews. When Max says to Bones "low overhead, high return: the first law of life," we are firmly on Jewish ground, although Mosaic or Talmudic wisdom has been replaced by business rules. Similarly, although the world of philanthropic donations is not specifically Jewish, when Seymour Berger asks Max to donate money for a Max Herschel Memorial Wing for Exotic Diseases, the reference is firmly Jewish.

The fact of Max's Jewishness is further demonstrated, indeed, made primary, by his frequent recourse to Yiddish. When he is admitted to the hospital he instructs his secretary how much she should tip to insure better service: "$20 for the Puerto Ricans; $50 for the *schwartzes*" [blacks—a term not necessarily derogatory but neither is it complimentary; he tells Stella to tip Jews even more]. In a quick explanation of how he talked Seymour into a risky business deal, he observes that "I couldn't move him without a little *schmeer*" [literally, spreading, as on a sandwich, but the implication of a bribe]. More richly revealing are two moments of intense anger, when Max bursts into Yiddish as a primal response. The first occurs when he learns that Seymour and Mike have sold off a valuable asset from a movie company Max is buying. In utter fury, he turns on Seymour and shouts: "*Goniff* [thief] . . . you *momser* [bastard] you!" The second outburst happens after he learns that Bones has married Steven Rutledge (Peter Weller), a young playwright. He first whines to his secretary, "Stella, I'm a dead Jew!" but then recovers and soon works himself into a lather with schemes of revenge. Threatening to entangle all of Bones's holdings legally, he declares, "and when she tries to sell her paintings: *gornisht* [nothing]!" When he is most upset, most hurt at his gut level, Max reverts to the *mama loshen* [mother tongue]; Yiddish reflects his most basic, true self.

The Jewishness of the milieu of *Just Tell Me What You Want* is further solidified by setting the film within show business, one of the few places where Yiddish words and phrases are still part of daily discourse. Although Max Herschel is an international industrialist, head of Herschel Industries, almost nothing is seen of his multifaceted holdings. Television and the movies comprise virtually all of the film's business background, yet Max's professed attitude appears distinctly against show business, and he directs numerous barbs at the movies. The remarks are in-jokes and result in a movie that makes fun of the movie business. Max proclaims, for example, that the movie industry is an idiot's business peopled by ding-a-lings and dreamers, and that "anybody who wants to make movies has no respect for money." It is both humorous and—for those who love the business—unfortunately true that Max intends to dump International Pictures and divest himself of all its holdings "except the negatives . . . the film library" when he acquires its parent company.

To this extremely Jewish milieu, Lumet and writer Jay Presson Allen, who together produced *Just Tell Me What You Want,* add the motif of a Jewish man's education of a shiksa. Max Herschel takes this quite literally through what he calls "Herschel's scholars," young women from the secretarial pool whom he takes under his wing, transforming the already pretty, wholesome midwestern women into sophisticated urbanites. He sends them to school, to orthodontists, and to fancy dress shops, turning them into visions of WASPish beauty and class. One such vision has gone sour on Max—his wife, Connie. First seen at a midwestern sanitarium, Connie returns to Max's palatial Long Island estate for their daughter's birthday party, tormenting him with her drinking and her disdain. At the dinner table, for example, she drops her expensive earrings and a diamond ring into wine glasses, as if to try and challenge her nouveau riche Jewish husband.

By the same token, the reeducation and transformation of Bones similarly backfires for Max. As the film begins, she attacks him, beating him with her purse and kicking him as he cowers in the face of her assault. Her voice-over prevents this scene from going further, instead leading into a flashback until the film comes full circle (a strategy Lumet also uses in *Serpico*). Bones's voice-over makes what is about to occur sound as if she were relating a fairytale, but clearly this is unlike anything in Hans Christian Anderson and more like the Brothers Grimm.

What began for Bones as a fantasylike existence of a poor Cinderella shiksa transformed by the Jewish prince (of the city) into a distaff version of himself evolves into a nightmare of recriminations and regrets that culminate in her attack on Max when he ties up her assets. The tragedy is that Bones has become too much like Max. They use the same (vulgar) expression when speaking about each other to Steven; each alleges that the other "doesn't know tit from tail about the movie business." When Bones confronts Max with the news of her wedding to Steven, she claims that "he is better than you . . . than us." Yet, as this is a comedy (with some admittedly dark overtones), Max and Bones do reconcile, and the film ends as they negotiate terms for their marriage. Max is too successful in transforming the shiksa; he makes her too cognizant of the weaknesses in other people and of the darker side of life.

It is this darker side of life that Lumet and Jay Presson Allen cannot entirely repress, a particularly Jewish response that suspects that the good times and the good life cannot last. This attitude is indicated humorously early in the film, with Max at home in his mansion, surrounded by domestic servants and company employees who await his every command. He walks over to an elegant silver server for a cup of coffee. When he discovers the coffee is cold, he exclaims, "I can't live like this! I can't live in this squalor!" Nothing is ever good enough; none of his success can overcome his feelings of inferiority. He whines like a baby when Bones leaves him and plots petty revenge, further revealing this aspect of his character.

A much darker vision of life subtly appears through the figure of Seymour Berger. As portrayed by Keenan Wynn, he is a man of great dignity and intelligence, but as the film progresses he sinks into ill-health and disillusionment. The beginnings of his decline are evident early in the film, when the aging Seymour, an Eastern European émigré movie mogul who has lost control of International Pictures, confides to Max that his grandson—Mikey—has been a great disappointment. Mike is homosexual and will never produce grandchildren. Although Max later laughs at Seymour's angst, his own relationship to his granddaughter shows him to be a typically doting grandpa, convinced that his progeny is the smartest little girl in the world.

Seymour eventually abandons New York for California, where he plans to speculate in real estate and enjoy a life-style that enables people to live forever. By the time Bones meets him at a Hollywood party late in the film, however, he is small and crippled in a wheelchair, now a widower. His wife died shortly after they moved to Los Angeles. The promise of California has certainly betrayed Seymour. His wife's death is a personal tragedy, and the death of his movie studio (and, by extension, the enormous changes within the movie industry since the glory days of the movie moguls) similarly constitute a tragedy in what had been a rags-to-riches success story. It is this injection of pathos, this recognition that life has a way of delivering a nasty surprise even to those who seem the most successful, that makes what is an otherwise amusing character sketch of the idle rich at work and play particularly Jewish.

Little is specifically Jewish in Lumet's two films of 1982: *Deathtrap* and *The Verdict*. The former, adapted from a hit play by Ira Levin, and the latter, adapted from a minor novel by the playwright David Mamet, represent Lumet's mere entertainments, although *The Verdict*, starring Paul Newman, was a smash hit. Aspects of these two diversions owe something to Lumet's vision of society and social justice. *Deathtrap* presents, for example, a sympathetic view of homosexuality, as apparent in *Dog Day Afternoon* and *Q & A; The Verdict* condemns the medical and the legal system for running roughshod and protecting their inner circles at the expense of those outside. *The Verdict,* moreover, represents a vision of one man's redemption, a down-and-out lawyer's escape from his past pressures and failures as he works to beat the odds and fight the system for his own sake as much as for his client's.

With *Garbo Talks* (1984), Lumet returns centrally and significantly to Jewish life in contemporary America. Like *Bye Bye Braverman* and *Just Tell Me What You Want, Garbo Talks* is another of Lumet's New York comedies, a film filled with the specifics of the city that so preoccupies him. The film focuses on Woody Allen's milieu, upper-class Manhattan, and revolves around a woman's attraction—indeed, her need—for movies, which give her a sense of meaning and transcendence. As in *Play It Again, Sam,* the protagonist identifies with the screen image of a movie star and, like Allen's film of a decade earlier, Lumet's film begins with his protagonist enthralled in front of a movie, mouthing the words from *Camille* (1932). Yet unlike *Play It Again, Sam* or, alternately, *The Purple Rose of Cairo,* the protagonist does not conjure up a filmic persona or have a movie character conjured up for her. Rather, a real movie star, one of such legendary proportions that she might as well be nothing more than an image on celluloid, becomes the protagonist's object of need and identification. The heroine's desire to meet Greta Garbo might be linked to the longing that the family has in *Radio Days,* to dine just once with the celebrities. Yet Lumet provides enough differences to make this film, although similar to Allen's, a variation on Allen's version of Jewish New York, show business, and the near-religious dimension of the movies.

One important difference is that although Lumet's image of the city shares much of the glamor and mystique of Allen's, it also represents a place of problems, which Allen typically ignores. An-

other difference is that Lumet's protagonist, Estelle (Anne Bancroft), is no wispy, dreamy, dreary housewife like Cecilia in *Cairo*,
nor does she spend her time cynically comparing her life to that of
her fantasy heroine's like the mother in *Radio Days*. Instead, she has
her own life. She is a fighter, a hard-as-nails, politically committed,
New York Jewish, left-wing intellectual; she is Allison Porchnik
from *Annie Hall*, grown older and with a sense of humor. Of
course, Lumet comically exaggerates her. Would a mother really
not cross a picket line to attend her own son's wedding? Not a
Jewish mother. Yet this comic tribute to the labor movement typifies how Lumet holds on to the political values of the Old Left, so
much a part of growing up Jewish in the 1930s.

Another critical difference between Lumet's understanding of
the place of popular culture in the lives of ordinary people and
Allen's vision of it is evident when Lumet delivers a rather sentimental conclusion. The notoriously reclusive movie star does indeed pay a visit to talk to the dying heroine. In a sense, Lumet
rewards his character's faith; her movie star redeems her life. Compare this to Gil Shepherd's betrayal of Cecilia in *The Purple Rose of
Cairo*. Allen's ambivalence about celebrity, his obsessive introspection about his own place within the constellation of stardom, never
permits his characters an unambiguous reward. Lumet allows his
heroine her moment of transcendence precisely because she has
been a genuine character, not one who gives meaning to her life
through entertainment. When her daughter-in-law exclaims that
Estelle's desire to meet Greta Garbo resembles a last wish, Estelle
testily retorts, "It's not my last wish. I have a lot more. I'm just short
on time." Lumet can reward his heroine because he feels unam-
biguously about the power of his entertainments, his art, to make a
difference.

If Lumet's art can make a difference, so, too, can his heroine's
life. As important as any other aspect of her existence, she is a
mother; she makes a difference, for the better, in her son's life.
While Cecilia, significantly, has no children, Estelle does. While Joe
in *Radio Days* becomes somebody despite his family, Estelle's son
Gilbert (Ron Silver) becomes an even better person during the
course of the film, not despite his mother but because of her. In
fact, Estelle becomes something like her idol, Garbo, when she redeems Gilbert's life just as Garbo lends a transcendent finish to
Estelle's. The film begins with its primary focus on Estelle and her
identification with Garbo. An animated sequence under the credits
traces the life of a woman. First she is a young girl playing with dolls

and watching movies, then she is a student protestor, a bride, and a mother. The transformations are all accompanied by stills from Garbo's films. Just as Garbo cut her career short at the height of her fame, so, too, Estelle's career as the protagonist of this film gets cut short by a brain tumor. The focus then shifts to Gilbert and his search for Greta Garbo to convince the actress to see his dying mother.

Through this quest for Garbo, a seemingly hopeless search that frustrates and humiliates him, Gilbert comes to understand how much his mother means to him and how much her life, her vision of its possibilities, saves his own. Gilbert starts the film as something of a schlemiel, a neo-Woody Allen whose marriage has deteriorated into loveless habituality. He inadvertently dips his tie into the morning coffee that he drinks alone while his wife (Carrie Fisher) sleeps in the nearby bed; he loses a taxicab on his way to work after a more aggressive commuter outmaneuvers him; he even loses his already small office at his dull accountancy job and must move to an even tinier cubicle without a window. By film's end this schlemiel is made whole precisely by sacrificing his false goals and attitudes and reaching a new understanding of himself as he undertakes the hopeless task of meeting Garbo.

Gilbert's quest for Garbo results in the further deterioration of his marriage and his further disillusionment with his job. It also involves him with another side to New York life—the eccentric, the dispossessed, the people who live in their memories, fantasies, and dreams. Gilbert meets not only the rich and protected, but also the poor and put-upon. He encounters an aging photographer who realizes that he has been a parasite on the lives of the famous; an old actress who cannot remember her lines but still shows class; and a quiet homosexual on his lonely way to Fire Island. These dreamers, like his mother, put Gilbert in touch with a vital part of himself, an essence dulled by his monotonous job and routine life. The impossibility of his mission reinforces how much life forces him to accommodate. More important, he sees a world in which people hold onto their dreams and illusions, maintaining both their hope and their integrity.

Gilbert's father, Walter (Steven Hill), long since divorced from Estelle, has not kept his integrity. He could no longer support Estelle's causes, no longer believe in the activism of their youth. While Estelle encourages unionizing among the hospital's nurses even though she is terminally ill, Walter remains with his new wife because she worships him. Lumet portrays another betrayer of true values, Lisa, Gilbert's wife, as a spoiled daddy's girl. Early in the film Estelle bitterly expresses dislike for Lisa, claiming that she spends her days playing tennis. Gil and Lisa part after she refuses to support his search for Garbo. When asked to help pay for one month's rent out of her trust fund, Lisa invokes her father's dictatorial assertion, "never touch the principal!" as virtually a biblical commandment. Leaving Gilbert and returning to her family in California, Lisa embodies all the negative stereotypes of the state that also are evident in Allen's and Mazursky's films.

After Gil's wife abandons him in a time of crisis, he begins a relationship with a beautiful blonde shiksa (Catherine Hicks) who supports his hopeless quest. Yet this is no stereotypical shiksa, but rather an eccentric who exercises on her office floor while Gil tries to talk facts and figures with her and who wishes to be an actress. Like Gil and Estelle, she sides with the dreamers rather than the planners. Lumet pointedly demonstrates that Jews and non-Jews alike can betray their social and familial duties and that both groups must keep the faith of solidarity, social activism, and romanticism.

Such is this Jewish mother's legacy. Instead of ruining her son's life by turning him into a sexual neurotic and keeping him an adolescent schlemiel in the tradition of Alexander Portnoy, she redeems and enriches her son's life. Gilbert discovers the link between familial love and social solidarity that enables him to take control of his life. This represents the film's most important insight; that Gilbert's quest succeeds is almost secondary. However, sacrificing his staid, middle-class life to fulfill his mother's dream enables Gilbert to succeed, giving rise to the statement that is the film's title. A famous advertisement for *Anna Christie* in 1930 exclaimed "Garbo Talks!" Yet Estelle monopolizes the conversation when she finally meets Garbo. Garbo does not talk until the very end of the film, when, upon meeting Gilbert in Central Park, she inquires, "How do you do, Gilbert." The fact that Garbo meets Gil's mother and speaks to him are miraculous. Estelle claims not to believe in miracles, yet she surely experiences one when Garbo visits her in the hospital. Gilbert's miracle is not so much that Garbo talks (to him), but that he finds a meaning in life. He finds significance in family, romance, and social responsibility.

Lumet demonstrates the link between family ties and social activism in *Garbo Talks*. He further explores this crucial connection, less comically but perhaps with equal subtlety, in *Running on Empty* (1988). Before making *Running on Empty*, a film about how politics

Garbo talks to Gil (Ron Silver) and Jane (Catherine Hicks).

intrudes on family life as much as family life should intrude on politics, he directed *Power* in 1986. A vastly underrated film at the time of its release, *Power* is worthy of more attention in light of the fact that sound bites and photo-ops comprise contemporary political campaigning. Like *Network*, *Power* focuses on the people behind the scenes of one of our most fundamental institutions: political campaigning and the democratic process.

It is possible to see both *Network* and *Power* as responses to the disappointments of the middle 1970s and into the 1980s as the promise of the 1960s faded under the weight of the "me generation" and the culture of greed that followed. As America turned to the Right politically, the 1960s itself came in for significant reconceptualizations. Blamed for everything from abortion rights, to drug addiction, to the perceived destruction of the family and family values, along with America's alleged decline as a world military and economic power, the 1960s became for America what the Jews symbolized for the Nazis when Hitler rose to power. This conservative rewriting of the decade was countered to some extent by a handful of American movies, most of them produced outside of mainstream sources. Led by John Sayles's literate, low-budget comedy *Return of the Secaucus Seven* (1979), other filmmakers took nostalgic, sympathetic, sometimes critical looks back at the turbulent times of Vietnam, the New Left, and hippies. Yet save for the character portrayed by Jeff Goldblum in Lawrence Kasdan's *The Big Chill* (1983), Jewish participation, even centrality, in New Left politics and countercultural life-styles is almost completely elided in this cycle of films (the exception being Paul Mazursky's films, especially *Willie and Phil*).

It was enough, perhaps, that some American filmmakers resisted revisionism and the temptation to scapegoat the decade's admitted excesses. But it was not enough for Lumet, for in films like *Daniel* and *Running on Empty* the 1960s remain a positive, idealistic attempt to resist America's drift toward materialism and dehumanization. In addition, Lumet attempts to bring the Jewish component of this millenarian generation firmly back into view.

Running on Empty specifically resists 1960s' revisionism precisely by its present-day setting and focus on a family, headed by a Jewish father, which maintains its values and beliefs but must act upon them in a different, dramatically constrained way. Mainstream reviews of the film (for example, those in *Time*, *Newsweek*, and *New York Magazine*) missed the manner in which Lumet and Naomi Foner, the screenwriter, insist that the values espoused in the 1960s still remain among many who participated in protests against the Vietnam War and in countercultural life-styles. This view runs deliberately counter to the myth espoused by the Right, that the hippies of yesteryear are the yuppies of today. By using the dramatic situation of a family forced to live underground, perpetually in hiding and forever changing identities to elude the FBI, *Running on Empty* shows how the values of the 1960s can, do, and should remain a constant in a changed and changing world.

As in *Garbo Talks*, a parent's values influence a son's choice in life. Here, however, Lumet adds his near-biblical conception of guilt, the injunction that the sins of the fathers are visited upon the sons. In this case, both of Danny's parents are guilty of a crime. As part of their activist protests against the Vietnam War, Annie (Christine Lahti) and Arthur (Judd Hirsch) Pope blew up a laboratory that manufactured napalm on their college campus. Unfortunately, a janitor at work in the building at the time was blinded in the blast. Wanted criminals since that tragic incident, the Popes became wandering Jews (only Arthur is Jewish, the name *Pope* seems an odd ruse to deny Jewishness or to inject irony), unable to find a permanent home. Yet within their constrained life-styles, the Popes work for local causes at home and at their typically blue-collar work sites. Although they must keep a low profile, their activism is characterized by such concerns as forming food coops or engaging in unionizing activities at their jobs. They hide from the FBI, but not from their responsibilities to family and community.

Their constrained life-style has, in a sense, turned their two sons into criminals. Danny (River Phoenix) and his younger brother Harry (Jonas Abry) have developed a sixth-sense about local police and the FBI. Indeed, the film begins as the brothers spot two field agents watching their house and alert their family that it is time to make a move. The boys cannot lead normal lives. Classmates must be kept at a distance and friendships must not deepen, for at any moment the family may move again and take on different looks, names, and lives.

The film's dramatic crisis arises when Danny's musical talents bring him to the attention of a sympathetic high school teacher, while his budding teenage sexuality brings him to the attention of the teacher's daughter, Lorna (Martha Plimpton). Danny's desire to attend Juilliard threatens the family with exposure. Worse for Lumet, it means that if Danny were, somehow, to go to college, he would essentially be separated from his family forever.

The centrality of the family to the Jewish experience—and the way in which the family transmits its values to its children—is an important part of Lumet's worldview. Thus the most deeply moving moments in *Running on Empty* come at points where Arthur and Annie recognize how their youthful idealism has tragically altered their lives. Arthur's pain when he recalls how he found out about his father's death, and his inability to see his ailing mother, forcefully illustrate the family's plight. The film's most affecting scene occurs when Annie must meet with her well-to-do father (Steven Hill) to ask if Danny can live with him while the boy attends music school. The recriminations exchanged for Annie's actions and her father's responses to them quickly become tearful acknowledgments of the pain of separation. Arthur's insistence that his family remain whole and stay together is admirable. His willingness to acknowledge that Danny must be permitted to live his own life, that Arthur's sin must not be passed on to Danny, and, therefore, that the family must be separated is Arthur's and Annie's tragedy. Lumet's strongest contention—that social activism and private life are linked inextricably—is demonstrated by the fact that the Popes maintain their values, which revolve specifically around the family.

The search for social justice, the tragedy of family separated by social forces, and the injunction to remember dominate *The Pawnbroker,* the first American film to confront the permanent scars of the Holocaust. Although earlier U.S. productions broached this subject, notably *The Diary of Anne Frank* (1959) and *Judgment at Nuremberg* (1960), the Holocaust always remained off-screen. For example, although Anne Frank perished in the Holocaust, the film ends with a ghostly freeze-frame of the still-together, still-alive family. *Judgment at Nuremberg* shows the Nazis being punished for the heinous crimes they committed before the film begins. *The Pawnbroker,* based on the novel by an American-Jewish author, Edward Lewis Wallant, presents the Holocaust directly, delivering harrowing scenes inside a concentration camp. These scenes, which occupy only about 10 percent of the film's running time, haunt the viewer. Although a number of subsequent films situated their entire running time within the death camps, few have the power to evoke the horrors, the utter dehumanization, of the camps as does *The Pawnbroker.*

Yet the fact that Lumet situated the bulk of the film outside the camps fueled a controversy. Many saw *The Pawnbroker* as part of a process Lawrence Langer contemptuously terms "the Americanization of the Holocaust." Judith Doneson agrees, observing that such films "utilize American symbols and language to convey an

American perception of the [European] Holocaust. . . . the Holocaust functions as a model, a paradigm, or a framework for understanding history. It is a metaphor that teaches a lesson" (Doneson 9). The lesson seems to be that "American society is responsible for the suffering of . . . blacks" just as the "good" Germans who did nothing during the war were responsible for the suffering of the Jews under the Nazis (Doneson 112). In essence, *The Pawnbroker* compares the situation of Jews under the Nazis to the situation of blacks and Hispanics in the contemporary ghetto. It also implicates the Jewish survivor, Nazerman (Rod Steiger), in the contemporary holocaust of racism, poverty, and victimization, which further fueled the fire of controversy.

Greater controversy surrounds the film now than when it was released. At the time, critics acclaimed its honest portrayal of the Holocaust; now, they condemn the fact that it yokes the Holocaust with contemporary issues. In 1965, *The Pawnbroker* was the only film of its time to portray the Holocaust; it was also almost the only film to depict urban racism. In its wake Hollywood produced numerous films about the Holocaust, although relatively fewer about racism. Thus, Lumet still remains a pioneer in bringing painful social issues before the movie-going public weaned on escapist entertainment in a society subject to a political process that favors symbols over substance.

Although adapted from a novel, *The Pawnbroker* stands as an archetypal Lumet film and, for that matter, an archetypal film of the Jewish experience in America.[10] Sam Girgus has discussed American-Jewish writers, many of whom strike what he calls a "new covenant" with America. "With the context of the rhetoric and ideology of America as the symbol of redemption, renewal, and revolution, the most influential Jewish writers of the past century constructed a narrative structure for the myth of America composed of symbols and metaphors relevant to the conditions of the modern American experience. . . . The hero of the piece is often Jewish and as such stands for an aspect of the modern condition, modern consciousness, or the modern sensibility" (17). The fact that this applies to *The Pawnbroker,* that the Holocaust becomes symbolic of the condition of modern America and that Holocaust survivor Sol Nazerman embodies an aspect of the modern condition, make the film controversial as well as uniquely Jewish American.

If Lumet and Wallant turn Nazerman into a symbol of the modern consciousness, a modern everyman, they do so without removing his Jewish specificity; more important, they do not remove the

Jewish specificity of the Holocaust. They neither universalize the Holocaust nor ever recall that Hitler's death machine destroyed other victims besides Jews. Sol's Jewishness remains central to the narrative. Lumet even incorporates the reality of contemporary anti-Semitism, bigotry that Hollywood had ignored almost totally since the late 1940s. Sol Nazerman might be a survivor only in the narrowest sense of that term, might indeed possess little that defines him as a feeling being. However the reason for his death-in-life is clearly, convincingly, and unabashedly presented in the most specific terms. He is a victimized man, one virtually destroyed solely because he is Jewish.

Like many of Lumet's protagonists, Sol Nazerman finds himself compelled by both social and personal history to remember, plagued by what Frank Cunningham eloquently calls "the insistence of memory" (39). Although the events of the Holocaust were essentially European, America's Jews account it (along with the establishment of Israel) as the fundamental, defining contemporary experience. As a survivor of the ineffable, Nazerman's compulsion to remember remains understandable, but no more or less so than the dysfunctional family members of *Long Day's Journey into Night,* the parents tormented by the memory of their son's death in *Murder on the Orient Express,* or the torment of the disturbed young man who maims the horses of *Equus.* Even the more mundane memories of the ambivalent comic heroes of *Bye Bye Braverman* are no less compelling than Nazerman's. Yet if Nazerman loses sight of the meaning of life, the need to fight for family ties and social justice, Lumet never does. The Holocaust thus becomes an event of uniquely tragic dimensions for Jews, as well as an opportunity to speak to the contemporary American condition.

Sol Nazerman is literally tormented by his memories of not only the death camps, but also the loss of his entire family and his friends. The film opens on the anniversary of his wife's death; throughout the days that pass within the film, Nazerman refuses to remove this calendar page. This memory, this remembrance, not only torments the shell-shocked survivor, but specific incidents of the Holocaust also intrude unbidden upon him. Lumet foregrounds memory from the start of the film, which opens with a scene that can only be understood retrospectively as a flashback, the ultimate significance and ultimate outcome of which is only gradually revealed. Viewers understand eventually that the film is structured by a series of flashbacks inspired by present-day occurrences, an important difference between the movie and its source novel. Gabriel Miller expresses this variation nicely: "Whereas in the novel the flashback memories come to him in his dreams, not triggered by any specific current incidents, in the film Sol's past recurs to him in his waking state, prompted by occurrences that remind him of related or similar happenings in the past" (185–86). That Lumet compares present-day happenings to events during the Holocaust becomes undeniable, yet this technique never denies their historical specificity or effects upon Nazerman.

Lumet inaugurates this strategy of present-day occurrences bringing forth horrific memories via flash cuts; in each instance almost subliminal edits reflect the impingement of memory upon Nazerman. The film's editor, Ralph Rosenblum, has noted the influence of Alan Resnais's *Hiroshima, Mon Amour* (1959) on the project. Graphic matches of events from the past, which begin with edits of four frames, replace a similar event in the present. Viewers are meant to understand the graphic matches as thematic matches, but that in no way diminishes their power.

A school-yard fence visually, and a barking dog aurally, inspire the first graphic match. From an event in Harlem, as a young boy tries desperately to climb a fence, only to be dragged down and beaten, Nazerman recalls a man trying to climb the barbed wire of a concentration camp fence, also to be dragged down and killed by a German shepherd as camp guards watch. As the opening moments of the film (which retrospectively compares a quiet summer's day in the present with a quiet picnic in the past ultimately shattered by motorcycle-riding Nazis), Lumet reveals the full significance of the fence scene only later. At the moment, the audience is horrified by the death of the Jewish prisoner and by Nazerman's sense of shocked helplessness. Later, the audience learns that the man was his best friend, Herman Rubin, whose wife is now his lover.

The sight of a pregnant young woman pitifully trying to pawn a ring she mistakenly thinks is diamond inspires a second matched edit between past and present. As she fretfully and frighteningly removes the ring from her finger, Nazerman's memory compels him to recall another young woman's ring callously removed by Nazi guards. The camera impassively, thus making the scene more powerful, pans across hands strung over barbed wire as Nazis remove rings from quivering fingers. A third matched cut occurs in the pawnshop as Jesus's girlfriend Mabel (Jamie Sanchez, Thelma Oliver) offers sex for sale to Nazerman in order to prevent her boyfriend from participating in the planned robbery of the pawnshop. The sight of this attractive woman degrading herself brings unbidden memories of his wife's sexual humiliation by the Nazis. As Mabel implores Nazerman to look at her bared chest, a Nazi guard more viciously commands Nazerman to look at Ruth, Nazerman's wife, similarly exposed as a Nazi soldier prepares to force himself on her.

Scenes in Harlem or in the pawnshop itself dominate the associative editing, but a sequence in the New York City subway gives rise to another shocking scene. As Nazerman retreats from his emotionally devastating meeting with Marilyn Birchfield, a sympathetic if somewhat naive social worker (Geraldine Fitzgerald), he heads for the anonymity of the underground trains only to be reminded of the cattle car that transported his family to the death camps. Rosenblum notes that Lumet packed the freight car so tightly with extras that the scene could only be filmed from above (161), an effective strategy that creates empathy with the debilitated Jews who stand shoulder to shoulder with no room to move or, it seems, breathe. Sol's son, David, slips from his father's shoulders, and Sol is powerless to reach down and retrieve the boy. Rosenblum claims that "Lumet tried to give the impression that the child was trampled to death" (162). Whatever its cause, however, the death is another instance in which Sol can do nothing to save his family, as was the case with Rubin on the barbed wire or Ruth's degradation and eventual, unseen death.[11]

Nazerman's death camp experiences leave him literally dehumanized, an unfeeling shell of a man. Bitterness and cynicism become his only genuine responses, as he completely cuts himself off from the warmth of human feeling and contact. As introduced in the first present-day section, Nazerman sits "lifelessly on a lounge chair" in a geometrically fenced-in yard (Cunningham, "Insistence of Memory" 40), already cut off from his surroundings by suburban row houses of a crushing sameness. Further, as seen in a longshot, the fences between the houses function as a reminder, again retrospectively, of the fences in the concentration camp. Viewers then experience Nazerman's almost palpable disgust with his inlaws, whom he lives with and supports.

In the only scene in which the in-laws appear, Nazerman's sister-in-law chatters mindlessly, and is grossly insensitive, about taking a trip to Germany, while his niece and nephew torment and tease each other. Gabriel Miller notes that "the bright, harsh sunlight of the suburban scene, contrasting sharply with the hazy lighting of the pastoral memory sequence that preceded it, heightens the effect of oppressive vulgarity created by their banal, selfish chattering" (182). This reading is a bit extreme. The in-laws are more normal, more typically middle-class American, than anything else. Lumet's point is to emphasize the monumental gap between Nazerman's experiences under the Nazis and the safety and ordinariness of life in the American suburbs. However, as Miller points out, the family is never seen again. "This opening scene . . . seems rather pointless here . . . since neither its characters nor its satiric flavor is to be encountered again in the film . . . it remains unclear why [the filmmakers] have bothered to introduce the family at all" (182–83). The family is a legacy from the novel; Nazerman demonstrates some fatherly feelings for his nephew, Morton, in the novel. His lack of such feelings for Morton in the film is thus notable, emphasizing his complete alienation from his family.

If he is alienated from his American family, the substitute family that Lumet proposes cannot replace them. The fatherly relationship with Morton is structurally replaced by Nazerman's relationship with his assistant, Jesus Ortiz, but it is only Jesus who desires a relationship, only Jesus who looks to Nazerman as his mentor and teacher. Nazerman feels no more or less for Jesus than for his own family. Similarly, his feelings about his wretched customers, who come to pawn their paltry belongings, verge on the disgraceful. He thinks about these people as the Nazis thought about Jews and refuses to engage in conversation with a heartbreakingly lonely would-be intellectual, or even pass some pleasantries with the energetic, optimistic Mrs. Harmon, obviously a regular customer pawning the remnants of a sad life. Yet Nazerman's motives are not strictly racist; he treats white customers (the woman with her wedding ring, a man with an oratory award) with as little compassion and respect as those who are black or Puerto Rican.

Alienated from his American family, and from the people with whom he interacts on the job, Nazerman similarly displays no emotional commitment to his mistress, Tessie. Indeed, her father, Mendel, berates Nazerman for his lack of feelings, angrily condemning the pawnbroker for his hypocrisy and refusal to face the past. Survivors like Tessie and her father maintain more humanity than does Sol, despite having survived their own horrors (it was Tessie's husband who was killed on the barbed wire). Nazerman simply closes the door on Mendel (Baruch Lumet, Sidney's father), responding to him as he responds to his feelings.[12] His mechanical love-making to Tessie contains no passion and no joy. Later, when her father dies, Tessie calls Nazerman, hysterical and confused. He simply tells her to bury the man, as Nazerman buries his own humanity beneath the crushing weight of his past.

Lumet matches this strategy of juxtaposing Nazerman's alienated present with his nightmarish past with another strategy of juxtaposition: he compares Nazerman's life to that of Jesus Ortiz. This choice further explains the elimination of Nazerman's individual family life in favor of an alternative one marked by optimism, energy, and love. To Nazerman's initial alienation from his American family, Lumet juxtaposes Jesus and his mother. Although they live in a tenement slum (Jesus bathes in the kitchen), Jesus and his mother engage in good-natured bantering. Jesus's faith in the future, in America, is indexed by his insistence that his Spanish-speaking mother use English. That Jesus has no father only makes his hope that Nazerman will be his mentor and teacher all the more pathetic and moving—and ultimately more futile and disappointing.

Lumet juxtaposes Nazerman's passionless relationship to Tessie to Jesus's love-making with Mabel. During their love-making Jesus speaks glowingly of his future as a businessman, his hopes and expectations that Nazerman will teach him how to make money, so that he may reject the petty crimes of his past and redeem Mabel from her life of prostitution. Mabel, although a prostitute, sees her actions as temporary, a means of helping her lover and thus not degrading. Mabel's offer of sex for money motivates Nazerman's unwelcome memory of his wife's forced labors. Significantly, the two scenes featuring Mabel occur soon after scenes that feature Tessie. In the first, she and Nazerman engage in joyless sex; in the second, she calls Nazerman about her father's death immediately after Nazerman has thought of his wife.

Jesus's desire to learn from Nazerman, and Nazerman's rejection of him—Jesus's life-affirming actions and Nazerman's death-in-life—seem to condemn the older man in the audience's eyes. Only his tormented past can explain, if not totally justify, his coldness and cruelty. For all the positive attributions of Jesus and the negative characteristics of Nazerman in the present, however, the film also carefully delineates Jesus's profound ignorance of historical Jewish tragedies, particularly the Holocaust. Jesus asks about the numbers tattooed on Nazerman's arm—if this is some sort of secret society. He has no idea of the horrors of Nazerman's past; even the tattoos that denote the Holocaust make no impression on him.

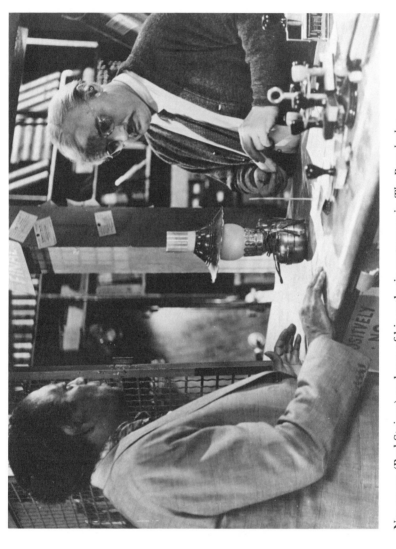

Nazerman (Rod Steiger) and one of his pathetic customers in *The Pawnbroker*.

Jesus also displays an innocent, culturally sanctioned anti-Semitism. At one point he asks Nazerman, "How come you people are so good at business?" It takes a moment for Nazerman to realize that the anti-Semitism that plagued his youth has recurred to confront him in the present. For once, however, he explains things, and some of the power and passion he obviously used to possess as a professor returns as he bitterly but eloquently lectures the Puerto Rican youth on the history of the Jewish experience in Europe, a history that forced Jews into mercantile and monetary pursuits when they were not permitted to own land:

> You want to learn the secret of our success, is that right? . . . First of all, you start off with a period of several thousand years during which you have nothing to sustain you but a great bearded legend. No, my friend, you have no land to call your own, grow food on, or to hunt. You're never in one place long enough to have a geography or an army or a land myth. All you have is a little brain, a little brain and a great bearded legend to sustain you and convince you that you are [pause] special, even in poverty. [Nazerman describes developing an obsession with monetary profit at the expense of desiring to own land, or even to see a child happy with a toy.] Suddenly, you make a grand discovery: you have a mercantile heritage. You are a merchant—you're known as usurer, a man with secret resources, a witch, a pawnbroker, a sheenie, a mockie, and a kike!

Nazerman's explanation of what he calls the Jewish mercantile heritage eliminates the other heritage of European Jewry—the intellectual heritage. Yet Nazerman was not a businessman before the Holocaust, but a professor, thus recalling and redressing the image of the Jew as moneylender and pawnbroker.

For all this supposed mercantile heritage, Nazerman is not especially good at business; he is not, in fact, even the owner of the pawnshop. Actually controlled by Rodriguez (Brock Peters), a Harlem gangster, the pawnshop operates as a front for Rodriguez's other, more profitable although unsavory and illegal, businesses, including prostitution. When Mabel reveals to Nazerman that she works for Rodriguez, he is inspired to take his only positive action thus far: he confronts Rodriguez and refuses to be complicit in the gangster's activities. The confrontation scene, constructed via the same use of flash cuts that indicate Holocaust flashbacks, clearly symbolizes Nazerman's continuing victimization. However, he must confront the fact that he is no longer a bystander, but an active participant in a new kind of Holocaust.

The Pawnbroker undeniably makes comparisons between the situations of Jews under the Nazis and people of color in contemporary America. The question becomes whether these situations are merely different, or are they differing. One standard by which critics judge the film revolves around the question of the Jewish specificity of the Holocaust and the unique magnitude of the event. Earlier Holocaust films such as *The Diary of Anne Frank* and *Judgment at Nuremberg* both succumbed to the universalization of the Holocaust, the Jew either representing all humanity or their extermination greatly deemphasized. *The Pawnbroker* remains open to the charge of the relativization of the Holocaust, the Jewish Holocaust becomes one among many, for example, those caused by Hiroshima, Cambodia, and Stalinism. Dorothy Seidman Bilik has criticized Wallant for equating the Holocaust with the contemporary ghetto: "If Wallant is using scenes of lacerating horror to point to the continuing presence of evil in the world, he is overstating his case. If he is drawing parallels, the extremity of the Nazi scenes undermines the similarities" (93). Alan Berger seconds this critique, claiming that "the American-born Wallant misreads and domesticates the Holocaust. He suggests that the Harlem ghetto, suburban New York, and the death camps are all points on the continuum of human misery. Overcoming this misery may be accomplished only through community with those people—Jews, Christian, black, whites—who care about others" (166–67).

Although the film indeed relativizes the Holocaust, Lumet also recognizes that the Holocaust is essentially unchangeable; tragically, it happened and its outcome may not be changed. The situation in urban ghettos, however, is eminently changeable, if only people would take notice. The horrors of the ghetto may pale by comparison to the horrors of the Holocaust, but they are horrors nonetheless. Good Germans stood by while Nazis brutalized and murdered Jews, but are not the urban poor, blacks and Hispanics, brutalized and murdered while society at large remains aloof? If it is too late to save the Jews, we can at least rectify the horrors in our own backyard. Who better than Jews to understand the horrors of contemporary society?

The other, perhaps more serious, charge leveled against the film is that the Jewish survivor becomes much like a Nazi himself—Nazerman, the Nazi man. The victim becomes the victimizer. In the current climate of oppression, the film singles out the Jewish survivor as being more guilty than others. It is apparent that Nazerman suffers almost unbearably as the memories of the Holocaust torment him. Yet it is still shocking when he derides his customers in language similar to the Nazis' description of the Jews. As a pawn-broker, he is that most visible symbol of oppression and greed. Yet surely Lumet understood such symbology. Surely he was aware that his Jewish hero has become a victimizer roughly comparable to the people who turned him into an ultimate victim. The tragedy of Nazerman is twofold: survive the Nazis a hollow shell of a man and to permit, even become complicit in, another oppressive situation. If Lumet singles out the Jew, it is because the Jew should know more; Nazerman is no worse than the rest of the "good Germans." Yet as a Jew, he should be better, he should not let it happen here. As Annette Insdorf observes, "Nazerman is not the only passerby who simply walks past the group of kids beating up a black boy" (*Indelible* 27). Lumet's point can only be that Jews have a special bur-den to bear witness to history, to remember, and to learn from it.

Along with the charges of relativizing the Holocaust and making the Jew a victimizer comes the charge of anti-Judaism. Judith Doneson, among others, finds an aspect of *The Pawnbroker* in which "Judaism . . . is indicted for its failure to provide spiritual suste-nance. Indeed, can it be coincidence that the name of the Puerto Rican assistant is Jesus? Judaism, it is intimated, lacks that essential ingredient of 'love thy neighbor' found in Christianity" (112). Ilan Avisar mounts an even more persistent attack on the film, finding it an "extreme example of Jewish self-hatred" and sees its basic prem-ise as a "bogus analogy between the horrors of the Holocaust and living conditions in Spanish Harlem" (122, 124). Avisar, who is of-fended by much else in the film, claims that it presents an essen-tially Christian vision. "Nazerman, because of his traumatic experi-ence at the hands of the Nazis, almost understandably behaves like one of his former tormenters: his name suggests that he is a kind of Nazi-made man. But at the end of the film, he is redeemed and is thus qualified to be looked at as the man of Nazareth" (125). Avisar sees the film as anti-Judaic, noting that it has been praised by a Christian theologian, as if such praise condemns Lumet's efforts.[13] Berger, too, takes up this charge of Christianizing Nazerman, not-ing, "Nazerman, whose name may be read as Nazarene, becomes fully human . . . only by becoming a kind of Jewish-Christian ev-eryman" (167).

The final image of Nazerman impaling his hand on the pawn-shop's receipt spike certainly leads critics to note the act's Christ-like implications and thus condemn the film for turning the Jewish survivor into a Christian, for allowing the symbolically named Jesus to be Nazerman's savior, and for transforming Nazerman into a

Christ-like figure. The symbolism is impossible to miss, and perhaps unfortunate as such. But it also functions as a symbol very much within the world of this film, a symbol primarily of Nazerman's return to feeling. He screams in agony as the sharp point pierces his flesh, a scream in excess, of course, of the pain he suffers. Yet Lumet does not choose this sharp spike arbitrarily, nor does he select it for its connotations. Rather, the spike is precisely what Nazerman has used to dismiss his clients derisively. They pour their hearts out to him—the old man who wants some intellectual conversation, the young woman who sells her wedding band, the drug-addicted anti-Semite—while Nazerman impassively impales their pawn tickets on the spike, killing their dreams as the Nazis killed his reality.

"I survived. I survived and they didn't." Such is Sol Nazerman's plaintive cry. So, too, the same might be said of Daniel, the eponymous hero of Lumet's 1983 film about the Jewish Old Left. Both Daniel and Nazerman, traumatized by past events, remain plagued by their memory of them. Virtually all of their families were destroyed in the past; they do not now feel much of anything, either inadvertently cruel or deliberately cut off from their present circumstances. As Stephen Farber notes of Daniel and Nazerman, "both characters have resolved to make themselves invulnerable to pain" (32). Tormented by the past and struggling to come to terms with it, Nazerman and Daniel are linked to other Lumet protagonists, but they also have a common bond. Their past tragedies have much to do with the fact that Nazerman and Daniel are Jewish.

The anti-Semitic madness of the Holocaust destroyed Nazerman's family; the anti-Semitic madness of the cold war and McCarthyism kills Daniel's parents. A State apparatus run wild, the bureaucratic killing machine of the concentration camps, murdered Nazerman's family. Daniel's parents, similarly put to death by the State (they are murdered with due process in the electric chair) die by a legal system corrupted, like the German Reich, by ideology and prejudice. Similarity of present circumstances due to similar past trauma not only links Daniel with Nazerman, but also leads one to wonder if Lumet consciously wishes to compare the Holocaust with McCarthyism, as he earlier compared the Holocaust to the ghetto. In *Daniel,* which spans the eras immediately before and after the war and features a character who served in the army during the war (Daniel's father, Paul), the Holocaust is conspicuous by its absence. It is referred to only in passing, by implication really, early in the film. Perhaps Lumet wished, thereby, to avoid both the direct comparison to the Holocaust (comparisons that would trivialize both events), yet remind his audience of America's own shameful bout with murderous anti-Semitism.

If the anticommunist fervor of the postwar era, which ultimately included anti-Semitism, cannot compare to the Holocaust, the events as they affect Daniel and the entire Isaacson family (based on the Rosenbergs) are tragic and traumatic nonetheless. If the anti-Semitism of members of the House Un-American Activities Committee (HUAC) was hardly as murderous as the hierarchy of the Nazi party, anti-Semitism nevertheless infested America and virtually destroyed the lives of many who survived the era. Ultimately *Daniel* and *The Pawnbroker* share a vision of how the past, despite its horrific traumas and guilt, must be overcome. In the earlier film, Nazerman's revelation is a painful and heartrending one, and we are uncertain what will happen next. In *Daniel,* the title character finds his revelation, his redemption, within the course of the film through confronting the past and coming to terms with the present. Indeed, the present allows him to accommodate the past. Life goes on, and people are either slaves to the past, innocent victims but victims nonetheless, or they are able to live meaningful lives, not despite the past but because of it.

The meaningful life that Daniel discovers continues the political activism of the past into the present. Because the film is set in the late 1960s, it delivers two past tenses for the present-day audience, a double dose of history. Like many of Lumet's films, *Daniel* is based on a novel, in this case, *The Book of Daniel* by E. L. Doctorow (1971). The novel's present coincides with the activist era of the 1960s. It would, of course, have been impossible to update the film's present to the 1980s and still retain the respective ages of Daniel and his sister, Susan, when their parents were executed in 1953. By choosing to adapt Doctorow's novel and retain its timeframes, Lumet structures the film so that it revives two levels of past politics. He offers two history lessons, both of which reclaim not only an American political legacy but also an American-Jewish political legacy.

Lumet's film strategy in *Daniel* functions quite similarly to the one he used in *The Pawnbroker.* The earlier film linked past and present by juxtaposing similar events. *Daniel* also cuts between past and present, as Danny Isaacson (Timothy Hutton) confronts the horrors of the past and the pain of the present. The primary point of comparison becomes the politics of the Old Left and the New Left, but Lumet saves that comparison—the conclusion that they are linked—for the ending. Another comparison is the way in which the State, which destroyed Rochelle and Paul Isaacson, threatens to do the same to their children, Danny and Susan (Amanda Plummer). Lumet juxtaposes Susan's stay in a psychiatric institution and Danny's visits to her there with the uncomfortable visits the children made to prison, where their parents awaited execution. Just as Paul and Rochelle will never leave prison alive, so, too, Susan's only escape from her institution is through her death. The most telling comparison comes through crosscutting between the respective funerals held for these victims of society: Paul and Rochelle are buried with a huge public funeral that acclaims them martyrs. Poor Susan is buried with only Daniel and their adoptive parents holding lonely vigil. As much of a martyr to a doomed cause as her parents, as much of a victim of discrimination and mass madness, she is a forgotten figure, abandoned by the people who once supported her parents. It is precisely this forgetting, this cultural amnesia, that Lumet seeks to redress.

The absence Lumet wants to redress, the presence he insists his audience recall, encompasses a veritable history of American-Jewish politics, which trace their activist roots to Yiddish-speaking immigrants, the world of the sweatshops and union organizing, and then to the City College of New York and the American Communist party. Early in the film Paul Isaacson (Mandy Patinkin) argues intricate political theory and tactics with another politically conscious young Jewish student in the hallways of City College. At another point, Paul take a beating from mounted police, whom he calls Cossacks when they charge him, for his militant support of striking workers. Rochelle (Lindsay Crouse), in her tenement flat, argues politics with her mother, who speaks Yiddish while Rochelle speaks English.[14] Paul and Rochelle eventually join the Communist party and hold party meetings at their house; they even take their children along to political rallies held at the beach or in the Catskill Mountains. Paul amusingly indoctrinates young Danny into the ways and means in which management exploits workers through a humorous disquisition on Joe DiMaggio's image on a box of Wheaties. Less amusingly, Lumet and Doctorow remind the audience that the elder Isaacsons' misguided idealism provided no excuse for the clear and vicious anti-Semitic, anticommunistic fervor of the cold war years.

Along the way Lumet also recalls the Jewish support for civil rights for blacks, not just in the 1950s and 1960s, but going back to the 1930s and 1940s. He does this in two sequences. The first focuses on Rochelle's conversation with her Yiddish-speaking mother. The young radical firebrand tells the tired, downtrodden, poverty-stricken woman with whom she lives that she has given $2 to the Scottsboro Boys, $2 the women can clearly ill-afford to part with. The second sequence finds Paul and Rochelle taking Danny on a party outing to Peekskill, New York, to hear Paul Robeson, whom Rochelle calls "the hero of the people," sing at an outdoor concert. The description of Robeson and the physical risk the family takes at the hands of redneck rowdies betray their sympathies and support for the black struggle in the United States.[15]

Lumet mirrors Jewish participation in the Old Left by Jewish participation in the New Left. This is seen through the character of Susan, who in one frail figure stands for the schizophrenic, confusing, yet idealistic 1960s. Although at film's start Daniel sneers at her latest project—she wants to form the Paul and Rochelle Isaacson Foundation for Radical Studies—the audience can appreciate the young woman's desperate search for meaning. She has embraced a variety of causes and pursuits, from Eastern religion, to psychedelic drugs, sexual promiscuity, and revolutionary politics. Susan's New Left sympathies are typical of those of many middle-class Jewish youths during the 1960s. They were the "red diaper babies," children of Old Leftists who disproportionately assumed leadership roles even while rejecting much of the Old Left's tactics and beliefs. Susan's tragedy lies in the fact that her life is empty because the State scapegoated her parents for their political beliefs and her own search for political values is unsatisfying. Her search will fail to fill the void that her parents' execution created not because the values she embraces are false but because she, too, willingly played the role of victim and remained a hostage to the past.

Daniel, on the other hand, can overcome the past, can embrace a set of political values with roots in the Old Left precisely when he drops the mantle of victimization. He does this by an active confrontation with his past. Unlike Sol Nazerman, with whom he shares a tragic memory of anti-Semitic madness that destroyed his family, Daniel seeks out the past, confronts it, and interrogates it, not to change the past but to accommodate it. Whereas in *The Pawnbroker* Nazerman's memories of the horror he has experienced come to him unbidden by graphic reminders in the present, Daniel's confrontation with the past is of his own choosing, his own efforts. He not only deliberately recalls past incidents, but also he seeks out people from his past. For example, he wants to learn more from the widow of the lawyer who defended his parents.

The film's climactic sequence comes, therefore, when Daniel

confronts the major witness the State used against his mother and father. Selig Mindish (Joseph Leon), dentist to the party, is in the present a broken old man, pitifully painting pictures in a Jewish old-age home in Southern California. When Mindish's daughter, Linda (Tovah Feldshuh), and her yuppie husband bitterly confront Danny when he dredges up memories they wish to keep buried, Danny's response turns to bemusement. Can Dr. Mindish really continue to exert power over him? Can this pathetic former radical remain a figure of terror for the now grown-up Danny Isaacson?

When Danny realizes that he has overcome the past in ways that Linda Mindish and her senile father have not, he comes to terms with the past and the present. Married and a father, Danny optimistically keeps his new family whole. He, his wife, and their child join a massive, peaceful demonstration; in a long-shot at film's end they merge with the quiet, hopeful crowd. Family provides Danny with a lasting political lesson that the State tried to destroy in a time of political madness. Yet he will continue the political responsibilities his first family imbued in him. Institutions may betray individuals, but Lumet views individuals as having the responsibility to fight the very injustices that threaten destruction.

What seems to be a message common to Lumet's previous films was overlooked in the controversy that immediately greeted *Daniel*. This controversy remains interesting primarily for the way it reveals the continued uncomfortableness of American Jewry and for the way it demonstrates how people implicitly view the power of cinema compared to the power of the novel.[16] On the latter issue, although *Daniel,* greeted by a firestorm of criticism, follows Doctorow's novel quite closely (indeed, the script is by Doctorow himself), the novel was virtually controversy-free. Criticism of the film, which was not leveled at the novel, revolves around the manner in which the story follows the case of Julius and Ethel Rosenberg quite closely and yet veers away from it significantly. Because the basic story and characters of the film all derive from the novel, why such hue and cry over Lumet's adaptation compared to Doctorow's original novel? Perhaps there exists an implicit belief, if not certainty, that a larger audience exists (potentially) for film than for a novel, therefore, film has a greater responsibility to "stick to the facts." Such an argument holds no compelling reasons for any serious study of cinema. The argument does, however, have a compelling subtext when we realize that cries for historical accuracy in cinema in the case of *Daniel* represent only the overt manifestations of an undercurrent of Jewish paranoia and fear similar to that which struck movie moguls and official Jewry precisely around the time of the Rosenberg case itself.

The case of Julius and Ethel Rosenberg, tried and convicted as "atom spies" and executed in 1953 for the crime of giving secrets to the Soviet Union, was part and parcel of the paranoia and fear of the cold war. Another manifestation of cold war hysteria was the blacklist within the film and entertainment worlds initiated by the HUAC hearings into possible communist influence in the motion picture industry. The HUAC hearings presented the movie studios, still under the control of first- and second-generation movie moguls, with an opportunity to show their all-Americanness by purging not simply communists, former communists, and communist sympathizers from their ranks, but by blacklisting anyone who would not cooperate as a "friendly witness" with the House committee. In part, their actions may be understood as the fear of a resurgent anti-Semitism with the not-uncommon (and not entirely unjustified) association of Jews with radical causes. This fear manifested itself quite similarly with official Jewry's reaction to the Rosenberg case, not so much with the trial as with the sentence. Few were willing to proclaim the Rosenbergs' innocence, certainly not official Jewish organizations, and one can hardly blame them for that. However, the death sentences were surely too extreme and, although not indicative of anti-Semitism (as HUAC's actions indisputably were), indicated paranoia that was out of control. Even if, as many believe, they were guilty, the Rosenbergs were clearly symbols. As sacrificial victims, the fact that they were Jewish carried many implications that the American-Jewish community should have recognized and fought against. That the judge who sentenced them to death, permitting a host of questionable legal maneuvers on the government's part, was himself Jewish only reveals the over-determination that many Jews felt to disassociate themselves from radical politics and proclaim an America-first attitude, regardless of its consequences.

In the case of *Daniel,* complaints of historical inaccuracy revolved precisely around the film's divergence from the Rosenberg case. As portrayed in the film, Paul and Rochelle Isaacson seem clearly innocent, victimized solely for their radical beliefs. That they, in some sense, become willing participants in their own sham trial, deliberately martyring themselves for their cause, condemns them as overly idealistic, not as bomb-throwing (or bomb-secret-giving) radicals. Yet the Rosenbergs were hardly picked at random by the anti-Semitic Federal Bureau of Investigation and executed merely for symbolic reasons. That they were guilty, that they intended to help the Soviets develop the atomic bomb, seems little in doubt, although how much they actually accomplished is quite questionable. Does society execute people for what they intend to do, however, or what they actually do?[17]

Thus the controversy over *Daniel* stemmed in part from the film's portrayal of the Isaacsons' absolute innocence and history's judgment of the Rosenbergs' basic guilt. Yet it is precisely in the unwillingness to acknowledge the film as fiction that American Jewry's paranoia emerges. Simply put, much of official Jewry was unwilling to condemn the State for its anti-Semitic, antiradical, even anti-American activities during the 1950s and chose, instead, to condemn an American-Jewish filmmaker for his attempts to condemn America's past. The result was to condemn *Daniel* to relative obscurity, its commercial prospects crushed by the very audience required to stimulate interest in a film with a political stance and a historical vision. As Woody Allen has it in *Stardust Memories*, "I love intellectuals. Like the Mafia, they only kill their own." The same might apply about the Jewish Left in America.

Notes

1. The only full-length study of Lumet's career is Cunningham's *Sidney Lumet: Film and Literary Vision*. The dominant approach is to examine Lumet's cinema from the point of view of his adaptations from literature and theater, while claiming authorship for the director nevertheless. Although the focus of emphasis is vastly different from this work, we are in basic agreement with the idea of Lumet as author.

2. The biographical data that follows is adapted from Bowles, *Sidney Lumet: A Guide to References and Resources*.

3. Much scholarly work remains to be done on television, especially the golden age, a subject of much nostalgia but little analysis of actual programs. The work of Herbert Brodkin remains fascinating terra incognita from the perspective of Jewish contributions to American television. For a detailed study of the reception of his miniseries "Holocaust," see Doneson 155–75.

4. As was the case with *The Pawnbroker*, Lumet came to this project rather late, replacing the director John G. Avildsen who had the standard "creative differences" with producer Dino de Laurentis (Bowles 28). However, Lumet's suitability for the project, as with *The Pawnbroker*, is abundantly clear; it is arguable that his work on *Serpico* inspired his interest in the similarly true-to-life story of *Prince of the City*, which he helped script. By the time he got to *Q & A*, Lumet was not only the film's director, but also its sole screenwriter.

5. Immediately before producing *Q & A*, Lumet made *Family Business*

(1989), the kind of film known in the trade as "high concept." One can imagine a studio executive giving Lumet the go-ahead to make the film on little more than the fact that it stars Sean Connery, Dustin Hoffman, and Matthew Broderick as three generations of a New York family. Although the film features a virtual hodge-podge of ethnicity—Hoffman, as Connery's son, is the product of a Welsh father and an Italian-Catholic mother; Broderick, as Hoffman's son, has a Jewish mother, herself played by a Hispanic actress (Rosanna de Soto)—little in the film is believable. Similarly, the idea of the sins of the father passed on to the son is again displayed but completely undercut by the film's total lack of credibility. For one of the few times in his career, Lumet made only a movie.

6. See Lumet, *The Hornes: An American Family*.

7. Show business is a small world, and perhaps it is not too much of a coincidence that *The Hospital* was directed by Arthur Hiller, whom Sidney Lumet replaced as the director of *The Pawnbroker* a few years earlier. By the same token, Lumet himself in 1955 had directed a production of G. B. Shaw's *The Doctor's Dilemma*, like *The Hospital* a satire on the medical profession (Bowles 9). Lumet would return to the institution of medicine and its corruption with *The Verdict* in 1982.

8. This metaphor for Diana's retreat from reality due to television is perhaps not the most apt one for the situation. Bugs Bunny was a specifically filmic creation of the early 1940s and not a product of television. It is doubtful that the Technicolor glories of the classic Warner Brothers cartoon character would have had a formative role on Diana as she grew up in the 1950s in front of the twelve-inch black and white screen of the typical American suburban home.

9. Bowles (32) notes that, once again, Lumet was not originally assigned to the project. This time he replaced John Badham, who departed late in pre-production, another victim of creative differences. What is most amazing is not Lumet's ability to take over and do a competent job on such short notice, but rather that, as with *Serpico* and *The Pawnbroker*, he was not the first choice for the project.

10. Auteurist-inspired criticism and our contention of Lumet's particular version of the American-Jewish experience should not blind us to the reality of *The Pawnbroker*'s production circumstances. Ely Landau originally signed Arthur Hiller (another American Jew) to direct this film, while he signed Lumet to direct *The Heart Is a Lonely Hunter*, which was to star Montgomery Clift. When the Carson McCullers adaptation fell through, Landau dismissed Hiller, who was ill at the time, in favor of Lumet for *The Pawnbroker*, which was already scripted and cast. See Rosenblum and Karen 139–40 and Bowles 19.

11. In the novel, David does not slip off Sol's shoulders; rather, holding onto Sol's leg, he slides down to the floor. We understand clearly that he slips on and eventually suffocates in the feces of the tightly packed Jews (Wallant 37–38).

12. Baruch Lumet was a star in the Yiddish theater before the war and thus, like Mendel, a survivor of a world lost forever.

13. Avisar's aversion to American films of the Holocaust, generally, makes him err when he observes that "such movies as *The Mortal Storm, The Young Lions, The Diary of Anne Frank,* and *The Pawnbroker* were major productions, featuring superstars in leading roles" (129). While certainly true of *The Young Lions* (with Marlon Brando and Montgomery Clift), surely neither Millie Perkins, who portrayed Anne, nor Rod Steiger, in the title role of Lumet's film, were ever, and certainly not at the time, superstars by any definition. Similarly, Lumet's film was produced independently by Ely Landau after it was rejected by MGM (itself long past its glory days) and distributed independently after various major studios passed on it (Rosenblum 164).

14. A conversation here which features two different languages recalls a chat between Jesus and his mother in *The Pawnbroker,* where the mother speaks Spanish and the son insists upon English. Jesus's and Rochelle's use of English is an index of their desire to assimilate, assimilation implicitly carrying in their minds the promise of fulfillment in the American mainstream. Compare this to a sequence in the later *Q & A* in which Nancy visits with her mother: both speak Spanish, an index of the failure of the myth of the melting pot.

15. It is typical of Lumet that he use two actual events to ground his fictional story in reality. The Scottsboro Boys (also known as the Scottsboro Nine) were nine black youths arrested in Alabama in 1931 and charged with rape. A series of trials over the next few years found them guilty until the conviction was overturned by the U.S. Supreme Court in 1935. The American Communist party was active in their defense. Paul Robeson's 1949 concert in upstate New York was marred by right-wing violence of a specifically racist and anti-Semitic nature, an incident that came to be known as the Peekskill riot (Kanfer 197–98). Equally as interesting as referencing such incidents is the fact that Lumet feels little compulsion to elaborate upon these occurrences. Rochelle attempts merely a few words of explanation to her mother to justify giving money to the Scottsboro Boys, while the fact that the Peekskill riot actually took place must be the work of memory, cinema, and books like this to recall.

16. The controversy played itself out in such articles as "The Movie *Daniel:* How Close Is It to History?" *New York Times,* Aug. 31, 1983, C-21; Andrew Sarris, "The Rosenbergs, the Isaacsons, and Thou" *Village Voice,* Sept. 6, 1983, 45; Richard Grenier, "The Hard Left and the Soft," *Commentary* 77 (Jan. 1984): 56–61; and Irving Howe, "The Troubles of *Daniel,*" *Dissent* 31, no. 1 (1984): 121–23.

17. One of the novel's motifs that is reproduced in the film involves Daniel's recitation of the various means of execution that past cultures have employed. Doctorow and Lumet want this litany of horrible killings, for example, drawing-and-quartering or the guillotine, to be compared ironically to the idea that somehow execution in the electric chair is more "humane." The motif pays off in the execution of the Isaacsons in events that lead up to the actual electrocution: they are strapped in the chair, the rubber cap is put on them, then the switch is thrown and their bodies twitch uncontrollably and horribly. This horror is literally doubled in the case of Rochelle (which is based upon Ethel Rosenberg's execution) when, after having thousands of volts sent

through her body, Rochelle does not die and requires a second execution. For a variation on State murder and an execution that requires a second try, see Nagisa Oshima's film *Death by Hanging* (*Koshikei*, 1970), not simply a tract against capital punishment but, like *Daniel*, a disquisition on State-sponsored prejudice and murder.

CHAPTER FIVE

Paul Mazursky: The Price of Freedom

Although he performed bit parts (*Fear and Desire*, 1953, *The Blackboard Jungle*, 1955) early in his professional career, Paul (né Irwin) Mazursky, like Woody Allen and Mel Brooks, began the formative part of his show business life as a comedy writer ("The Danny Kaye Show," 1961–69) and comic performer (Igor and H, and the Los Angeles Second City troupe). As with Allen and Brooks, he maintains rare personal control over his work; he has directed all but one of his own screenplays and has never directed another writer's script. Like Sidney Lumet—but to a lesser degree—Mazursky's initial directorial efforts also came in television ("The Monkees," 1966–68), rather than in film. But unlike these other American-Jewish directors, Mazursky focuses his vision almost exclusively on members of America's white, middle-to-upper-middle-class, subjects, he contends, that "are as noble . . . as the Medicis or the farmworkers" (Haller 85). His well-educated, well-fed characters possess enough self-consciousness to perpetually analyze the quality of their lives and enough money to alter their life-styles radically. With roughly equal portions of censure and compassion, Mazursky chronicles the feelings, beliefs, and fears of this segment of society from the 1950s until the present.

Throughout his unique tracing of American culture as experienced by this socioeconomic group over four decades, Mazursky employs many Jewish central characters as representative figures, usually identifying them as such but sometimes simply dropping subtle verbal and visual clues about their ethnic identity. In addition, Mazursky's films revolve around many of the American-Jewish motifs discussed previously, even when his central characters are not Jewish. In fact, Mazursky's movies chart the evolution of this Jewish segment of American society: from the late 1940s' immigrant enclaves of Coney Island and the Bronx in *Enemies, A Love Story;* to the 1950s of Brooklyn neighborhoods and bohemian Greenwich Village lofts in *Next Stop, Greenwich Village;* to the 1960s of the South Bronx and the Jewish wanderer's search for enlightenment in *Willy and Phil;* to the 1970s of radical-chic parties and the disaffected Jewish lawyer in *Blume in Love;* to the 1980s of Beverly Hills and the fragmented Whiteman family in *Down and Out in Beverly Hills;* to the 1990s and the bickering Fifers in *Scenes from a Mall.* Such a sustained and original body of work makes Mazursky one of the most important interpreters of the Jewish experience within American society, an individualistic artist whose filmic explorations of this unique cultural interaction create particular issues as well as universal themes.

In an interview with Freida Lee Mock and Terry Saunders for the American Film Foundation's television program "Words into Images: Writers on Screenwriting," Mazursky succinctly characterizes his films as examining "freedom, and the price of freedom; change, and the price of change." He contextualizes his remarks by citing the period after World War II as pivotal in the course of American social history: "We were suddenly told after World War II that you could do things differently if you wanted to. . . . There's now this possibility: freedom. . . . Can the middle class handle all the freedom it's now being offered? Does anybody really change? . . . My pictures are about a reaction in the United States against and to authority, a re-assessment of moral values and social mores, of how people live."

Such a response to this era of immense social and political upheaval—as is the case in the works of Allen, Lumet, and Brooks— characterizes a decidedly Jewish sensibility acutely attuned to both the subtle and the broad shifts in cultural directions. To one degree or another, all these film artists chart how people set adrift without the sustaining life jackets of organized religion and cultural traditions float, swim, or drown in a seemingly endless sea of possibilities. But more than any of these other American-Jewish filmmakers, Mazursky's pictures persistently explore an issue that obsesses Jewish thinkers in every culture into which Jews have assimilated—be it Babylon or Egypt, Spain or Germany—and one that informs the central core of much American-Jewish thinking: the price of freedom.

From 1881 onward, when the great mass of Jewish immigrants streamed to the shores of the United States, Jewish writers and intellectuals immediately recognized that the major question for the American-Jewish community was no longer, as it had been in most other countries of the world, how to survive in the face of overt hostility. Rather, the question in America became whether or

Director Paul Mazursky and friend.

not to retain a distinctly Jewish identity, or even how to retain it, within the fluid American class and economic structure that threatened to dissolve discrete group ties and totally absorb Jews. For example, when the 1961 National Opinion Research Center survey placed intermarriages between Jews and gentiles at a historic high of 10 to 15 percent, the conservative rabbi Robert Gordis calmly responded that such increases were "part of the price modern Jewry paid for freedom and equality in an open society." In fact, the increasingly strong dichotomy between America as the Promised Land of economic salvation and the Gomorrah of spiritual peril played an important role in the subsequent history of the East European immigrants.

Mazursky usually does not deal specifically with the price of freedom in regard to the dangers or advantages of intermarriage or the split between Judaism and Jewishness. He does, however, demonstrate the "partially inside-partially outside" perspective that Jewish artists have assumed over the centuries and in many different societies. They become the Other who, however outwardly assimilated into a culture, still feel emotionally removed from it, to some degree or another, by virtue of allegiance to a minority religion. Such a marginal position inevitably creates tension and anxiety, but it also filters personal creativity through a psychologically bifurcated lens, a unique viewpoint that acknowledges the power (and absurdity) of any given situation. Although certainly not a stranger in a strange land, Mazursky still engages with American social life as both an enthusiastic participant and a detached observer. His camera work and his screenplays distance Mazursky from the situation under examination, be it modern marriage, contemporary mores, or current fads. For example, no true villains exist in Mazursky's pictures. Although he insightfully notes the flaws of a particular character, he always finds some redeeming quality.

In the majority of Mazursky's films, tensions arise when a character discovers that something or someone dramatically alters his or her life. Initially, most characters neither plan nor contemplate freedom from the regular habits of a lifetime. Instead, these dramatic transformations result from one blindingly brief moment, a single, thoughtless action or a chance encounter that initially finds the character frightened by present loss rather than exhilarated by the possibility of future choice. For example, in *I Love You, Alice B. Toklas!,* the life of Harold Fine, an up-tight lawyer, alters after he casually meets a young hippie, much in the same way that Willy and

Phil's accidental encounters with each other and then Jeannette forever remold the lives of all three characters, and Jerry's arbitrary selection of Dave Whiteman's pool in which to commit suicide changes the lives of everyone in *Down and Out in Beverly Hills*. These seemingly brief encounters all force characters to contemplate new ways of living and loving. As Mazursky observes in his interview with Mock and Saunders, "does anybody really change? Americans tend to believe in miracles, psychologically: I'm going to EST; I'm being Rolfed; I've become a Buddhist; I'm no longer a Jew; I'm born again. We could name thousands of them. Two years later the person is off and gone to another one. It's a very American thing. . . . The hope for change is in me too, so probably in my writing the hope for change is there to some degree." Such changes may last a few short months, a period of years, or become permanent, but each springs from an accidental meeting with another person.

Sometimes an event not a person becomes the catalyst for change. In *Bob and Carol and Ted and Alice* four friends must readjust their values after one couple's weekend encounter session, while in *Moscow on the Hudson* Vladimir's spontaneous decision to defect transfigures his life. On a larger historical level, the fanatical Nazis forever alter Herman Broder's comfortable East European existence in *Enemies, A Love Story*. In addition, just as he adjusts to America, complete with both a wife and a mistress, Herman's first wife, believed to have been killed in a concentration camp, reappears to destroy his neatly reordered new life. Several of Mazursky's other films pivot around marriages that instantly snap under the weight of discovered infidelity, leaving one (or both) former partners staring into the abyss of freedom: Steven's wife catches him in bed with his secretary in *Blume in Love;* Erica's husband admits his affair and asks for a divorce in *An Unmarried Woman;* Phil discovers his wife's liaison with his boss in *Tempest;* and Nick Fifer confesses his infidelity in *Scenes from a Mall*. Harry, in *Harry and Tonto,* gets equally jolted when his apartment building is demolished and he must find a new place to live, as does Jack Noah, who assumes an entirely new identity after being forced to impersonate a dictator in *Moon over Parador.*

In almost all of these films, characters move from a well-known to a basically unfamiliar space, their altered environment representing the crucial psychological changes they are experiencing, the physical manifestation of their emotional search for new values and identities. All of Mazursky's characters struggle in the midst of transitions, wandering as Matthew Arnold puts it, "between two worlds, one dead, / The other powerless to be born." In each movie, events beyond the control of Mazursky's characters open doors to possibilities that were uncontemplated previously.

Before analyzing Mazursky's two most overtly Jewish movies, *Next Stop, Greenwich Village* and *Enemies, A Love Story*, in detail, an overview of his work will demonstrate how American-Jewish characters and motifs dominate his movies. With the exception of *Moscow on the Hudson* and *Enemies, A Love Story*, two films in which recent immigrants strive to become middle class, Mazursky rarely ventures beyond the confines of the world inhabited by his white, middle-to-upper-middle-class characters, although he often employs secondary or minor characters to call the basic assumptions and moral values of his protagonists into question. Most Mazursky characters, although not independently or outrageously wealthy, have enough money to live quite comfortably. They could be termed yuppies and, at least before the chance encounter or thoughtless action transforms their lives, such a label might be reasonably accurate. But Mazursky's characters quickly move beyond this cultural stereotype and its connotations of bourgeois morality, monetary obsession, vapid escapism, and designer consumerism. The event or person that alters their lives forces them to redefine and reevaluate their priorities, a process that brings an honest reappraisal of their strengths and shortcomings.

Anti-Semitism, a motif that figures prominently in the works of such other American-Jewish filmmakers as Woody Allen, Mel Brooks, and Sidney Lumet, never appears in Paul Mazursky's pictures. Perhaps this subject is just too psychologically painful, too disruptively emotional, for Mazursky to incorporate into his human comedies of modern American life. After all, his sensibilities focus most comfortably on social rather than political concerns and on present problems rather than past history. Then, too, Mazursky's films explore issues of assimilation rather than separateness, and anti-Semitism, on both a private and a public level, tends to isolate Jews from the rest of American society. It might be (although one can hardly imagine so) that Mazursky has little personal experience with this issue, that anti-Semitism never engages his artistic consciousness so it does not affect his characters' lives. Yet the very fact that Mazursky's characters never experience anti-Semitism, much as Bill Cosby's upper-middle-class Huxtable family never experiences racism, clearly demonstrates how much these figures see themselves as part of American culture.

Mazursky cowrote *I Love You, Alice B. Toklas!* (1968) with his comedy partner Larry Tucker, and Hy Averback, not Mazursky, directed the film. Harold Fine (Peter Sellers), a successful Jewish lawyer whose parents once owned a candy store in Brooklyn, succumbs to the nubile charms of Nancy (Leigh Taylor-Young), a lovely young hippie. The infatuation turns the up-tight, conservative Harold into a free-living hippie (Mazursky himself makes the first of his signature cameo roles, here as a hippie). His transition from courtroom to commune allows scriptwriter Mazursky to satirize various Jewish characters and institutions. Harold's brother, Herbie (David Arkin), a California beach bum, represents the rootless young Jews of the 1960s, endlessly searching for spiritual meaning in their lives while ignoring the significance their own religious and cultural heritage might play in their quest for self-knowledge. (Mazursky would later expand on this group via the character of Willy in *Willy and Phil*.) Herbie, for example, wears the burial outfit of the Hopi when he attends a funeral, although he displays little knowledge of Jewish burial rituals.

Harold's girlfriend, Joyce Miller (Joyce Van Patten), has one main goal in life: to marry Harold. As such, she embodies rapacious, social-climbing Jewish girls whose lives revolve around trapping and marrying successful professional men, no matter how unsuitable. Harold's mother (Jo Van Fleet) is a typical Hollywood version of the Jewish mother; she uses guilt to manipulate Harold and stacks his cupboards with Manischewitz products, from egg noodles to gefilte fish, that he never uses. His father (Salem Ludwig) speaks fondly of Franklin D. Roosevelt and the New Deal yet is ineffectual and emotionally distant. Finally, Mazursky parodies a lavish Jewish wedding ceremony, here performed by twin cantors, and the reception that follows complete with a gigantic Star of David atop a large mound of green gelatin.

Mazursky's focus, however, remains on Harold's inability to find peace and meaning in either a pin-striped or a long-haired existence, losing his way in a world devoid of traditions and ethical morality. He bolts from the ceremonial *chupa* (canopy) on his wedding day to search for spiritual enlightenment and sexual fulfillment. Harold finds the straight world too confining, for he has the heart of a hippie, and the alternative culture too loose, for he has the head of a corporate lawyer. While with Joyce, Harold longs for the freedom associated with Nancy. While with Nancy, he tries to lock her into a confining relationship more rigid than Joyce demanded of him. Harold searches in vain for some compromise that will provide a measure of independence without foregoing all sense of responsibility, but at the movie's conclusion he is alone, unable to marry Joyce or to sustain a relationship with Nancy.

I Love You, Alice B. Toklas! includes many of the Jewish motifs that have been discussed previously. Such Yiddish expressions as *mishpocheh, meshuggener,* and *facocked* abound in the film, indicating the background of the film's characters. In fact, Mazursky claims that Warner Brothers initially feared that the film was too Jewish and would, therefore, not be a financial success. Clearly, the picture focuses on social alienation and family relationships, issues around which even Harold's fantasies revolve. In one particularly vivid LSD trip, he sees his mother and father living as hippies, his partner (Herb Edelman) and Joyce making love, and his Mexican clients as cantors singing Hebrew melodies. Early in the film, Harold drives around and around a parking garage, searching for a spot to leave his car. Finally, he finds a space. But when he returns to take Joyce home, Harold discovers that another car has pinned him in, and he cannot move his automobile. Such is life for Harold Fine. Either he ceaselessly circles or statically remains locked into one position.

Even with his long hair, love beads, and flowing robes, Harold still cannot free himself from the inculcated desire to please his teachers; he must forever be the smart little Jewish kid in the front-row seat, as a conversation with his guru indicates.

> *Guru:* Who are you Harold? Do you know who you are?
> *Harold:* I'm trying, Guru, I'm really trying.
> *Guru:* When you stop trying, then you'll know.
> *Harold:* Well, I'm trying to stop trying.

His relationship with Nancy fares little better than his desire for enlightenment. He wants to be monogamous; she, as the butterfly tattooed on her leg indicates, wants to be free. Even their esthetic tastes differ sharply. Nancy enjoys experimental art films like *Mondo Teeth,* a parody of Andy Warhol's movies that contains no people, simply teeth. Harold prefers to stay at home and read. For Mazursky, Harold's attempt to change himself represents a misguided if totally understandable process, but his radical shift in lifestyles leaves him unable to exist in either world. Even at the film's conclusion, he remains unsure about how to live his life. Merging, not excluding, remains at the center of all Mazursky's films about freedom and change, as his characters learn to incorporate what is good about their old lives with what is positive about their new lives. This typically Jewish issue permeates the fiction and nonfiction writing of American Jews, who strive to merge what they deem useful from their heritage with what they see as positive about American society.

Bob and Carol and Ted and Alice (1969), like *I Love You, Alice B. Toklas!* written by Mazursky and Larry Tucker, deals with a similar social set; Harold Fine and Ted Henderson probably see each other in court every so often. On the surface, however, Mazursky's directorial debut film is far less Jewish than the previous picture and is his least overtly Jewish work, the only one that contains no clearly identified Jewish characters. Bob (Robert Culp) and Carol (Natalie Wood) Saunders, along with their best friends, Ted (Elliott Gould) and Alice (Dyan Cannon) Henderson, never discuss their religious or cultural heritage. They initially involve themselves with little beyond their jobs, pool-side barbecues, families, and dinners at nice Italian restaurants. Yet the film's advertising slogan, "Consider the Possibilities," remains an apt, one-line summation of all Mazursky's subsequent pictures. The slogan simultaneously presents an invitation (think how things could be better if you did this); a warning (you'd better contemplate the consequences before you do this); a dare (challenge yourself to do this); and a directive (you must think about doing this). At one point or another, all of Mazursky's major characters feel compelled to at least contemplate their lives from another angle and reconsider the choices of a lifetime.

Bob and Carol and Ted and Alice follows the activities of a couple who discover a new system of values and incorporate these alternative principles into their straight, upper-middle-class lives. While doing research for his documentary, Bob takes Carol to spend a weekend at an Esalen-type retreat atop a scenic California mountain. There they engage in a marathon encounter session that motivates them to commit themselves to emotional and sexual truthfulness. Returning to Los Angeles, Bob and Carol share these insights with their closest friends, Ted and Alice. In particular, Carol reveals that Bob had an affair while on business in San Francisco. This revelation initially shocks and then infuriates Alice, so much so that she enters psychotherapy to explore her hostility. Eventually, however, she comes to accept Carol's open attitude toward Bob's infidelity, as well as Carol's brief affair with an attractive young tennis teacher. Ted, on the other hand, becomes so overwhelmingly titillated by Bob's story that he begins to fantasize about having a similar sexual encounter and eventually does.

Finally, the couples journey to Las Vegas for a weekend, their unspoken agenda "to hear Tony Bennett and have an orgy." In what became an iconic, if rather ironic, symbol for the swinging sixties, the four climb into bed together, determined to prove that their new permissiveness empowers them to stretch beyond the narrow, conventional values of marital monogamy and sexual fidelity. Bob begins kissing Alice, and Ted does the same with Carol. Yet a close-up of Bob, uncomfortably watching his wife kissing his best friend, forces viewers to share an extended moment of disquieting contemplation, silently and uneasily realizing the limitations of personal liberation in an era of social openness. Poised on the brink of self-discovery via communal orgasm, the four sense that switching partners would cross too far beyond the emotional and psychological boundaries that govern their lives; they decide to leave the bedroom without having sex. The film ends with a Fellini-esque moment as people in the hotel parking lot (including cowriter Tucker), in a repeat of the encounter-group exercise, walk around and stare deeply into each other's faces while "What the World Needs Now Is Love, Sweet Love" swells ironically on the soundtrack.

The first sequence in *Bob and Carol and Ted and Alice* aptly depicts a constant Mazursky theme, as well as one of the more powerful motifs used by Allen, Brooks, and Lumet: an exploration of the new values that usurp the role of traditional religious precepts. Bob and Carol drive their Jaguar XKE to the mountain-top shrine that draws pilgrims searching for modern miracles to cure contemporary psychological ills. On the soundtrack, the "Hallelujah Chorus" accompanies their pilgrimage. This is the new Lourdes. Here, penitents bathe in the holy water of churning hot tubs and sit naked in the Lotus position, meditating in the California sunshine. When the soundtrack shifts from the "Hallelujah Chorus" to "I Know That My Redeemer Liveth," one accompanying image shows a woman shampooing a bearded, long-haired man as both sit naked in a hot tub. To rinse the lather, she dunks his head under water, an ironic baptism. By juxtaposing this deeply religious music, mostly associated with Christmas and hence the birth of Christ, with modern secular rituals like encounter marathons and psychotherapy, Mazursky shows how humans hunger for change through miraculous cures and magical potions that still exert profound influence over rationality and convention. *Bob and Carol and Ted and Alice,* and to some extent all of Mazursky's subsequent films, explores the borders of change, or, perhaps even more important, whether true and permanent change is possible.

Bob and Carol and Ted and Alice, a huge critical and commercial success, made more than $30 million in its initial release, garnering rave reviews and premiering as the opening entry at the prestigious New York Film Festival. Such acclaim, although certainly welcomed, pushed Mazursky into the glare of the public spotlight; along with the high praise for his first film came the lofty expectations for his second. He was no longer a fresh-faced novice, a clever young director with the surprise hit of 1969. He now faced a public, a press, and a production company that expected him to deliver another financial and creative hit. It is not surprising, therefore, that the storyline of *Alex in Wonderland* (1970, the last film cowritten with long-time partner Larry Tucker) contains obvious biographical parallels to this period in Mazursky's personal life and artistic development. In it, a film director (Donald Sutherland), whose first film is a smash, must learn how to handle his good fortune and, more frighteningly, to decide what he can possibly do to match his initial effort.

The film demonstrates how much the humanistic, neorealistic films of the 1950s and 1960s influence Mazursky's pictures. Most of his films contain seeds, and sometimes even roots, from the European master filmmakers: Fellini (*Alex in Wonderland* and *Bob and Carol and Ted and Alice*); Truffaut (*Next Stop, Greenwich Village* and *Willy and Phil*); DeSica (*Harry and Tonto*); Renoir (*Down and Out in Beverly Hills*); Visconti (*Blume in Love*); Antonioni (*Tempest*); and Lubitsch (*Moon over Parador* and *Enemies, A Love Story*). Part of this strategy, no doubt, springs from Mazursky's innate feeling for tradition, a Jewish perspective that looks to a European heritage for a sense of enduring culture and sophisticated values.

On a more practical level, Mazursky clearly finds the modestly budgeted, more personal European style of filmmaking particularly conducive to his own desire to explore what he labels "inner journeys," looking to the European cinema's history of character studies rather than to the American cinema's obsession with violence, space-aged special effects, and repetitive genre formulas. Although a Fellini-esque view of life permeates his pictures, a comic perspective on this cockeyed caravan of life, Mazursky's strongest affinity is with Truffaut: "The two filmmakers share a critical, but ultimately optimistic, view of life, approached from an oblique, metacomic angle. Their films are primarily character studies that stress the importance of those off-moments when revelation takes the form of the smallest smile, or an unexpected caress, or the lighting of a pipe" (Corliss, "Poet" 55). Such European sensibilities strengthen Mazursky's films and endow his characters with a depth and resonance absent in most modern American pictures.

In *Alex in Wonderland,* which many critics derisively dismissed as a feeble attempt to make an American *8½,* both Fellini and Jeanne Moreau (accompanied by music from *Jules et Jim*) appear as themselves, but they also signify various approaches to filmmaking that captivate the imagination of Mazursky and his fictional counterpart. Yet Mazursky fully understands the danger of slavishly imitating even these revered cinematic forebears. By superimposing his own directorial credit over Cracker Jacks, M&Ms, Baby Ruths, and other items in a theater-lobby candy counter, he wryly undercuts his own celluloid confections, as well as acknowledges a public that hungrily gobbles up his creations to satisfy a momentary sweet tooth. As he tells Mock and Saunders, "I'm afraid of pretense. . . . I want to be a clown. I don't want to be taken too seriously, yet I want you to know that underneath it I'm very serious. I want to be amusing. I want to be honest. I want to be sincere. I want to make money. . . . I like to make 'em laugh and make 'em cry and tell an interesting story."

In addition, he clearly satirizes Alex's pretentious search for a "significant" theme—a quest that encompasses biographies of Malcolm X and Lenny Bruce, pictures about Native Americans, stories about Cortez and the Aztecs, fantasies about blacks taking over Los Angeles, and the war in Vietnam. As Diane Jacobs notes, *"Alex in Wonderland* is not Mazursky pretending to be Fellini. . . . It is Mazursky yearning toward Fellini, laughing at himself, and continuing to yearn" (*Hollywood Renaissance* 167). Thus, the picture opens with a quote from *Alice in Wonderland* that perhaps indicates Mazursky's state of mind during this period. The shaken Alice responds with obvious confusion to the Caterpillar's sharp demand ("Who are you?") that she identify herself: "I-I hardly know, Sir, just at present—at least I know who I *was* when I got up this morning, but I think I must have been changed several times since then."

Alex, following the white rabbit of success, also falls down the rabbit hole and emerges into a world over which he exerts little control and that becomes ever more "curiouser and curiouser." In much the same manner as his literary counterpart, he has "been changed," the language indicating how outside forces rather than personal choices instigate spontaneous shifts in action and perspective. He might well agree with the irritated Alice who, in further conversation with the contradictory Caterpillar, hastily replies, "Oh, I'm not particular to size . . . only one doesn't like changing so often, you know." Immediately after the film's revealing epigram, the audience hears and then sees Alex in close-up, reciting Hamlet's "To Be or Not to Be" soliloquy. The camera slowly pulls back to reveal him delivering the speech to his uncomprehending young daughter while both splash in the bathtub. With this movement from *Alice in Wonderland* to *Hamlet*, Mazursky quickly establishes the film's dialectic: the decontextualizing constant of change versus the immobilizing fear of decision making.

Thus, throughout the course of the movie, Mazursky's alter ego finds himself increasingly incapable of doing precisely the activity that most commonly and clearly defines him: directing. His world swirls about him as he helplessly searches for a point of reference. Like Lewis Carroll's fictional heroine, Alex's wonderland (Holly-wood) becomes a place where magical dreams and jarring night-mares collide in the same crowded space. Fantasies turn facts into fiction, friends alter their identities and drift in and out of his life, questions go unanswered, houses unbought, and important con-versations become tangled in grade B (*Riff Raff,* 1936) movie dia-logue on television. Both protagonist and viewer find it more and more difficult to distinguish real from reel life. Discussing the "New Hollywood" with James Monaco, Mazursky displays an al-most nostalgic yearning for the "Old Hollywood" dominated by Jews: "you begin to think of Jack Warner and Sam Goldwyn and Harry Cohn as intellectual giants . . . because they would say things about story, content, conflict, drama, and they had emotions still from the streets, from their own lives" (375). Yet, as with Hamlet, Alex cannot bring himself to make a decision. He remains unable to choose subject matter that might allow him a modicum of influ-ence over personal and professional events, or at the very least the comforting illusion of artistic control.

Although Mazursky never labels the director Alex Morrison as Jewish, he identifies several of the film's characters as such. Alex's mother, for example, speaks with a decidedly Jewish intonation. When she suddenly appears atop a white horse in the midst of a Fellini-esque fantasy, Alex asks her, "What are you doing here?" "Mr. Fellini called I should come," she replies, adding lethally, "sure, he called; you're the one who never calls." His best friend, André (André Philippe), searches throughout the film for an iden-tity, finally becoming an orthodox Jew complete with yarmulke and phylacteries. He tells Alex, "if you want a movie, read the Bible. Every page is a movie. You could do Solomon." In one of the film's warmest scenes, André and Alex celebrate the Sabbath by the sea, the two men singing "Shabbat Shalom" and drinking wine from kiddush cups. André's search for identity returns him to his cultural past, to Judaism. Alex, although appreciating (indeed, taping) this religious experience, still remains personally unfulfilled and uses the occasion to take his first acid trip. Another friend, Leo (Michael Lerner), is described as a "Jewish fascist" when he rejects Alex's idea for a movie about blacks, even though Alex's fantasies depict hopelessly naive and sometimes blatantly racist stereotypes about black sexuality, violence, and music. These imaginary film sequences, if meant to communicate Alex's thoughts for his next picture, demonstrate that he is obsessed with sexually infantile characterizations and superficially apocalyptic images.

Finally, Mazursky casts himself as Hal Stern, an obnoxious studio executive whose pseudo-hip sixties patter ("heavy cats," "I dig, I dig"), long hair, and bell-bottom jeans disguise a sleazy producer with bad table manners and even worse story ideas: He suggests a musical *Huck Finn*. (This was, of course, before the popular Broadway musical *Big River*.) When Alex admires a Chagall lithograph in Hal's office, the voracious producer tries to give him the picture, a crude and transparent attempt to ingratiate himself with the hot young director. The fact that Chagall is one of the few major Jewish painters adds to the scene's cultural and religious ambience. "Just *do* for me" begs Stern, who succeeds in totally alienating the far-less-effusive Alex. Unlike Alfred Hitchcock, who also cast himself in small roles within his own movies, Mazursky continually gives himself obnoxious roles, perhaps culminating in his appearance in drag as the dictator's mother in *Moon over Parador*.

Alex in Wonderland revolves around a series of questions about identity (Who are you?); work (What are you planning to do next?); personal choices (If you had only three kinds of food for the rest of your life, what three foods would you pick?); and feelings (Why am I so sad?). At its center, as in most of Mazursky's films and those of his fellow American-Jewish directors, is a pervasive sense of dislocation, an alienation of feeling that even success cannot assuage. Alex's daily life pales before his fantasy life, and he remains incapable of integrating his imagination with his everyday activities. Thus, his family life, another pervasive theme in Mazursky's pictures, suffers even as his professional life prospers. By virtue of his successful first film, Alex gains the freedom to choose the subject matter for his next project, but this apparent liberty immobilizes him. Once again, a Mazursky character finds freedom constraining rather than liberating. Alex may not be identified as Jewish, but the milieu in which he works, the friends with whom he surrounds himself, the questions he raises, and the feelings he experiences all speak to the American-Jewish experience.

As *Alex in Wonderland*, which presents the portrait of a director incapable of directing his own life, uses a literary text as a point of departure, so, too, *Blume in Love* (1973), which revolves around a divorce lawyer who cannot handle his own divorce, employs a similar device. The earlier film's title emphasizes the dislocations, fantasies, and strange inhabitants—reminiscent of Lewis Carroll's frightening and magical Wonderland—that exist in Mazursky's equally scary and enchanting Hollywood. The latter movie's title, however, references the most famous outsider in modern literary history: Leopold Bloom, the Jewish advertising space salesman who wanders around Dublin in *Ulysses*. (The title also plays, ironically, on the popular tune and Jack Benny's theme song, "Love in Bloom.") The very name *Stephen Blume* combines the first and last names of the novel's two male figures, Stephen Dedalus and Leopold Bloom. In addition, Stephen (George Segal) and Nina (Susan Anspach) Blume plan to call their child Molly, a direct reference to Leopold Bloom's adulterous wife. Mazursky, of course, reverses the initiator of sexual infidelity from Joyce's Molly to his Stephen. Furthermore, he attempts a cinematic equivalent of Joyce's stream-of-consciousness method, incorporating internal monologues that directly reveal Stephen's thoughts through voice-over dialogues.

The movie begins with Stephen Blume, another of Mazursky's Jewish lawyers, sitting disconsolately in an outdoor cafe in Venice, musing to himself about espresso and love. "Love is like a miracle; you can't hide it," he thinks, "but to be in love with your ex-wife is a tragedy." The narrative then unfolds through flashbacks, as Stephen describes how he met Nina Cashman, a social worker, at a trendy fundraiser for Hispanic farmworkers; how they fell in love and married; how Nina found him in bed with his black secretary and divorced him; how she fell in love with Elmo (Kris Kristofferson), an easy-going, hippie singer; how Stephen weaseled his way into their relationship and struggled to get Nina back; how he ultimately raped her; and how Nina is now about to give birth to his child. As he concludes his tale, Stephen glances across the Piazza San Marco, where he and Nina had spent much of their honeymoon, and sees his pregnant former wife walking toward him. "I'm not your wife," she tells him, but they tenderly embrace and, as Nina goes into labor, she and Stephen hurry off to the hospital to deliver their baby. Mazursky thus establishes his milieu as similar to that in his previous, or for that matter his subsequent, pictures. "I wanted to deal with the middle class romantically. The middle class, I feel, is a class which is never dealt with romantically, although the passion which is felt there is as grand a passion as in the movies we used to see with Grace Kelly" (Fox 30). Again, we find big-city, college-educated, professionally successful, currently-in-analysis characters who eat in nice restaurants, believe in liberal causes, and experiment with new life-styles. They live the *Life* magazine version of the American Dream, but they lack inner peace and emotional stability.

Blume in Love contains other aspects characteristic of Mazursky's films. Mazursky again plays the bit role of a figure who has distinctly Jewish characteristics; this time he is Blume's uptight legal partner, Kurt Hellman. Donald F. Mulich, Mazursky's own psychiatrist, again appears as an analyst when Nina undergoes therapy. As Harold Fine sought freedom in the arms of the uninhibited Nancy, a girl totally different from the aggressively Jewish Joyce in *I Love You, Alice B. Toklas!*, so Nina finds liberation in her relationship with the laid-back, former convict Elmo, a distinctive change from the hyperactive lawyer Blume. Nancy and Elmo both represent shiksas, clearly delineated gentile "Others" who function as dramatic foils to the film's Jewish characters because their personalities, values, looks, and ambitions represent such polar opposites. Mazursky, to one degree or another, uses this device of comparing and contrasting Jewish with non-Jewish characters in almost all of his pictures, particularly *Next Stop, Greenwich Village, An Unmarried Woman, Willy and Phil,* and *Down and Out in Beverly Hills.* At moments even the food takes on a Jewish flavor, as it does in several other Mazursky pictures, for example, Blume brings Nina bagels, an act the writer-director himself describes as "a love token, a message of peace, a peace offering, to get back into the house" (Tuchman 71).

Mazursky and other American-Jewish filmmakers compulsively explore several themes that appear in *Blume in Love.* Stephen, like so many of Mazursky's characters, finds his life drastically changed as the result of one thoughtless and (from his point of view) meaningless event: his afternoon tryst with a secretary. He becomes free but at a terrible emotional price. In addition, many of Mazursky's characters—particularly Stephen, Harry (*Harry and Tonto*), and Jessica (*An Unmarried Woman*)—find themselves stranded without partners in a middle-class society that revolves firmly around couples. Herman Broder (*Enemies, A Love Story*), of course, has the opposite social problem; he is married to three women at the same time. These characters exist in emotional exile that allows little personal stability and even less fulfillment. Stephen Blume, like his two literary namesakes in Joyce's *Ulysses,* wanders in search of human connections. They wander the back alleys and pubs of Dublin; he searches the streets of Los Angeles and the piazzas of Venice. Although the lush strains of the theme from *Tristan und Isolde* accompany Stephen's apparent reconciliation with Nina, she recognizes that she is the mother of his child yet not his wife, signalling a new, potentially difficult, relationship that is easier to imagine than live.

Seventy-two-year-old Harry Combes (Art Carney), the central figure in *Harry and Tonto* (1974, cowritten with Josh Greenfeld), is another of Mazursky's wanderers. A retired high school teacher with a love of Shakespeare, he is a widower who still mourns for his beloved Annie. Harry and his cat, Tonto, are forcibly evicted from his soon-to-be-demolished New York City apartment building. At first, Harry tries living with Bert (Phil Bruns), his eldest son, in a crowded suburban setting. When this fails, he first visits his cynical, four-times-divorced daughter (Ellen Burstyn) in Chicago and then his nearly bankrupt son (Larry Hagman) in Los Angeles. The cross-country odyssey, creating a genre that Pauline Kael dubs the "geriatric picaresque," allows Harry to meet an array of intriguing characters: a sixteen-year-old runaway (Melanie Mayron), a friendly hooker (Barbara Rhoades), and even an Indian medicine man (Chief Dan George). The most touching detour, however, occurs when he visits Jessie (Geraldine Fitzgerald), his first love. A once-beautiful dancer who performed with Isadora Duncan, Jessie now lives in a nursing home, a victim of neglect and senility. Harry gallantly, and quite movingly, dances with her, tenderly ignoring the fact that she fails to remember him.

After Tonto dies, Harry decides to live alone near the ocean. For Mazursky, this decision represents a distinct change, a positive evolution from Harry's earlier refusal to abandon his beloved New York City apartment. Although the changes in his life have not been of his own choosing, Harry has survived his trial by catastrophe; he has made peace with himself and the world. Toward the end of the picture, he meets another cat-lover (Sally F. Marr, Lenny Bruce's mother), an aggressive widow who suggests that they pool social security checks and remarks, "if you hadn't told me, I'd have thought you were Jewish." Anyone familiar with Mazursky's other pictures might well agree, although Carney is Irish. In the film's final scene, Harry helps a child (Mazursky's own daughter) make a sand castle on the beach. Such an activity, shot against the backdrop of the setting sun, provides a complex but seemingly apt visual metaphor for Harry's renewed commitment to life's promises and pleasures. It simultaneously reminds viewers that such things must eventually be washed away by the unceasing ebb and flow of life.

Although, like Alex and the characters in *Bob and Carol and Ted and Alice,* Harry is not Jewish, Mazursky populates the film with secondary characters who are Jews, including the cat-lover and the runaway Ginger. Most important, Harry's best friend in New York City, Jacob Ribotowski (Herbert Berghof), is a Polish Jew who spouts Marxist slogans ("Capitalist bastards!") while following the progress of his investments on the New York Stock Exchange. Harry treats Jacob as something of a substitute for Annie, someone with whom he can share his anxieties and frustrations. In fact, Harry feels free enough to discuss his sexual dysfunction with Jacob, admitting to him that "those days are over."

Even those persistent quirks so evident in Mazursky's other films appear in *Harry and Tonto.* For example, Harry is another frustrated performer; he does impressions of various singers for Tonto, telling the cat how he always wanted to go into show business. It is no accident, therefore, that one of the first places he visits in Hollywood is the Walk of the Stars. Mazursky again casts himself in an obnoxious role, this time as a male hustler. Harry's friendship with LeRoy (Avon Long), a black maintenance man, is reminiscent of the other characters of color in Mazursky's films (for example, *Bob and Carol and Ted and Alice* and *Moon over Parador*), a list that contains both sympathetic and stereotypical figures.

Principally, *Harry and Tonto* explores the breakdown of the modern family, the fragmentation of family life generated by time, age, distance, and freedom. Although this theme is not uniquely Jewish, it clearly permeates the work of American-Jewish directors from Edward Slomon to Steven Spielberg. It also rests at the heart of most of Mazursky's pictures, whether from the points of view of successful middle-aged couples with children (*Bob and Carol and Ted and Alice, Down and Out in Beverly Hills,* and *Tempest*); creative artists (*Alex in Wonderland*); young marrieds (*Blume in Love*); single young men (*Next Stop, Greenwich Village* and *Willy and Phil*); middle-aged women with children (*An Unmarried Woman*); immigrants (*Moscow on the Hudson*); or survivors of the Holocaust (*Enemies, A Love Story*). In a 1978 interview with Terry Curtis Fox, Mazursky speaks precisely to this point: "For me, the central things in my life have been my family and my work. I've two children and I've been married twenty-four years. That warmth and closeness obviously means something to me . . . it's my preoccupation" (30).

Harry and Tonto, however, is the single Mazursky film to examine this fragmentation from the point of view of the older man, the patriarchal figure who surveys the checkered record of his children's lives with a mixture of regret, resistance, and resignation. Harry finds that father often doesn't know best, and even if he does, the kids rarely listen to him. Such a truth, although painful, is also strangely liberating. It frees Harry from the curse of continual, debilitating parental responsibility and allows him to struggle for his own independence. Although *Harry and Tonto* certainly functions structurally as a picaresque tale, it works thematically more as a bildungsroman (chapter 1) in which an older, rather than the traditionally younger, character learns, matures, and evolves over the course of the travel narrative.

An Unmarried Woman (1978) also functions, like many of Mazursky's pictures, as a bildungsroman, allowing him to explore the consequences of introducing freedom and change into his by-now-familiar social and economic territory. The narrative, written by Mazursky and nominated for an Academy Award, reverses the premise of *Blume in Love;* this time it is the experience of the female, rather than the male, marriage partner after the husband (Michael Murphy) commits adultery and the couple divorces. Like Harry, Erica Benton (Jill Clayburgh) suddenly finds herself without a partner in a world comprised of couples, although she must also contend with a bitter teenage daughter Patti (Lisa Lucas). Her three close friends (Kelly Bishop, Linda Miller, and Pat Quinn) provide a degree of emotional support as they espouse varying approaches to male-female relationships—from taking a much-younger lover, to tolerating a husband's infidelities, to shunning men, to drinking too much. Support is also given by a compassionate female therapist, Mazursky again using a real psychiatrist (Penelope Russianoff) for the role. Erica, after a one-nighter with an egotistical artist (Cliff Gorman), begins a loving affair with Saul Kaplan (Alan Bates), a sensitive and sexy painter who asks her to spend the summer with him in Vermont. Not yet ready to attempt this type of everyday relationship, Erica refuses to make a commitment but agrees to see Saul on a less encompassing level.

Like many of the other directors discussed in this book, Woody Allen and Sidney Lumet in particular, Mazursky's roots are decidedly urban. He sets a large proportion of his films either in Los

Angeles or New York. *An Unmarried Woman,* for example, opens and closes with spectacular aerial shots of New York City and along the way tours Manhattan, from Rockefeller Center to Chinatown, from the East River Drive to Wall Street, from Fifth Avenue bars to Greenwich Village lofts. Erica's financial status, as well as her connection with the art world through her job in a Soho art gallery, allow Mazursky to take viewers into the bars, galleries, lofts, offices, and restaurants that make New York City unique. As he states, "something about the pace of life, the energy here, the taxis, walking and lunches . . . make people different" (Fox 31). For Mazursky, the urban environment represents a social, emotional, and economic fluidity impossible to find in less frantic settings. It's "part magic, part filth."

The character of Saul Kaplan, which Mazursky considered playing himself before concluding that he was not a sufficiently romantic figure, represents a distinct physical and emotional departure from the Jewish males who populate Mazursky's previous pictures. Whereas in his earlier films Mazursky juxtaposed conservative, rather repressed Jewish figures (Harold Fine and Stephen Blume) with liberated, more expressive gentiles (Nancy and Elmo), here the Jewish painter represents the sensitive, creative man as opposed to Erica's philandering, three-piece-suit former husband. In addition, Saul specifically relates, albeit humorously, his initial artistic impulses back to his ethnic origins: "My father had a shop in what would be the Lower East Side of London. One day when I was about six, my parents had a row and my mother threw a pickled herring at my dad. It missed and splattered all against the wall. I took one look at that pickled herring and that's when I decided to become an abstract expressionist." As a parting gift with both ethnic and oedipal overtones, Erica presents Saul with a jar of pickled herring, which he immediately splatters against the nearest wall. Mazursky, himself, is well aware that Saul represents a clear break from earlier, more traditional Jewish film figures: "I was brought up in a very Jewish neighborhood, but the Jewish thing in America has changed: I think the Jewish alienated schlemiel hero is a thing of the past" (Fox 31).

In *An Unmarried Woman,* Mazursky sees middle-class life in the same manner as Erica views her club meetings: "a cross between 'Mary Hartman' and Ingmar Bergman." He recognizes that the possibility of change, both in a social and in a psychological sense, is double-edged. When the potential for change is not a true psychological reality, a certain amount of fear and anxiety is eliminated.

Freedom, the ability to change, radically alters even the most com-
placent of lives. As Mazursky observes about Erica's husband Martin, "the poor sucker. He doesn't know what to do next. He's made
money, he's earned respectability. . . . He's got a beautiful wife, a
nice child, he's doing well, he lives okay. . . . The possibility of
change exists all around him. He's been fed it" (Fox 32). Not knowing "what to do next" plagues many of Mazursky's middle-class
characters, and he remains one of the few directors who deals with
the "real feeling" of middle-class life, an existence he describes as
being "on the edge of soap opera and the edge of real; it's alienated
and confused, almost tragic" (Fox 30).

Mazursky's next movie, *Willy and Phil* (1980), deals even more
explicitly with characters who have trouble deciding "what to do
next." Willy (Michael Ontkean), a Jewish high school teacher who
wants to be a jazz pianist, and Phil (Ray Sharkey), an Italian photographer who becomes a commercial director, meet at a Bleecker
Street Cinema screening of *Jules et Jim* (1961) in 1970. "They shared
a sense of humor, they hated the war in Vietnam and they loved
Truffaut," says Mazursky on the film's soundtrack, enough reasons
to become friends. Soon, both men fall in love with Jeannette (Mar-
got Kidder), a film editor who comes from Kentucky. Jeannette
moves in with Willy, but she sleeps with Phil, which does not stop
Willy from marrying and having a daughter with her. Finally, all
three, plus the child, end up in Phil's luxurious Malibu Beach
house, an uncomfortable ménage à trois that satisfies none of their
individual needs. Jeannette soon tires of the three-way affair and
takes her daughter back to New York. Followed by Willy and Phil,
she rejects both of them for Igor, a Russian immigrant who is
making a movie called *Moscow on the Hudson* (which became the title
of Mazursky's later picture). In the film's last scene, Willy and Phil,
now older and more conservative, go to see *Jules et Jim* once more,
afterward marveling at the outlandish costumes of the younger
patrons lined up to watch *The Rocky Horror Picture Show*.

Mazursky structures much of his movie around the ethnic interaction between his Jewish and Italian characters, along with their
shiksa from the South. Usually, this interplay assumes a jocular
tone; for example, Willy accuses Phil of wanting to "be a Jewish
intellectual" and asks the fashion photographer to call up some
Presbyterian models so they can get laid. Later, Willy describes his
bar mitzvah to Phil, and Phil tells him about growing up in an
immigrant Italian household. When Willy and Jeannette get into a

fight, she accuses him of feeling sorry for himself. "It's an old Jewish tradition," he answers. After Willy returns from his spiritual adventures in Maui and India, he immediately wants a corned beef sandwich, a bagel with lox and cream cheese, and a *New York Times*.

In the terrible and disturbing scene following Jeannette's departure, however, Willy and Phil discover that even the best of friends harbor ethnic stereotypes that can eventually erupt from beneath a civilized veneer. By hurling such words as "Jew boy and guinea," "wop and kike," "spaghetti head and Christ killer" to hurt each other, Willy and Phil cross an invisible boundary that forever alters their conceptions about their friendship. Their argument is, quite obviously, about Jeannette, as well as an explosion of the repressed jealousy each feels about the other's relationship with her, yet the particular form of these attacks speaks to the inherent underlying tensions and cultural stereotypes present in every interracial, interreligious, interethnic relationship.

Mazursky's Willy is a modern wandering Jew. His drifting search for "answers" leads him to a country farm in up-state New York, a commune on a Hawaiian beach, and an ashram in India. Yet he never quite knows the questions he should be asking. "Did you find enlightenment?" Jeannette finally asks him. "No," he sadly responds, "I just lost a few pounds." Willy finds contentment of even a limited sort only in various unions with people he loves most in the world—Jeannette, Phil, and his daughter. Despite his desire to engage in meaningful relationships, however, Willy remains unable to make a lasting commitment to any concrete ideal or specific person. He is symbolic of the intellectual Jew, searching for significance everywhere but in his own heritage, much like Mazursky's earlier depiction of Harold's hippie brother in *I Love You, Alice B. Toklas!* At times, Willy seems unsure of how Jewish he is. When, for example, he finds a Volkswagen he likes, Willy hesitates to buy it because the car is made in Germany. "Are you Jewish?" the car dealer (Helen Hanft) asks him. "Sort of," he mumbles, "I was bar mitzvahed and go to Passover seder once a year." "Is your mother Jewish?" presses the saleswoman. "Yes," Willy answers. "Then you're Jewish," she concludes.

Willy's mother (Jan Miner) is indeed Jewish. When Willy brings Jeannette home to visit his parents in Brooklyn, Mrs. Kauffman serves chopped liver as if to test Jeannette's attitude toward this decidedly Jewish delicacy. She then alternately brags about her son's IQ of 135 and scolds him for not eating enough. Her major worry is that Willy and Jeannette are not married. Although she tries to be "modern" about this whole situation, Mrs. Kauffman pesters the couple to set a wedding date.

For all her familiar traits, however, Willy's Jewish mother accepts these revolving relationships far easier than does Phil's domineering Italian mother (Julie Bovasso). She demands to be taken back to the airport on the day she arrives in California and discovers that Jeannette and Phil, along with Willy's child, all live together. When Jeannette finally agrees to do just that, Mrs. Demeco turns to her intimidated husband (Louis Guss) and triumphantly crows, "See, she didn't want us here in the first place." Yet for all the fun he has at their expense, Mazursky clearly admires the older generation's commitment to family and—by extension—to their ethnic heritages. Their frustrations, however loud and overbearing, spring from genuine concern and love. They see that Willy, Phil, and Jeannette find peace and contentment unattainable ideals in their jobs, marriages, and misfortunes. Neither Phil's business success nor Willy's wanderings make them very happy. The end of the picture finds the two men as they began it, watchers observing the actions of others.

At least on the surface, Mazursky's next picture, *Tempest* (1982), seems to depart from his previous works. Incongruously, the premiere satirist of modern, urban, middle-class angst turns to Shakespeare, rather than to the headlines, for his inspiration. (Coincidentally, Woody Allen also made his Shakespeare-inspired comedy, *A Midsummer Night's Sex Comedy,* in 1982.) The Greek flavor of the film, which probably owes its origins to Mazursky's new writing partner Leon Capetanos, appears out of sync with either Mazursky's preceding or subsequent films: a small island of feta cheese floating in a sea of lox and bagels. Upon closer examination, however, even this apparently atypical film reveals a prevailing Jewish consciousness, an unspoken state of mind that animates it as much as its clearly stated Shakespearean source. This is the only film in which Mazursky overtly confronts the issue of diaspora in a physical as well as a psychological manner.

Mazursky's primary character is a brooding architect, Phillip Dimitrious (John Cassavetes), whose dream of designing great buildings has dwindled to constructing lavish Atlantic City casinos for the mob, while his desire for a happy home life has degenerated into mortal combat with his wife and his possessiveness with his child. Suffering a midlife crisis as he careens toward a mental, physical, and spiritual breakdown, he mistreats and finally leaves his actress wife Antonia (Gena Rowlands), whom he discovers is having an affair with his gangster boss Alonzo (Vittorio Gassman). With his teenaged daughter, Miranda (Molly Ringwald), and platonic girlfriend, Aretha (Susan Sarandon), a free-spirited, American singer he picks up in Athens, Phillip retreats to a rocky, isolated Greek island inhabited only by a lusty goatherder, Kalibanos (Raul Julia). There the three live for the summer, as Phillip attempts to piece together his shattered life by designing and overseeing the building of a small Greek amphitheater.

Then a sudden storm, one seemingly conjured up by Phillip/Prospero, shipwrecks his former boss, his boss's son Freddy (Sam Robards), and his estranged wife on the island. This particular sequence stirred up squalls of critical outrage, but Mazursky's dramatic intentions seem quite legitimate: "The storm is a bit of insanity made real. Phillip thinks he can do anything. When you believe strongly enough, magic *can* happen. It's just that he's not in control. He thought he was God, but was not. He's just another sap. And sometimes you can't handle your problems until you understand who you are" (Rosenthal 50). Eventually, all are reconciled: Phillip with Antonia, Alonzo with Aretha, and Miranda with Freddy. In the final scene, Phillip, Antonia, and Miranda arrive in New York City to begin their life anew.

Mazursky, as is his practice, sprinkles secondary Jewish characters and specifically Jewish references throughout the film. For example, Trinc (Jackie Gayle), Alonzo's hired comic, clearly represents Jewish comedians who have a Borscht Belt background. In a wonderfully comic clash of cultures, Aretha sings "Hava Nagilah" to a camera-clicking Japanese audience in an Athenian bar. She later tells Phillip about her first husband: an Israeli swimming instructor from Tel Aviv, which is "ridiculous since Jews don't think they can float."

As he does in almost all of his pictures, Mazursky himself performs a Jewish role, Terry Bloomfield, a Broadway musical producer who wants to hire Antonia for his next play. (Betsy Mazursky, the director's wife, plays Bloomfield's wife.) Once again, Mazursky involves himself in the film's most uncomfortable and unpleasant sequence: a drunk and abrasive Phillip disrupts and then destroys Antonia's party by dancing around the room with the disconcerted Bloomfield. Although Phillip apologizes for his actions, even sinking to his knees to beg his wife's forgiveness, Bloomfield and the other guests quickly scurry from the room, their faces expressing sympathy for Antonia and disgust for her husband. However these small touches and secondary portraits seem less connected with the main action and central issues of *Tempest* than such elements in Mazursky's previous work. They seem to be reflexive rather than responsive ingredients that contribute relatively little to the picture.

Like most of Mazursky's other films, *Tempest* revolves around family life, a dominant American-Jewish motif. As James Monaco notes, there is "an underlying sense of community in Mazursky's movies . . . most often expressed in its basic unit: the family" (380). Indeed, even if, like Larry in *Next Stop, Greenwich Village*, Mazursky's figures choose to leave their families, they eventually coalesce into groups representing some form of extended family structure. The very titles of most Mazursky pictures demonstrate the importance he places on these units, as they "announce the group [or] they announce the situation, which is usually a dilemma" (Monaco 380). So it is in *Tempest*. Phillip and Antonia break apart under the strain of work and growing older, but they immediately fling themselves into entangled group relationships equally familial as that just dissolved. In fact, Antonia's search to reclaim Miranda and somehow reconstruct at least part of her family puts the film's ultimate conflict into resolution. For Mazursky, therefore, families are the most satisfying (and the most painful) of social groupings, a Jewish perspective that appears consistently throughout his movies.

What is most interesting about *Tempest* is Phillip's decision to leave his birthplace and seek his cultural homeland, a narrative structure that forces Mazursky to confront the issue of exile (here, self-imposed as differentiated from Shakespeare's Prospero being set adrift by Antonio) from an American-Jewish perspective. On a biographical level, one could easily draw an analogy between Phillip, the frustrated creator forced to compromise his visions to finance his projects, and Mazursky, the pressured director forced to make business deals to finance his pictures, thus establishing an emotional link between the director and his character. "I want to quit. I want to get out. To travel, dream, wander" yells Phillip, and his journey leads him back to his spiritual roots in Greece. But for an American with a cultural heritage drawn from another country such an attempted escape presents immense psychological, intellectual, and spiritual problems. Although it is possible to identify with the culture of one's ancestors, the identification relates to the traditions and customs associated with that culture rather than to the actual day-to-day life in a foreign country. Although Phillip returns to his ancestral homeland, attempting to purify his art by recreating Greek style and form, he never fully integrates himself into the fabric of another society, as his "colonization" of Kalibanos demonstrates. The conclusion of the film, with its beautiful helicopter shots of the Manhattan skyline, heralds the return of Phillip and his family to New York City, an acknowledgment that, for American-Jewish artists, home must be the United States, not some dimly nostalgic vision of life recounted by an aging relative to an impressionable youngster.

Moscow on the Hudson (1984), in almost direct opposition to *Tempest,* revolves around a man immigrating to, rather than seeking refuge from, the United States. Vladimir Ivanoff (Robin Williams) plays a saxophone in a Moscow circus band. While in Russia, he stands in endless lines waiting for shoes that do not fit, meager portions of whatever food is available, and toilet paper that feels like cardboard. He and the other five members of his close-knit family squeeze uncomfortably into a cramped apartment, and Vladimir must ritually bribe a cloddish KGB agent (Savely Kramarov) to maintain his barely tolerable job of "playing for the tigers and bears." Trapped in a society of suffocating individual paranoia and artistic repression, Vladimir resists primarily through his music, enthusiastically singing forbidden Duke Ellington songs and furtively playing American jazz. The only bright spot is his loving family, particularly his irreverent grandfather (Alexander Beniaminov). As Vladimir points out later in the film, "in Russia I did not love my life, but I loved my misery because it was mine."

During the circus's visit to New York City, Vladimir spontaneously defects while shopping at Bloomingdales, requesting political asylum "between Estée Lauder and Pierre Cardin." Leaving his best friend (Elya Baskin), his family, and his ordered life, he initially lives with the black security officer (Cleavant Derricks) who befriends him, joining a family that is emotionally and generationally similar to his own in Russia. Vladimir works at a series of jobs that range from selling hamburgers, to washing dishes, to running a hotdog stand, to driving a limousine, and finally earns enough money to rent a small apartment of his own. He also falls in love with an Italian salesgirl (Maria Conchita Alonso) and adjusts, however uncomfortably at moments, to life in New York City. Realizing both the positive and negative aspects of urban existence in the United States yet still maintaining a nostalgic affection for Soviet culture, Vladimir ultimately grasps the abbreviated version American Dream available to immigrants in the 1980s.

Although Vladimir and his family demonstrate no particular religious affiliation, *Moscow on the Hudson* seems clearly inspired by the plight of Russia's Jews. In fact, the original inspiration for the film came from a story told to Mazursky by Vladimir Toukan, a Soviet Jew studying filmmaking in America, who convinced the director to take him along as part of the crew of *Tempest*. Furthermore, Mazursky and cowriter Leon Capetanos expressly interviewed groups of Russian-Jewish immigrants in Los Angeles and New York City; they even incorporated into their script some portions of the various experiences related to them by these newly minted Americans. In addition, Mazursky and Capetanos traveled in Russia for three weeks, spending most of their time in Moscow, Leningrad, and Kiev. (Mazursky would journey to Russia again during March of 1990, bringing *Enemies, A Love Story* as part of the first Jewish Film Festival, an outgrowth of the San Francisco Jewish Film Festival, ever held in the Soviet Union.) Given Mazursky's fascination with Jewish culture, it seems quite probable that at least some of the Russian citizens who invited him into their homes on his first trip were Jewish. Evidence of this inspiration exists within the film itself as well. In one brief scene, Vladimir guiltily watches and then turns away as KGB agents hustle Jewish protestors into an ominous black sedan. On first viewing, it is unclear whether Vladimir responds simply as any wary Russian would, unwilling to get involved in such public protests, or whether his response is specifically that of a Russian Jew, afraid of being associated and ultimately dragged off with these so-called Refuseniks. Once in America, Vladimir receives a letter from his family. Because the letter is delivered by a Jewish Russian immigrant, the event constitutes direct evidence that his relatives have at least tangential ties with the Jewish community in the Soviet Union.

Moscow on the Hudson preaches an almost total assimilationist philosophy that stretches back to the great melting pot concept that dominated American attitudes toward immigration until the 1960s. In an interview about the "authenticity" of his picture, Mazursky tells Eleanor Blau: "If you came to New York from another country, you'd be shocked—not in a bad way—at how ethnic it really is. All the colors and types would seem extremely exotic compared with what you were used to. . . . What I'm saying is that it's possible for immigrants to be integrated into society and have a good life. That's not true in other countries" (11).

Mazursky's America, at least his vision of urban America as symbolized by the polyglot community that comprises New York City, teems with the vitality of new citizens: a Cuban lawyer, Italian cosmetics salesperson, black security guard (from Alabama), Chinese television reporter, Korean cabdriver, Mexican dishwasher, Indian physician, Filipino nurse, and Jamaican civil servant. "When you speak English," Vladimir asks a fellow immigrant, "does your mouth hurt?" In one of the movie's most unabashedly patriotic scenes, a dejected Vladimir enters a coffee shop soon after he is mugged. Angered by this experience, he speaks pessimistically about America's seemingly hollow promise of liberty and freedom. Soon, however, his entire mood alters as the various immigrants in the shop begin reciting sections from the Declaration of Independence. Responding to the harsh criticism of this and several other Capra-esque scenes, Mazursky declared: "Some people have trouble with the so-called patriotism in the film. I have no trouble. I suppose they think a glib, cynical anti-Americanism would be more chic. We are working awfully hard at thinking this country stinks. . . . But look at the freedom here. Look at the power of that freedom. It's awesome" (Blau 11). Clearly, these are the sentiments of an artist shaped by the Great Depression and World War II, rather than by the Vietnam War and the riots of the late 1960s.

For Mazursky, the difference between Russia and the United States, at least on a personal, day-to-day level, becomes that between a restrictive society as opposed to one that offers choices. The social and political philosophies that structure each country have repercussions on every element of American and Russian society; they characterize all the institutions that affect daily life. Although Mazursky clearly finds the system in the United States far superior to that in Russia, he realizes that such a plethora of choices can overwhelm newcomers. Vladimir, for example, hyperventilates upon discovering the innumerable brands of coffee available to him in the supermarket. Other times the potentiality to accomplish a goal means having to face failure. When, for example, Vladimir finally gets to play music with his musical idol, an event impossible to imagine in his native land, he fails to impress the aging jazz man, a bitter lesson about the limitations of his musical talent. Some illusions are best left untested Mazursky tells us or, to put it another way, because one has the freedom to do something does not necessarily mean he or she should do it.

Although *Moscow on the Hudson* overflows with paeans to the freedom inherent in American life, Mazursky remains keenly aware of how easily democracy turns into indulgence. A country that allows its citizens so many material choices—from rows of cof-

Vladimir Ivanoff (Robin Williams), a Russian defector, is protected by Bloomingdale's security guard (Cleavant Derricks) against the KGB agent (Savely Kramarov) in *Moscow on the Hudson* (1984).

The Whitemans (Bette Midler and Richard Dreyfuss), contemporary lost Jews, throw a party in *Down and Out in Beverly Hills* (1986).

fee at the supermarket to a Bloomingdale's overflowing with capitalist treasures—runs the danger of complacency and selfishness. In another of his "schmuck" cameo appearances, Mazursky himself embodies this danger. He plays Dave, an obnoxious Jewish tourist on the beach of the Fountainbleau Hotel in Miami. (His wife is played by the film's casting director, Joy Todd.) Intent only on his own material comforts, the loutish Dave totally ignores the condition of the almost drowned Orlando Ramierez (Alejandro Ray); he orders a drink from the Cuban refugee and complains about the service of waiters who do not speak English. People from somewhere else comprise most of the citizens of this "strange and wonderful country," but Mazursky warns of the danger of former immigrants not being hospitable to newer arrivals. Such a seemingly endless diversity of personal possibilities, material choices, and societal freedoms can camouflage the dangers present in American life. Thus, when faced with the isolation and brutality of life in urban America, Vladimir can only shake his head and slowly remark, "at least in Russia I knew who the enemy was."

In Mazursky's next film, *Down and Out in Beverly Hills* (1986), freedom has produced indulgence, resulting in an emotional wasteland of damaged egos, wounded intellects, and dysfunctional relationships. His central Jewish couple, the Whitemans, pursue the American dream; in fact, they grasp it in a headlock and squeeze. They have moved, as Mazursky describes an earlier film, "from an ethnic neighborhood to a dream house in the suburbs to EST to Buddhism" (Haller 83). Dave (Richard Dreyfuss), king of the coat hanger manufacturers, lives in a Beverly Hills mansion, drives a Rolls-Royce, and provides his family with every possible material need. So why is his wife Barbara (Bette Midler) unable to relax? Why is his daughter Jenny (Tracy Nelson), who attends posh Sarah Lawrence, unwilling to eat? Why is his son Max (Evan Richards) afraid to explore his sexual preferences? Why does his dog Matisse (Mike) need a shrink (Donald F. Muhich, once again) for his "pre-anorexic condition"? Some tentative answers surface after Dave saves a down-and-out bum, Jerry Baskin (Nick Nolte), from drowning in his pool and convinces him to sojourn in the Whiteman household. (Mazursky and cowriter Leon Capetanos based the film on Jean Renoir's 1932 classic, *Boudu Saved from Drowning*, although their happy ending ignores the original's more complex conclusion.) Jerry brings each character what he or she needs, from manly bonding, to sexual fulfillment, to personal confidence, to mature understanding.

The Whitemans are clearly Jewish. Dave sprinkles his conversation with echoes from a distant past: such Yiddish expressions as *putz, nudge, facocta,* and *schmuck.* His father was a communist in the 1930s, not an uncommon political allegiance for Jews during that economically depressed period. Late one evening, Jerry and Dave reminisce about a shared Brooklyn background (although, because Jerry continually fabricates his past, we can never assess the truthfulness of his tales), and they cement their relationship over generous helpings of bagel, cream cheese, tomato, onion, and lox sandwiches. Dave tearfully recounts his boyhood days growing up around the hallowed Ebbets Field and how he cried the day the Dodgers forsook the grimy Brooklyn streets for the palm-treed elegance of Los Angeles. Of course, he never recognizes that he made a similar exodus from the ethnic neighborhood of his New York City youth to the culturally bland Beverly Hills of his adult years. His glossy L. A. Dodgers jacket, for example, bears little resemblance to the bygone world of "Dem Bums" that he physically and figuratively left behind. Dave's parents, present at a lavish Thanksgiving Day feast early in the picture, appear equally Jewish (Mrs. Whiteman is played by Dreyfuss's real-life mother, Geraldine), as does Sidney Waxman (Mazursky in another bit part) as the Whiteman's pushy accountant who sees walking on hot coals as a tax deduction rather than a spiritual experience. So many small details of Jewish life pile up that one begins to wonder by what difficult-to-pronounce Eastern European name the Whitemans were called before they changed to a more "acceptable," good for business, and WASP-like variation.

Yet beneath the surface humor of Mazursky's portrait of the financially successful Jews of the 1980s lurks a disturbing indictment of a generation bereft of its cultural, religious, and ethical moorings. Dave, a balding, middle-aged Duddy Kravitz with an itch he still cannot scratch, started out hawking lingerie from the back seat of his car and eventually made millions supplying coat hangers to large motel chains. His whole life revolves around achieving material wealth. Once obtained, his possessions provide only minimal emotional solace. In fact, Dave really has quite little to do at work: his modern, mechanized assembly line—assisted by foreign workers—mindlessly hums along, efficiently spewing out coat hangers for millions of Holiday Inn customers.

With all his financial security, Dave still yearns for something more, something he cannot articulate but that he knows is missing. Although he looks happy, his medicine cabinet bulges with bottles of Pepto Bismol, which he compulsively swigs to calm his perpetually upset stomach; he drives an expensive car but feels sinful about owning it; he treats his family and friends to a sumptuous Thanksgiving Day meal but cannot forget the starving people in the world. Yet for all his upper-class, liberal guilt, Dave's proudest social achievement is a comprehensive dental plan for his employees. Thus his daily life provides evidence of the symptoms, if not the disease.

Mazursky defines Dave's relationship to his family in material rather than emotional terms. His nonexistent sex life with his wife gives him the excuse to sneak downstairs during the night to have sex with the Mexican maid (Elizabeth Pena), an uncomfortable image harking back to slave owners sexually oppressing their female slaves. His children either avoid or embarrass him. Of all the characters in the film, Dave most clearly identifies with the lyrics from the Talking Heads song ("Once In a Lifetime") heard on the film's soundtrack: "You may ask yourself what are you doing here./You may ask yourself how did I get here./It's the same as it ever was."

Unlike the generations of Jewish fathers who precede him on the screen, Dave Whiteman has little control over his children, and they demonstrate little respect, or even gratitude, toward him. His contact with them is limited, most spent pampering his elusive daughter and yelling at his rebellious son. Such a dysfunctional Jewish family life is a far cry from earlier screen stories that, like *The Jazz Singer* (1927), *His People* (1929), *Symphony of Six Million* (1932), or *Molly* (1951), present family members fighting furiously among themselves but still demonstrating love and respect for each other.

If Dave represents a middle-aged Duddy Kravitz, Barbara becomes a Brenda Patimkin thirty years after the ending of *Goodbye, Columbus*. She certainly possesses few of the traits that characterize, sometimes to their detriment, previous generations of celluloid Jewish mothers. More concerned with her long fingernails, expanding waistline, and faddish spiritual advisers than about her family's well-being, she mirrors the stereotypical fears and foibles of an aging Jewish-American Princess. For example, Mrs. Whiteman knows that Dave sleeps with Carmen, the maid, but does nothing to stop it. At times she reverses roles with her domestic servant even further and clears the table after dinner while Carmen sits and enjoys dessert. Unlike the traditional portrait of the emotionally suffocating Jewish mother who ladles out guilt and matzoh ball soup in equal portions (a picture Mazursky drew with deadly accuracy in *Next Stop, Greenwich Village*), Barbara detaches herself from her son and daughter. She is more concerned over Matisse's refusal to eat than over anything relating to her offspring, oblivious to the fact that her daughter also has eating problems and that her son's behavior is hostile and antisocial. Although she has time and money to do whatever she wants, Barbara never defines her role, that of a contemporary Jewish wife and mother.

The Whiteman children reflect the problems of their unsettled and insecure parents. Dave sees so little of Jenny that she becomes "nothing but a blur with a nice smell." She may well have chosen to attend college in the East to get away from her bizarre family life. Dave's "little girl" also appears to be anorexic, a condition Mazursky describes as "a disease that's been around for a long time, has become really fashionable in the last decade and a half . . . when people can afford the luxury of being that neurotic" (Tuchman 18). Jenny does not understand her parents, makes no effort to get to know them as adults, and even refuses to introduce them to her boyfriends. Until Jerry's intervention, she describes herself as "a bitch, a total princess." Max, unlike his sister, desperately wants to communicate with Dave and Barbara but is so alienated, emotionally isolated, and psychologically paralyzed that he can do so only through a series of vitriolic videos that show his parents constantly yelling at him. He fears that his parents will not accept his sexual choice and that he never measures up to his father's expectations. Thus, the Whitemans are less a family than a series of related neuroses, each feeding off the other. Externally, they mirror America's assimilated Jews during the Reagan era; internally, they reflect the destruction of traditional American-Jewish family structure.

Being totally assimilated Jews, the Whitemans never consider using their ethnic culture, their religious and moral heritage, to help resolve their problems. Instead, an accident of fate delivers them a scruffy messiah, Jerry Baskin. Jerry is Dave's physical and psychological opposite: Dave is short and dark whereas Jerry is tall and blonde; Dave overachieves whereas Jerry underachieves; Dave has all the material comforts whereas Jerry has few; Dave hates his dog whereas Jerry loves his and even attempts suicide when he cannot locate him; Dave's whole life revolves around work whereas Jerry lets his considerable talents go to waste; Dave is Jewish whereas Jerry clearly is not. In fact, Jerry's introduction to the Whitemans comes through Christian symbology, that is, the baptism and rebirth ritual in the swimming pool that both saves his life and forever alters that of his somewhat befuddled hosts. The same image reappears near the movie's conclusion, this time comically undercutting the Whitemans' pretentious party for some visiting Chinese businessmen interested in buying Dave's coat hangers. At this same event, Jerry assumes the ultimate Christian role, Santa Claus. The persona is apt because he dispenses emotional gifts to the various members of the household: friendship to Dave, sexual fulfillment to Barbara, self-esteem to Max, self-awareness to Jenny, and political consciousness to Carmen.

The manner in which *Down and Out in Beverly Hills* uses Jerry reverses the traditional role of the Jew as ethical role model for a modern world obsessed with material wealth and dedicated to quick-fix solutions. In this environment, the Jew functions as an apparent failure, but one whose ethical values raise him above those who cheat, lie, steal, and injure others to achieve economic success. As Morris Bober, the long-suffering neighborhood grocer in Bernard Malamud's *The Assistant,* observes, "this [Jewish Law] means to do what is right, to be honest, to be good. This means to other people. Our life is hard enough. Why should we hurt somebody else? For everybody should be the best, not only for you or me. We ain't animals. This is why we need the Law. This is what a Jew believes" (124).

Such a vision, in one form or another, often operates in movies containing Jewish characters, as well as in literature. For example, Jewish soldiers function as moral centers of the action, often speaking the lines that foreground the picture's message in such war dramas as *The Purple Heart* (1944), *Pride of the Marines* (1945), and *The Young Lions* (1958). Similarly, Jewish victims of Nazi horrors in such films as *Diary of Anne Frank* (1959), *The Juggler* (1953), *Judgment at Nuremberg* (1961) and *Voyage of the Damned* (1979), or of American anti-Semitism in *Crossfire* (1947) and *Gentleman's Agreement* (1947), are often eloquent reminders of inhumanity and intolerance. The Jewish victims remain inherently more ethical than their persecutors. Even in the comedies of Woody Allen which, like *Annie Hall* (1977) and *Broadway Danny Rose* (1984), poke fun at the director's neurotic Jewish protagonists, Jewish figures usually appear more ethically sensitive, more torn between the highs and lows of daily existence and conscious of life's moral paradoxes, than do his emotionally and morally bland gentiles. *Down and Out in Beverly Hills,* however, reverses this traditional pattern of Jew teaching gentile how to behave responsibly.

Indeed, the gentile's role as teacher of values to the nouveau riche Jews caused some critics to attack *Down and Out in Beverly*

Hills' moral perspective. Mashey Bernstein, for example, petu-lantly harangues Mazursky about his ethnic attitudes and views the movie as the latest example of Mazursky's long-standing disdain for Judaism: "Mazursky's comedic glove holds a knife aimed at the Jew's jugular. . . . Mazursky does not mourn the loss of ethnic iden-tity, but rather advocates its demise. He falls prey to the ultimate Jewish fantasy: the quest for universalism. *Down and Out . . .* marks a new low in the saga of the assimilation of the American Jew" (42–43). Such a point of view ignores the subtle shading in Mazursky's pictures. Jerry has not forever cured all the ills of the Whiteman household, any more than Bob and Carol find absolute truth in their encounter weekend, Steve and Nina leave all their troubles behind them, Erica and Saul totally resolve their fundamental dif-ferences, or Phillip and Antonia live in permanent domestic tran-quility. Jerry is the Whiteman's latest (not last) spiritual fad, their new guru until something, or someone, offering greater fulfillment comes along.

Mazursky clearly sees America as different from European countries in that separation of church and state creates a fluid so-cial structure that frees Jews to experience economic blessings as well as emotional turmoil. The American Jews in Mazursky's films do not cling to traditions that united their ancestors yet isolated them into small enclaves within whatever political system they lived. Mazursky's generation of filmmakers forsakes traditional rit-uals but offers no encompassing value system to replace tradition. For him, moral and emotional uncertainty is the price of freedom, the price Jews pay for their willingness to play a larger role in the social, economic, and political contexts that surround them.

Moon over Parador (1988) is a departure for Mazursky, in that he abandons New York City and Los Angeles for the mythical Carib-bean island of Parador. When the island's gluttonish dictator, Al-berto Simms, dies unexpectedly, the country's chief of secret police, Roberto Strausmann (Raul Julia), forces a second-rate actor, Jack Noah (Richard Dreyfuss), to impersonate the deceased ruler, as-suming the country's elite ruling class can maintain their grip on power by manipulating the frightened performer. Madonna Men-dez (Sonia Braga), the dictator's voluptuous mistress, quickly rec-ognizes the switch and the reasons for Strausmann's desperate ploy but perpetuates the charade to influence Noah/Simms into making land reforms and democratizing the country. Complicating matters is the presence of the man who actually makes foreign and domes-tic policy decisions for Parador: a CIA station chief (Jonathan Winters) masquerading as a retired American businessman. Eventually, however, Noah realizes the precariousness of his role-playing and arranges for a fake assassination followed by a secret flight to the United States. Safely back in New York City, he once again assumes the comparatively humdrum life of an often-out-of-work actor, ruefully realizing that his finest performance was played before an audience unaware of his performance.

Many Mazursky characters have a direct, or at least a tangential, relationship to show business. Some simply fantasize about a life performing for others. Harry (*Harry and Tonto*) wanted to be a singer and constantly does impressions of famous actors, while his first lover danced in Isadora Duncan's company. Erica (*An Unmarried Woman*), too, once aspired to dance, as her impromptu rendition of "Swan Lake" early in the picture demonstrates. In the same film, Saul's status as a renowned painter makes him a media personality similar to those in show business. In a later sequence, Erica and her friends sprawl on a bed, reading the Sunday *New York Times* and looking at portraits of famous women film stars. Their conversation about how they lack self-esteem, and, conversely, how Bette Davis and Katharine Hepburn never did, speaks to their confusion of reality with fantasy. The scene further functions as a sly commentary on how cinema offers easy fictions to solve complex realities (a reflexive moment in a movie that does precisely the same thing). Willy (*Willy and Phil*) also harbors secret ambitions to perform, although as a jazz pianist rather than a singer. Phil's work as a fashion photographer and then director of television commercials brings him, too, into daily contact with show business.

Still other characters in Mazursky's films live out creative fantasies, usually functioning successfully (or at least semisuccessfully) in the competitive show business environment. For example, Bob (*Bob and Carol and Ted and Alice*) works as a documentary filmmaker, and Alex (*Alex in Wonderland*) directs feature movies. Both make enough to live comfortable, upper-middle-class lives, unlike the drifter Elmo (*Blume in Love*), whose songwriting career keeps him on public assistance. Larry (*Next Stop, Greenwich Village*) leaves home to pursue a creative dream and, at the end of the film, abandons New York for a part in a Hollywood picture. His major reason for moving from Brooklyn to Greenwich Village is to find emotional and psychological freedom to pursue a career in acting. Antonia, an already established actress, and Aretha, a café singer, interest Phillip in *Tempest,* while in *Moscow on the Hudson,* Vladimir dreams of being a jazz saxophonist, plays in a circus band, and entertains Lucia's fantasy of being a television personality. Finally, Jerry (*Down and Out in Beverly Hills*) claims he was an actor, and Dave's next-door neighbor (Little Richard) is a famous singer.

Jack (né Noah Blumberg) Noah represents what Larry might eventually become: a little-known actor who, although he has had some success, spends most of his time going from one casting call to the next. His serendipitous role as president of a country, pretending to rule while actual power resides with rich, nearly anonymous men banded together behind the scenes, becomes an obvious satire of Ronald Reagan's terms as president. Mazursky further implies that Strausmann (with his obvious German name) and those who actually govern Parador, while using the president as a figurehead to assuage the masses, are direct descendants of Nazis who fled to South America after the fall of the Third Reich. One even confides that he is afraid of ending up in an Israeli court. In addition, Mazursky's bit part as the dictator's mother, given his previous portraits of Jewish mothers (*I Love You, Alice B. Toklas!, Next Stop, Greenwich Village, Willy and Phil, Down and Out in Beverly Hills*) as well as his obsession with psychoanalysis, brims with Freudian ramifications. Her/his relationship with the dictator echoes Mazursky's previous mothers, most of whom struggled to reconcile their children's new ideas with their own Old World values. Yet upon returning to Parador from an extravagant shopping spree in Paris, she expresses her ennui, sounding very much like a world-weary director when she observes that "everything is ruined by repetition."

Scenes from a Mall (1991) breaks little new ground other than matching two icons of American-Jewish pop culture: Bette Midler and Woody Allen. He plays Nick Fifer, a successful sports agent celebrating a wedding anniversary with his wife of sixteen years, the marriage counselor-turned-bestselling author Dr. Deborah Feingold-Fifer. On the surface all seems fine, as the two prosperous Jews juggle brisk walks together, separate telephone lines, demanding answering services, and reasonable lovemaking with astonishing dexterity. Trendy, liberated, aging yuppies, they display little outward connection to Jewish religion or culture, preferring sushi, surfboards, and skiing to more traditional pursuits. As in most Mazursky pictures, however, calm outward appearances disguise inner turmoils; the deconstruction of the relationship, the movie's central section, is not surprising. Mazursky's subject is again the angst of modern American life among the wealthy, as each half of this seemingly content couple turns into a raving lunatic. First Nick and then Deborah confesses infidelity: he with a secretary and she with a prominent colleague (Mazursky, again in a cameo role). In light of such revelations, their quiet day together, shopping in the mall, quickly evolves into chaotic episodes of breakups and make-ups. The Fifers' sweet-sixteen celebration degenerates into an acrimonious series of recriminations that reveal their deep-seated animosities and repressed hostilities. Clearly, we are in familiar Mazursky territory, from the juxtaposition of old-time Christmas songs and new-era melodies, to the large Menorah in the midst of the elaborate Christmas decorations, to the randy moment of oral sex while watching *Salaam Bombay*.

During his entire directing career, Paul Mazursky has incorporated almost all of the Jewish motifs discussed in chapter 1. Several, such as family life, assimilation-alienation, and urban life, inform the central vision of his pictures and reappear in film after film. In addition, many of the characters, attitudes, and themes within his films spring from a decidedly Jewish perspective, a worldview colored by the fact that he is a Jew within a Christian culture. Other elements and motifs seem almost tangential in Mazursky's works, functioning more as communal atmosphere, as unstated ethnic context or even as in-jokes for alert viewers. In a few films, the Jewish elements seem simply a given, not much more important than a character's height or hair color. Yet Mazursky's particular sensibility remains dependent on an apparent paradox, his simultaneous distance from and embrace of American middle-class life. Such a balancing act becomes possible because of his cultural heritage. Like the work of Woody Allen, Mel Brooks, and Sidney Lumet, Mazursky's films cannot be separated from the Jewish context that informs them and from Mazursky's personal sense of himself as an American and a Jew. However assimilated he may be, Mazursky's work reveals a deep-seated concern, an artistic obsession, with things Jewish.

These concerns are central in Mazursky's two most explicitly Jewish films, the autobiographical *Next Stop, Greenwich Village* (1976) and the adaptation of Isaac Bashevis Singer's novel *Enemies, A Love Story* (1989). Thirteen years separate the two projects, and a close examination of each reveals how Mazursky's attitudes change over the years. The earlier film, a remembrance of growing up Jewish in America from the vantage point of middle age (Mazursky was forty-six when he made the film), presents a decidedly ambivalent portrait of Jewish home life, almost totally ignoring the religious element of Judaism. Mazursky's Larry Lapinsky finds the

Mazursky directs Bette Midler and Woody Allen in a segment of *Scenes from a Mall.*

trappings of Jewish religious life irrelevant to his daily existence; for him, it is an accident of genetics, not a moral imperative. The latter movie, completed as Mazursky approached sixty, delves far deeper into the intricate connections between Jews and Judaism, as well as the immense chasm separating those Jews who experienced the Holocaust firsthand and those who sat safely in America while Hitler exterminated European Jewry. Here the characters are obsessed with their relationship to God and religious Judaism. Taken together, the films demonstrate Mazursky's continual concern with issues central to Jewish life in America. They also chart his deepening exploration of complex issues that remain at the heart of the American-Jewish experience, topics that join as well as separate Jews from their Christian neighbors.

Next Stop, Greenwich Village tells the tale of Larry Lapinsky's (Lenny Baker) move away from suffocating home life with his parents toward independence in his own Greenwich Village apartment. The account echoes the director's own exodus and development: "It was a memory of my friends and experiences in the early Fifties. And, like any memory I've ever got, it's a very high mixture of fact and fiction" (Applebaum 16). The picture opens in 1953, as Larry packs his suitcase, the final step in leaving his parent's Brownsville home (Brownsville is a section of Brooklyn where Mazursky also grew up). On the wall, framed, hangs his Certificate for Achievement in College Theater presented by the Varsity Players of Brooklyn College (Mazursky's alma mater), as well as pictures of him in various roles from different college productions. Completing this collage of memories are Brooklyn Dodger pennants. Larry takes a yarmulke out of his dresser, places it on his head, contemplates his image in the mirror, and then throws the yarmulke back into the drawer. Later, on the subway ride to the Village, he jauntily puts a beret on his head. The new has replaced the old, the foreign has displaced the familiar, and Greenwich Village has no place for religious leanings.

Larry's parting, however, is made difficult by his overbearing mother (Shelley Winters), who forces Larry to feel intensely guilty over "deserting" his parents. Although he keeps repeating that "I'm not gonna argue with you Mom," Larry becomes more and more upset by his mother's hysterical antics. He gets little support from his father (Mike Kellin) who, uncomfortable with any displays of negative emotion, passively reads the *Daily News* and tries to ignore the chaos surrounding him. Finally, when she refuses to kiss him goodbye, Larry erupts in anger: "Jesus Christ," he screams, "will you stop! You are not going to make me feel guilty!" He storms out of the house and makes his way to fame and fortune in a new environment, the music shifting from the operatic arias that fill his Brooklyn home to the Dave Brubeck and Charlie Parker melodies characteristic of Greenwich Village. Yet he cannot leave his mother totally behind; "Oh boy, am I guilty," he mutters as he stands in front of his new apartment house, admitting to himself what he refuses to tell his mother.

Once in Greenwich Village, Larry gets a part-time job in a health food store (as did the young Paul Mazursky) and collects an odd assortment of bohemian friends. One thing in his life does not change, however; he remains faithful to Sarah Roth (Ellen Green), his long-time girl friend in Queens. Now that he has his own apartment, the two can freely make love any time they want, but Sarah seems more interested in washing her hair and keeping her makeup fresh than in enjoying their newfound independence. "Do you love me?" asks the confused Larry after she rebuffs his advances. "I told you I might get a diaphragm," snaps Sarah as though her "sacrifice" proves the depth of her feelings. When they finally do make love, Larry asks her, "Was I funny or was I great?" and Sarah responds, "you were fine," as if commenting on a new play that is acceptable but not particularly moving or inspiring. Her sarcasm reveals a deeper dissatisfaction with both their physical and their emotional relationship, as she cynically refers to their lovemaking as a "comedy act together."

For Sarah, going to bed with Larry is primarily an act of rebellion against her stolid and oppressive parents, as well as against the social values she feels compelled to uphold. Rather than an act of personal commitment, or even one of sheer physical abandonment, Sarah's sexual relationship with Larry remains a shiver of excitement that momentarily enlivens her boring environment. "I love you," Larry tells Sarah as they make love early in the movie; her response, a resounding silence, speaks volumes about her feelings. Later, after Sarah admits that she loves his "friend" Robert (Christopher Walken) and has gone to bed with him, a distraught Larry slaps her and then pathetically says once again, "I love you Sarah." "I know," she replies. Sarah allows Larry to make love to her on the front porch of her Brooklyn home, even though he uses no contraceptive, because this location seems both more daring and disrespectful of her parents. Later, when Sarah becomes pregnant, Larry offers to marry her. She says she will think about it but instead has an abortion without discussing it with him.

In many ways, Sarah falls prey to the dominant mores of female behavior in the 1950s. For example, when she finally reveals that she lied to Larry and did sleep with her previous boyfriend, she claims, with some justification, "it's what you wanted to hear." At the film's conclusion, Sarah still lives at home and continues lying to her parents about where, and with whom, she spends her nights. She, unlike Larry, is unable to break from her conventional environment and middle-class morality, preferring hypocrisy to direct confrontation with her parents. While Larry dreams of becoming a star, Sarah wonders if she should go to an analyst. Indeed, as the picture progresses, she seems more and more an unlikely match for Larry's expanding sensibilities: "I think about suicide once or twice a day," he tells her. "That's natural," she responds calmly, "thinking about suicide makes you feel talented. You feel like a Dostoevskian hero."

Larry also has problems with his friend Robert Fullmer, a self-styled poet and intellectual. Mazursky constantly compares and contrasts the dark, very Jewish Larry with the blonde, very gentile Robert, whose intellectual ability, good looks, and introspective sensitivity clash with Larry's ebullient, and far coarser, personality. While Larry struggles to obtain even menial acting jobs, Robert effortlessly gets his poems published in *Sewanee Review*. But Robert eventually reveals himself as superficial, egotistical, and weak, an effete poseur who preys upon the desperation of lonely, older women to obtain a living. Another friend describes him: "Gigantic ego. A man who thinks everything in skirts is in love with him. Charm. Guile. Poetry. Hate." Robert's intelligence, so admired in the earlier segments of the movie, becomes an emotional escape as the picture progresses. It is a bright, gleaming weapon that destroys, rather than heals, other people. For example, this icy narcissist forces everyone to play the "Truth Game," a slim pretext for savaging his friends' fragile egos. Later, he seduces Sarah with little thought about Larry and no concern about her feelings for him. "Have you ever been in love?" Larry asks him, trying to understand why he would seduce and then so cruelly abandon Sarah. "I don't think so," Robert replies, adding somewhat lamely, "What can I tell you; people get hurt." Robert evolves into the most negative character in *Next Stop, Greenwich Village*. His intellectual affectations, disguises for emotional sadism, draw people to him whom he then exploits, damages, and refuses to take responsibility for destroying. As Larry finally realizes, "underneath that pose, there's just more pose."

The Jewish mother (Shelley Winters) comes to visit her son in *Next Stop, Greenwich Village* (1976).

Larry's conflicts with Robert and Sarah, however, remain less heated than his constant clashes with his mother. Although he physically departs his parents' home for the free, bohemian life of Greenwich Village, Larry never psychologically leaves his mother behind. Indeed, the film is often a compendium of Jewish mother-son conflicts, with enough pop Freudian psychology thrown in to delight any armchair psychiatrist. The weekly visits that Larry's parents pay him in his new apartment betray the lack of communication that plagues the family. The three sit silently; his good-natured but ineffectual father reads the *Daily News*, his emotionally volatile mother listens to her opera records and cries, and he, duty-bound, stares out the window, wishing he were elsewhere. Of course, Mrs. Lapinsky ritually brings her son presents each Sunday, ranging from lox and challah to tooth powder and underwear. Before each uncomfortable visit between a mother who still views her son as a child and a son who sees his mother as simply a dispenser of guilt, Larry imitates his mother, knowing precisely what she will say and how she will respond to each situation. He is, of course, absolutely accurate. During these moments, Mazursky captures the historical and emotional gulf that exists between generations, here particularized as the uncrossable chasm between second- and third-generation Jews.

When his parents show up uninvited at his rent party, Larry seethes in quiet embarrassment. His fears that his mother will make a fool of herself—and therefore of him—give way to anger when his friends readily accept Mrs. Lapinsky and she becomes the life of the party. In particular, her semiseductive dance with Bernstein, a homosexual black who claims his mother named him after her Jewish employers, infuriates Larry, perhaps because he resents seeing her with another "child" or, for that matter, playing a role other than one he can assimilate.

The rent party marks the first occasion that Sarah meets Mrs. Lapinsky. "At least you're a Jewish girl," she says to Sarah, adding, "if it were up to my son, we'd never meet; he's ashamed of me." "No, he's not," responds Sarah, "he's afraid of you." "Miss, don't be such a wise guy" is the retort. Mrs. Lapinsky eventually cajoles Sarah into admitting that she and Larry sleep together, then behaves hysterically and threatens never to see them again. Realizing that he must calm her down, Mr. Lapinsky soothes her by saying, "Don't worry. She's a nice Jewish girl. She was lying." Once his parents leave, Larry contemplates the evening's psychic damage: "Great God in Heaven help me! Help a poor Jewish boy. Help my twisted brain. . . . The crazy thing is that while it's happening I see the humor of it. No matter how insane it gets, there's still the funny side." He then goes on to claim that his mother invented the Oedipus complex.

Larry's fantasies about his mother contain suppressed sexuality and anger. In one, he recites Shylock's famous "Hath Not" speech before members of his acting class. Disgusted by his weak performance, Mrs. Lapinsky actually takes over Larry's role before the class, reciting the same lines but receiving an enthusiastic response from Larry's classmates. Basking in their applause, Mrs. Lapinsky does a little tap dance, holding up her skirt high enough to reveal her garters. In his fantasies, Larry's mother succeeds where he fails. Earlier in the film, Larry plays a scene from Clifford Odets's *Golden Boy* with a beautiful, blonde woman in his acting class. In his most oedipal fantasy, his mother plays opposite him in the same segment and, in a particularly passionate moment, he grabs her, bends her over backward, and kisses her on the lips. In a later fantasy, Larry sees himself reciting Hamlet's "To Be or Not to Be" soliloquy before a hostile audience that pelts him with pies. His mother joins them, shouting, "Be a doctor!" Such dreams indicate Larry's love-hate relationship with the figure Mazursky describes as "my own mother, this very powerful woman. Tremendous energy that was not used, not plugged in. So it fizzled all over the joint. That silver cord tremendously overdone is bad. But no cord—is worse" (Tallmer 13).

To Mazursky's credit, however, he never turns Mrs. Lapinsky into a raging Sophie Portnoy. As Pauline Kael notes in her review of *Next Stop, Greenwich Village,* she is no crass castrator: "Mrs. Lapinsky pours so much brute emotion into every small detail of her life that she has lost all sense of proportion; everything to do with her becomes of world-shaking importance. Her unused brains have turned her into a howling freak, but you can recognize in her the sources of her son's talent and wit" (*Lights* 128). Her sensitivity reveals itself as she weeps while listening to her opera records, tearfully telling Larry how her one desire is to go to the Metropolitan Opera House and actually see her favorite opera singers. When Larry prepares to leave New York for Hollywood, where he has been offered a small acting job in a movie (as was budding actor Paul Mazursky in 1954), Mrs. Lapinsky tells him about his roots, although in seriocomic form: "You come from good stock. Your grandmother snuck across the Polish border buried under sacks of potatoes. The guards put bayonets into the sacks, but she never cried out. That's where you came from." She then hands Larry some apple strudel to eat on the plane trip to California. "You're a funny lady, ma" observes Larry, to which she responds with uncharacteristic candor, "My life has not been very funny."

By the film's conclusion, Larry, unlike the still-resentful Alexander Portnoy, has learned to accept his mother's foibles. "I'm not angry anymore," he tells his long-suffering father, "I'm crazy, not angry." Perhaps even more important, he compromises with his mother's obsessions, agreeing to write often and call every day. Mrs. Lapinsky, too, has changed. She accepts Larry's decision to follow his dreams, telling him as he leaves to tell Clark Gable that she always loved him and admonishing, "Larry, be a good actor." Thus, by the end of the film, Larry recognizes what his mother has done to him, as well as understands her actions as expressions of love, however misguided.

In the Village, Larry finds the intellectual fellowship and emotional support missing at home. His sojourn allows him to accept his mother more readily, opening him to the real humanism that converts his anger to a mature compassion. Unlike Portnoy, Larry is not crippled by his life within a "Jewish joke." Although it creates problems, such a life also strengthens Larry and provides him with confidence in his own talents. Thus, unlike his friend Robert, he never resorts to emotional cruelty or needs to prove his superiority by destroying others. Mazursky, through his portrait of Larry, never loses sight of the insecurity, guilt, and frustration derived from this Jewish background. But, as his films display, he recommends neither total assimilation nor blind cynicism. Humor remains Mazursky's recommended perspective. The distinction between humor and joking is articulated through the acting teacher (Michael Eagan), who critiques Larry's early performance: "Joking is the American actor's disease. It's the American person's disease. Because what you're doing is keeping reality out so that it won't touch you. The worst kind of joking you can do is to keep life out. Commenting. Editorializing. Joking. Terrible. Don't do it. It's fatal." Mazursky desperately tries to "keep life" in his pictures, and his humor captures, not excludes, it. His films present portraits drawn from his Jewish roots and lessons learned from his Jewish perspective of the world.

Although certainly not Mazursky's best film, *Next Stop, Greenwich Village* represents an important key to understanding the Jewish perspective that informs all of his pictures; it is his attempt to record his passage from Brooklyn to Greenwich Village to Hollywood. Such a journey represents much more than simply a physical change; it is psychological, emotional, and sociological transition that shapes Mazursky's comic worldview. The movement also charts the crucial role that Mazursky's Jewish background plays in transforming his unique sensibilities that are expressed so powerfully in his movies. For Mazursky, the angst implicit in growing up Jewish in America leads either to anger or to craziness—or to some mixture of both. Using these descriptors as poles, one could easily plot the spectrum of Jewish comedians from the benign, homespun humor of Sam Levinson, comedy that simply exaggerates daily life and makes an audience feel warm nostalgia, to the acerbic wit of Lenny Bruce, which outrages as it attacks fondly held beliefs. Bright points along this spectrum that (with the notable exception of black comics) defines American comedy could be placed next to the names of such American-Jewish humorists as Sid Caesar, Woody Allen, Mel Brooks, Joan Rivers, Judy Holiday, Norman Lear, Jerry Lewis, Roseanne Arnold, Milton Berle, Jack Benny, Danny Kaye, Goldie Hawn, Shelley Berman, David Brenner, George Burns, Eddie Cantor, Rodney Dangerfield, the Three Stooges, Buddy Hackett, Alan King, Jackie Mason, the Marx Brothers, Albert Brooks, Elaine May, Fanny Brice, Smith and Dale, Carl Reiner, the Ritz Brothers, Mort Sahl, Henny Youngman, Soupy Sales, Bea Arthur, and many many more. All of these distinctive comic talents, to one degree or another, managed to mold either their anger or their craziness (more often than not an amalgam of both) into public personas that acknowledged resentment and madness and somehow changed their personal traumas into performances and monologues that the rest of America recognized, laughed at, and rewarded.

Enemies, A Love Story represents Mazursky's deepest and most overt exploration of complex Jewish issues connected to the horrors of the Holocaust. Based on Nobel prize-winner Isaac Bashevis Singer's 1972 novel, his first book exploring a post-Holocaust world and his first set in the United States, the film's black comedy revolves about three women and one man whose lives are irrevocably altered and affected daily by the trauma of surviving the Holocaust. Herman Broder (Ron Silver), the well-educated son of a wealthy Polish landowner, spends World War II hiding in a cramped hayloft and cared for by his family's former servant, Yadwiga (Margaret Sophie Stein). Out of gratitude, he marries his gentile savior, and they travel to America to begin a new life in Coney Island. Herman finds work ghostwriting speeches, articles, and book chapters for Rabbi Lembeck (Alan King), a Manhattan religious leader more interested in business deals than in spiritual salvation.

Quickly bored with Yadwiga's simple-minded, peasant mentality, Herman begins a torrid affair with Masha (Lena Olin), a beautiful but neurotic concentration camp survivor living with her mother (Judith Malina) in the Bronx. Masha remains married to, but separated from, Leon Tortshiner (Paul Mazursky), a small-time con man who claims to be an important scientist. After Masha informs Herman about her pregnancy, they marry in a Jewish ceremony although he never divorces Yadwiga (whom he wed in a civil ceremony). In the midst of this emotional ferment, Herman's first wife, Tamara (Anjelica Huston), suddenly appears to throw his life into even greater turmoil. Eye-witnesses had told Herman, and he had accepted their reports, that she and their two children had been shot in Auschwitz. But the resourceful Tamara outwitted her persecutors by hiding among dead bodies and then crawling to freedom, eventually escaping to Russia and finally finding her way to New York City and Herman.

It is readily apparent why Singer's novel, with its delicate blend of the comic and the tragic, its powerful female characters, and its examination of the price of freedom, attracted Mazursky immediately. Yet in bringing this particular work to the screen, he faced, for the first time in his career, two intimidating challenges: adapting the work of a world-renowned author and dealing with the Holocaust. The usual estimate is that from one-fourth to one-fifth of all feature films have been literary adaptations, yet few outstanding films have been made from superior novels. The standard explanation of the cinema's inability to transform great books into great films remains that a notable work of literature has achieved its fullest artistic expression in that form and, by its very nature, part of its noteworthiness resides in the author's ability to manipulate language.

According to this view, no filmic adaptation of an important literary work could ever match the power and sophistication of the original source material. The best adaptations are provocative interpretations, the majority are pale illustrations, the worst are willful acts of sabotage. A more enlightened position holds that superior film adaptations of literary works seek the spirit rather than the letter of the original source. Here, as the literary critic Martin Battestin argues, analogy is the key: "striking analogous attitudes and finding analogous rhetorical techniques" (36). In this manner, directors become not merely illustrators of the written text, but artists in their own right who draw inspiration, rather than slavish imitations, from original sources.

Mazursky's (and cowriter Roger Simon's) film adaptation of Singer's novel remains extremely faithful to its original source. Singer's exact language has been carefully transposed into dialogue and his verbal pictures into visual representations. Yet one particular image clearly demonstrates Mazursky's sense of visual analogy: the Wonder Wheel, a gigantic ferris wheel that dominates the Coney Island landscape. Here, he subtly uses a concrete image to communicate an abstract idea present throughout Singer's work, the cyclical nature of history and the persistence of evil: "The idle promises of progress were no more than a spit in the face of the martyrs of all generations. If time is just a form of perception, or a category of reason, the past is as present as today. Cain continues to murder Abel. Nebuchadnezzar is still slaughtering the sons of Zedekiah and putting out Zedekiah's eyes. The pogrom in Keshneniev never ceases. Jews are still burned in Auschwitz" (Singer 165).

At various points throughout the picture, Herman stands motionless, staring out the window of the cramped apartment he shares with Yadwiga, mesmerized by the hypnotic lights and perpetual rotations of the Wonder Wheel. Mazursky even concludes the film with an image of a still-revolving mechanical ride. Yet for all its illusion of movement, deceptive grace, and apparent power, the wheel never takes its passengers anywhere. Its revolutions ultimately deposit them precisely where they entered its ceaseless pattern of circles. By naming such a contraption a "Wonder," the film comments ironically on the gullible nature of human thinking, a habit of mind that perceives uniqueness where there is only duplication. Such a pattern of perpetual evil fashions human history into a series of circular repetitions rather than of linear evolutions, an endlessly repeated cycle of destruction followed by escape followed by destruction—precisely how many philosophers view the history of the Jewish people. Unlike those who view humankind as evolving and becoming more civilized, Singer and Mazursky see it as trapped on the Wonder Wheel, repeatedly turning through time in a continuously recurring pattern.

In addition to problems of adaptation, Mazursky clearly knew about the debate raging around the fictional representation of the Holocaust. Some prominent thinkers, such as the critic George

Steiner, claim that silence is the only adequate response to such unspeakable atrocities, because they are "the kind of thing under which language breaks" (*Language* 352). Others, like Elie Wiesel, argue that fiction is wholly inadequate to depict this event: "A novel about Auschwitz is not a novel, or else it is not about Auschwitz" (314). Going one step further, the theologist Michael Wyschogrod believes that no art is "appropriate" to the Holocaust, since art takes the sting out of suffering (68). Such positions have been basically ignored, as artists in every medium struggle with the ominous implications of modern history's most compelling and troubling event. The flood of books, movies, and television shows dealing with the terrible legacy of the Holocaust has increased since the 1960s.

Yet some problems persist, and objections have been raised. Filmmakers, as Ilan Avisar argues, have displayed an "unresolved tension between verisimilitude and . . . the stylistic imposition . . . [of] melodramatic narration, existentialist mood, or mythical pattern" (181). Putting such tendencies in a harsher light, Lawrence Langer accuses American artists in general (and Hollywood filmmakers in particular) of "moral oversimplification" by attempting to affirm the "tragic dignity of the individual man" in so many works about the Holocaust: "How much darkness must we acknowledge before we will be able to confess that the Holocaust story cannot be told in terms of heroic dignity, moral courage, and the triumph of the human spirit in adversity. . . . There is no final solace, no redeeming truth, no hope that so many millions may not have died in vain. They have" (214).

Mazursky's subject matter allows him to sidestep many of these dilemmas because he focuses on the life of survivors rather than the death of victims. The film, like Singer's novel, contains no dramatic scenes of tortured, beaten, or burning bodies; no film documentation of hair, teeth, and articles of clothing stolen from the dead and arranged in neat piles; no horrific sequences of sexual, medical, or emotional brutality; and no staged segments of emaciated inmates stuffed into cramped barracks. Only in its opening few minutes does *Enemies* resemble films that employ such commonly accepted icons of atrocity, as Herman dreams about Nazis searching his hayloft refuge in Lipsk. In fact, Mazursky demonstrates admirable restraint by not striving for the visually shocking and employing close-to-clichéd graphic images to convey the horrors of life under the Nazis. However, as insightful writers such as

Singer have demonstrated, these horrors do not cease with physical liberation; they simply change from physical to psychological tortures. The mind, not the body, becomes the battleground.

None of the story's characters can imagine a life without persecutors. Masha, even amid the tranquility of the Catskills, wonders ironically, "Where are the Nazis? What kind of world is this without Nazis? A backward country, this America." Herman sees Nazis in New York City and plans how he could survive them this time. This state of constant paranoia permeates the film, as it does Singer's novel. For these Holocaust survivors, the mentality embodied by the Nazis can never be permanently defeated, only temporarily subdued. America offers them no enduring rest, no vision of inviolate freedom, but simply a fleeting respite from persecution. Their peace of mind has been another casualty of the war, their psyches now as imprisoned and tortured as were their bodies.

Thus Mazursky, with Singer as his guide, demonstrates no desire to shock through with visceral images. He reaches for something far more subtle, the indelible mark that such a horrific experience leaves upon everyday existence. Initially, this manifests itself in the feeling of not being part of this world, of being a ghost. All of the characters express this sentiment at one time or another. "Anyone who's gone through all that I have is no longer part of this world," Herman tells Rabbi Lambert, who rejects Broder's point of view as unnecessarily pessimistic and accuses him of merely "playing a role." In so doing, Lambert represents the American Jews who never personally experienced the Holocaust and thus can never fathom the maimed psyche of those who did. He becomes another of those blustering American pragmatists who blithely advise Europeans to forget about the past and get on with their lives. Such trite phrases seem to Herman a blasphemy on the ashes of the tormented.

Herman's job as a ghostwriter for Rabbi Lambert, therefore, is an apt metaphor for his emotional state. As he later tells Tamara, "The truth is that I'm still hiding in an attic right here in America." As one who also suffered, Tamara not only understands Herman's feelings but also replies by unknowingly repeating parts of his statements to Rabbi Lambert: "I really no longer think of myself as being part of this world . . . two dead people certainly needn't have any secrets from one another." Such feelings place the characters in a state of almost total psychological exile, a diaspora of the spirit and the soul, because their experiences during the Holocaust permanently cut them off from the rest of humanity.

How do mutilated psyches like those of Herman, Masha, and Tamara deal with everyday reality? First, no survivor of the Holocaust ever feels totally secure, on either a physical or a psychological level. They remain forever haunted by the knowledge that a seemingly safe world, one in which the rules appear clear and understandable, can suddenly change into a hostile, life-threatening place of horror where neighbors become oppressors and friends become informers. For example, Herman never shakes himself free from his cruel fantasies about Nazis occupying New York City and forcing him to find a protective hayloft once again. Shifah Puah, Masha's mother, always wears black to mourn the memory of her murdered husband, parents, sisters, and brothers.

Masha, whom the Nazis brutalized sexually, talks constantly about suicide, often expressing her guilt about not being cremated like so many other Jews. After the death of her mother and the desertion of Herman, Masha eventually does swallow enough sleeping pills to kill herself, leaving a note that holds no one responsible for her death. Suicidal thoughts also flood Tamara's thoughts. Claiming that she is without hope, and "one dies of that more quickly than of cancer," she tells Herman that she is already a corpse and must die. Unlike Masha, however, Tamara finds some sliver of hope in the birth of Yadwiga's child, named Masha, and the three women form what Lawrence Friedman labels "the nucleus of a reborn Jewish community. . . . Their symbolic reconstitution of the family invokes the ancient Jewish formula for survival" (174).

In addition to living with his Nazi fantasies, Herman copes with the legacy of the Holocaust in several other ways, none particularly effective. For example, Herman's life has become a series of elaborate evasions, an ever-increasing web of misrepresentations, lies, deceits, and falsehoods that create a counter-reality to whichever actual reality he must endure at any given moment. Herman becomes a pathological liar, a man who fabricates deceptions as naturally as he eats breakfast. He lies out of habit. Such an existence, of course, makes Broder easy prey for the dybbuks of paranoia; his life in America remains as filled with the fear of exposure as was his life in Poland during the Nazi occupation. "I'm caught in a vise and can't free myself" he tells his original wife. When Masha demands that he marry her, fully knowing that he is already married to Yadwiga, Herman replies, "I'll be afraid of every policeman in the street." "You're afraid anyhow," she replies.

With each new lie invented to conceal past untruths comes a

stronger fear of exposure. Yet Herman Broder cannot stop lying. To live in a world of truth is to acknowledge that such a value actually exists, that civilized human life is characterized by a unified acceptance of shared realities and enlightened by the morality of great thinkers. This belief rings false to a man who knows that it is possible to be "a Spinozaist and a Nazi." Such a belief can never be accepted by a man whose wife and children seemingly have been brutally murdered, whose seemingly ordered world has been turned on its head, who has been forced to seek a new life in a strange and foreign country, and who feels compelled to marry a woman he never loved. The experience of surviving the Holocaust has forever fragmented Herman's vision of the world, forcing him to have alternative realities available just in case the current one is ripped away again.

Finally, one other important element ties Mazursky, both philosophically and emotionally, to Singer's tale of post-Holocaust fragmentation: the unrelenting conflict between faith and doubt. In Mazursky's previous films, such a conflict inevitably occurs on a secular level. That is, the film's characters commit themselves to some sort of cultural or philosophical position, and the director satirizes them. "Americans like to believe in miracles," Mazursky told Mock and Saunders, "we tend to believe we are going to get saved." As a writer-director, Mazursky accepts the sincerity of his characters' searches for salvation but rarely gets swept up in their causes. His tone remains that of the sober man at a party where everyone else is at least slightly drunk. Bemused, he watches from the outside, chiding his characters for their enthusiastic excesses and shaking his head at their pretentious antics.

Mazursky's characters all hope for change and seek ways to make their lives more meaningful. Yet their creator seems unable to share their faith in any one approach to life and its conflicts. Much like Woody Allen, Mazursky cannot ignore the absurdity inherent in every system of belief. The result, to appropriate Lawrence Friedman's term to describe Herman Broder, is a kind of "moral schizophrenia." Mazursky wishes to believe in something but is unable to commit himself to anything (153). His desire to place his faith in some belief system, evident in the more emotional scenes of his films, constantly battles his intellectual skepticism, evident in his satire of precisely those same beliefs.

In *Enemies*, the conflict between faith and doubt occurs on the religious level rather than the secular. The characters, all of whom have suffered at the hands of the demonic Nazis, acknowledge their ambivalence about accepting easy descriptions of a benevolent God. Masha, for example, argues that "If God allowed the Jews of Europe to be killed, what reason is there to believe he would prevent the extermination of the Jews in America? God doesn't care." As if to emphasize her point, whenever Masha talks of the German atrocities she runs to the mezuzah on her door and spits on it. "The true God hates us," she tells Herman, "but we have dreamed up an idol who loves us and has made us His chosen people" (Singer 205). The equally tormented Tamara believes that "the merciful God in whom we believed does not exist. . . . If God was able to watch all this horror and remain silent, then He's no God." Traumatized by the deaths of her children and others, Tamara believes that souls exist, God does not. Only the simple Yadwiga maintains an uncritical acceptance of divine existence and providence, beseeching Herman to help her convert to Judaism and conceive a child with her. Both acts mirror both her faith and hope as she strives to side with the persecuted rather than the oppressors and bring new life into a world obsessed with the dead.

Herman, typically uncertain, veers from one set of beliefs to another. At first, he rebels against anything Jewish, ignoring the Sabbath and telling Yadwiga that "there is no God . . . and even if there were, I would defy him." He does fast on Yom Kippur, but will not attend religious services because he cannot bring himself to be like one of those "assimilated Jews who only go to synagogue once a year." Slowly, he changes his position. He admits that there may be a God, but that He is quite powerless: "If a God of mercy did exist in the heavenly hierarchy, then He was only a helpless godlet, a kind of heavenly Jew among the heavenly Nazis" (Singer 212).

Eventually, the appearance of Tamara and his attempt to break with Masha lead Herman to plunge anew into Jewish studies, enjoining himself to go back to the Torah, the Gemara (the Babylonian Talmud), and the other Jewish books. He finds that "on these pages dwelt his parents, his grandparents, all his ancestors" (Singer 237). Herman faces his deepest doubts, claiming "even if one were to doubt the existence of oxygen, one would still have to breathe. One could deny gravity, but one would still have to walk on the ground. Since he was suffocating without God and the Torah, he must serve God and study the Torah" (Singer 236). Yadwiga, totally surprised by her husband's abrupt embrace of orthodoxy, rejoices as Herman agrees to allow her to convert to Judaism, as well as to attempt to have children with her. "If we don't want to become like the Nazis," he scolds Yadwiga, "we must be Jews."

Herman's fervent rededication to Jewish study, like his commitment to monogamy, is brief; he returns to Masha, and his feelings of "presuicidal gloom" return. Once more, God becomes nothing but an "Almighty Sadist." Even in the midst of the Passover service, while reciting the Haggadah with Tamara and the now-pregnant Yadwiga, Herman feels the ceremony to be nothing but a game, an expression of nostalgia. Eventually, Herman leaves everyone, including the reconstituted Jewish family formed by Tamara, Yadwiga, and the infant Masha. Although he sends money to help Yadwiga defray expenses (a sympathetic action added by Mazursky and absent in the novel), Herman's abandonment of his child demonstrates, even more than his marital duplicity, his inability to confront any serious moral responsibilities. Yet the very fact that Yadwiga's and Herman's child is born the night before Shevuot, a holiday that commemorates the date when God's will was revealed to the Jewish people through the Ten Commandments and a new covenant was reaffirmed between the Jews and God, attests to the possibility that spiritual survival may exist even after the Holocaust.

Paul Mazursky understands that his Jewish roots and experiences, although particular to that specific culture, tie him to the rest of middle-class America. As Frank Rich astutely observes in a review of *Next Stop, Greenwich Village*, "as the American Jew has chosen or been forced to play roles that will enable him to fit into his society—to assimilate—so affluent Americans have more and more had to choose among the ever-proliferating roles that the culture creates for their consumption; like Jews who have left behind their ghettos, the heroes of Mazursky's films leave behind their middle-class identities to try and fit into the new revamped America that emerged out of the social traumas of the 1960s" (5).

In a sense, then, Mazursky's most important characters are all Jewish because they all face the terrors and pay the price of freedom. After all, how different on an emotional and psychological level is that quintessential 1960s' couple Bob and Carol from Willy and Phil in the 1970s or Larry and his bohemian friends in the 1950s? Are the romantic dreams of Stephen Blume that far removed from those of Philip Dimitrious, Harold Fine, Dave Whiteman, Erica Benton, or Nick and Deborah?

Although Vladimir Ivanoff and Herman Broder remain Mazursky's only actual immigrants, all his central characters find the constantly shifting terrain of American life difficult to negotiate. All invent and reinvent their identities and play various roles. As they ceaselessly shift from one set of values and priorities to the next, Mazursky's characters create and then reformulate ever-changing collages of ethical positions, points of view, and emotional ranges. They all wrestle with how to handle the social liberation so intrinsic to American life, so omnipresent in this age of opportunity. Such issues continue to haunt Mazursky. Perhaps that is why so many of Mazursky's movies end with images of escape and the feeling that things are resolved only temporarily. "The most difficult thing to do," Mazursky told an interviewer, "is to laugh with compassion." Such a goal, in many ways, represents a Jewish perspective on the world. In attempting to do precisely that, Paul Mazursky repeatedly draws upon his Jewish roots as both metaphor and inspiration to chart middle-class America's response to freedom and change.

CHAPTER SIX

Too Much at Home in America?

Because our definition of being a Jewish filmmaker in America depends upon more than the mere fact of being born to Jewish parents, other American-Jewish filmmakers, at least those of the same generation as Woody Allen, Mel Brooks, Sidney Lumet, and Paul Mazursky, should deal with many similar subjects and themes. That is to say, we chose to write about Allen, Brooks, Lumet, and Mazursky; other directors could have been selected to illustrate our claims that being a Jewish filmmaker in America means examining or being attracted to certain issues and images. We focused upon these four men primarily because of the varied manifestations of Jewish issues and themes across their impressive bodies of work.

As alternatives to Allen, Brooks, Lumet, and Mazursky, we might indeed have examined the careers of four other directors who grew up in a Jewish-American milieu before the war: Elaine May (b. 1932), Mike Nichols (b. 1931), Arthur Penn (b. 1922), and Carl Reiner (b. 1922). In so doing, we would note how Elaine May's early career in show business, partnered with Mike Nichols, resembled Woody Allen's as it revolved around stand-up comedy and took as its subjects emerging life-style trends and popular culture fads and fallacies. Nichols and May were noted not simply for their verbal facility, but for the way they captured much of the urban angst of male-female relationships in the changing society of the late 1950s and early 1960s.

May's first two directorial efforts sprung from the new freedom Hollywood filmmakers experienced in the wake of increased agitation for equal opportunities and the breakdown of the old studio system, as she became the first major woman director since Ida Lupino after the golden age of Hollywood had ended. More significantly, *A New Leaf* (1971) and *The Heartbreak Kid* (1972) remain two of the most piercing and perceptive studies of Jewish self-hatred ever committed to celluloid. In the earlier film, May herself plays a bumbling wallflower, a scientist so clumsy and hopeless that she seems a distaff version of Harry Langdon's comical man-child of the late silent era or Woody Allen's schlemiel. In the latter film, she cast her daughter, Jeannie Berlin, opposite Charles Grodin in a story (adapted by Neil Simon from a work by Bruce Jay Friedman) about a newlywed couple. The new husband, on his honeymoon, develops an immediate distaste for his socially and sexually inept wife while he becomes foolishly attracted to an archetypal shiksa (Cybill Shepherd). Some would argue that *The Heartbreak Kid* is more an exercise in self-hatred than a study of it, a complaint with which Woody Allen is familiar. One also has to wonder who but a Jewish director would dare make *Ishtar* (1987), a film which equates U.S. foreign policy in the Middle East with show business; who else would understand so intimately the deepest fears of small-time entertainers and the deepest absurdities of American political policy?

The career of May's former comic partner Mike Nichols offers equal insight into the legacy left by growing up Jewish in America. Nichols came to the United States in 1939, the son of a Russian doctor who fled to Germany after the Russian Revolution, and who fled with most of his family when his adopted homeland began its state-sponsored anti-Semitism in the late 1930s. Nichols betrays little of the immigrant in his speech and behavior, and nothing in his total assimilation into mainstream show business. Yet he keeps a critical eye on the culture to which he came as an outsider. Nichols has built a film career as impressive as any contemporary director's, yet its particularities fit well within the motifs of American-Jewish life and art. His background in New York City, in show business as a comic, and in the New York theater, a background he shares with our subjects of study, is evident in his early films and has remained constant across a wide range of subjects. His film debut in 1966, *Who's Afraid of Virginia Woolf?*, not only betrays his roots in the theater but also, like his own stand-up comedy, cuts to the heart of man-woman relationships. The impact of Nichols's adaptation of Edward Albee's now-classic play was even more profound than the fact that it introduced a major new director to the film world. Like the work of an earlier Jewish émigré, Otto Preminger, whose films *The Moon is Blue* (1953) and *The Man with the Golden Arm* (1956) did much to erode the restrictions of the old production code, Nichols's film forever ended the code's control of Hollywood. But it was *The Graduate* (1967), his second film, that not only established his career as a filmmaker but also had an even greater impact upon American moviemaking.

Can anyone doubt that Dustin Hoffman's Ben Braddock, the graduate of the title, is Jewish, just as the sensibility behind the camera is equally Jewish? This film on the cutting edge of youthful alienation, the rejection of middle-class life and values ("plastics!") and recognition of the hollowness of individual achievements is the hallmark of an American-Jewish culture that both prizes and decries bourgeois beliefs. The centrality of the family in this film, and its equally potent rejection, represents a classic instance of the ordeal of civility and the guilt of shame. It is more the sensibility behind the camera that makes *The Graduate* a brilliant film, and a particularly Jewish one, than the inchoate angst of the protagonist. Nichols recognizes, as Ben does not, the contradictions of youthful protest and rebellion. The youth culture of the 1960s (in which Jews were abundantly represented) arose only out of overly loving and supportive families and because of the era's material wealth.

Nichols's most characteristic auteur quality has been not simply social satire, the puncturing of life-style trends à la Paul Mazursky with whom he shares much in common, but an ability to detail the situation and status of women. Nichols's Jewishness thus translates to a solidarity with oppressed classes, as Brooks and Lumet in particular also reveal, with a special insight and sympathy for women. This ability appears as early as his third film, *Carnal Knowledge* (1971). Again, the American-Jewish film director is not solely responsible for all his films; an American-Jewish writer is also part of giving voice to the traditions. Here Jules Feiffer, whose political cartoons for more than three decades devastated the hypocrisies of government, examines the middle-class male ego with equally devastating results. By focusing on the fears and foibles of men, and how their insecurities and insensitivities hurt their partners in love and marriage, Nichols expresses his solidarity with women.

Later films bring him closer to women's issues as he creates a bildungsroman from women's coming-of-age stories, especially coming of age in the sense of a political, social, and personal maturity. *Silkwood* (1983), based on a real-life incident and subjected to the same public scrutiny and debate about cinema's ideal relation to history as Lumet's *Daniel* of the same year, typifies Nichols's concerns, here with questions of social justice and responsibility. While the characters in such films as *The Graduate* and *Carnal Knowledge* are played and written, if not specifically identified, as Jewish (Art Garfunkel's character in the latter is explicitly Jewish), *Heartburn* (1987) foregrounds the Jewishness of its central characters in a combination bildungsroman and roman à clef based upon the writer Nora Ephron's marriage to the journalist Carl Bernstein. And what, for that matter, could be more Jewish than a coming-of-age story set in Hollywood, the subject matter of Nichols's *Postcards from the Edge* (1990), based upon another roman à clef, this one by Carrie Fisher?

The Jewish derivation of Nichols's concern with the status of women is the most interesting in one of his most popular films, *Working Girl* (1989). The film reads like a displaced examination of the Jewish struggle for economic and social success in America, with its focus upon a girl who comes over by boat to Manhattan (the ferry from Staten Island replacing the steamer from Europe) possessed of an inappropriate accent, hair style, and clothing, along with a desire to succeed in a world that is unwilling to give her a chance and judges her precisely on those external characteristics. Tess (Melanie Griffith), the allegorical stand-in for immigrant Jewry at the turn of the century, finds that her biggest obstacle to success is another woman (i.e., another Jew). The most revealing scene, therefore, occurs when Katherine (Sigourney Weaver), Tess's boss and betrayer, speaks German on the telephone. Her conversation symbolizes Katherine not as a Nazi, but as a German Jew assimilated in America before the influx of Eastern European Jewry and embarrassed by the *ostjuden* pouring into America, with their bad manners and ostentatious differences. Clearly, the film codes Katherine as WASP and Tess as working-class ethnic and thus addresses social class, an issue that most American films are loathe to present. But the power of Katherine's image compared to Tess's comes from these allegorical connotations. Furthermore, Tess desires to succeed on Wall Street, among the last arenas to accept Jews. The fact that her victory seems a rather small one, literally a tiny office in one corner of a huge downtown office building, further reinforces the allegory of Jewish success in America, which began modestly enough by making inroads based on ability and desire into all facets of mainstream life.

If there are similarities between Elaine May and Woody Allen, and between Mike Nichols and Paul Mazursky, Arthur Penn may likewise be equated with Sidney Lumet. Fewer than two years older than Lumet, Penn was also born in Philadelphia and, like Lumet, saw active duty in World War II (as did Mel Brooks). Like Lumet he trained as an actor and spent his formative years learning his craft as a director in the golden age of television. As did Lumet (and Nichols), Penn continued to work in theater while he labored in television and even throughout his early career in feature films.

Penn's feature film directorial debut, *The Left-Handed Gun* in 1958, was almost simultaneous with Lumet's in 1957. His primary filmic concern has been with outsiders, with those who feel alienated from an oppressive system, a characteristic he also shares with Lumet. Perhaps the most classic expression of alienation may be found in Penn's 1962 film version of the play he originally directed for the stage: *The Miracle Worker*. This story of Helen Keller's attempt to fit into society despite her handicaps might not be an allegory of Jewish assimilation into the American mainstream, based as it is upon fact and taking nothing away from Keller's heroic and inspiring efforts, yet surely the director's attraction and commitment to the tale bespeak a commonality of experience.

Penn's career similarly boasts of other films committed to revealing the undercurrents of American society, exposing its hypocrisies, decrying its failures, and sanctifying its successes. *Mickey One* (1965) is the closest thing to a film version of one of Kafka's tales that the American cinema has ever produced, not coincidentally set in the world of stand-up comedy as a metaphor of alienation and self-doubt. And if Mike Nichols produced one of the key films of the contemporary cinema with *The Graduate* in 1967, that same year saw Arthur Penn direct the other key film: *Bonnie and Clyde*. The movie's stylistic panache may be owed to the French New Wave, but the theme of alienated youth was strictly American Jewish. Penn's affinities with the outcast hippies of *Alice's Restaurant* (1969), the oppressed Indians of *Little Big Man* (1970), and the existential detective of *Night Moves* (1975) further contribute to his virtual obsession with outsiders and marginalized people. Although Penn's only specified Jewish character remains David Levine (Michael Huddleston), the comic member of the gang in *Four Friends* (1981), almost all his figures and most of his films clearly demonstrate many of the motifs of American-Jewish life discussed previously. Penn's career has been well analyzed by other scholars, although not from the perspective of Jewishness. Unfortunately, he has been unable to sustain his status over time, unlike Lumet and the other directors discussed previously.

Another American-Jewish entertainer who has consistently managed to keep himself in the forefront, whether as a writer, actor, or director, has been Carl Reiner. The similarities and connections he shares with Mel Brooks are not simply striking, they are deliberate. They were, after all, writing partners on "Your Show of Shows" along with other major American-Jewish comic authors (Reiner was also an on-air talent) and co-creators of a series of classic comedy sketches on records and guest spots on television, the 2,000 Year Old Man. Reiner's first film, an adaptation of his autobiographically derived play *Enter Laughing* (1967), focuses upon a Jewish protagonist and is set in the Broadway theater. Reiner's second film, *Where's Poppa?* (1970), is even more overtly Jewish, featuring one of the screen's most hilariously memorable (if negative) portraits of a Jewish mother. Like Brooks, much of Reiner's later screen comedy revolves around parody, drawing upon classic Hollywood for its humorous spoofing. In this respect, Reiner's work may also be linked to Woody Allen's early films. Reiner's *The Man with Two Brains* (1983) seems clearly derived from one of the films-within-the film of *Stardust Memories*. Alternately, *Dead Men Don't Wear Plaid* (1982) anticipates Allen's *Zelig* in its deft integration of contemporary actors in period footage.

Allen, Brooks, Lumet, and Mazursky are thus more paradigms than exhaustive examinations of all the examples of how being Jewish in America affects one's filmic sensibilities. We might, indeed, have examined yet another set of directors. Sydney Pollack, born in 1934, was trained as an actor in New York (although he was born in South Bend, Indiana) and got his start as a director in television. His career, characteristically Jewish, is marked by interest in show business in such films as *The Electric Horseman* (1979) and *Tootsie* (1982); sympathy for the alienated outsider in *Jeremiah Johnson* (1972); fellow-feelings for the downtrodden and oppressed in *They Shoot Horses, Don't They?* (1969); sensitivity for cultural difference and universal truths in *The Yakuza* (1975); and a welcome reversal of the shiksa archetype in *The Way We Were* (1973), in which the idealized WASP image is male while the woman is the ethnic other. Pollack has also entered the arena as an actor; his most sustained performance thus far has been under Woody Allen's direction in *Husbands and Wives*. Similarly, we could consider the career of Barry Levinson (b. 1932) whose take on ethnic, urban Baltimore in *Diner* (1982), *Tin Men* (1986), and *Avalon* (1990) make him the Woody Allen of the mid-Atlantic states. Joan Micklin Silver also deserves mention, especially for *Hester Street* (1975), her feminist slant on the immigrant experience in the New Old Country, and *Crossing Delancey* (1988), her perceptive treatment of a Jewish career woman who finds her roots. As equally Jewish in its own way is Silver's underrated *Between the Lines* (1977), which deals with a New Left counterculture newspaper in Boston in the late 1960s.

There is, then, no shortage of American-Jewish filmmakers who were born and raised before the war and came of age in a Holly-

Sydney Pollack directs a scene in New York City.

wood much changed since its Golden Age. A question that remains concerns how younger American-Jewish filmmakers have been affected by growing up in an America much changed since the subjects of this book came of age. If we define the Jewish time in America as a series of lived experiences common across a generation, born in the 1920s and 1930s, that grew up primarily in New York City and its environs, it remains to be seen if these formative experiences similarly affect younger Jews. Alternately, do younger Jews have a set of common experiences that define them as Jewish, even if the experiences may differ from those of their immediate predecessors? For example, although today's Jewry remains an urban community, it hardly qualifies as a specifically New York community. For that matter, more of America is urban than was true in the 1920s. Has the shift to urbanization made Jews of the rest of America? If it is true that anti-Semitism is hardly a defining characteristic of growing up in America, how has the lack of overt and constant exposure to this venal racism made younger Jews different than the older generation, or different from a mainstream non-Jewish social segment similarly free of discrimination directed against it?

As we were writing this chapter, the Council of Jewish Federations released their National Jewish Population survey, the most comprehensive study ever taken of the Jewish population in the United States. Based on 2,441 interviews in forty-nine states, the polling procedures allowed for equal representation among Jews from small towns and major population centers, while it concentrated on a spectrum of critical issues that defines the American-Jewish community. Some highlights from these responses, particularly those that relate to areas covered in previous chapters, provide evidence of shifting values and beliefs. Take, for example, the basic but quite startling statistic that 90 percent of American Jews were born in this country, with one-third born between 1946 and 1964 (the years of the baby boom). Equally fascinating are the intermarriage figures. Since 1984, fewer than half of Jewish marriages involve partners who were born Jewish, and the survey found increasing acceptance of intermarriage, even among those who practice the religion in some overt manner. Less surprising, the remarkably high levels of education within the American-Jewish community continue. More than 50 percent of Jewish men (compared to 24 percent in the population as a whole) and more than 45 percent of Jewish women (compared to 17 percent in the population as a whole) graduate from college, while the number of Jews engaging in family businesses has declined dramatically to only 3 percent. All these factors indicate the continued professional status and personal acceptance of Jews into all facets of American life.

Jewish geographical distribution has also shifted, in some cases as dramatically as the high intermarriage rates. Forty-four percent of Jews now live in the Northeast, 23 percent in the West, 22 percent in the South, and 11 percent in the Midwest. These figures mean that the South and the West have doubled their Jewish populations since World War II, while the Midwest has lost one-fourth of its former Jewish population. Equally interesting are the issues of self-definition and discrimination. For example, four times as many Jews practice religion as claim they are secular, 4.4 million to 1.1 million; yet, many more respondents chose "cultural" or "ethnic" than "religious" to describe what it means to be Jewish in America. As far as attitudes and fears about prejudice, Jews across the spectrum (79 percent) perceive anti-Semitism as a serious problem in the United States, although a mere 5 percent have personally experienced work-related discrimination. Politically, 45 percent of the Jewish population still sees itself as liberal, 20 percent lists itself as conservative, and 30 percent call themselves middle of the road. Even though the total Jewish population of America numbers around 5.5 million people who live in 3.2 million households in which at least one family member is Jewish or had a Jewish parent, these statistics paint a rather different portrait of the current American-Jewish population than that which formed the cultural milieu of Allen, Brooks, Lumet, and Mazursky.[1]

For the sake of argument, let us claim that there might be such a thing as a younger generation of American-Jewish filmmakers (i.e., directors born after World War II who are part of the preceding statistics) without yet situating a number of filmmakers within this group. As we began this book by defining Jewish life in America for someone born here during the 1920s and 1930s, we can also examine Jewish life in America for a postwar generation, especially in light of the National Jewish Population survey. The question of assimilation versus alienation has resolutely and firmly been answered by the facts that Jews are accepted in virtually every walk of American life and the intermarriage ratio approaches 50 percent, which has done much to eliminate the need for the image of the shiksa.[2] By the same token, Yiddish as a language and as a culture has virtually disappeared from the normative experience of American Jewry, reduced to a lexicon of a dozen words or so in American

English. If the nation has not achieved the melting pot ideal in its entirety, the language certainly has.

Other defining characteristics of American Jewry, such as the Holocaust and Israel, although not eroded for the better (such as the disappearance of all but the most ignorant anti-Semitism) or the worse (such as the loss of *Yiddishkeit*), have shifted meaning. The Holocaust, as Michael Berenbaum has demonstrated, has been Americanized without losing its specifically Jewish dimensions (3–42). More significantly, as the last generation of survivors dies, all that is left are images of the event. Indelible though they may be, they are hardly the tormented flesh and blood of the last remnants of an entire civilization destroyed by madness. Inevitably, the Holocaust, that is, the destruction of European Jewry, becomes one among too many attempted genocides. Moreover, the memory of powerlessness associated with the Holocaust has been replaced by an image of a triumphant, militarily strong Jewry, Israel, in the minds of America's younger Jews.[3]

Yet even in the case of Israel, the civil religion of American Jewry cannot be a defining characteristic of American-Jewish life. The break between segments of American Jewry has not been caused simply by political and moral disagreements over Israeli policy on the occupied territories and the *intifada*. Rather, the growing recognition that American-Jewish culture is fundamentally different than Jewish culture in Israel is responsible for the rift. There was always something untenable in defining an American culture by another culture, another nation. Yet as Israel was created primarily by East European Jewish culture, many Americans felt a kinship with the new state; indeed, many had kin there. As the direct experience of the Holocaust fades in Israel, as the majority of its citizens (not including the ongoing revolutionary influx of Russian Jews) are now those born and raised there, an Israeli culture with its own integrity has arisen. It is no surprise that this has happened, and it is also no surprise that there should be little connection to a Jewish culture that is specifically, indeed archetypically, American.

Israeli culture as separate from American-Jewish culture, that is, Israel as a nation unto itself, has shifted the image of diaspora and exile in the American-Jewish consciousness. That American Jews do not consider themselves in exile, that they remain in the Diaspora, means fundamentally that America is home to American Jewry. As Michael Berenbaum observes, "vicarious Jewish existence through identification with the State of Israel is not sufficient to nurture another generation of American Jews" (156). American

Jews find their values outside of Israel, outside of the concept of exile while remaining within the Diaspora.

The issue of self-hatred, too, has shifted. The elimination of the image of Jews as victims, powerless in the face of a hostile majority, has naturally increased Jews' sense of self-esteem. So, too, has the conscious choice to remain in America and be an American that refusal to make *aliyah* to Israel implies. Although we have no statistics to indicate, for example, a decrease in plastic surgery ("nose jobs") among adolescent Jewish women, it is probable that such show business icons as Barbra Streisand and Bette Midler enhance the status of Jewish women as sex symbols and superstars. Woody Allen, Dustin Hoffman, Richard Dreyfuss, as well as Kirk Douglas, Paul Newman, and James Caan, among others, have done the same for Jewish men. We see no repetition of the famous Milton Berle declaration when, after having a nose job, he maintained "I cut off my nose to spite my race. Now I'm a thing of beauty and a goy forever!" Intermarriage rates must also be factored in because Jews have proven attractive mates to non-Jews.

Given the increased presence of film and television stars and the notion of celebrity in postmodern America, not to mention the continued crucial participation of Jews behind the camera and in the executive offices, show business remains a viable aspect of American-Jewish life and art. Thus it is no surprise that Jewish entertainers continue to thrive. But non-Jews predominate in many traditionally Jewish fields of entertainment. The world of stand-up comedy, for example, has seen a Jewish generation come and go, as has the world of the Broadway musical. Similarly, where young Jews might have considered participating in professional sports, especially boxing, baseball, and basketball, during the 1920s and 1930s, Jewish participation in these sports remains at a minimum. There is only one Jewish player in the National Basketball Association, and most Jews who play American college basketball are Israelis.

The same may be true of political activism. Although at one time the Left, either Old or New, offered potent attractions to Jews, members of the current mainstream are not likely to be attracted to the margins. When people today think of Jews in politics, they likely think of the American Israel Public Affairs Committee (AIPAC), a potent reminder that Israel has not entirely disappeared as a communal force for American Jewry, but a far cry from the heady days of the Communist party or the yippies. Jews seem more likely to be senators, judges, or the secretaries of state or defense than radicals with a bomb. How much longer will American Jewry "live like Episcopalians and vote like Puerto Ricans" (Berenbaum 164)?

If Jewish life in America has changed, if the formative experiences of postwar American Jews differ from their prewar counterparts, and if the defining characteristics of Jewish life in America have shifted since the 1960s and 1970s, what motifs, if any, would a contemporary American-Jewish filmmaker employ? Would these motifs speak to a Jewish culture, a Jewish tradition, in the same way as had earlier ones? To begin to answer this, it is necessary to consider the most prominent younger Jewish director of our time, the most commercially successful director, Jewish or not, in history: Steven Spielberg.

Spielberg has told *American Film* magazine about why he undertook a film adaptation of Alice Walker's seminal novel *The Color Purple* in 1988:

> Kathleen Kennedy, the president of my company . . . gave me Alice Walker's book. She said, "Look you're going to think I'm crazy. But if you don't hate this book, I think it will make a wonderful movie, and I think you should direct it." She gave me some background: "You know it's a black story. But that shouldn't bother you, because you're Jewish and essentially you share similarities in your upbringing and your heritage." I had some anti-Semitic experiences when I was growing up that Kathleen knew about, including prejudice and everything else I had to go through at one particular high school.[4]

Spielberg's mother confirms his exposure to anti-Semitism as a youth and has wondered if she was mistaken in moving her family from Cincinnati to Scottsdale, Arizona, where they were bothered by neighborhood children who stood outside their home and yelled, " 'The Spielbergs are dirty Jews. The Spielbergs are dirty Jews' " (Bernstein, *Jewish Mothers* 4).

His adaptation of Walker's novel surely confirms a continuing legacy of positive Jewish-black relations based on the shared experience of prejudice. Yet, to many, Spielberg's motivations were clearly less inclined toward feelings of solidarity between oppressed ethnic groups and more toward seeking greater respect from critics and other filmmakers by turning his attention away from escapist, neoadolescent fantasies to an obviously more "serious" subject. Perhaps the most characteristically Jewish element

Steven Spielberg, representative of the new generation of American-Jewish directors, with Whoopi Goldberg in *The Color Purple* (1985).

in his choice of *The Color Purple* is the fact that he made it because he felt guilty for his tremendous, indeed unprecedented, previous successes.

Spielberg's cinema seems to demonstrate his unwillingness to focus overtly on Jewish characters, although his mother was raised as an orthodox Jew amid other relatives who were part of the Yiddish theater and vaudeville.[5] If we wish to make the case that in some sense *E.T.* (1982) represents an eloquent parable of the immigrant experience, what are we to make of the fact that E.T. not only phones home but also goes home? One might claim that Spielberg manifests a palpable sense of the loss of religious certainty in the abandonment, or the inability to accept, Judaism seen in the desperation on the part of the characters in *Close Encounters of the Third Kind* (1977), whose desire to uncover the truth, to believe, borders on the hysterical. This seems to be a case of displacement and acknowledgment that Jewish issues like prejudice, the outsider-immigrant, and the loss of religiosity must be handled through the black experience or through genre efforts. Initially, this acknowledgment seems to have eerie similarity to the first generation of Jewish directors in America, those European émigrés whom studio moguls essentially forbade to tackle Jewish issues. Or is something else behind Spielberg's retreat from Jewishness?

Understanding this issue necessitates consideration of Spielberg's most overtly Jewish-themed films: *Raiders of the Lost Ark* (1981) and *An American Tail* (1986). The former, as much a product of the non-Jewish George Lucas as the Jewish writers involved (Philip Kaufman and Lawrence Kasdan) and the Jewish director, reads as Jewish insofar as it postulates the existence of the Ark of the Covenant of Hebraic Law, literally, the casket containing the Ten Commandments. The Ark, however, is surely the only Jewish component of the film. Even with its focus on Nazis and its use of Judaic mythology, the film never confronts Nazi anti-Semitism directly. Similarly, the film's climax, where the power of the Ark is let loose to destroy the group of Nazis who have bedeviled and finally captured the heroic Indiana Jones (whose very name bespeaks all-American, heartland U.S.A.), is nothing other than escapist wish-fulfillment, an adolescent revenge fantasy. Its puzzling concluding scene, where the Ark is bureaucratically condemned to be forgotten amid a host of other boxed-up and walled-in weapons, undercuts the idea of the Ark's unique power. The conclusion, obviously derived visually from the ending of Orson Welles's *Citizen Kane* (1941), which Spielberg greatly admires, thus seems more homage than meaningful commentary. That the Ark, a weapon from God, did not save Europe's Jews, and that it is now hidden away by the U.S. government, are perhaps commentaries on the death or disappearance of God in a post-Holocaust universe. This would certainly link Spielberg with Woody Allen, who wonders in *Hannah and Her Sisters* why a Jewish God would permit the Nazis to exist and writes in *Tikkun* that he never experienced the Holocaust directly yet thinks of nothing but revenge.

Although the Jewish specificity of *Raiders of the Lost Ark* is modulated by being merely implied, its implications are admittedly hard to miss. Yet this is even further undercut by *Indiana Jones and the Last Crusade* (1989), the third entry in the Indiana Jones cycle which, although it again uses Nazis as a villainous force, makes the quest uniquely Christian, the search for the Holy Grail, the cup from which Christ drank at the Last Supper. Thus, the Nazis are the enemies of all religions and people, universal symbols of evil, not simply the most malevolent force to which the Jews were ever exposed. The best Spielberg can muster is Indy's comment about the Nazis: "I hate these guys."

A similar strategy of universalizing the Jewish experience may be found in the animated *An American Tail*, a film that primarily belongs to its writer-director, Don Bluth. However Spielberg's involvement with this seemingly Jewish-themed story must also be considered as reflective of his view of the Jewish experience in America. Using the by-now standard animated film technique of anthropomorphizing nature, *An American Tail* focuses on a family of Jewish mice, the Mousekawitzes, who flee Russian pogroms and come to America. The film is simultaneously specific about the Jewishness of the Mousekawitzes and covert about the issues surrounding immigration. As the film begins, Cossacks attack a Jewish household, while Katsacks attack the Jewish mice within the household. Nowhere does the film explain the anti-Semitic nature of Cossack attacks, the irrational viciousness of the pogroms; by using cats to attack mice the historical specificity of Russian anti-Semitism is displaced onto the natural animosity of cats toward mice. The mouse family's dream of freedom from fear is expressed in their song "There Are No Cats in America." As it turns out, however, there are cats in America. Are we then to conclude that the reality of anti-Semitism does indeed exist in America?

The specifically anti-Semitic nature of the Cossacks/Katsacks' attack on the Russian-Jewish mice is similarly displaced onto the natural antipathy of cats for mice when the Mousekawitzes meet mice from other European nations, also en route to America in the belief that there are no cats there. Jewish immigration from Eastern Europe is thus conflated with Italian and Irish immigration (in the form of mice representing these national and ethnic groups), thereby universalizing the Jewish experience, removing its specificity, and linking Jews with other ethnic groups. The film thus pays tribute to America for its largesse. Although there are cats in America, the film's climax sees all the ethnic mice banding together and banishing them. *An American Tail*, then, wants to have it both ways; it uses the historical specificity of Russian anti-Semitism and the mass migration of Russian Jews to America as it denies the uniqueness of the Jewish experience in favor of universalizing it. It does so precisely by its use of mice to displace the ethnic and historical realities behind anti-Semitism and the mass immigration of Eastern European Jews.[6] Spielberg's seeming reproduction of the strategy of displacement by the European émigrés of the first generation of Jewish directors in America is actually the Jewish assimilation into the American melting pot. All ethnic groups, Jews, Irish, and Italian alike, are now all one and the same.

American Jews are products of an overwhelmingly middle-class background that is generally suburban and in communities across the nation. With little direct experience of anti-Semitism in their formative years, with little conflict over being a hyphenated American, with little pressure from within the community to hold onto religious beliefs but little pressure from without to give them up, American Jewry is a comfortable, satisfied group. Certainly, they are cohesive, but their cohesion revolves around choice; they are not God's chosen people, but self-chosen and without stigma. Thus the motif of Judaism itself has shifted. To be a practicing Jew is a matter of choice (and a wide range of choices present themselves in American Judaism), with little pressure to subscribe from parents who are primarily secular and little pressure to abandon from a gentile world.

Judaism might indeed not be a civilization in America today, but merely one religion among many. This viewpoint does not necessarily subscribe to Jean-Paul Sartre's famous dictum (in *Anti-Semite and Jew*) that Jews are Jews because non-Jews call them Jews. Nor is it to claim that the disappearance of American Jewry is imminent. Many made this claim in the face of America's largesse only to see American Jewry retain its identity, at least in some form. This viewpoint does recognize, however, that art evolves out of tension. If American-Jewish filmmakers born during the 1920s and 1930s did not feel in outright conflict with America, at least a struggle was perceptible in their lives and thus expressed in their art. It may be the case that while American Jewry continues to thrive it does so in relative harmony with the mainstream. Indeed, perhaps American Jewry is part and parcel of the mainstream as Jews. Is a postwar generation of American Jews, one united by nothing other than assimilation into the American mainstream, likely to produce a characteristically Jewish mode of expression? Is it likely to be defined by a group of films and filmmakers with remarkably similar characteristics, distinguishable from their non-Jewish peers? Or have we seen the last flowering of an American-Jewish cinema?

Notes

1. These statistics come from the *Syracuse Jewish Observer,* June 12, 1991, 6, 24.

2. The rather sanguine view of contemporary Jewish life is contradicted by Dershowitz (*Chutzpah*), whose main point seems to be that there is a good deal of anti-Semitism in America, and Jews are at fault not for causing it but for too often allowing it to go unchallenged. It may also be that anti-Semitism and other negative or ambivalent images of Jewry are on the rise in America, which may thus have impact on the generation of Jews who came of age during the 1980s.

3. For a rather eccentric but challenging discussion of how powerlessness has been replaced by the image of the Jew-as-warrior, see Breines, *Tough Jews.*

4. "Dialogue on Film: Steven Spielberg," 14.

5. Spielberg's mother speaks longingly of her own father, an immigrant from Russia, and of an uncle who was a Yiddish Shakespearean actor (Bernstein 3–4).

6. The use of mice to represent Jews is a strategy manifested in a more challenging and extraordinary format by Art Spiegelman in "Maus," a story of the Holocaust, and Holocaust survivors, told in comic-strip form. The Jews are mice, the Germans cats, the Poles pigs, and the Americans dogs. Spiegelman's decision to tell this story in comic-strip form represents a strategy of displacement, as the events are autobiographical in nature. His parents were interned in Auschwitz (which he renames Mauschwitz), and much of the story revolves around Spiegelman's attempt to form a relationship with his father. Yet as he himself points out, the use of these specific creatures has a basis in the historical context: "the Nazis [spoke] of the Jews as 'vermin,' for example, and plotted their 'extermination.' And before that back to Kafka, whose story 'Josephine the Singer, or the Mouse Folk' was one of my favorites . . . and has always struck me as a dark parable and prophecy about the situation of the Jews and Jewishness" ("Mighty 'Maus'" 148).

References

Adler, Bill, and Jeffrey Feinman. *Mel Brooks: The Irreverent Funnyman.* Chicago: Playboy Press, 1976.

Allen, Woody. *Four Films of Woody Allen: Annie Hall, Interiors, Manhattan, Stardust Memories.* New York: Random House, 1982.

————. *Getting Even.* New York: Warner Paperback Library, 1972.

————. "Random Reflections of a Second-Rate Mind." *Tikkun* 5 (Jan.–Feb. 1990): 13.

————. *Side Effects.* New York: Random House, 1980.

————. *Without Feathers.* New York: Random House, 1975.

Alter, Robert. *After the Tradition: Essays on Modern Jewish Writing.* New York: E. P. Dutton, 1969.

————. *Defenses of the Imagination: Jewish Writers and Modern Historical Crisis.* Philadelphia: Jewish Publication Society of America, 1977.

Altman, Sig. *The Comic Image of the Jew: Explorations of a Pop Culture Phenomenon.* Rutherford: Fairleigh Dickinson University Press, 1971.

Applebaum, Ralph. "Experience and Expression: Paul Mazursky." *Films and Filming* 24 (Aug. 1978): 10–16.

Arendt, Hannah. *The Jew as Pariah: Jewish Identity and Politics in the Modern Age.* New York: Grove Press, 1978.

Atlas, Jacoba. "New Hollywood—Mel Brooks." *Film Comment* 11 (March–April 1975): 54–57.

Avisar, Ilan. *Screening the Holocaust: Cinema's Images of the Unimaginable.* Bloomington: Indiana University Press, 1988.

Barth, Fredrik, ed. *Ethnic Groups and Boundaries: The Social Organization of Culture Difference.* London: George Allen and Unwin, 1969. (Results of a symposium held at the University of Bergen, Feb. 23–26, 1967.)

Battestin, Martin C. "Osborne's *Tom Jones:* Adapting a Classic." In *Man and the Movies,* ed. W. R. Robinson. Baton Rouge: Louisiana University Press, 1967.

Baumgarten, Murray. *City Scriptures: Modern Jewish Writing.* Cambridge: Harvard University Press, 1982.

Bellow, Saul, ed. *Great Jewish Short Stories.* New York: Dell Publishing, 1963.

Benayoun, Robert. *The Films of Woody Allen.* Translated by Alexander Walker. New York: Harmony Books, 1986.

Berenbaum, Michael. *After Tragedy and Triumph: Essays in Modern Jewish Thought and the American Experience.* New York: Cambridge University Press, 1990.

Berger, Alan. *Crisis and Covenant: The Holocaust in American Jewish Fiction.* Albany: State University of New York Press, 1985.

Berger, Phil. *The Last Laugh: The World of the Stand-Up Comics.* New York: Limelight Editions, 1985.

Berlin, Isaiah. *Jewish Slavery and Emancipation.* Herzl Institute, Pamphlet no. 8. New York: Herzl Press, 1961.

Bermant, Chaim. *The Jews.* New York: Times Books, 1977.

Bernstein, Fred. *Jewish Mothers' Hall of Fame.* Garden City: Doubleday, 1986.

Bernstein, Mashey M. "Whitebread and Whitemeat in Beverly Hills." *Midstream* 32 (Aug. 1986): 42–43.

Bilik, Dorothy Seidman. *Immigrant-Survivors: Post-Holocaust Consciousness in Recent Jewish American Fiction.* Middletown: Wesleyan University Press, 1981.

Blau, Eleanor. "The Ethnic Authenticity of 'Moscow.'" *New York Times,* May 22, 1984, C-11.

Blau, Joseph L. *Judaism in America: From Curiosity to Third Faith.* Chicago: University of Chicago Press, 1976.

Blau, Zena Smith. "The Strategy of the Jewish Mother." In *The Jews in American Society,* ed. Marshall Sklare. New York: Behrman House, 1974.

Bloom, Harold. "Jewish Culture and Jewish Memory." *Dialectical Anthropology* 8 (Oct. 1983): 7–19.

Boelhower, William. *Through a Glass Darkly: Ethnic Semiosis in American Literature.* New York: Oxford University Press, 1987.

Bowles, Stephen. *Sidney Lumet: A Guide to References and Resources.* Boston: G. K. Hall, 1979.

Brater, Enoch. "Ethics and Ethnicity in the Plays of Arthur Miller." In *From Hester Street to Hollywood: The Jewish-American Stage and Screen,* ed. Sarah Cohen. Bloomington: Indiana University Press, 1983.

Braungart, Richard G. "Family Status, Socialization, and Student Politics: A Multivariate Analysis." Ph.D. diss., Pennsylvania State University, 1980.

Breines, Paul. *Tough Jews: Political Fantasies and the Moral Dilemma of American Jewry.* New York: Basic Books, 1990.

Brode, Douglas. *Woody Allen: His Films and Career.* Secaucus: Citadel Press, 1985.

Buber, Martin. *Israel and the World.* New York: Shocken Books, 1948.

Buckley, Gail Lumet. *The Hornes: An American Family.* New York: Knopf, 1986.

Burton, Dee. *I Dream of Woody.* New York: William Morrow, 1984.

Carter, E. Graydon. "The Cosmos According to Mel Brooks." *Vogue* 177 (June 1987): 220–21.

Caughie, John, ed. *Theories in Authorship: A Reader.* London: Routledge and Kegan Paul, 1981.

Chametzky, Jules. "Elmer Rice, Liberation, and the Great Ethnic Question." In *From Hester Street to Hollywood: The Jewish-American Stage and Screen,* ed. Sarah Cohen. Bloomington: Indiana University Press, 1983.

Clum, John. *Paddy Chayefsky.* Boston: Twayne, 1976.

Cohen, Sarah Blacher, ed. *Jewish Wry: Essays on Jewish Humor.* Bloomington: Indiana University Press, 1987.

Cooper, Arthur. "Mel Brooks: Chasing Rabbits." *Newsweek,* April 22, 1974, 98.

Corliss, Richard. "Paul Mazursky: A Poet for People Like Us." *New Times,* April 3, 1978, 52–58.

———. "Paul Mazursky: The Horace with a Heart of Gold." *Film Comment* 10–11 (March–April 1975): 40–41.

Corrigan, Robert W., ed. *Comedy: Meaning and Form.* New York: Harper and Row, 1981.

Cuddihy, John Murray. *The Ordeal of Civility: Freud, Marx, Lévi-Strauss, and the Jewish Struggle with Modernity.* New York: Basic Books, 1974.

Cunningham, Frank. "The Insistence of Memory: The Opening Sequences of Lumet's *Pawnbroker.*" *Literature/Film Quarterly* 17, 1 (1989): 39–43.

———. *Sidney Lumet: Film and Literary Vision.* Lexington: University Press of Kentucky, 1991.

Davidowitz, Moshe. "The Psychohistory of Jewish Rage and Redemption as Seen Through Its Art." *Journal of Psychohistory* 6 (Fall 1978): 273–84.

Dawidowicz, Lucy S. *The Jewish Presence: Essays on Identity and History.* New York: Holt, Rinehart and Winston, 1977.

Dearborn, Mary V. *Pocahontas's Daughters: Gender and Ethnicity in American Culture.* New York: Oxford University Press, 1986.

Dembo, L. S. *The Monological Jew: A Literary Study.* Madison: University of Wisconsin Press, 1988.

Dershowitz, Alan M. *Chutzpah.* Boston: Little, Brown, 1991.

Desser, David. "The Cinematic Melting Pot: Ethnicity, Jews and Psychoanalysis." In *Unspeakable Images: Ethnicity and the American Cinema,* ed. Lester D. Friedman. Urbana: University of Illinois Press, 1991.

———. "Parody and Ethnicity: Genre Transformations in the Films of Woody Allen and Mel Brooks." Paper given at annual meeting of Society for Cinema Studies, New Orleans, April 1986.

"Dialogue on Film: Steven Spielberg." *American Film* 13 (June 1988): 14.

Dinnerstein, Leonard. *Uneasy at Home: Antisemitism and the American Jewish Experience.* New York: Columbia University Press, 1987.

Di Pietro, Robert J., and Edward Ifkovic, eds. *Ethnic Perspectives in American Literature: Selected Essays on the European Contribution: A Source Book.* New York: Modern Language Association, 1983.

Doctorow, E. L. *The Book of Daniel*. New York: Bantam, 1979.

Doneson, Judith E. *The Holocaust in American Film*. Philadelphia: Jewish Publication Society, 1987.

Doroshkin, Milton. *Yiddish in America: Social and Cultural Foundations*. Rutherford: Fairleigh Dickinson University Press, 1969.

Ebel, Henry. "Adapting to Annihilation." *Journal of Psychoanalytic Anthropology* 3 (Winter 1986): 67–89.

———. "Being Jewish." *Journal of Psychohistory* 8 (Summer 1980): 67–76.

Ehrlich, Howard. "Observations on Ethnic and Intergroup Humor." *Ethnicity* 6 (Dec. 1979): 383–98.

Eisen, Arnold M. *Galut: Modern Jewish Reflections on Homelessness and Homecoming*. Bloomington: Indiana University Press, 1986.

Elkin, Michael. "Jews on TV: From the Goldbergs to Hill Street's Cops." *Jewish Exponent,* June 28, 1985, 24–29.

Elman, Yishrael. "Intermarriage in the USA." *Jewish Social Studies* (Winter 1987–88): 1–26.

Erens, Patricia. *The Jew in American Cinema*. Bloomington: Indiana University Press, 1984.

———. "You Could Die Laughing: Jewish Humor and Film." *East-West Film Journal* 2 (Dec. 1987): 50–62.

Erikson, Erik. *Childhood and Society*. New York: W. W. Norton, 1963.

Farber, Stephen. "Daniel." *Film Quarterly* 37, 3 (1984), pp. 32–37.

Fein, Helen. *Accounting for Genocide: National Responses and Jewish Victimization during the Holocaust*. Chicago: University of Chicago Press, 1984.

Feldstein, Stanley. *The Land That I Show You: Three Centuries of Jewish Life in America*. Garden City: Anchor Press/Doubleday, 1978.

Feuerlicht, Roberta Strauss. *The Fate of the Jews: A People Torn Between Israeli Power and Jewish Ethics*. New York: Times Books, 1983.

Fisch, Harold. *A Remembered Future: A Study in Literary Mythology*. Bloomington: Indiana University Press, 1984.

Flashner, Graham. *Fun with Woody: The Complete Woody Allen Quiz Book*. New York: Henry Holt and Company, 1987.

Fleischman, Philip. "Interview with Mel Brooks." *Maclean's,* April 7, 1977, 6–10.

Fox, Stuart. *Jewish Films in the United States: A Comprehensive Survey and Descriptive Filmography*. Boston: G. K. Hall, 1976.

Fox, Terry Curtis. "Paul Mazursky Interviewed." *Film Comment* 14–15 (March–April 1978): 29–32.

Freud, Sigmund. "Jokes and Their Relation to the Unconscious." 1905. In *The Standard Edition of the Complete Psychological Works of Sigmund Freud,* trans. and ed. James Strachey and Anna Freud. Vol. 8. London: Hogarth Press, 1953.

Friedlander, Saul. *Reflections of Nazism: An Essay on Kitsch and Death*. New York: Harper and Row, 1989.

Friedman, Lawrence. *Understanding Isaac Bashevis Singer*. Columbia: University of South Carolina Press, 1988.

Friedman, Lester D. "Celluloid Assimilation: Jews in American Silent Movies." *Journal of Popular Film and Television* 15 (Fall 1987): 129–36.

———. *Hollywood's Image of the Jew.* New York: Frederick Ungar, 1982.

———. *The Jewish Image in American Film.* Secaucus: Citadel Press, 1987.

———, ed. *Unspeakable Images: Ethnicity and the American Cinema.* Urbana: University of Illinois Press, 1991.

Gabler, Neal. *An Empire of Their Own: How the Jews Invented Hollywood.* New York: Crown Publishers, 1988.

Gay, Peter. *A Godless Jew: Freud, Atheism and the Making of Psychoanalysis.* New Haven: Yale University Press, 1987.

Gerber, David A., ed. *Anti-Semitism in American History.* Urbana: University of Illinois Press, 1986.

Giannetti, Louis D. *Masters of the American Cinema.* Englewood Cliffs: Prentice-Hall, 1981.

Giles, Paul. "The Cinema of Catholicism: John Ford and Robert Altman." In *Unspeakable Images: Ethnicity and the American Cinema,* ed. Lester D. Friedman. Urbana: University of Illinois Press, 1991.

Gilman, Sander L. *Difference and Pathology: Stereotypes of Sexuality, Race and Madness.* Ithaca: Cornell University Press, 1985.

———. *Jewish Self-Hatred: Anti-Semitism and the Hidden Language of the Jews.* Baltimore: Johns Hopkins University Press, 1986.

Girgus, Sam B. *The New Covenant: Jewish Writers and the American Idea.* Chapel Hill: University of North Carolina Press, 1984.

Gitlin, Todd. *The Sixties: Years of Hope, Days of Rage.* Toronto: Bantam Books, 1987.

Glazer, Nathan. *American Judaism.* Chicago: University of Chicago Press, 1972.

Goldman, Albert. "Laughter Makers." In *Jewish Wry: Essays on Jewish Humor,* ed. Sarah Blacher Cohen. Bloomington: Indiana University Press, 1987.

Goldscheider, Calvin. *Jewish Continuity and Change: Emerging Patterns in America.* Bloomington: Indiana University Press, 1986.

Goldstein, Sidney. "American Jewry, 1970: A Demographic Profile." In *The Jew in American Society,* ed. Marshall Sklare. New York: Behrman House, 1974.

Gordon, Milton M. *Assimilation in American Life: The Role of Race, Religion, and National Origins.* New York: Oxford University Press, 1964.

Grenier, Richard. "Woody Allen on the American Character." (Review of *Zelig.*) *Commentary* 76 (Nov. 1983): 61–65.

Guttmann, Allen. *The Jewish Writer in America: Assimilation and the Crisis of Identity.* New York: Oxford University Press, 1971.

———. "Out of the Ghetto and on to the Field: Jewish Writers and the Theme of Sport." *American Jewish History* 74 (March 1985): 274–86.

Haller, Scott. "The Happily Married Man Who Examines the Shaky State of Marriage." *Horizon* 4 (May 1978): 82–87.

Heilbut, Anthony. *Exiled in Paradise: German Refugee Artists and Intellectuals in America from the 1930's to the Present.* New York: Viking Press, 1983.

Henderson, Brian. Review of *Broadway Danny Rose. Film Quarterly* 39 (Spring 1986): 46–50.

Hendra, Tony. *Going Too Far.* New York: Doubleday, 1987.

Herman, Simon N. *Jewish Identity: A Social Psychological Perspective.* Sage Library of Social Research 48. Beverly Hills: Sage Publications, 1977.

Heschel, Abraham Joshua. *God in Search of Man: A Philosophy of Judaism.* New York: Meridian Books, 1959.

Higham, John. *Send These to Me: Jews and Other Immigrants in Urban America.* New York: Atheneum, 1975.

Himmelfarb, Harold S. "Patterns of Assimilation-Identification Among American Jews." *Ethnicity* 6 (Sept. 1979): 249–67.

Hirsch, Foster. *Love, Sex, Death and the Meaning of Life: Woody Allen's Comedy.* New York: McGraw-Hill, 1981.

Holtzman, William. *Seesaw: A Dual Biography of Anne Bancroft and Mel Brooks.* Garden City: Doubleday, 1979.

Howe, Irving. *World of Our Fathers.* New York: Harcourt, Brace and Jovanovich, 1976.

Hutcheon, Linda. *A Theory of Parody: The Teachings of Twentieth Century Art Forms.* New York: Methuen, 1985.

Insdorf, Annette. *Indelible Shadows: Film and the Holocaust.* New York: Random House, 1983.

————. "Take Two: *To Be or Not to Be.*" *American Film* 5 (Nov. 1979): 80–81, 85.

Isaacs, Harold R. "Basic Group Identity: The Idols of the Tribe." *Ethnicity* 1 (April 1974): 15–41.

Jacobs, Diane. *. . . but we need the eggs: The Magic of Woody Allen.* New York: St. Martin's Press, 1982.

————. *Hollywood Renaissance.* South Brunswick: A. S. Barnes, 1977.

Jameson, Fredric. *Signatures of the Visible.* New York: Routledge, 1990.

Johnson, Paul. *A History of the Jews.* New York: Harper and Row, 1987.

Joselit, Jenna Weissman. "Modern Orthodox Jews and the Ordeal of Civility." *American Jewish History* 74 (Dec. 1984): 133–42.

————. *Our Gang: Jewish Crime and the New York Jewish Community, 1900–1940.* Bloomington: Indiana University Press, 1983.

Jowett, Garth. *Film: The Democratic Art.* Boston: Little, Brown, 1976.

Kael, Pauline. "The Artist as Young Comedian." *When the Lights Go Down.* New York: Holt, Rinehart and Winston, 1980.

————. "Harry and Tonto." *New Yorker,* Jan. 13, 1975, 74–82.

Kanfer, Stefan. *A Summer World: The Attempt to Build a Jewish Eden in the Catskills, from the Days of the Ghetto to the Rise and Decline of the Borscht Belt.* New York: Farrar, Straus, Giroux, 1989.

Kaplan, Mordecai. *Judaism as Civilization.* New York: Macmillan, 1934.

Kehr, Dave. "Funny Peculiar." *Film Comment* 18 (July–Aug. 1982): 9–11.

Knox, Israel. "The Traditional Roots of Jewish Humor." *Judaism* 12 (1963): 327–37.

Kovel, Joel. "Marx on the Jewish Question." *Dialectical Anthropology* 8 (Oct. 1983): 31–46.

Kristal, Marc. "Brooks' Bookshop." *Saturday Review* 9 (July–Aug. 1983): 24–28.

Langer, Lawrence. "The Americanization of the Holocaust on Stage and Screen." In *From Hester Street to Hollywood: The Jewish-American Stage and Screen,* ed. Sarah Cohen. Bloomington: Indiana University Press, 1983.

Lax, Eric. *Woody Allen: A Biography.* New York: Alfred Knopf, 1991.

Lees, Gene. "The Mel Brooks Memos." *American Film* 3 (Oct. 1977): 10–18.

Levin, Nora. *While Messiah Tarried: Jewish Socialist Movements, 1871–1917.* New York: Schocken, 1977.

Lewis, Anthony. "The Jew in Stand-up Comedy." In *Jewish Wry: Essays on Jewish Humor,* ed. Sarah Blacher Cohen. Bloomington: Indiana University Press, 1987.

Liebman, Arthur. *Jews and the Left.* New York: John Wiley & Sons, 1979.

Lipset, Seymour Martin, and Gerald Schaflander. *Passion and Politics: Student Activism in America.* Boston: Little, Brown, 1971.

Long, Marion. "A Night at the Movies." *Omni* (June 1987): 45.

Mailer, Norman. *Cannibals and Christians.* New York: Dell Books, 1966.

Malamud, Bernard. *The Assistant.* New York: Farrar, Straus and Cudahy, 1957.

Malin, Irving. *Jews and Americans.* Carbondale: Southern Illinois University Press, 1965.

Manchel, Frank. *The Box-Office Clowns.* New York: Franklin Watts, 1979.

Markfield, Wallace. *To an Early Grave.* New York: Simon and Schuster, 1964.

Memmi, Albert. *Dominated Man: Notes Towards a Portrait.* New York: Orion Press, 1968.

———. *The Liberation of the Jew.* New York: Orion Press, 1966.

"Mighty Maus." *Rolling Stone,* Nov. 20, 1986, 148.

Miller, Gabriel. *Screening the Novel: Rediscovered American Fiction in Film.* New York: Frederick Ungar, 1980.

Mitchell, Lisa. ". . . and Please Love Melvin Brooks or How a Little Guy from Brooklyn Grew up to Be the Comic Genius of the '70s." *Saturday Evening Post* 250 (May 1978): 63.

Mock, Fredia Lee, and Terry Sanders. "Word into Image: Portraits of American Screenwriters." American Film Foundation, 1981.

Monaco, James. *American Film Now: The People, the Money, the Movies.* New York: Oxford University Press, 1979.

Moore, Deborah Dash. *At Home in America: Second Generation New York Jews.* New York: Columbia University Press, 1981.

———. "Defining American Jewish Identity" In *The Annual of American*

Culture Studies Prospects, ed. Jack Salzman. Vol. 6. New York: Burt Franklin and Company, 1981.

Nash, Manning. *The Cauldron of Ethnicity in the Modern World.* Chicago: University of Chicago Press, 1989.

Neusner, Jacob. *American Judaism: Adventure in Modernity: An Anthological Essay.* New York: KTAV Publishing House, 1978.

———. *Stranger at Home: "The Holocaust," Zionism, and American Judaism.* Chicago: University of Chicago Press, 1981.

Novak, Michael. *The Rise of the Unmeltable Ethnics: Politics and Culture in the Seventies.* New York: Macmillan, 1972.

Oring, Elliott. *The Jokes of Sigmund Freud: A Study in Humor and Jewish Identity.* Philadelphia: University of Pennsylvania Press, 1984.

Oz, Amos. "Make Peace Not Love." *Reform Judaism* 18 (Spring 1990): 7, 46.

Ozick, Cynthia. *Art and Ardor: Essays.* New York: Knopf, 1983.

Patai, Raphael. *Tents of Jacob: The Diaspora—Yesterday and Today.* Englewood Cliffs: Prentice-Hall, 1971.

Petsonk, Judy, and Jim Remsen. *The Intermarriage Handbook: A Guide for Jews and Christians.* New York: Arbor House, 1988.

Philipson, Ilene. *Ethel Rosenberg: Beyond the Myths.* New York: Franklin Watts, 1988.

Pinsker, Sanford. "Mel Brooks and the Cinema of Exhaustion." In *Jewish Wry: Essays on Jewish Humor,* ed. Sarah Blacher Cohen. Bloomington: Indiana University Press, 1987.

Pogel, Nancy. *Woody Allen.* Boston: Twayne, 1987.

Rich, Frank. "Still Crazy After All These Years." *New York Post,* Feb. 7, 1976, 5–7.

Robinson, David. *Chaplin: His Life and Art.* New York: McGraw-Hill, 1985.

Roiphe, Anne. *Generation without Memory: A Jewish Journey in Christian America.* Boston: Beacon Press, 1981.

Rosenbaum, Jonathan. "Notes Toward the Depreciation of Woody Allen." *Tikkun* 5 (May–June 1990): 33–35, 98–100.

Rosenblum, Ralph, and Robert Karen. *When the Shooting Stops . . . the Cutting Begins: A Film Editor's Story.* New York: Viking, 1979.

Rosenfeld, Alvin H. *Imagining Hitler.* Bloomington: Indiana University Press, 1985.

Rosenthal, David. "Mazursky: Movies for Grown-ups." *Rolling Stone,* Oct. 28, 1982, 48–50.

Roskies, David G. *Against the Apocalypse: Responses to Catastrophe in Modern Jewish Culture.* Cambridge: Harvard University Press, 1984.

Rosten, Leo. *The Joys of Yiddish.* New York: Pocket Books, 1970.

Roth, Philip. *Reading Myself and Others.* New York: Farrar, Straus and Giroux, 1975.

Rotundo, E. Anthony. "Jews and Rock and Roll: A Study in Cultural Contracts." *American Jewish History* 72 (Sept. 1982): 82–107.

Rovin, Jeff. "Film." *Omni* (Aug. 1981): 28, 112–14.

————. "Last Word." *Omni* (July 1981): 130.

Royce, Anya Peterson. *Ethnic Identity: Strategies of Diversity.* Bloomington: Indiana University Press, 1982.

Sanders, Ronald. *Shores of Refuge: A Hundred Years of Jewish Emigration.* New York: Henry Holt, 1988.

Sarris, Andrew. "Films in Focus: Is Woody Strictly Kosher?" *Village Voice,* Feb. 10, 1987, 47.

————. "Picking the Funny Bone." *Village Voice,* March 14, 1974, 71, 74.

Schermerhorn, R. A. "Ethnicity in the Perspective of the Sociology of Knowledge." *Ethnicity* 1 (April 1974): 1–14.

Schulz, Max F. *Radical Sophistication: Studies in Contemporary Jewish-American Novelists.* Athens: Ohio University Press, 1969.

Shapiro, Karl. *Poems of a Jew.* New York: Random House, 1958.

Shechner, Mark. *After the Revolution: Studies in the Contemporary Jewish-American Imagination.* Bloomington: Indiana University Press, 1987.

————. "Dear Mr. Einstein: Jewish Comedy and the Contradictions of Culture." In *Jewish Wry: Essays on Jewish Humor,* ed. Sarah Blacher Cohen. Bloomington: Indiana University Press, 1987.

Shelley, Mary. *Frankenstein.* Edited by M. K. Joseph. Oxford: Oxford University Press, 1971.

Sherman, Bernard. *The Invention of the Jew: Jewish-American Education Novels (1916–1964).* New York: T. Yoseloff, 1969.

Shohat, Ella. "Ethnicities-in-Relation: Toward a Multicultural Reading of American Cinema." In *Unspeakable Images: Ethnicity and the American Cinema,* ed. Lester D. Friedman. Urbana: University of Illinois Press, 1991.

Shuman, R. Baird. "Clifford Odets and the Jewish Contest." In *From Hester Street to Hollywood,* ed. Sarah Cohen. Bloomington: Indiana University Press, 1983.

Sicher, Efraim. *Beyond Marginality: Anglo-Jewish Literature After the Holocaust.* Albany: State University of New York Press, 1985.

Siegel, Larry. "Playboy Interview." *Playboy* (Oct. 1966): 135.

Silberman, Charles. *A Certain People: American Jews and Their Lives Today.* New York: Summit Books, 1985.

Singer, Isaac Bashevis. *Enemies, A Love Story.* New York: Avenal Books, 1982.

Sklare, Marshall. *America's Jews.* New York: Random House, 1971.

————, ed. *The Jew in American Society.* New York: Behrman House, 1974.

————, ed. *Understanding American Jewry.* New Brunswick: Transaction Books, 1982.

Slide, Anthony. *Aspects of Film History Prior to 1920.* Metuchen: Scarecrow Press, 1978.

Smith, Gavin. "Sidney Lumet: Lion on the Left." *Film Comment* 24 (July–Aug. 1988): 32, 34–38.

Sollors, Werner. *Beyond Ethnicity: Consent and Descent in American Culture.* New York: Oxford University Press, 1986.

Solotoroff, Ted. "American-Jewish Writers: On Edge Once More." *New York Times Book Review,* Dec. 18, 1988, 1, 31–32.

Spiegelman, Art. *Maus: A Survivor's Tale.* New York: Pantheon, 1986.

Sragow, Michael. "The Not-So-Flip Side of Mel Brooks." *Rolling Stone,* Oct. 14, 1982, 57.

Stam, Robert. "Bakhtin, Polyphony, and Ethnic/Racial Representation." In *Unspeakable Images: Ethnicity and the American Cinema,* ed. Lester D. Friedman. Urbana: University of Illinois Press, 1991.

————. *Subversive Pleasures: Bakhtin, Cultural Criticism, and Film.* Baltimore: Johns Hopkins University Press, 1989.

Stein, Howard F. "Culture and Ethnicity as Group-Fantasies: A Psychohistoric Paradigm of Group Identity." *Journal of Psychohistory* 8 (Summer 1980): 21–51.

————. *Developmental Time, Cultural Space: Studies in Psychogeography.* Norman: University of Oklahoma Press, 1987.

————. "Ethnicity, Identity and Ideology." *School Review* 83 (Feb. 1975): 273–300.

————. "Judaism and the Group Fantasy of Martyrdom: The Psychodynamic Paradox of Survival Through Persecution." *Journal of Psychohistory* 6 (Fall 1978): 151–210.

Steinberg, Stephen. *The Ethnic Myth: Race, Ethnicity, and Class in America.* New York: Atheneum, 1981.

Steiner, George. *The Death of Tragedy.* New York: Alfred A. Knopf, 1961.

————. *Language and Silence: Essays on Language, Literature, and the Inhuman.* New York: Atheneum, 1967.

Suleiman, Susan, ed. *The Reader in the Text.* Princeton: Princeton University Press, 1980.

Tallmer, Jerry. "Paul Mazursky: The Village as It Was." *New York Post,* Jan. 31, 1976, 13–14.

Tiefenthaler, Sepp. L. "The Search for Cultural Identity: Jewish-American Immigrant Autobiographies as Agents of Ethnicity." *Melus* 12 (Winter 1985): 37–51.

Tuchman, Mitch. "Down the Hatch in 'Beverly Hills.'" *Film Comment* 22 (Feb. 1986): 16–19, 71–72.

Tynan, Kenneth. "Mel Brooks: Frolics and Detours of a Short Hebrew Man." *New Yorker,* Oct. 30, 1978, 46–50 + .

Veblen, Thorstein. "The Intellectual Pre-Eminence of Jews in Modern Europe." In *The Portable Veblen,* ed. Max Lerner. New York: Viking Press, 1948.

Wallant, Edward Lewis. *The Pawnbroker.* New York: Harcourt, Brace and World, 1961.

Warshow, Robert. "Poet of the Jewish Middle Class." *Commentary* 1 (May 1946): 17–22.

Weinberg, Sydney Stahl. *The World of Our Mothers: The Lives of Jewish Immigrant Women.* Chapel Hill: University of North Carolina Press, 1988.

Whitfield, Stephen J. *American Space, Jewish Time*. Hamden: Archon Books, 1988.

———. "Our American Jewish Heritage: The Hollywood Version." *American Jewish History* 74 (March 1986): 322–40.

Wiesel, Elie. "For Some Measure of Humility." *Sh'ma*, Oct. 31, 1975, 314–15.

Wild, David. *The Movies of Woody Allen: A Short, Neurotic Quiz Book*. New York: Perigee Books, 1987.

Wisse, Ruth R. *The Schlemiel as Modern Hero*. Chicago: University of Chicago Press, 1971.

Woll, Allen L., and Randall M. Miller, eds. *Ethnic and Racial Images in American Film and Television: Historical Essays and Bibliography*. New York: Garland Publishing, 1987.

Woocher, Jonathan S. *Sacred Survival: The Civil Religion of American Jews*. Bloomington: Indiana University Press, 1986.

Wood, Robin. "Gods and Monsters." *Film Comment* 14 (Sept.–Oct. 1978): 19–25.

———. "Return of the Repressed." *Film Comment* 14 (July–Aug. 1978): 24–32.

Wyschogrod, Michael. "Some Theological Reflections on the Holocaust." *Response* 9 (Spring 1975): 65–68.

Yacowar, Maurice. *Loser Take All: The Comic Art of Woody Allen*. New York: Ungar, 1979.

———. *Method in Madness: The Art of Mel Brooks*. New York: St. Martin's Press, 1981.

Young, Charles. "Seven Revelations About Mel Brooks: A Study in Low Anxiety." *Rolling Stone*, Feb. 9, 1978, 32–36.

Yudkin, Leon. *Jewish Writing and Identity in the Twentieth Century*. New York: St. Martin's Press, 1982.

Zenner, Walter P. "Jewishness in America: Ascription and Choice." In *Ethnicity and Race in the U.S.A.: Toward the Twenty-first Century*, ed. Richard D. Alba. London: Routledge and Kegan Paul, 1985.

———. "Lachrymosity: A Cultural Reinforcement of Minority Status." *Ethnicity* 4 (June 1977): 156–66.

Zimmerman, Paul. "The Mad Mad Mel Brooks." *Newsweek*, Feb. 17, 1975, 54–58 +.

Zoglin, Richard. "Manhattan's Methuselah." *Film Comment* 22 (May–June 1986): 16–20.

Index